George Porter

The letters of the late father George Porter, S. J., Archbishop of Bombay

George Porter

The letters of the late father George Porter, S. J., Archbishop of Bombay

ISBN/EAN: 9783337017965

Printed in Europe, USA, Canada, Australia, Japan

Cover: Foto ©Lupo / pixelio.de

More available books at **www.hansebooks.com**

THE LATE

FATHER GEORGE PORTER, S.J.

Archbishop of Bombay

LONDON: BURNS & OATES, Limited.
NEW YORK: CATHOLIC PUBLICATION SOCIETY CO.
1891

HAD the late Archbishop of Bombay been a Frenchman, no doubt a lengthy biography of him would long since have appeared. For such a work the numerous letters, which notwithstanding his many and varied occupations he found time to write, would have furnished abundant material. In England we are less eager to embark on these literary enterprises, and to us it has seemed that the publication without comments or additions of as many letters from Father Porter as could be collected would furnish the best record of him that could be given.

And this we may hope will be a more satisfactory record than a Biography. Biographies tell us a good deal about their subject, but it does not follow that they represent him as he was. How often does our estimate of a man, even of a saint, depend on the skill, or lack of skill of the writer, who has undertaken to portray him! It is from the writings, and especially from the letters of a man, that we gain the truest insight into his character. Father Porter's letters show his habit of looking at things, the judgments he formed, the largeness of his sympathy, his method of dealing with souls, the untiring kindness he manifested to all who had recourse to him for guidance, the universality of his interest in the questions of the day. Thus naturally they disclose the man himself as no biographer could depict him for us.

Of his exterior life there is little to be said. There was little in which it would be distinguished from that of any other Father of the Society of Jesus, till the day came when he was summoned to resign his work in England and to undertake the burden and the dignity of the Episcopate in India.

In the nineteenth century, no less than in the sixteenth, the vows taken by the followers of St. Ignatius are no unreal ones; and with the almost certainty of a speedy death as the consequence of his obedience to the Sovereign Pontiff, Father Porter was ready at a moment's notice to leave all that he most cared for on earth, not friends and associations and native country only, nor even the life of unusual activity and labour that he was leading, but what as a true Jesuit he valued above all things, the poverty and obedience and obscurity of the religious life.

The present volume consists of letters written during the last ten years of his life, comprising a series from Rome and Fiesole, and a larger series from India during the two years and a half of his Episcopate. A few letters of an earlier period are printed in the Introductory Chapter.

Of those who were asked to contribute to the collection but few comparatively responded. A not unnatural hesitation was felt by many to make public what they cherished as their own peculiar property. Some were influenced by the fear that their *incognito* would not be preserved, and others by the mistaken idea that advice which was intended for one could not be in any way applicable to another. Not a few who might have been willing to contribute may never have been asked. The Editors take this opportunity of saying that in the event of a second series being called for, such contributions would be most gratefully accepted.

CONTENTS.

CHAPTER I.

INTRODUCTORY 1

Advice to a novice immediately before her Profession. Courage in facing a change of work. Value of employment. Graces to be frequently prayed for. Exercise of the presence of God. The wisdom of waiting quietly. Patience and kindness; most necessary in a Superior. Boys' Home in London. Value of home life. Pilgrimage to Paray. Life at Manresa. Infirmities of temper. How to meet faults and failings. Association of the Perpetual Lamp. A bazaar. Carlsbad. On overcoming jealousy and evil thoughts. The oldest shrine of the Sacred Heart in England. Family meeting at Exeter. On the death of a mother. A proposed charity. Temptations. Rule of life. Time for all things. Consolation under trials. *L'Apostolat de la Souffrance.* How to do things well. Advice on Particular Examen. Books on the Blessed Eucharist. Letter on the death of a father. To a Sister of Mercy on completing the half of her Jubilee. Connection of health with the spiritual life. How to deal with spiritual troubles and temptations to abstain from Holy Communion. Retrospective. Spiritual counsels.

CHAPTER II.

LETTERS FROM ROME 36

Departure for Rome. Padua. Relics at Venice. S. Ambrogio, Milan. Fiesole. Sacrilege and reparation. German College, Rome. San Lorenzo. Audience with the Pope. Celebration in Rome of the twenty-fifth anniversary of the definition of the Immaculate Conception. S. Andrea al Quirinale. Lord Bute's English Breviary. How to get a love of prayer. Christmas in Rome, the Cribs Samuel and Robert Isaac Wilberforce. Father Ramière's book on the Apostleship of Prayer. Books on the Passion. St. Bernard's Sermons on the Feasts of our Lord. Spiritual dangers arising from overmuch work. Subjects for Easter meditations. The pilgrimage to the Seven Churches. Lenten preachers and Holy Week in Rome. The Decrees in France against the Religious. July in Rome. Probable movements. Advice for a Retreat. The French Government and its persecution of the Jesuits. Ruskin's *Mornings in Florence.* Italian translations of the Fathers. Peace of mind essential for gaining profit from a Retreat. Meditations on the Psalms. Carlsbad again. Father Porter no longer Superior at Manresa.

CHAPTER III.

LETTERS FROM ROME 64

Journey to Rome. The Passion Play at Ober-Ammergau. Advice about Confession. Execution of the decrees against Jesuits in France. Republican intolerance and irreligion. Ludolph of Saxony. Condition of souls outside the Visible Church. Each soul *capable* of receiving truth. Visits to Cardinals. Bad people, the minority in the world. There is more good than bad in every one. The First Commandment. How to deal with souls. Life and writings of P. Marquet. A long letter about faith. An act of faith as distinguished from the habit of faith. The act of faith an act of the *understanding*. The preparation for faith. The office of the will. The progress of faith illustrated in the sixth chapter of St. John. Reasons why some people, though leading good lives, never receive the faith. How to meet difficulties and temptations against faith. How to strengthen the *habit* of faith. Père Matignon Sur le Surnaturel. The Roman spring. Healthiness of Rome. "A pearl of great price." Perseverance in the means of grace. The preachers of the Mese di Maggio in Rome. Conclusion of his Roman business. Father Porter in Paris. The mortification and conquest of self-love implied in following certain rules necessary for attaining peace of mind. The devil's game in France.

CHAPTER IV.

LETTERS FROM FIESOLE 88

Journey to Florence. Religious affairs in Paris. Scruples. Supernatural virtues. Comforting considerations when difficulties are suggested against revelation. On acquiring the virtue of faith. The Breviary for Advent. Tuscan religious customs. How devotions to the Blessed Sacrament and to the Holy Souls became united in Tuscany. The Nun of Kenmare. Answers to three questions. 1. Whether our Lady and the Apostles were baptized? 2. How is the Immaculate Conception proved? 3. What is the meaning of St. John x. 16? Why our Lady suffered from the effects of original sin. Whether Jesuits govern the Church. Feeling of lonesomeness. Meaning of the Immaculate Conception. The devil's interference in our daily life. On cherishing a desire for the spirit of prayer and for perfection. Evil of hurrying. Latin studies. Tuscan Christmas. Beauty of Fiesole. Mr. Spence. Cartier's *Life of Fra Angelico*. Cornoldi's Philosophy. Counsels—to be faithful in prayer, not to expect a sensible faith, and how to avoid being overwhelmed with business, &c. The death of a religious Superior. Despondency a bad adviser. A desolate sick-bed. Worries and prayer. The prayer of petitions. Da Ponte's *Spiritual Guide*. Abbé Guthlin's *Doctrines Positivistes en France*. Tediousness and stupidity of positivists. Climacterics. Management of health. Simplicity in confession.

CHAPTER V.

LETTERS FROM FIESOLE 114

Beginning of summer. Engravings of Hieronymus Wierx. Arrival and speedy departure of Father Weld. Visit to the Bagni di Lucca. The *cicala*. Lessius, *De Divinis Perfectionibus*, and *De Divinis Nominibus*. How to teach English Composition and History. The Corpus Christi processions. The writings of Mr. Allies. Penitential cure at Monte Catini. Visit to Lucca. The *Sacro Volto*. Symonds' Renaissance in Italy. Advice to a Sister of Charity. Pisa. Pistoia. The work of a retreat compared to that of an etcher. Anxiety to be avoided. God's action on the soul in retreat. Nothing equal in interest to a human soul. Liberalism and the *Univers*. Disquieting thoughts. Dissatisfaction with self, when good, when evil. Pleasure in life. Faith. Discouragement. Savonarola. What is necessary to constitute sin. Beauty of the vintage. Contrition. A wet September in Italy. On realizing truths. Connection between faith and hope. A conversion to Catholicism, what wonders of grace it implies. Hopes about Heaven and motives for encouragement.

CHAPTER VI.

LAST LETTERS FROM FIESOLE 137

Instance of a truth *believed* but *realized* in various degrees, sometimes very imperfectly. The Florentine painters and their realization of the Divinity of Jesus Christ. Degeneration of Modern Art. What to do when uncertain about our duty. How to acquire a habit of decision. Palmer's Notes of a Visit to the Russian Church. Life not wasted because spent in attending to prosy duties. St. Jerome's Letters. Mgr. Freppel. Samuel Wilberforce. Life of Bishop Mazenod and privations of missionaries. Translations of the Fathers by the early Tractarians. Evil of vagueness in spiritual matters. New Year's note of encouragement. Devotions for Lent. Helps for the memory. Gibbon's plan. Life of Mgr. de Ségur. Father Weld's movements. Illness of Mgr. Rogerson. Holy deaths. Bougaud's works. The Immaculate Conception. Hettinger's *Apologetik*. Temptations. Necessity of rest. Sunshine after storms. Reliquaries in the Baptistery of Florence. Advice to a Superior. Reopening of the Duomo at Fiesole. Procession of *Corpus Domini* at Careggi. The facciata of the Duomo at Florence. Death of the architect. Visit to the Convent of St. Domenico. Balmez and Cornoldi. A Retreat, the Exercises of the First Week, their importance. Return of Father Weld. Siena. How to measure progress in our spiritual life. The Sisters of Charity at Siena.

CHAPTER VII.

LETTERS FROM VARIOUS PLACES 165

Work at Rome. Announcement of speedy return to England. Hints for meditation. Commentaries on the Psalms. The Third Order. Happiness of a convert. The Last Judgment. London. Devotion to the Holy Souls. Obedience. Opening of the New Oratory, London. Dr. Wace's Preface to Luther's primary works. Maclear's evidential value of the Holy Eucharist. Short notes of counsel. Plans for Sept. 1886. Pusey and Meyrick on our Lady. Prayer of petitions. The Scotch Synod. Journey to Florence. Turin. San Girolamo again. Storm on the Lac du Bourget. Return to Paris. Caro's books on Positivism. St. Bernard, depth and devotion of his writings. Montmartre. Notre Dame. Works of Father Franco.

CHAPTER VIII.

LETTERS ON RELIGIOUS VOCATION 183

First Series. Importance of forming a high idea of the religious state. Rules for the examination of conscience, for Communions, for times of depression. *Christian Perfection.* Evil of over-doing self-examination. Fidelity to inspirations. Prayer for guidance. Acts of Love. Evidence of God's education of the soul. How to prepare for the sacrifices of religious life. Craving for affection. Consolations and desolations. Fidelity the great virtue necessary in times of desolation. Congratulations on the vocation being given. Certainty that trials will come. Happiness of being called to the religious life even at the eleventh hour. What God really asks. Regular soldiers as distinguished from the militia. On the death of a young nun. Encouragement to perseverance.

Second Series. Calmness indispensable for forming a decision. Holiness of the married state, but superiority of the religious state. No one should embrace the religious state without a call. Different forms a call may take. Indications of a true vocation. A vocation may be genuine, though imposing a very hard sacrifice. Mistake of assuming that nuns must be narrow-minded, scrupulous, and ignorant. Natural affections implanted by God. True love of relatives helps true love of God. Scruples. Encouragement to aspire to religious life. Use of time. Devotion to the Sacred Heart. Vocation distinctly manifested. Abundance and variety of work to be found in the Order of the Sacred Heart.

CHAPTER IX.

SPIRITUAL COUNSELS. NOTES OF A SERMON PREACHED AT A PROFESSION 208

Spiritual Counsels on the way to cure scrupulous fidgets. On the frequentation of the sacraments. Holy Purity. To one troubled with scruples. Confession. Patience with temptations. Despondency. On how to distinguish between temptations and sins.

CHAPTER X.

FROM LONDON TO BOMBAY 220

Nomination to the See of Bombay. Farewell Notes. Journey by Lourdes to Fiesole. A word of consolation. Peacefulness of Fiesole. Arrival at Loreto. Impressions of Lourdes. Last Mass in Farm Street. Partings are not separations. On board the *Assam*. Fidelity to rules in times of trial. Description of the Santa Casa. The Church's work in Bombay. From Alexandria to Suez. A night at Suez. The Suez Canal. On board the *Peshawur*. From Aden to Bombay. Uneventful voyage. Arrival in Bombay. Welcome. Celebration of the Queen's Jubilee. Sermon at the Cathedral. The Jesuit Colleges. Feeling of bewilderment. Population of Bombay. Hindoo cemetery.

CHAPTER XI.

ALLAHABAD AND THE ARCHBISHOP'S SERMON 237

Journey to Allahabad. The Council and the Consecration. Garden-party. Vegetation of India. Fort Chapel. Work. Minor crosses and patience.
Sermon on the Catholic Hierarchy in India. The Church, Christ's Kingdom upon earth. How it differs from the kingdoms of the world. Its independence. Its form. Its vicissitudes. The normal organization of the Church. The Episcopate in communion with the Apostolic See. How the Pope provides for the government of countries where for various reasons a regularly constituted diocese cannot exist. Difference between Bishops and Vicars Apostolic. Substitution by Leo XIII. of twenty-five regular sees for the vicariates previously existing in India. Review of the past history of the Church in India. Advantages which will ensue from the establishment of the Hierarchy.

CHAPTER XII.

FIRST MONTHS OF THE EPISCOPATE 255

The order of the day. Reminiscences of the last weeks in London and of the journey. Account of the Hindoos. Description of Fort Chapel, of the Archbishop's residence and commissariat. Hindoo ideas about the Blessed Eucharist. Arrival of the "precious mitre." Embarrassing variety of languages. Colleges and charitable institutions. On guarding against despondency. Description of Bombay and its inhabitants. Khandala. The gift of tongues. The Hindoo religion. Rukmabai. Child-marriages. Mahommedan women. Parsee women, their emancipation. Parsee persecution of converts to Christianity. Novelty of Bombay life. Pectoral cross. Hindoo marriages. Miss Martineau. The clergy. The native Christians. Graces that come in sickness. The rainy season. Excessive moisture. Indian customs. Feast of Corpus Christi. Proposed volume on Marriage. Portugal and India. The first Pastoral. Consecration of the Archdiocese to the Sacred Heart.

CHAPTER XIII.

LETTERS FROM BOMBAY 295

Retreat at Kirkee. The responsibilities of a Bishop. *The Eternal Truths*, by Father Pergmahr. Description of house at Kirkee. Proposed work on Marriage. French Mission in Madura. Magnificence of Bombay: some account of its inhabitants. The crozier. The spiritual work of advancing life. Commissions for books. Galliffet's *Adorable Heart of Jesus*. *Was ist Christus*, by Father Roh. *The Throne of the Fisherman*. Faith strengthened by familiarity with the History of the Church. The Indian *Messenger*. More commissions for books. Hints for a private retreat. The writings of Mr. Allies. Unconsoling aspect of Bombay. Argument for Christianity derived from the spectacle of the non-Christian world. Patience under spiritual distresses. Meditation on the Divine Perfections. Mahommed's description of God. Consolations in a sudden death. Secret of contending with despondency. First moments after death. Father Humphrey on Christian Marriage. The Freemasons' persistent attacks on Marriage. Advice for a proposed treatise on the Divine Perfections. Projected visit to Karachi. Reminiscences of Lourdes. The Foundlings' Home and the cholera. The weather.

CHAPTER XIV.

KARACHI. BHAUNAGAR. AHMADABAD 320

Extent of the diocese of Bombay. The Archbishop of Goa's Pastoral. Decree from Rome. Visit to Karachi. Meeting with Lord and Lady Dufferin. St. Thomas of Aquin and the Missal and Breviary for Corpus Christi. Piranesi's prints of Rome. Purgatory. Worshippers of idols. Mahommedan hatred of idolatry and of learning. Mahommedan preachers. M. le Play's writings on social questions. Simple rule for those who wish for consolation. Prize-books. Visit to Bhaunagar. Gaorishanker. His present mode of life. Ahmadabad and its interesting remains. The grace of patience. Visit to the monastery and temple of the Swami-Naryan sect at Ahmadabad. Anniversary of appointment to Bombay. Celebration of Christmas. The climate. Words of encouragement. Two communities of nuns. Numerous conversions in the diocese of Calcutta and in Madura. Darwin's autobiography. Journey to Goa given up. Further account of the Hindoo monastery at Ahmadabad. The Epiphany. Benefit that may be derived from spiritual privations. Life of the Foundress of the Filles de la Croix. Father Baur, miracle related by him. His experiences as a missioner. St. Bernard's Homilies. Promise of the statue of Our Lady of Lourdes from Farm Street. Expedition to Juvem and Tara. Celebration of the Pope's Jubilee. Mosquitoes. The worse torments of Africa. Advice to an invalid. Few opportunities of preaching in Bombay. Sermon at St. Anne's. Remedy for discouragement. Darwin. Life of Père Liebermann. Account of work and diocese. Mahommedans. How and when to measure spiritual progress. The Archbishop's experience of the preceding twelve months. A religious of the Filles de la Croix. Her adventures in a jungle. "A Brahmin of the highest caste." An Anglican clergyman and the light of the Gospel.

CHAPTER XV.

THE LENTEN PASTORAL AND BEGINNING OF SECOND YEAR OF INDIAN LIFE 355

Subject of Pastoral, and extract from it. Importance of Prayer. Special graces that cannot be obtained without Prayer. No limit to what God is ready to give to those who ask. Life without Prayer, not the life for which man was created. How Prayer gives a foretaste of Heaven. Mental Prayer. Vocal Prayer. The Psalms. What we should pray for. How to meet desolation arising from physical weakness. An old nun's story. Archbishop Regan's sermon. Hindoo catechumen. A great loss to the Mission. Faith cannot be trifled with. Lord and Lady Reay's visit to the Bandora Orphanage. Death of the Emperor of Germany. Charity of non-Catholics. Great heat.

Custom at the death of a Parsee. Extract from Mère Theodorine's journal. Bradley's *Lectures on Job*. Conversions in India. A little lesson of hope. Hindoo Christians' attachment to customs. Difficulty of making changes in religious observances. The Apostleship of Prayer. Clergy retreat. Khandalla. Mary always our Model. The new Emperor of Germany. Advice to an invalid. Spiritual Extreme Unction. The Pope's Jubilee—a grand fact. Trials of a Bishop's life. Dean Bradley's mode of writing. Lesson about God that sufferers may learn from Job. An Armenian church. Pagan superstitions. Dr. Ullathorne's fatherly care for his nuns. Rosmini's Philosophy and the Condemned Propositions. The *Spectator* and Hutton. F. D. Maurice. Da Ponte.

CHAPTER XVI.

THE ARCHBISHOP'S ILLNESS. MAHABULESHWAR. GANESH KHIND. KIRKEE 382

Confidence in God. Journey to Poona and Mahabuleshwar. Visit to Lord and Lady Reay. Interest manifested in Mr. Luke Rivington's conversion. The worries of wealth. Reviews of *Robert Elsmere*. Consideration shown to unbelievers. Malarial fever, and removal to Kirkee. Kindness of Lord and Lady Reay. Hope. God nearest to us in dark hours. Papal Decree on Boycotting and the Plan of Campaign. What to do when everything is a trouble. Portrait of St. Ignatius. On sanctifying sickness and helplessness. Ganesh Khind. Death of the Emperor Frederick of Germany. James Martineau's writings. Hettinger on the Apostolic See. More helps for strengthening hope. The Pan-Anglican Synod. Sir Henry Maine's *Ancient Law* and *Village Communities*. Bright's *Progress to Democracy*. Visit to the Cowley Fathers at Poona. *Life of Lady Georgiana Fullerton*. Kirkee. Feast of St. Ignatius. The Prerogatives of St. Peter. "Without St. Peter there can be no Church." The Lambeth Conference. Mr. Rivington's *Plain Reason*. Return to Bombay. Difficulty of taking exercise.

CHAPTER XVII.

END OF SECOND YEAR AS ARCHBISHOP 404

German as a language for theology. The Pan-Anglican Synod and Bishop Ryle. The Land Question. A tiger-killing Colonel. Ghastly story of Indian life. Encouragement and advice. Counsels to an invalid. Fear of death. Extreme Unction not to be delayed. The Parsees—customs at their New Year. The Chinese and their payment of debts. Death of the Very Reverend Thomas Porter, S.J. *Robert Ellesmere*. *Moral Philosophy*, by Father Rickaby. Father Clarke's Manuals of Catholic Philosophy. Famine. Reception of the Pope's Letter in Ireland. Mr. Luke Rivington's *Plain Reason*. The English Edition of Lady G. Fullerton's Life. Scrapes. Pages of Indian life. The Divine Presence. Suggestions as to conversation. Omnipotence of prayer. Retreat at Bandora. The thought of death, pleasant. Visiting the poor in England. Value of literary occupation. St. Peter Claver. *The Holy See and the Wanderings of the Nations*. A marriage arranged by nuns. Pastoral visitation. Culvem. Dissatisfaction with self, good, if not morbid. Motives for thanksgiving. A second account of the visit to Culvem. Contempt for the body practised by St. Peter Claver. The loss of faith. Comforts and self-indulgence. Duty must come before mortification. Discouraging thoughts. *Il Diritto Naturale* of Taparelli. Druzbicki's *Devotions to the Sacred Heart.* Distribution of prizes at Bandora. Benediction and Mass. Second anniversary of the nomination to Bombay.

CHAPTER XVIII.

COMMENTS ON BOOKS, WITH A PREFACE TO THE TRANSLATION OF HETTINGER 431

Growth and fluctuations of devotions. Devotion to St. Joseph; graces that have come from it. Constant expansion of the faith. The way to get rid of disquieting thoughts. What an invalid may do. A line of encouragement. Blessings of sickness. Temptations and difficulties. The prayer of physical helplessness. Trial of Bishop King. Translation of Hettinger completed and forwarded to England. The native Press; its disregard to truth. The Malabar Syrian Christians. Life of Gaorishankar. Manuals of Catholic Philosophy; their sale in Bombay. How to behave in serious illness. Graces given through Extreme Unction. *The New Antigone*. A conversion. Father Clarke's *Logic*. Father Dalgairns' Preface to the *Lives of the Fathers of the Desert*. Life of Mère Marie de Sales Chappuis. Archbishop Ullathorne, his death, his interest in nuns and knowledge of religious life. An Easter meditation. The Mandatum. Maundy Thursday in Bombay. Ritualists and their impatience of authority. Archdeacon Farrar. The Constitutions of the Vatican Council. Preface to Hettinger.

CHAPTER XIX.

LAST LETTERS 462

Indisposition. Move to Khandalla. Trials of convalescence. How sickness sanctifies. Catholicism, the only remedy for India. Liturgy for Pentecost. The jungle and its aborigines. Storm at Khandalla. Sanyasis, their penances. How much can be effected by moderate work. Change to Poona. Suppressed gout and its effects. Rev. A. Richardson's *Catholic Claims*. Contemplated work of the Papacy. Power of music. Despondency. Pleasantness of Poona. Short visit to Bombay. Puzzle solved about "An Impossible Precept." A Hindoo's idea about the two chief sacraments. Conversions at Chota-Nagpore. Rules of Election. *Life of Ozanam*. Attack of fever. Enjoyment of the beauties of nature. Ritualists and the Royal Supremacy. Dr. Pusey's Life. Return to Bombay. W. G. Ward. Bryce's *American Commonwealth*. The Sacred Heart Convents in Australia. Mrs. Montgomery's theological books. *The Nun of Kenmare*. Wilfrid Ward's Life of his father. Moisture of the weather. To a Nun on her Profession. To visit Rome a great grace. Devotion of the early Christians to our Lord's Glorified Life. *The Grammar of Assent*. The ways of Providence. Sunday and the European mail. The Religious life and life in the world. Unhealthiness of Poona. Plans for the future which were cut short by death.

CHAPTER I.

INTRODUCTORY.

Advice to a novice immediately before her Profession. Courage in facing a change of work. Value of employment. Graces to be frequently prayed for. Exercise of the presence of God. The wisdom of waiting quietly. Patience and kindness; most necessary in a Superior. Boys' Home in London. Value of home life. Pilgrimage to Paray. Life at Manresa. Infirmities of temper. How to meet faults and failings. Association of the Perpetual Lamp. A bazaar. Carlsbad. On overcoming jealousy and evil thoughts. The oldest shrine of the Sacred Heart in England. Family meeting at Exeter. On the death of a mother. A proposed charity. Temptations. Rule of life. Time for all things. Consolation under trials. *L'Apostolat de la Souffrance.* How to do things well. Advice on Particular Examen. Books on the Blessed Eucharist. Letter on the death of a father. To a Sister of Mercy on completing the half of her Jubilee. Connection of health with the spiritual life. How to deal with spiritual troubles and temptations to abstain from Holy Communion. Retrospective. Spiritual counsels.

OF letters written by Father Porter before 1879, only a few have reached the editors, and these are for the most part short; but, as they contain much that is characteristic of the writer, they are inserted as an introduction to the fuller and more complete series which date from his departure for Rome in October, 1879.

TO A NOVICE IMMEDIATELY BEFORE HER PROFESSION.

St. Beuno's, June 11, 1861.

Dear Sister in Christ,
P.C.

Many thanks for your little note and the good news it brought. I congratulate you most heartily on your happiness and on your securing St. Aloysius for the patron of your profession. It is a huge blessing to be allowed to give oneself to Almighty God by the vows of religion, and if you endeavour to be faithful to your vocation, you will appreciate the privilege more and more every day you live. I shall have great pleasure in offering up the Holy Sacrifice for you on the happy feast, and during your retreat I will make a memento for you and for the other good Sisters who are to have the same happiness, both in the Mass and in the Office. In return I will ask you to remember me in your prayers.

In conclusion you will allow me to give you a word of advice. First, as regards your retreat, if you should find at times, or even throughout the whole retreat, that you do not experience that sensible devotion which you think you ought to have on so important an occasion, do not be discouraged. It is quite natural that when the soul has been for a period in a state of expectation, a reaction should set in, and mind and body will prove unequal to the last effort. Sometimes too God allows such a dryness to keep alive the feeling of humility, and to impress the lesson that we are absolutely dependent on Him. Therefore, if God sends you great sensible fervour, receive it humbly and thankfully; if He withholds it, resign yourself to His holy will, and do not be disheartened, for He does not look so much to the *feeling* of devotion as to the desire of the heart to make Him the best return possible for His countless mercies and graces.

Again. Do not allow the feeling of your unworthiness to frighten you too much, that is to say, so much as to interfere with meditations or other spiritual duties, or so much as to cause any doubts for the future. The feeling is a right one, we ought to strive to keep it always alive; but it need not, and it ought not, to frighten us too much. If you direct it properly, it will assist you very much in your spiritual life. The way is to argue from your own nothingness and unworthiness to the necessity of leaning wholly on the mercy of God. And the more fully you realize your unworthiness, the stronger will be your motive to trust that the Divine mercy will not be wanting to you. If Jesus Christ has chosen me, unworthy as I am, to serve among the princes of His people, surely He will supply what is deficient in me. Our counterpoise to our nothingness must be trust in the goodness and riches of the Sacred Heart: the thought of our own misery should always provoke an act of confidence. Happy will you be in your religious vocation, if you strengthen yourself by this double thought, your own unworthiness and the loving mercy of the Sacred Heart. May our Lord and His Blessed Mother accept the consecration of yourself you are about to make.

Again begging a share in your prayers, I remain,

Yours very truly in Christ,

GEORGE PORTER.

TO A SISTER OF MERCY.

Liverpool, Aug. 14, 1864.

Now that you have made your retreat, I trust that you are ready to take up your cross.

No doubt it is very hard work to tear oneself from an old work and make a complete transfer of thoughts and affections to another.

Take courage; though the present work is distasteful and trying to you, yet it is more important, higher in the sight of God.

St. Ignatius lays down the maxim, *Bonum est majus, quod universalius*, that is the greatest good which is the more general. God's glory is more advanced by the sanctification of —— than that of ——

This is supernatural consolation for you. Go for

counsel to the Blessed Sacrament. Pray to their Guardian Angels.

Remember me very kindly to —— and all the community.

St. Francis Xavier's, Liverpool,
Aug. 22, 1866.

Thank you for your note. I am glad you find more to do now and more to learn. Depend upon it, every piece of housekeeping and management you learn now, will be of use hereafter. Spend your time patiently and cheerfully as well as you can. Years spent usefully and well-filled pass quickly and happily. You will soon find yourself at the term of your wishes. Your chief anxiety should be to make the most of the time that you have. Make the most of it for your health, and give yourself every chance of becoming strong. Make the most of it for your mind. And I need not add, make the most of it to advance in virtue, and practise now some of the self-denial which hereafter will be necessary to you.

Convent of Mercy.
[No date.]

My dear Child,

P.C.

During the last fortnight I have been constantly on the move. Yesterday I began a retreat in this Convent, and to-day I give you the benefit of the quiet I enjoy.

I trust you will not be disappointed with regard to your retreat. It is not unfrequently the case that private retreats are felt to be dry, especially when one commences somewhat out of condition, bodily and spiritually.

Pray every day for the grace of perseverance. I always ask the grace to die in the Society, at the Elevation of the Chalice, and the grace not to lose the spirit of the Society. There are certain graces which we ought to pray for often—not to be lost for ever; to persevere in religion; not to fall into mortal sin. And these are commonly given to frequent and earnest prayer.

Pray for me, and may God bless you.

Yours very sincerely in Christ,

GEORGE PORTER.

St. Francis Xavier's, Liverpool,
September, 1868.

My dear Child,

September has set in with its more than usual quantum of work. Even on the 6th I am snatching odd moments to answer letters of August. Vaubert's treatise is the best I know of on the Presence of God. Without effort, and pleasantly, the thought of God should rise soon to the mind. Study to combine this exercise with certain practical tendencies, viz., when you recollect yourself before God, animate yourself to fervour. "Let us not degenerate," &c., or think of God's goodness, what can I do to prove my love and my devotedness to Almighty God? or borrow a motive from the past. I have been so negligent, I must be all the more fervent in the time to come; or merely humble yourself—"God be merciful to me a sinner." "Jesus, Son of David, have mercy on me."

You ask for a spiritual book. Get Dupont, *Le Guide Spirituel;* translated by Brignon, re-edited by Gaydon. There you will find some nuts worth the cracking! Pray for me.

May God bless you.

St. Francis Xavier's, Liverpool,
Sept. 8, 1870.

I wish you a very happy feast to-day. This day 29 years ago I entered the Novitiate: the day is a dear one to me.

You are not philosopher enough. Fruit does not fall till it is ripe, and fruit takes time to ripen. And you should be wise enough to wait with calmness and quiet for the appointed hour. Meanwhile pray God's will may be done and that all may be arranged for the best. I will join my prayers to yours. You must not be impatient nor too eager. May God bless you.

111, *Mount Street, Dec.* 25, 1871.

Thank you for your kind wishes and for your kind note received this morning. In return I wish you a very merry Christmas and a happy New Year. Try and spend it well and make a resolution to maintain the ground you have gained. With time, patience, care and prayer, you will succeed. I promise you that much. May God bless you.

111, *Mount Street, April* 14, 1872.

As you truly say, time flies. Here is Sunday again, and I am very much afraid I have not written to thank you for all the pains you took to discover whether poor —— was alive or dead. I think you will give me credit for *intending* to discharge this debt of gratitude even if I failed in the performance. I am very much obliged.

You must practise patience in your new post, wish people at Jericho, and speak as mildly as possible. Keep a great store of kind words, gentleness for the good, excuses for the thoughtless, encouragement for the bad, cheerfulness for all. . . Only your house is full of blind people, I should counsel you to have all over the house in large characters, "Kind words break no bones." These homely proverbs often teach sound wisdom. What would I not give to recall all the nasty, snappish, bitter speeches I have perpetrated in my time. You are younger and beginning life; take warning from me in time and try to be the best natured Superior in the Order. I will pray for you that you may have the grace of kind words and kind thoughts.

I met K—— the other evening at the Archbishop's conversazione. He was looking as well as usual, talked about the education business, &c. He gives a good account of your father's recovery and also of poor ——, who has gone dreadfully into the blues with his measles and touch of bronchitis. K—— tells me all his family get very low when they fall ill.

On Thursday I dined at B——'s and met there N——. He is now a man of business and talks tall about risks and averages and good years and bad years. I think he will take to work kindly enough in time, but his heart still yearns with great simplicity after the country, the moors, &c. N—— is a sample of a good-hearted lad, seems never out of humour, and since he has travelled has so much to say for himself. . . . I am getting all right again. One of these days I will tell you of my Boys' Home—no seeking of mine—it was forced upon me.

111, *Mount Street, April* 28, 1872.

I thank you, though somewhat tardily, for your kind wishes on St. George's day. I am glad to know that you don't forget me and that you give me a corner in your prayers.

I send you a circular for my new hobby here—a Boys' Home. When you come up next month I must take you to see it. Prices are not the same here, my rent is £120 per annum. The Home is only just beginning. I expect it will quickly fill; plenty of grand people profess to be interested in it, and I think funds will be forthcoming. I have some already to meet my first year.

When you decide on the London trip, remember to give me some notice, as I should like to keep myself free for one day with you at least, if not more. London keeps me busily engaged all day. You say nothing about yourself, your health, or anything else. Perhaps you reserve all for your London visit.

P.S.—Not to copy your omission, I will add that my health is much improved.

111, *Mount Street, Oct.* 27, 1872.

Now that you have my brother's opinion almost identical with mine, you may feel quiet in following the direction I gave you, viz., decide nothing, try to sanctify your daily duties, and overcome the faults of which you are conscious. Life is not wasted because it is spent at home; on the contrary, home life is to thousands the opportunity of sanctification given by Almighty God; in it they are to become great saints. If God really calls you elsewhere He will make His will known when the time comes. Continue your practice of the motto, "Kind words break no bones." God bless you.

111, *Mount Street, April* 22, 1873.

I thank you for all your kind wishes for St. George's day, and for all your kind prayers. I am better again, at least I have had no return of the pain for the last four days. The doctor has treated me abominably; for two days kept me without a crumb of solid food, and since then persists in starving me. The result you may imagine, bones, nothing but bones.

Manresa House, Roehampton,
Sept. 22, 1873.

I was very glad to hear your family was so well represented at the pilgrimage, and I am particularly glad you were there. From all I can see and hear the pilgrimage was a grand act of religion. I hear from some of my London friends that many of the more religious Protestants have expressed themselves much pleased with the success. I am very much obliged to you for remembering me in your prayers and at Holy Communion when you were at Paray. The offer of the relic of Blessed Margaret Mary I accept with many thanks. I shall be happy to receive it, and I shall prize it as my memento of the famous pilgrimage.

Manresa is very quiet, but my life is a most busy one. I am kept occupied from morning till night. You must come here when next you pay a visit to London. You will find the scenery beautiful (Richmond Park is spread out before us), the grounds charming, and our chapel a perfect gem. My health continues excellent, and I give myself a better chance of taking my sleep more regularly now. I have almost come to pity the poor wretches doomed to live in cities.

Notwithstanding what you say of the infirmities of temper surviving the pilgrimage, I shall continue to hope that they have been well taken in hand and are in a fair way to be permanently cured. As to the green-eyed monster jealousy, whom you think you have seen lurking about the grounds, set on him at once and poison him with extra doses of kindness to the person whom he wants to turn you against. A little generosity and nobleness of conduct in time will quickly free you from his visits. He is only dangerous when he is petted and pampered and encouraged.

It is not so hard to be good, if you don't let yourself be cast down by your faults and failings. Only learn to repent well and a holy life becomes much easier. We all fall often, that is to be expected, we are weak and we are surrounded by temptations. When we fall we ought not to be surprised as if we had expected never to fall again. We ought not to be cast down, but we ought to make our self-accusation. "There you are again. My God, forgive me. I wish I had not offended Thee. I wish I had kept my resolution. I will begin again. O God, help my weakness." See whether this plan won't help you.

Manresa House, Roehampton, S.W.,
Sept. 25, 1873.

Dear Rev. Mother,

P.C.

I feel much obliged to you for thinking of me and inviting me to become a member of the Association of the Perpetual Lamp of ——, and thankfully accept the invitation and undertake to say an annual Mass for the intentions of the Association.

If ever I can be of use to you or to any of your community, you may count on my answering any questions, or indeed helping you in any way I can.

My new office somewhat confuses me. I have a community of more than 30 novices, 20 students, and some 10 veterans of one kind or another. My time and thoughts are fairly occupied.

I am glad to hear you have quite recovered your strength. God is pleased that I should keep my place in the "cripple squad," so I must practise patience as well as teach it. I am mostly able for a good day's work, but every now and then I have a heavy fall, which staggers me for two or three days. I can see sickness is a good school, so I say, God's will be done.

None the less I am very much obliged to your community for their good prayers for my recovery.

God bless you all.

     Yours very truly in Christ,

       GEORGE PORTER.

Manresa House, Jan. 12, 1874.

I did not write my usual Sunday letter yesterday, as I knew you would be engaged with your bazaar, and could not find much time to write or read letters.

Rather cross, I imagine, just now; unless you have made an extraordinary start with the new year and met your first cross of 1874 with a double preparation of patience. Well, console yourself. You will work very hard; you will be far from being satisfied; you will probably apprehend a fiasco, but somehow on the day itself every one will appear to be delighted and the result will be a splendid collection. There is my little prophecy for your bazaar: tell Miss —— I have written it and mean to pray that it may be verified.

Of course spirituals must suffer "a leetle" during these periods of pressure, when the work is too much and the hands are too few; but secure the Mass, the Beads, and the Night Prayers, and do them as leisurely and devoutly as you can, and you won't be much the worse the week after the bazaar. . . .

When you recover from the bazaar fever, tell me how the dispensary goes on. I have my doubts as to the wisdom of that institution, and feel curious to learn how it works. The public dispensaries give medicine so cheaply to the poor, I should have thought you could not easily compete with them. On the other hand, it may bring you into contact more with the sick and the infirm.

Wishing you a very successful bazaar and a big blessing for yourself,

I remain yours very truly in Christ,

GEORGE PORTER.

Hotel, Rheinischer Hof, Carlsbad,
June 7, 1874.

I fear I left England without writing to wish you good-bye and to ask for your prayers. You can understand the bustle I was in during the few last days of my stay at Manresa, and that many things were left undone which I had good intentions of doing; so I shall not trouble you with any long apologies, but throw myself on your good nature and charity.

I left London on Friday, the 29th of May, reached Cologne on Saturday evening, spent the Sunday at Cologne, heard High Mass in the Cathedral, and saw some of the churches. Monday I was on the rail from 9 a.m. till nearly midnight. On Tuesday I was moving early and reached Carlsbad about 10.30 a.m.

The place is in a pretty neighbourhood, and the walks through the woods are most inviting. The visitors are here in crowds; people say there are quite 4,000, in which case the visitors outnumber the natives, who are put down at 3,800. As far as I can make out, the present set of visitors are mostly Germans, and of these a very large proportion must be Jews, if one may rely on Jewish noses and faces. They seem business people, are very dressy, very vulgar, very uninteresting. My circle of acquaintance is limited. . . . I do not care to add to it. What with the waters, my prayers and my books, the days are well filled and slip away quickly enough.

I get up at 5, say Mass at 6, begin the waters a quarter before seven, take four tumblers (a quarter of an hour's interval after each), and after the last walk for an hour. At 9 I breakfast on a few rusks and *café-au-lait* (a moderate portion); from 10 to 1, I say Office, write to friends, read a little; at 1 I go to dinner, see *The Times*, take an easy stroll; towards 5 I go to my hotel, say more Office, read, &c., till 7, when I sup; the supper consists of bread and wine.

I cannot make much of the priests here: they do not seem disposed to be social. There are some nuns, not many; what Order they belong to I do not know; their dress is black; I do not think I shall go to see them; my German is not of the best, and priests and nuns in this country do not know French or English. When at Cologne I visited a convent of your Sisters at Nippe, a suburb of Cologne; one of the nuns, the sister of a London friend of mine, was able to speak English; the convent had something of the look of Carlisle Place. I shall expect to have a letter from you before I leave. Remember me very kindly to Sister Superior. I hope she did not return too soon; the cold in May was severe for a brief period. How goes the Particular Examen? Now you have Sister Superior home all will be *couleur de rose*. God bless you.

Manresa House, July 26, 1874.

I am happy to tell you that I am really better for my visit to Carlsbad. I stayed out my four weeks there, according to the advice of my English doctor. The Carlsbad doctor advised five weeks, because he said the waters agreed with me, and probably I should not be able to get to Carlsbad again next year. The waters punished me severely, but I did not experience any bad effect beyond that usually produced. The journey home tired me greatly. At any time the distance is considerable; then the heat was fierce, and lastly, at the end of a month at Carlsbad, the patient is not in a very vigorous state. And so, though I broke my journey for three or four days in Saxony, and then again for a couple of days at Cologne, and again for a day at Folkestone, I was not worth much when I reached Manresa. Now I am beginning to pluck up, and as a sign of life, I am undertaking to answer my letters, which have been rising like a mountain before me during the last fortnight. My English doctor thinks I have gained by my trip, and thinks I shall gain still more during the next three months.

I was sorry to miss you when you were in London. I should have been very glad to have had a chat and heard all about yourself and everybody. I am much obliged to you for remembering my intentions at Notre Dame de Lourdes, and for securing me some of the water from the Grotto. In return I will not forget you at the Holy Sacrifice. God bless you.

Manresa House, August 20, 1874.

I am in my retreat, and for that reason I did not answer your letter sooner. The news of Mr. ——'s sudden and unexpected death filled me with sorrow. I always hoped that he would make his peace with God, before going to his account. I do not despair.

> Between the saddle and the ground
> He mercy asked and mercy found.

There is always time for hope, but such a death terrifies me. I shall not forget —— in my prayers. She has a claim upon me.

Now to your troubles. The thoughts of jealousy I advise you to treat with great contempt. You cannot shut them out; so when they come say to yourself: "A pretty idea indeed. Shall I be so mean as to repine at

———'s success?" When you are calm, reason with yourself on the base nature of jealousy and firmly resolve never to give in to it, and pray for grace against it. Then keep the greatest vigilance over yourself, not to show jealousy in look, in word, or in deed. Sometimes thank God that ——— gets on so well and is so liked. Again, when you think you fail, have no friends, &c., say: "I must be content to live in a corner. God does not wish me to succeed, probably in mercy, for success might turn my head. I won't care to please the world. I will try to please Jesus Christ, and find my delight in my duties, in occupation, in prayer.

As for the evil thoughts, I have so uniformly remarked in your case that they are dependent on your state of health that I say without hesitation, begin a course of Vichy and Carlsbad. Observe, I say, a course, *i.e.*, take a dose for a week, or even a fortnight. This will do more for you than a bucket of dandelion or herb-tea, though they are also good. So much for the principal remedy. Meanwhile, have constant occupation of mind and hand: take plenty of moderate outdoor exercise, but beware of fatiguing yourself. Don't let your strength fall too low by going too long without food. When the temptation importunes you, say slowly: "Heart of Jesus, Thou lovest. Thou art not loved. Would Thou wert loved." And lastly, persuade yourself that you are not likely to offend God grievously without knowing it, and that in your actual dispositions you are not likely to offend Him grievously at all. I hope your next account will be more hopeful. God bless you. Pray for me.

Manresa House, Nov. 16, 1874.

Dear Rev. Mother,

Many thanks for the photo of the sanctuary of the Sacred Heart. I will try to get the history of the

Pilgrimage into the *Messenger* for December. But (1) I should like Mr. Powell (give me his correct name, *John*, or whatever it is, and his abode, Bristol, Bath, as it may be) to send me a description of his decoration.

(2) I should like you to find out the date when Dr. Milner dedicated the first Chapel of the Sacred Heart.

(3) The year when St. Marie's, Oscott, was opened.

(4) The year when the Sisters of Mercy took possession of Maryvale.

(5) Tell me whether the hymn of the Perpetual Lamp has been published in any periodical. If you will send me all this quickly, I will make up a paragraph for you.

(6) Add name of Rector of Bishop's Seminary: also of Vice-Rector, also say where Seminary is, what date it was opened.

(7) Did the pilgrims receive Holy Communion, hear Mass, assist at Benediction? What?

(8) Was Act of Reparation said? All these points are worth noting. Send me back this list of questions with answers.

You ask me to send you a novice, with a something of a dower. I regret to say I do not know of any.

Between 18th and 25th November, write to me at 3, Bartholomew Terrace, Exeter. My father and mother keep their golden wedding, and I am going to spend a few days with them. Pray for them. Also for my new novices, who begin their month's retreat on the 25th.

In conclusion, allow me to recommend to you the *Perfect Lay-Brother* (Oates and Co.). It contains much that would make a perfect lay-sister, a being much wanted.

Give my kindest remembrances to each and all of your community. Though I cannot visit you now, I do not forget that you have a claim on my unworthy prayers.

Believe me, yours very truly in Christ,

GEORGE PORTER.

Answers to the above questions were forwarded to Father Porter, and he wrote, as he kindly promised to do, an interesting article "On the oldest Shrine of the Devotion to the Sacred Heart of Jesus, in England," for the *Messenger of the Sacred Heart*, December, 1874, which we here reprint.

The readers of the *Messenger of the Sacred Heart* will learn with pleasure that the oldest shrine of the Devotion to the Sacred Heart of Jesus in England is still kept up, and draws devout clients from all parts of the old midland district.

This shrine consists of a small chapel, built or dedicated to the Sacred Heart by Dr. Milner, at Oscott College (now Maryvale), in the year 1816: the exact day on which this consecration was made has not been preserved.

The east end of the chapel is lighted by a circular window, in which Dr. Milner caused to be placed a stained glass representation of the Sacred Heart of our Lord. The glass was painted in Rome, and possesses some interest as being the first stained glass subject placed in a window previously to the revival of the art of glass painting in England.

When the College was removed from Old Oscott to St. Marie's, Oscott, the Sisters of Mercy were invited to establish their orphanage at Old Oscott. It has flourished there since the 11th of November, 1851, the day on which the Sisters took possession, as the Maryvale Orphanage.

The Sisters have ever religiously preserved Dr. Milner's little sanctuary of the Sacred Heart; and last year they founded in connection with it an Association called the Perpetual Lamp. More than a thousand persons have joined the Association, and no fewer than eighty priests are numbered among the members. The little sanctuary has been richly decorated under the direction of Mr. John Powell, Bristol. The reredos has been cleverly altered so as to admit a decorated figure of the Sacred Heart. The decorations have been carried throughout the whole of the wall surface of the chapel, producing a very pleasing effect. The Perpetual Lamp burns day and night (1) in reparation for all the sins now committed; (2) to obtain graces for England, and especially the grace of conversion; (3) for all the intentions of those who belong to the Association.

Dr. Ullathorne, the venerated Bishop of Birmingham, cherishes the traditions of his diocese; and no sooner had he opened his new Episcopal Seminary, at Olton, Solihull, near Birmingham, than he hastened to consecrate it to the Sacred Heart. In his discourse on the occasion, his lordship told the young students of St. Bernard's Seminary, of Dr. Milner's little Chapel of the Sacred Heart at Maryvale, and recommended them to make a pilgrimage to a shrine of so much interest.

Accordingly, on St. Edward's day, the feast of their Rector, the Very Rev. E. Ilsley, the young seminarists were conducted by the Rector and the Vice-Rector, the Rev. Dr. Barry, to Maryvale. The students gathered round their Superiors before the altar of the Sacred Heart, and joined in the Litany and the Acts of Consecration and Reparation, which were read aloud by the Rector. The orphans sang the hymn, "To Jesus' Heart all burning," and the "Hymn of the Perpetual Lamp." Benediction of the Blessed Sacrament followed, and the seminarists of St. Bernard's, having left their offering of candles at the shrine, returned to Solihull.

May this act of devotion to the Sacred Heart draw down a rich blessing on the first generation of St. Bernard's Seminary! Since then a pilgrimage to Maryvale has been organized among the students of St. Marie's, Oscott.

The readers of the *Messenger* will not forget that the Devotion to the Sacred Heart found a powerful advocate in Dr. Milner. Father de la Colombière, of the Society of Jesus, had learnt the Devotion from the Blessed Margaret Mary Alacoque herself, and had been its Apostle in England. But the merit of reviving the Devotion, and spreading it in this century in England, is due in the first place to Dr. Milner.

Manresa House, Nov. 30, 1874, 7 p.m.

Our Exeter meeting was a very pleasant one. My father and mother, two sons, two daughters, two sons-in-law, two grandsons. And, thank God, all in good health and trying to save our souls. Excuse more. I have five-and-twenty people in retreat. I was going to forget to say that I said Mass for you this morning. God bless you. Kindest remembrances to all.

TO ——, ON THE DEATH OF HER MOTHER.

Manresa House, 1875.

I condole with you on your great loss. As the days pass by you will know more fully what a void has been made in your life. The very grief you feel in the first days, and the necessary preparations you have to attend to, will not allow you to judge of the full extent of your loss. But when all is quiet, and the grave has closed over your mother, and the long evenings succeed each other, then you will know what a gap has been left. Death is an unwelcome visitor—no questioning the fact. You can only break the blow he has dealt, by thinking how good your mother was, and how much you owe to her care, and by remembering that death will come to you very soon (at least, it will seem soon, however long you may live), and by resolving to lead a holy life: these thoughts will pluck out the sting of death.

You may reproach yourself that you were not as dutiful as you ought to have been, but don't worry yourself with unavailing regrets; the very best reparation you can make will be trying to imitate the genuine virtues of your mother. She knows now all your goodwill as well and better than if she were still with you.

In your last letter (last but one) you tell me you feel a dread of going to Holy Communion. You may rest assured this is a temptation. Read À Kempis, book iv., chapter x. And, you may be satisfied, if you could talk with your mother and she were able to tell you all she now knows, she would urge you to persevere in Holy Communion. Whether this dryness in your prayers be the result of bad health, or low spirits, or be merely a trial which God sends you to rouse you to greater exertions, one thing is certain, it is not the time in which you ought to make any alterations in your rule of life. No: so long as this dryness lasts, be as faithful as possible in your rule in approaching the sacraments, and don't omit any of your prayers. Before long, I hope God will give you back some of your spirit of devotion, and you will feel happy again in trying to fulfil your duties. I shall be glad to hear from you when you have time to write.

TO A YOUNG MAN IN THE WORLD.

Manresa House, April 7, 1875.

My dear ——

Your proposed charity is a good one, it has my entire approval.

I will tell you one that I think still better. Pay for a poor respectable boy at College. If you are fortunate in your choice you may get a good novice for Manresa.

I have several here who came directly from ——

You may know such a boy, or Father —— might point out one to you.

I consider the education of one novice a better work than the education of sixty poor children.[1]

Believe me, yours very truly,
GEORGE PORTER.

Manresa House, April 23, 1875.

I am quite ashamed of myself to find that I have two of your letters to answer. I have been dreadfully busy and indeed I am still the same. In the first place I must thank you for your kind wishes on my feast-day and for all your good prayers. My health continues very good. I am equal to a long day's work, and I do not often stand in need of a rest, which is a great improvement on what I was this time twelvemonth. I consider it not a little matter to have got through the winter without a break-down. You have not been so well. I fear the cold must have tried you, and so will the spring. You must persevere in the use of Carlsbad and Vichy, that is your salvation. I hope you have a supply always at hand.

By this time I hope your more troublesome temptations have abated and you are able to go to Holy Communion with some feeling of devotion and some comfort. The great matter is not to allow yourself to be hindered from Holy Communion, and when you go, say your prayers as quietly and as well as you can. The Holy Communion

---

[1] This was a common saying of Father Porter's. "Because," he used to say, "the education of one novice may prove the salvation of a thousand poor children."—EDITOR.

must do you good, even though God may allow you to think It has done you none. Then you ought to try and make Holy Communion your great comfort, the one refuge to fly to when you are tempted and bothered or put out by servants. If the devil saw that you acted in this way, he would soon desist from annoying you about Holy Communion.

Then as regards troublesome thoughts, dispel them by making an act of the love of Jesus Christ. Say the words slowly and calmly, and you will break the backbone of the temptation.

Tell —— that I shall be very glad to see him. Cannot you coax him to bring you with him? God bless you.

Manresa House, Dec. 14, 1875.

You won't find the use of the little book for Particular Examination so irksome once you get into it, and you will soon discover the advantages it brings.

You write that you do nothing beyond your beads and night prayers. What about the meditation or the reading in its place? Once start the rule of life, and I think I may promise you that the whole day will fall into its place as naturally and as quietly as possible. You must not yield to discouragement nor trouble yourself about what others do or don't do. Begin the rule, and you will find your whole life changed and wonderfully improved.

A thousand wishes that you may all enjoy a happy Christmas.

WRITTEN TO A YOUNG MAN IN THE WORLD.

Manresa House, Roehampton,
Dec. 28, 1875.

My dear ——

Just a line to thank you for your Christmas card and to wish you a happy New Year.

Some time ago you wrote me about a new undertaking you had in hand. I hope it prospered to your heart's content. I did not forget the intention at the Holy Sacrifice.

I hope you keep your health; and I hope you have made some progress in practical philosophy and learnt to take work a little more quietly.

I think the one fault your mamma found with you was that you were too anxious.

There is time for all things if we don't go too fast.

Believe me, my dear ——

Yours very truly,

GEORGE PORTER.

Manresa House, Feb. 24, 1876.

I am very afflicted to hear of your trouble, I do not think you are much to blame, if at all.

And from what you tell me, I feel little doubt the poor child left this world with all the benefit of the sacraments. Besides she was so good and so patient, you may reasonably hope that God would take care that her soul should not be lost. I will say Mass for her to-morrow. Her death is very distressing, but then there are many circumstances which inspire hope.

However, you may take a lesson which I have long since learnt. Always incline to the side of giving the sacraments too soon. I have never seen cause to regret having administered them too soon. I think they are *often* administered too late.

You come in for a good share of troubles. I take that to be a sign of predestination, only make good use of your trials, be patient and don't grumble. You say you are destined to suffer. Suffering is by no means the worst destiny in this life, only bear it well and it will be the making of you.

If you enjoy the privilege of much suffering, you should get the book of P. Lyonnard, *L'Apostolat de la Souffrance.* I met a person living in the world who had taken a vow always to take what brought most suffering. Think of that!

I am rather amused that you find in —— and her jealousy a reminder of your earlier days. You may apply a lesson from your own experience. I suppose you were most helped by any patience and forbearance which was shown to you. Scolding never did you good. A great deal of kindness was not thrown away. You will end some day by writing instructions to Superiors who have subjects that are ever so little exigeantes.

I hope your head keeps well amid all your troubles. Try and get your sleep regularly: nothing like rest for a wearied head.

Manresa House, March 17, 1876.

In answer to yours of the 12th, I enclose you a mortuary card of my dear mother; her anniversary was on Monday. I meant to have sent you the card as a reminder: pray for her. I hope she is in Heaven, but the prayers won't be lost.

Don't be afraid of death; it is often very painful, but God always gives abundant graces at the last; that is my firm belief. Work away now at your own sanctification, and do what you can for the souls of those who are placed under your charge. When your turn comes, you will have help to prepare you for the journey to the land of which we know so little. I am glad to hear you have gone into your new building. I hope you have given the walls time to dry. It is just possible that I may pay you a visit before Easter, and see all your improvements. I am to preach the Three Hours at Manchester. Holy Week is not exactly the season for novice-masters to take trips, and very probably I shall only have time to run to Manchester and back again. If I can manage to get to —— I will do so.

You say you wish you could get into a way of doing things well. Don't do anything in a hurry, but give plenty of time to each duty, as much time as the rule requires or the work demands. You are none the worse for liking to do things well; only say to God you want to do them well, because it is His work; repress any little whisperings of vanity or desires of approbation, contenting yourself with God's approval.

If you do not get on well with your Particular Examen, change it to this form. At the beginning of each hour or of each important action say the prayer, "Jesus, meek and humble of Heart, make my heart like to Thine," and mark every omission as a fault: the marking is an important part of the Particular Examen. This prayer is indulgenced, and you may acquire a habit of frequently using it: this prayer, and not trying to do two things at the same time, and not getting hurried, will work wonders in your meditations and prayers.

I am sorry to hear you find a difficulty in Holy Communion. Have you Crasset's *Entretiens sur le Saint Sacrement*? or Mons. de la Bouillerie's *Meditations sur l'Eucharistie*? It would do you good to read these or any other devout book on the subject, to get up your desire for this food of the soul. Good-bye now. God bless you.

Manresa House, July 19, 1876.

I wish you a happy feast. I have just said Mass for you, that you may become a worthy child of St. Vincent.

You ask me to tell you in confidence if I am going to be Provincial this time. I keep no secrets from you, so I will tell you I am not going to be Provincial. I think Divine Providence watches over the Society too mercifully, ever to allow my being named to that weighty office. Pray for me that I may become less unfit for my present post, which is more than enough for my poor shoulders.

If it was not that I feel the office of Master of Novices too much for me, I should ask you to pray that I might hold it to the end of my iife.

Manresa House, August 31, 1876.

I believe I never thanked you for your birthday letter. Accept my best thanks now for your letter, for your good wishes, and for your good prayers.

In answer to your last of yesterday. (1) Yes, read a spiritual book instead of meditating, but take care to read it slowly, avoid galloping over the pages, and dwell on the good thoughts, sometimes making an act of faith, of love of God, of love of your neighbour, of hope, of sorrow, of purpose of amendment. Sometimes instead of reading, take the Psalter and say the Penitential Psalms, or some of the other Psalms, or the Psalter of Jesus, or the Rosary of the Seven Dolours, or any other vocal prayer to which you feel a devotion.

(2) Begin the rule of life as soon as you can, if not completely, as far as you can; the longer you delay it, the harder you will find it.

In your previous letter you proposed to send me your Particular Examen book every month. Do so; this little practice will keep you up to the mark. I dare say now you wish I had forgotten your offer; never mind, send the book, and I will see how you go on. God bless you.

Manresa House, Roehampton,
Nov. 14, 1876.

Shortly after sending my letter yesterday, I received the news of your father's happy death, at fourteen minutes past midnight on Saturday. This morning I offered up Mass for the repose of his soul.—R.I.P.

Very unexpectedly Father C—— has just paid me a visit. I now send you as much as I can remember. He scarcely left your father during his illness: he was with him through Friday night and Saturday night; he gave him Viaticum on Thursday, Friday, and Saturday. His devotion in Holy Communion was very remarkable. When he received at 5 a.m. on Saturday, he could scarcely speak a word, but after his Holy Communion for at least five minutes he prayed aloud with a clear distinct voice, making his thanksgiving so that all could hear him. These were the last articulate words he was heard to utter.

For some few hours on the Saturday, he started from time to time, and opened his eyes wide as if he beheld some unwelcome sight. Each time Father C—— and those in the room said three Hail Marys; that always calmed him, and in the end, the agitation, whatever it was, quite ceased. He suffered no pain.

Father C—— thinks he was quite conscious to the last; he gave three long breaths, and looked round at every one, and so died. Your mother and —— held his two hands; the others were praying round the bed.

The Protestant nurse seems to have been wonderfully impressed; at first she left the room when prayers were said, but the last day and night she remained constantly by the bedside, sobbing audibly and quite overcome.

Father C—— tells me that your father to the last tried to have a smile on his face for every one around him. He says he never saw a more edifying death, and never saw one so cheerful and free from sorrow.

Your mother bears up well. She leaves to-day for —— with two of your sisters. There will be a Requiem in Farm Street to-morrow: the Provincial and Socius are going in from this house: I will go, if I can, but 9.30 a.m. is an early hour.

If I hear more I will send it to you. God bless you. Take courage to serve God now with more fervour. "My father hath left me, but God hath taken charge of me."

TO A SISTER OF MERCY.

Manresa House, Roehampton,
January 27, 1877.

My dear Child,

P.C.

I will say Mass for you on the 29th. May you live to complete the other half of your Jubilee.

I congratulate you on having happily come to the end of the first half. How many graces and blessings have been crowded into 25 years! Probably not all made the best of. Still, O Lord! your servant has believed in the Ever Blessed Trinity, Father, Son, and Holy Ghost, and now repents of all commissions and omissions, negligences and infidelities, promises amendment, and prays for grace to make better use of the future.

"Heart of Jesus! Thou lovest. Thou art not loved. Would Thou wert loved." Resume your march on the 30th of January to this war-cry: it will carry you well on the road.

On the occasion of your Jubilee I may flatter your self-love a little, little bit. Though so long since you had written, I had not forgotten the writing. I knew it at the first glance.

I do not know when I shall appear at —— again. I cannot often leave the noviceship. When I do come I hope to see a goodly muster of my old friends.

With kindest remembrances to —— and all the community, wishing you, my dear child, a very happy feast on the 29th and many graces,

I remain, yours very truly in Christ,

GEORGE PORTER.

Manresa, March 3, 1877.

I see I have allowed a fortnight to pass without answering your letter. Since December, my work has quite beaten me. I doubt whether I can ever get back to my level. I have not answered my Christmas letters yet: there seems to be some danger of their standing over till Christmas twelvemonth. Your last letter, however, must have an answer.

From what you say I come to the conclusion that your health is the cause of your present bad humour and jealousy. Are you following up Dr. C——'s prescription? Better far to eat meat on Good Friday than to live in war with every one about us. I fear much you do not take enough food and enough rest. You stand in need of both, and it is not wise to starve yourself into misery. Jealousy and all similar passions become intensified when the body is weak. I believe a little beef-tea judiciously taken would make a great difference. I cannot find any other explanation for the change you remark in yourself. Many persons are unwilling to believe that spiritual matters depend so much on the state of the health. You must try to improve your health and fight on: matters won't mend if you yield to troubles. Begin now. Lent is a holy time. Pray hard to overcome yourself; give up what pleases you and do what pleases others, and you will quickly find your good dispositions will return. I shall hope to have a brighter account. God bless you and strengthen you.

Collegio Germanico, Roma,
June 11, 1877.

I hope to be back at Manresa before the end of this month or early in July. Be quite satisfied: I was not consecrated in May, and still hope to get to my grave a simple priest, S.J. As I am too far from the General and the Provincial, I will not venture to send you any news.

Your spiritual troubles would very soon be diminished, perhaps quite disappear, if you could adopt a very simple rule: go on as if all is right and all will be right. Say your prayers, read your reading notwithstanding distractions, interruptions, infidelities, omissions: above all, as well as you can, be regular, follow a rule about Holy Communion and Confession. Disregard your scruples, take it for granted you have contrition and all necessary dispositions and your Communions will give you strength and courage. Lastly, try to be patient with yourself, others will be patient with you. I fear you do less because you cannot do as much as you would wish to do: the wise plan is to do what we can and to leave the rest to the mercy of God.

The heat here is very great just now. The Romans say we have the July heats in June this year. July or June, it is a respectable heat. Rome has been very interesting and is so still; the Jubilee, the pilgrimages, the exposition go to make up a picture one must have seen in order to understand. I consider I have been fortunate in visiting Rome at this time. I keep very well.

Manresa House, Nov. 25, 1877.

You must not be disheartened. If you persevere with the Particular Examen you will soon become pretty accurate in marking your defects, and you will find you have made real progress before many months have passed. As to Confession and Holy Communion, I still repeat, keep to your rule, never stay away through repugnances, &c. I know it is hard to be faithful, but be assured that if you give in now, the day is not very distant when you will remain away for *whole years*, one of the greatest calamities that could possibly happen to you. I have seen more than one such case. The very violence of your temptation to stay away is a proof that the devil means great mischief. You must not give in. Read that chapter of À Kempis (slowly) every day till Christmas Day, and pray that you may surmount your temptation. Indeed, it would do you good to read some of the other chapters of the fourth book.

Yesterday my father kept his seventy-seventh birthday. I spent a few hours with him on Thursday and Friday, after giving a short retreat at Westbury convent. He was very well and in good spirits. To-night I begin the thirty days' retreat. How well that would suit you: it would certainly put you right.

Father Jones has returned from Jamaica, not very well in health. He gives a good report of Father Thomas. God bless you.

Manresa House, Feb. 23, 1879.

My dear Child,

I owe you a long letter, or rather a series of letters. In the first place, you will ask me why I have remained so long without writing to you. I really cannot tell you. I have been very busy, but my work does not justify my long silence. I have wanted to write; but sometimes I did not think to write when I had the time, and sometimes when I did think, I had not the time. When you were so good as to send me that little book on first confession, then I resolved most firmly to despatch a long letter, and say how badly I had behaved, and how ashamed I felt, and how resolved I was to do better; and here I am writing that confession in the year of grace 1879! I am very much ashamed of myself: a sort of fatality comes over me when I once neglect a correspondent, it seems as if I never could put myself right. One thing I do feel, though I have behaved like a brute, you will forgive me, if I promise that I will try and do better, a promise which I make very sincerely, and now I have broken the ice, I hope I shall be faithful to my word. I dare not ask the date of my last letter; but how many great events have happened since that time!

My brother Thomas sent to Jamaica; it was thought he was to be made a Bishop. I am sure he congratulates himself that expectation has not been fulfilled; he is still a simple priest, Vicar-Apostolic, with power to give Confirmation. He likes his work, and is doing a great good out in the island: he keeps his health, though he has grown very thin. Since his departure from Europe, my dear old father has gone to his long home: he died on my birthday, the 28th of August. He had reached a fair old age: infirmities were creeping upon him; God gave him the grace of a very happy death, so we can look back with thankfulness on the many years he was spared to us, and feel grateful that he was taken at a time when a prolonged life would have brought much suffering. And he escaped, too, the total loss, or nearly the total loss, of all he had in this world. What he had, was mostly invested in shares of the West of

England Bank. Mrs. M—— will have told you that this bank has failed. . . . And what have I been doing all these years? quietly living at Manresa, never very strong, but able for my day's work, and having every day so filled I can never get through all that is before me; and for all I know, I may remain here till I die. I wish you were coming to England this year, that I might show you our beautiful garden. Perhaps a kind Providence may have that consolation in store for us; may it be so. It is just possible I may go to Rome again this spring, after Easter; but I do not expect to make such a long stay as I did in 1877. Now I have given you pretty nearly all my budget of domestic news, I will add one circumstance which took back my memory nearly twenty-two years, and will take back yours. On Saturday, I sent off two Fathers to give a mission at St. Mary's, Handsworth. Do you remember 1858 (I think that was the year) when Father Lambert and I were sent on a similar errand? good Father Grosvenor being then the chaplain. Many of my most valued friendships date from that mission. The despatch of two others to the same spot after an interval of twenty years brought many pleasing memories. I must ask now how you are, how you are getting on? You must put me up in all your contemporary history. I scarcely dare ask how temporal matters stand with you and your friend: this terrible war, now the plague, the unsettlement of all commerce must involve private individuals in great suffering and losses. Do you ever see Mad. v. O.? I have not heard from her for years; my thoughts always run to Halbendorf, when I get as far as Dresden. I shall send you by this post a most charming little book, which I have lately met with. When you have read it, kindly let the Countess see it. Remember me very kindly to her, to Mdlle. Hedvige, to the boys, and to little Mary. Shall we ever meet again at Krippen, and cross the frontiers to have the blessing of Mass?

Write and tell me you forgive me. I will never suffer so long a space to break into our correspondence. God bless you.

Pray for yours truly,
GEORGE PORTER, S.J.

Manresa House, July 18, 1879.

I write to wish you a happy feast to-morrow. I shall say Mass for you, and give a large memento to Sister Superior and to all my friends in your congregation, and to the congregation itself. May God prosper you and all you undertake for His honour and glory.

I must now say something on your last spiritual letter. The subject of your Particular Examen I fully approve: when one yields to the habit of grumbling, it is easy to magnify grievances to one's own mind. As À Kempis says, to bear annoyances in silence is a grand matter.

As to your meditations, I fancy the fault is not that you are wanting in zeal or effort; it is that you do not vary the form of your prayer. Sometimes you should make more affections of the will; at other times, more petitions, at other times more colloquies; sometimes be more passive, at other times take your meditations in complete sentences. Variety is a wonderful help in meditation: it does not entirely shut out distractions, but it diminishes them, and secures greater fruit from prayer.

So, in preparing for Holy Communion, vary your preparation: sometimes use one set of prayers, another day take a different set; on a third day prepare by meditation. Keep yourself alive, and this easily, without

Holy Communion. 35

violent efforts. Have you a method of recalling Holy Communion on the day before and the day after you receive? *e.g.*, whenever you say, "Give us this day our daily bread," whenever you visit the Blessed Sacrament, &c. It is true you are nearly forty, and much remains to be done; but you have done a good deal. Thank God for all His mercies to you, confess your shortcomings and your miseries, resolve to do better or to try and struggle on. Life will soon come to an end, and when the end appears you will see your time has not been lost.

I wanted to send you a book for St. Vincent, but it is not printed yet; it will be soon, and then I will send you a copy. Meanwhile, continue to read the *Conferences of St. Vincent:* you can have nothing better for you.

CHAPTER II.

LETTERS FROM ROME.

From Oct. 1879 to Sept. 1880.

Departure for Rome. Padua. Relics at Venice. S. Ambrogio, Milan. Fiesole. Sacrilege and reparation. German College, Rome. San Lorenzo. Audience with the Pope. Celebration in Rome of the twenty-fifth anniversary of the definition of the Immaculate Conception. S. Andrea al Quirinale. Lord Bute's English Breviary. How to get a love of prayer. Christmas in Rome, the Cribs. Samuel and Robert Isaac Wilberforce. Father Ramière's book on the Apostleship of Prayer. Books on the Passion. St. Bernard's Sermons on the Feasts of our Lord. Spiritual dangers arising from overmuch work. Subjects for Easter meditations. The pilgrimage to the Seven Churches. Lenten preachers and Holy Week in Rome. The Decrees in France against the Religious. July in Rome. Probable movements. Advice for a Retreat. The French Government and its persecution of the Jesuits. Ruskin's *Mornings in Florence*. Italian translations of the Fathers. Peace of mind essential for gaining profit from a Retreat. Meditations on the Psalms. Carlsbad again. Father Porter no longer Superior at Manresa.

Manresa House, Sept. 26, 1879.

I have been ordered to start for Rome next Wednesday, and you may imagine my hands are quite full. Manresa is crowded to excess. Twenty-four new novices joined on the 7th. On the 8th we had sixty-four novices in the house; since then our patriarch novice, Father Stevenson, aged seventy-three, has taken his vows. Father Morris takes the place of Master of Novices during my absence.

You will get on better with Father —— in the course of time. When he comes to understand your difficulties better he will show himself very kind to you. I will pray for you during my stay at Rome that you may get on better with him. So much depends on your being happy with your confessor. I consider it a very worthy object of prayer. Give my kindest remembrance to all at home. God bless you.

San Girolamo, Fiesole, Oct. 14, 1879.

I slept in Padua on Sunday evening and said Mass for you and yours in the *santuario* on Monday morning. What a glorious spot! The Masses succeeded each other from 5 a.m. till noon, and there was at every Mass something of a congregation, sometimes a large one, sometimes a smaller one. Then at the end of the Mass the pilgrims crept behind the altar to kiss the tomb of Il Santo, or to put their hands or their foreheads against the marble case which contains his body.

The Church of Santa Justina, close to the *santuario*, I found very interesting. The church is a noble one; empty I may say, but rich in very precious relics.

Venice surprised me most in the matter of relics, so numerous and so precious. I said Mass at our old Church of the Assunta at an altar where lies the head of St. Gregory Nazianzen, the thigh-bone of St. Cristoforo, and I don't know how many other great saints. Then almost every church possessed some great treasure in this way; unhappily I could not find a printed guide which gave the catalogue of these riches. Venice in her day evidently took a deep interest in securing good relics whenever they were to be met with. I saw nearly all the larger churches and several of the collections of paintings. The paintings were so numerous, and my time was so limited, that I was rather bewildered by them. I had no idea there was so much worth seeing at Venice.

A somewhat curious and antediluvian usage was observed on the Sunday I spent there. Two *parocchi* were inducted into their parishes, the houses were hung with flags; at 2 p.m. the *capi di famiglia* all went to kiss the hand of the new parish priest. At night there was an illumination. Not a nineteenth century practice. Very novel too was the sensation of going about in the gondolas, and breathing an atmosphere without any dust.

At Milan I was fortunate enough to fall in with a very intelligent ecclesiastic who showed me through that most interesting old Church of S. Ambrogio. I saw the relics of the saint, gorgeously vested in a shrine which contained too the bodies of SS. Gervase and Protase, discovered by St. Ambrose. . . . On my way through France I stayed at Aix-les-Bains. Lady Londonderry was there. We joined in an excursion to the Lake of Annecy, and I saw at Annecy the relics of St. Francis of Sales and St. Chantal, also the chapel in which St. Francis of Sales received the vows of St. Chantal. In Venice, by the way, I came upon a grand relic, the heart of St. Francis of Sales, which is preserved by the Nuns of the Visitation at the Monastery of St. Joseph.

On the 14th (I am continuing this on the 15th) I reached Fiesole, which looks very lovely. Here I am in the midst of many old friends. Very Rev. Father General is wonderfully well and hearty. Three of the Fathers are past 80 years of age. They are all moving soon after 4 a.m.—an hour, as an English novice once complained, at which no respectable fowl rises. They are most edifying.

Perhaps the Government annoys our people rather less than before; they are very busy confessing, preaching, and giving retreats. If the good done is on a small scale, a great deal is done. One must not expect much from a Government which issues bank-notes for 5*d*.

Collegio Germanico, Roma,
Nov. 3, 1879.

I write a short note, principally to say that I will not forget Mr. Dean's anniversary, the 7th of November. On that day I will offer up my Mass for him. It is as nearly as possible twenty-three years ago since I made his acquaintance on the steamer going from Marseilles to Civita Vecchia. He came up to me and asked me if I was Mr. Ferguson, and when I rejected the insinuation, he pretty nearly as much as said to me, Well, who are you then? He was only fishing for an acquaintance. R.I.P., an honest man and a confessor for the faith.

What a dreadful sacrilege that was at Brighton. God is very long-suffering. We cannot understand how He permits much that takes place in His Mystical Body; or what is done to His Eucharistic Body. But then, how much He allowed to be done to His natural Body, to His Sacred Humanity! We can only tremble and adore, and offer what reparation is in our power: the reparation called forth by the outrage has possibly pleased Him more than the outrage offended Him. Anent your idea of being allowed to have the Blessed Sacrament, I think the Bishop would grant you leave for a few days occasionally, on condition that the chapel were kept very securely. You may have to pay for your privilege in crosses and sufferings, which seem so hard before they come, and which God generally helps us to bear very well when they do come.

The German College is in the Via del Seminario, close to S. Ignazio: it goes from the Piazza of S. Ignazio to the Piazza of the Rotunda: and the German College is close to the Palazzo Serlupi. I am very happy here, and shall be quite content if I am left here: there is some danger of a German Bishop coming, and then I may have to turn out. However, I have been offered a room at the North American College, in the Via dell' Umilta, at the foot of the Quirinal. They had their retreat last week, and I gave them an instruction at 3 p.m. every day, for something like three quarters of an hour: so they look on me as a friend.

I have just been to San Lorenzo, the cemetery, to see the chapel fitted up for Ours, and to say a *De profundis* for the thirty-eight who lie there. The chapel is very simple, but beautifully contrived. I preferred the old crypt under the church, where a man was laid in the tufa, in the most Christian grave I have ever seen, exactly on the model of the catacombs. The piety of the Romans struck me this evening. There were crowds flocking to San Lorenzo, the tramway organized a special service, and many I saw on their knees. The month of the Holy Souls is observed with great devotion. I usually say my Mass at San Ignazio, either on the altar under which rests St. Aloysius, or that under which Blessed Berchmans rests. I have also said Mass in the room of St. Ignatius. How many holy associations Rome presents to keep one's fervour alive. Pray I may use this grace.

Collegio Germanico, Dec. 22, 1879.

It is high time I should answer yours of the 20th November. I have been very much occupied since then, never overwhelmed with work, but with my hands always full. From the heading you will see I am still at the Germanico: no Bishop has come, and I imagine I am safe during this cold weather, though two of our English Bishops (Hexham and Salford) have chosen this wild winter for their official visits to the Eternal City. It will be delightful if I am left undisturbed for the rest of my stay in Rome, which, by the way, threatens to run on, perhaps to Easter. . . . The weather is very cold for Rome, but there is no snow, no ice, the air is dry, the atmosphere beautifully clear, the sun bright and genial for several hours, and walking is most pleasurable. The pleasure is lessened when you return to your house and sit down to your table, on a brick floor, without anything like a fire nearer than the kitchen. I wear three or four suits of clothes, and so contrive to keep fairly warm, all except my fingers, which become chilly after much writing. The weather is very healthy, and I find myself perfectly well and in the best of humour, even jolly.

I must tell you of our audience. I say *our* because I went in under the wing of Father Jones. We had Leo XIII. all to ourselves for twenty minutes. He is not like the photo which I saw in England. I send you a small photo which I can vouch for as a faithful likeness. The face is a marked Italian face; mouth and nose both very prominent: the forehead is intellectual, the eyes are dark brown, large, clear, and honest: he is not a handsome man, but he has a noble presence, and with his spare, upright figure, his well-defined head and eyes, Leo XIII. looks a man who works, both brain and will, to some purpose. He was very gracious: asked many minute questions about the Society in England, and then explained in great detail the order of procedure which was to be followed in our business. At the end of our interview I asked his blessing for a number of my friends, among others for you and your family. I shall ever cherish a pleasing recollection of that audience.

The twenty-fifth year of the definition of the Immaculate Conception was well kept in Rome: in half a dozen of the largest churches there was a novena of preparation. The Pope invited our Father Gallerani from Florence to preach the novena in the Gesù. The church was crowded every day at 11 a.m. On the feast itself, not only was the church crowded, but the piazza of the Gesù as well. The doors of the church were closed for fear of an accident. The illumination was magnificent. I am not an enthusiastic admirer of fireworks in churches, but I confess this illumination of the Gesù was fine. People said there were ten thousand lights: the decoration and the illumination were the gift of some noble Roman lady (some say the Duchess of Garzioli): they did not cost less than £800. There was not the slightest sign of a disturbance: the feast is a holiday in Rome, and though it fell on a Monday, the day was generally observed, nearly as well as a Sunday. The illumination at night, I am told, was general. No attempt at a counter-demonstration was made, in fact everything passed of happily.

You say that you take it for granted we have been deprived of S. Andrea on the Quirinal. In a way we have been deprived of the church: a secular priest has charge of it, but our Fathers do a certain amount of work there. Of the house we retain, curiously enough, a portion, which is set apart for the South American College. Victor Emmanuel allowed us to have it without rent up to 1880. King Humbert leaves us as tenants paying a high rent. Rather hard to be turned out of half your house, and then be compelled to pay a high rent for the other half; however, we are glad to remain even under these conditions, rather than be turned out into the streets. The rooms of St. Stanislaus are in the part left to us. . . .

Have you been tempted to purchase a copy of Lord Bute's English Breviary? if so, you will find in the antiphons for Advent and for Christmas Day abundant matter for meditation, and matter in keeping with the season of the year, and matter, too, which will throw light on your Scripture readings. It is rather late to ask you how you have been during Advent? I fear the cold has tried you to a degree that does not help piety or prayer. Under those circumstances, piety mainly consists in bearing patiently the cold one cannot escape from, and struggling in some way through one's prayers. Wishing you many graces and joys of Christmas, and begging a share in your prayers, I remain,

Yours very truly,

GEORGE PORTER.

Collegio Germanico, Roma, Dec. 22, 1879.

This ought to reach you on Christmas Day. I suppose the cold and heavy frosts will still delay it a day at least. In any case I wish you and all a very merry Christmas and a happy New Year.

The cold here I find most intense; outside I don't mind it, the air dry, the atmosphere is wonderfully clear, there is no snow, and walking about you easily keep yourself warm, but in the house, with brick floors, windows and doors never well-fitting, no fire of any description, one does get cold. I am now wrapped up in a small mountain of clothing, with a blanket around my legs, mittens on my hands, and it is as much as I can manage to hold my pen. However, I am very well: the weather is healthy.

Looking back on the past year you may, I think, thank God that matters have gone on better with you. Only keep up your courage, and understand what you are aiming at, and you will still do very well.

Poor old —— was a great friend of mine. With a fine temper of her own: or the remains of what had been a fine temper, she was an honest body, perhaps hated her enemies, but certainly loved her friends.

In answer to your kind offer to send me a paper, I shall be very glad to receive the *Catholic Times*. The Italian papers don't know how to give news, in fact, I pass days without looking at a paper, and I don't think I am anything the worse for it, and I am quite sure a great deal of time is saved. Good-bye. God bless you.

Collegio Germanico, Roma,
Jan. 3, 1880.

My dear Child,

You have my best wishes and prayers for the New Year: may it bring you many graces and consolations, and grace to bear the trials that may come.

I thank you for all your good wishes to myself, except the one regarding the post of Provincial. I pray that cross may never be laid upon my shoulders. I am happy to tell you there is not a word of truth in the rumour of my appointment.

On the 25th of November, Father Jones and I had our audience. I asked His Holiness's blessing for you, and all the community; he gave it very graciously.

Father Jones left me early in December for Malta, Cyprus, Gibraltar; at present he is in Malta. He hopes to be in London about the middle of the month. I remain here to see the end of our business. Pray that it may end A.M.D.G. and for the good of religion.

The weather has been very cold; and as you know, when it is cold in Rome, religious suffer; there is absolutely no provision made for such a contingency. Thank God, I am very well, notwithstanding the cold.

——'s move to Cabul may be the making of him; his is a case for the Irish rule of driving down hill, "Hit him and hould him." Hardship and hard work tame the wildest creatures on the road.

To come to yourself. Might it not be a good subject for your efforts this year, to aim at getting a love of prayer and holy reading; to learn to settle down for a regular talk, short or long, as time will allow, with our Lord in the Blessed Sacrament; or at your praying place in your cell. It is in this way that prayer becomes a real stay to our life; we must be able to open our hearts to God, as to our friend, our father, our counsellor, our everything. We have made a great step forward when we can see God in everybody, and in every event, when He becomes a living reality to us, of Whose presence and nearness to us we become intimately conscious. There will be no presumption or rashness in turning your thoughts in this direction; no going beyond one's grace. How far you advance on the road, will depend on the progress you make in this union with God, and on the grace He gives you: to advance on the road ever so little is a great gain.

Quietness, order, having times of rest—all these help you towards the same end.

Everything kind to Rev. Mother and the Mothers Assistants. God bless you. Pray for me.

Collegio Germanico, Jan. 6, 1880.

. . . The Piedmontese have put a stop to what formerly was a pleasing accompaniment to a Roman Christmas. The peasants from the Abruzzi used to troop into Rome about a fortnight before Christmas, with a primitive form of that primitive instrument, the bag-pipes, and go up and down Rome playing novenas before the Madonnas and singing some simple Noels. They were always welcomed as the *pfifferi*, the heralds of Christmas. Poor fellows, the last I saw of the tribe was in London; a pair of them were piping their

Christmas carols to an unbelieving, gaping crowd of cockneys, who took more interest in their well-made legs, cased in sheep-skin, tied on with cords, than in their songs or their music. I hear that many of them now push their way as far as France, and there meet with sympathy and coppers. What has grown to be an intolerable nuisance is the celebration of Epiphany; from *Ave Maria* on the vigil till far into the morning of the festival all Rome, young and old, rich as well as poor, swarm in the streets with the most braying of cheap trumpets; the din and annoyance are incredible. I suppose there was a custom of this kind in Papal times, but I have no recollection of the babel we have had this year. The cribs are some of them most beautiful, artistic and devotional both; I have been this evening to see the one at S. Francesco di Ripa, and one in a small private house, 25, Via dei Genovesi, in the same neighbourhood. How I should like to transport some of these, even one of them, to London; they would do good; the utter realism of the Roman faith would be respected even by the unbeliever. My companions were two prosy, matter of fact Lancashire priests; they were quite mastered by the simple, homely, yet artistic versions of the wonderful tale of Bethlehem, as much as any of the Romans who crowded round in great delight. Such numbers flocked to the *presepio* of 25, Via dei Genovesi, that *gens d'armes* were stationed there to keep some sort of order.

The biography of Bishop Wilberforce would have little interest for me. I agree with you, there was no spark of true Catholic thought or feeling in the man: it was remarked that shortly before he met with his sad, sudden end he had spoken of the Catholic Church with a bitterness which he had not shown before, but which betrayed the utter want of sympathy, perhaps worse even, by which he was animated. In 1856, I knew here, and venerated and loved, his brother, Robert Isaac, a simple, grand soul, made of the stuff out of which Doctors of the Church are created; a man, I should think, the very opposite of his brother. . . .

When you are in special want of help, go before the Blessed Sacrament and tell your trouble to our Lord; there is so much direction to be had from Him, if we would only seek it and talk over our affairs with Him. Who can understand us so well? Who can help us so efficiently? You need not fear any contrivance of the devil in this difficulty. Go on as well as you can. God will take care of you.

On Thursday I am to preach at S. Andrea della Valle. During the Epiphany Octave there is a series of sermons in various languages, and Mass is said in various rites to represent the calling of the Gentiles; my sermon is the English contribution to the series. Good-bye. God bless you. Pray for me.

Collegio Germanico, Jan. 31, 1880.

. . . I recommend for your Lenten exercise the perusal of Father Ramière's *Apostleship of Prayer;* not so much with the view to engage you to enter into that Association (which, however, is an excellent one) as to urge you to much prayer, and above all to many petitions for yourself and others. We don't ask enough, not fervently enough, nor frequently enough. The first part of Father Ramière's book is an eloquent exhortation to prayer and to petitions. Bury your *bête noire* about making yourself miserable; take the crosses which God sends with patience and resignation, believing you deserve more, pray very fervently, often remember the Passion of our Lord, and leave all else to God.

Father Louis de la Palma is a book I recommend on the Passion; also Sister Emmerich; and with one or the other the Gospels themselves, the very text. The Stations I also recommend; or any plain, homely practice of devotion to the Five Wounds of our Lord, or the Seven Dolours of His Blessed Mother, or the Rosary. Holy Communion as often as you can: this is the first of all methods of honouring the Passion: "Do this in remembrance of Me." And if things are too comfortable at home, invite some torment to spend a few days with you.

I do not expect to return before Easter. My time is usefully spent here. I want to be at Manresa, but I cannot complain that I am kept at Rome. . . .

Collegio Germanico, Feb. 19, 1880.

This evening I have posted to your London address a copy of the Sermons of St. Bernard on the Feasts of our Lord, in an Italian translation. The Italian is by a Dominican, Cavalca, of the classic "trecento" age, a holy man, a classic author in the Italian language. The edition is by the Jesuit, Father Paria, my very good friend. This book you will read, I hope, with much pleasure and profit. I shall be glad to know how you get on with it. I have come on something of a mine of these old Italian translations. . . .

. . . I have no very decided news for you as yet in our business. Father Ballerini is not ready, and the Commission will not commence its labours till he is quite ready. The Bishops of Clifton and Salford are still in Rome.

I have made several very interesting visits to the Catacombs, with a man who knows them very well. To-morrow I am going through the Christian Antiquities at the Lateran Museum with him. . . .

[No date.]

The retreat won't be put off very long, I hope: one of your greatest spiritual dangers is having too much to do, you get worried, and then prayers cannot go so well. The Particular Examen on not speaking impatiently would get on very well if you were not overwhelmed with work. Do try to secure for yourself some respite during the day. Your prayers may become a rest, if you will take them very leisurely and devoutly, and especially if you will give more time to vocal prayer than to meditation. The imagination more easily runs riot when you have too much to do, too much work for the brain. At times of extra work, you stand in need of more repose and of more food. The faith you still have, and plenty of it: only keep down the work and the distractions which prevent the life of faith, with its consolations. The life of faith cannot go on without peace of mind: remember that truth.

Rome, March 7, 1880.

For a change in meditation you may take scraps from the Missal, from the Masses of Easter Week, from the Introits, the Collects, from Epistles and Gospels, and from the Prose, *Victimæ Paschali*. The Masses for Easter Week and those for Pentecost Week suggest to me more consolation and hope than any portion of the liturgy in the year.

My business here will not, I trust, drag on till July. I hope to get away about Pentecost. Cardinal Manning arrived on Monday. He will give an impulse to Roman slowness; at least, I hope he will. I have been six months absent from Manresa. The novices will forget me; and those who joined in September have hardly ever known me: an arrangement which does not console me. I have had one of my old attacks; but not a very violent one; it was the result, I imagine, of the long, sharp winter. I feel no effects of it now.

Remember me very kindly to your mother. I never pass the Piazza Campitelli without thinking of Mr. Palmer, and somehow your mother is always associated in my mind with the memory of that holy man.

I will not forget poor Sister ——.—R.I.P.

Collegio Germanico, April 1, 1880.

Buona Pasqua! Though I fear you will only receive my Easter greeting on Low Sunday. I have had an inundation of work for the last few weeks, and to-day, in order to make up some arrears in my correspondence, I have given up a pilgrimage to the Seven Churches, in which the ninety German students and their Superiors have joined. Perhaps some consideration of the distance to be walked weighed with me, the Seven Churches being S. Pietro, S. Lorenzo, S. Maria Maggiore, S. Croce, S. Giovanni Laterano, S. Sebastiano, S. Paolo fuori le Mure, and then home to S. Saba: a six hours' performance. I am not certain that I have given you the churches in the right order, but if you look at a map of Rome, and see where they are situated, you will come to the conclusion that they cannot be visited without a great deal of walking, unless the pilgrim takes refuge in the omnibus or *carrozzella*, a very undignified proceeding on a penitential walk.

P.S.—The visit to St. Peter is made overnight.

I hope you were able to attend the Holy Week services at Farm Street, and that you found them to your taste. Here I confined myself to the Gesù, where the ceremonies were performed by the German students.

The rubrics were carried out most exactly, and their singing, strictly Gregorian, was very fine. They are ninety in number; they have amongst them many fine voices at present, and they are fortunate in possessing a most competent choirmaster. I was very edified and delighted with the ceremonies. Of the Lenten preachers I cannot say very much; the preacher at the Gesù was admired by many and attracted immense congregations. I confess he did not please me. He pelted his audience with eloquence; there was no repose, no light and shade in his sermon; an unbroken glare from beginning to end, or a wild, unchecked torrent. I like to be able to draw my breath in peace sometimes during the course of an hour. One preacher, Father Rizzoli, pleased me; he had good matter, beautiful language, but he fell short of the orator, for he talked, very wisely, very pleasantly, and very deliberately, but he never got beyond talking.

Rome was very crowded with visitors, English and French, including two thousand French pilgrims and a detachment of Cook's tourists. As a rule they behaved very well. The Italians behaved much better than usual. The *employées*, who are counted here by thousands, and the soldiers approached the sacraments in great numbers. On Maundy Thursday I visited some of the most beautiful sepulchres. Everywhere I encountered crowds on the same errand: it is true the Annunciation fell on the same day, which turned the Maundy Thursday into a day of obligation and closed the shops and set free a large portion of the population; add that the evening was a lovely Roman spring evening, and some explanation is given for the crowds, but I think the crowds were larger than could be accounted for by those circumstances. Altogether I was edified and consoled. The throng at St. Peter's, I am told, was unprecedented.

Father Ballerini is getting near the end of his work:

when it is fairly out of his hands, I shall know my prospects of returning to England. . . . When you write I shall be glad to know whether you have been able to read any of St. Bernard, and how you have liked him. If your Italian proves serviceable to you, I shall be able to give you some nice reading when I come back. I have bought several Italian books of much merit.

You may have heard I was unwell. It was nothing very serious: one of my old attacks, probably the result of the long severe winter. Thank God, it is all passed now and I am quite recovered.

Collegio Germanico, May 8, 1880.

Welcome to Italy! always supposing that your plans have not been interfered with and that you really are at Florence. I do not know where you draw the line on the thermometer, but I do not complain as yet, though the heat in Rome has been unusual for the end of April and May's first week. Heat suits me; it seems to set the spirit free. I can work better and longer when there is a genial sun overhead and the shutters are partly closed. Just now we are passing through some showery weather, which takes the place of the rain we ought to have had during winter. Strangely enough, between the intervals of the showers the heat is greater, or I ought to say, perhaps, there is a feeling of sultriness. The Romans expect that the weather, when it is settled, will not be so oppressive.

You ask me whether I am likely to be at Fiesole; I do not see any prospect of my being called thither. Father Ballerini has finished all his writing. We are now delayed by the printing; that too must soon come to an end, and then the Commission will commence its labours. The Pope will do all in his power to keep the proceedings secret. I think he is displeased at all the paragraphs which have found their way into the papers. The English Episcopate is strongly represented. Besides the Cardinal we have Dr. Vaughan, Dr. Clifford, Dr. Patterson. Monsignor Patterson will be consecrated to-morrow; then Cardinal Howard goes with them very zealously; lastly, Lady ——, whom these wicked Romans call a "matriarch," smiles upon Rome, and is kind to her friends.

If the opportunity offers, won't you make a *Scappata* to Rome? the catacombs I fancy are closed now till the autumn, it would not be safe to visit them; but there are always shrines above ground. There will be some good functions; if nothing else there will be the month of May, as long as it lasts, and then there are the treasures of art.

Rome is preparing for a General Election, or rather Italy; the papers wish to make an agitation and the loungers about the Piazzas are whipping themselves into action, but the general public is wonderfully apathetic and indifferent. We want a Gladstone to stump the provinces, or some one province. . . .

The priests and religious in France are in no little anxiety about the 29th of June, when all are to disperse. All the communities in France have agreed not to ask for authorization; some fifty congregations of men are united on this line of conduct: the communities of women, and they must be still more numerous, follow the lead of the men. The Government is in a fix: my own belief is that it will find itself pushed on to the last extremity by the factions of Gambetta and Clemençeau, one more violent than the other. I hear Victor Hugo has declared in favour of liberty for the religious, especially of religious women who belong to the contemplative orders. The famous decrees of the 29th of March must be violent when they drive Jules Simon and Victor

Hugo to defend religious. There is a Frenchman here who is posted up in every phase of the controversy; with his help I have learnt many details which are very interesting. I dare not commit them to a letter, as the officials here make very free with what passes through the Post Office.

You say you consider your patience has been fairly exercised during the month of April. I congratulate you on the opportunity you have had; nothing helps one on in spiritual life so much as patience. No delusions come in there: every trial borne with patience is so much clear gain for this life and the next; it brings merit and grace here and earns a crown for hereafter. Among other precious books I have bought is an old substantial volume on Patience; it is written in Italian, so you will be able to manage it.

When you come to Pentecost, do not forget to make your readings and meditations on the Mass for each day of the week; I think I said to you the liturgy for that week and for Easter week is one of the most suggestive which occurs during the whole year. . . . By anticipation I wish you a happy Pentecost, with many gifts and graces from the Holy Ghost.

Collegio Germanico, May 30, 1880.

. . . Father Ballerini has at last finished his part of the work and finished it very well. On Tuesday in Whitsun week the copies were sent to Cardinal Nina, and by this time the Commission has entered on its labours: it remains to be seen how soon they will finish. Old Romans predict that all the parties to the controversy, cause, or whatever it is to be called, will be at their posts in Rome next November: and certainly the traditions of the past favour these prophets. On the other hand, Leo

XIII. is a brisk governor and he is known to wish for a speedy decision. Cardinal Manning too, who is a power out here, clamours for a speedy termination. Though the heat has fairly set in, His Eminence says he does not find it warm enough, and Bishops Vaughan and Clifford declare they won't move till the affair is ended. So it is just on the cards that I may get away before the end of July.

In any case, I shall not make myself unhappy. My time is very fully and very pleasantly and I hope very profitably occupied. Providence takes me away from my post, and Providence will look after the novices in my absence.

The very busiest time for me is at an end for the present, but a gust of work may come down on me at any moment. During the whole month of May I have not been to hear a single sermon. It is quite true there is no very attractive preacher in Rome at present; but, if there had been, I should have been much exercised to get to him.

You say your meditations don't get on very well. Interrupt them for a time and try the Masses of Pentecost week, or that of Corpus Christi, and use them by the second method of prayer, or even by the third. By the way, I hear that a great treasure has been found, the Mass and Office for every day of the octave of Corpus Christi, composed by St. Thomas of Aquin. At present we have only the Mass and Office for the feast and Lessons for each day during the octave. From these I imagine the liturgy for the octave will be very rich. It has been printed quite lately, or is going to be printed shortly: I only heard it from a Minor Osservante last week.

To come back to the meditations. A change to the second method is often useful, and especially when one is on a journey, away from the accustomed surroundings. Perhaps St. Bernard's Sermons on the Feasts of our Lord may help you during the month of June. I hope you continue your Communions; don't be kept back from them by any aridities or trials. . . . Good-bye. Pray for me.

Collegio Germanico, July 11, 1880.

My dear Child,

When you receive this, you will probably have finished your schools and commenced your holidays. Make the holidays a real rest, and give spirituals their share in the rest; there is, as you know, endless repose and strength in meditation and prayer and reading, when we go to them and give ourselves up to them calmly and attentively and devoutly. *Attente ac devote,* as we pray at the beginning of the Divine Office. A good rest, a good retreat, and a reasonable programme of work for next year, will find you in September well prepared for the coming year.

It is just possible that I may return to England for the next few months, but I shall not leave Rome before the end of July, perhaps not before the Assumption. When my programme is made out for me, I will send you a postcard. Cardinal Manning has started for London. Dr. Clifford has been called back by the illness of his brother, Lord Clifford. Dr. Vaughan is reported to be going to Perugia. He has sent his secretary, Monsignor Gadd, to Manchester. After July no great work will be done by our Commission.

I suppose we must all meet here again next November, and I shall not be surprised if the decision is postponed till 1881. Rome is a grand school for learning patience!

The summer heats have fairly commenced. Yesterday we had 31° or 32° centigrade in the afternoon, and that is respectable Roman heat. In the worst of the summer, the thermometer will stand at 34°: in exceptional years it has gone to 37° or 38°.

The mere heat is bearable enough. When the Sirocco or African wind blows, then the heat becomes trying. The Romans are very sensitive to it; their nervous system quickly warns them that Africa is blowing upon them, and the more delicate suffer from depression and *malaise*. At present the Sirocco does not make much impression upon me, but in proportion as I become acclimatized, I shall feel its power more and more. Up to the present, I call the weather delicious; the sky is cloudless and bright, and the air is clear.

What troubles the Holy Father has everywhere on hand, France, Belgium, Germany, Italy. Our Fathers in France met their fate with great dignity. I expect the persecution initiated by the Government there, will cause the downfall of the Reds.

Pray very hard. How many reasons we have to pray fervently. Good-bye. God bless you. Pray for me.

Rome, *July* 14, 1880.

You have had reason to complain of my long silence. It is very long since I last wrote to you; in truth all my correspondence has fallen into confusion. I sometimes wonder whether I shall ever get straight again. This Roman business pushes everything else into a corner. . . .

You ask me about my future movements; do I think it likely I shall have returned to Manresa by the 22nd of this month? We are now at the 14th. It seems to me highly improbable that I can return for the 22nd. I rather think that the Provincial intends to recall me for some time during September and October, but nothing has been fixed as yet. When I receive my orders you shall have a postcard. Perhaps I may see you before I return to Rome in the autumn.

You must not be alarmed by what the papers say about the heat. The warm weather has indeed commenced, but it is very bearable so far. During the day the thermometer runs up to something near 90°, but I never leave the house, if I can help it, till 6 or 7 p.m., and then there is a pleasant breeze. About 7 a.m. I close my shutters, admitting only as much light as I require for reading or writing. At 4 p.m. the shutters are thrown open. To tell the truth, I find the weather delightful. I am very well.

We have reached the turning-point in the year. I don't know whether you are aware that the genuine Romans count twenty-four hours to the day, and the day begins with the *Ave Maria* half an hour after sunset. For the last month *Ave Maria* has been 8.15 p.m., to-morrow it will be at 8 p.m., and it continues to fall back till January, when it will be 5.15. A Roman would call 8.30 this evening a quarter of an hour of the night, 10.15 two hours of the night, and so on. But the hottest and the most trying season is to come yet, during August and the first half of September. What wind there is comes from Libya, bringing a hot, suffocating fine dust.

Don't fret about not being a nun. You would have been in your coffin long ago, if you had made the attempt. God means you to do some good in the world before you leave it.

When I had an audience with the Pope, I asked his blessing for you all. Tell all. I don't think I have any further news for you. I hope we may meet during the autumn. If we do, then I can tell you anything I have passed over in this letter.

Advice for a Retreat.

Collegio Germanico, July 18, 1880.

I suppose you will join the retreat on the 22nd. I write this in the hope that it may reach you in good time. I will say Mass for you on St. Anne's day, the 26th, which comes during the retreat, that you may make it well, and obtain an increase of confidence and courage. Take it quietly; dwell on those two affections, hope and courage; make many acts of both during every meditation, pray for an increase of them, seek out motives for one and the other—but all calmly and quietly, allowing the thoughts and feelings to sink into your soul. In free time, instead of much reading, find out the Psalms which dwell most on these virtues, and study them very leisurely. Don't think that the greater part of your life has been passed without doing any good; it is very certain you might have made better use of your time, often make acts of contrition for loss of time, but then, don't think so much of the past as of the present and the future. What your hand can do now, that do; wish it were better done, but leave it to the mercy of God, and turn your thoughts to what comes next. Living much in the present gives a healthy tone to our spiritual life. At any rate, make the retreat a new *point de départ, da capo*.

You were right in supposing that Cardinal Manning would find it warm enough before the end of July: you have him again in London. Dr. Clifford was called back to England by the serious illness of his brother. Dr. Vaughan remains.

The Commission won't hold any sessions before November; but in November all the preliminary work will have been gone through. Some busy heads are at work in cool spots, outside Rome; and some are at work in Rome. I rather expect to return to England for some two or three months, and then come out again to Rome for November. I have not received marching orders as yet. When they do come, I will send you a post-card to say what my movements will be.

After all, the French Government has carried the decrees into execution: no doubt they have disgraced themselves in the estimation of all moderate men and of all true Liberals. In all probability, the other Orders and communities will be dealt with very soon. Thank God, our Fathers have met their persecution with dignity and fortitude: they have the consolation of thinking they are condemned, when Barabbas is amnestied. It is an honour to be pursued by the Government which grants wholesale pardon to the heroes of the Commune. Some sanguine people hope that the French Government will recall the Fathers. I cherish no such hope: the *canaille* of the Revolutionary party will compel the Ministry to carry out the whole of the anti-Christian programme. And the Ministry is pliant enough to accept any measure, provided sufficient pressure be applied from without. We shall see worse things yet in Paris.

When you were at Florence, did you fall in with Ruskin's *Mornings in Florence*, or a title with something of that sound and meaning? Ruskin is not a favourite of mine, as a rule, but I read one of those small volumes, and became more reconciled to the man than I had been before. His imperturbable self-satisfaction survives, but he has glimpses into the soul of Christian art which are precious. He has felt the spell of the thirteenth century upon him, and one knows little of the soul of Christian life and art till the great factors of that age have been understood. I think *Mornings in Florence* would interest you.

You never say a word about the Sermons of St. Bernard: I am afraid you have not had the courage to attack them. If you care for them, there are stores of the

Fathers covered up in good Italian translations, and I would soon get together a valuable library for you—a resource to fall back upon, when you want to rouse yourself by strong reading, by the words and thoughts of the giants of our race. *Addio.* God bless you. Pray for me.

Victoria, Carlsbad, August 29, 1880.

You see I have left Rome. I am on my way to England. The Provincial kindly offered me a month at Carlsbad. I willingly availed myself of the opportunity to repeat the course of waters which on two former visits did me so much good. I arrived here on August 9th, and shall leave on September 6th. On the 12th or 13th I hope to visit Ober-Ammergau and witness the Passion Play: about the 16th I shall report myself in London. As my stay in England must necessarily be a brief one, I shall not take up my residence in Manresa. I must content myself with some flying visits. My present instructions require me to be in Rome early in November. It is possible, but not probable, that I may have to anticipate that time. I hope I shall be able to see you before my return to Italy. . . .

. . . Your letter of the 13th was forwarded to me from Rome. I am glad you managed to keep yourself in peace during your retreat. Peace, or at least the effort to keep peace of mind, is a necessary condition to obtain much help from a retreat in all those cases in which no great battle has to be fought out, no vocation to be decided, no important resolution to be taken. You would like a retreat especially directed for persons who cannot leave the world, and who wish to sanctify themselves there. Such a retreat would be a great boon; perhaps the nuns at Roehampton may some day see their way to retreats for particular classes. The large gatherings which they have now do not allow of many special applications. You must accept the inevitable and make the best of it, till such time as you can have better.

You seem to find the Psalms and the *Imitation* furnish good matter for meditation. Why not follow up your *attrait*? Why not, occasionally at least, select some verse for your daily meditation, either in the form of a regular meditation, or according to St. Ignatius' second method of prayer? A verse of the Psalms or of the *Imitation* so meditated becomes, if I may say so, a property for life; after a good meditation, the mere reading of the verse, or the recollection of it, in a single moment brings back all the thoughts, all the pious affections, all the good resolutions of the meditation.

When I go back to Rome, I will look for St. Bernard's Treatise on the Degrees of Humility, in Italian. I think it must have been translated. . . . At Manresa I have a MS. translation of the treatise in English: on my return I will try to remember it, and I will lend it to you, till I can find an Italian translation.

On my way from Rome, I spent one long day at Perugia, in the company of a very dear friend, who knows it thoroughly. It was a large undertaking for a single day, but I saw much which delighted and edified me.

The rest of the journey I ran through; the route through Austrian Tyrol, from Ala to Innsbruck, was new to me, and very beautiful it was.

I don't know whether you have ever visited Carlsbad. The country is very beautiful. The first fortnight we had changeable, chilly weather, for the last week it has been fine autumn weather, with cold mornings and bright days. Carlsbad is surrounded with immense pine forests, which are most attractive. They are laid out with gravel walks for miles and miles, and they are kept

with as much care as a garden: a small army is employed
in sweeping them every day. I take all my meals in the
open air, at a Restauration which looks on one of these
forests. It is an object of the same endless interest as
the sea, always changing, never the same, impartially
telling the tale of cloud or sunshine. The life is penitential. I rise at 4.30, say Mass at 5.30, begin to drink
the waters at 6.30. My allowance is four tumblers, with
a quarter of an hour's walk after the first three glasses.
After the fourth I plunge into the forest with my breviary,
and walk and pray for an hour. The silence, the solemnity of the woods, help my prayer. About 8.30 a light
breakfast of Kaffee recht (*i.e.*, rather more coffee than
milk) and dry bread, the best bread I have ever seen:
dinner at 12, supper at 7, rest 9.30. In the intervals
I read, write, or walk: an idle life to lead for a month.

Sept. 26, 1880.

I reached London at 8 a.m. on the 23rd, but found
instructions calling me to the north. At 8 p.m. I was at
St. Beuno's, in North Wales. I hope to return to town
in a few days, and I will then write and say when I can
go to see you.

You have heard, or perhaps you have not heard, I
am no longer Superior at Manresa. I hold a roving
commission till the Roman business is ended, and the
Roman business may be concluded in a few months,
or it may drag on for years. I went twice to Ober-
Ammergau, but I must keep my histories and my
impressions for my visit. *Addio.* God bless you.

CHAPTER III.

LETTERS FROM ROME.

From Nov. 1880 to May, 1881.

Journey to Rome. The Passion Play at Ober-Ammergau. Advice about Confession. Execution of the decrees against Jesuits in France. Republican intolerance and irreligion. Ludolph of Saxony. Condition of souls outside the Visible Church. Each soul *capable* of receiving truth. Visits to Cardinals. Bad people, the minority in the world. There is more good than bad in every one. The First Commandment. How to deal with souls. Life and writings of P. Marquet. A long letter about faith. An act of faith as distinguished from the habit of faith. The act of faith an act of the *understanding*. The preparation for faith. The office of the will. The progress of faith illustrated in the sixth chapter of St. John. Reasons why some people, though leading good lives, never receive the faith. How to meet difficulties and temptations against faith. How to strengthen the *habit* of faith. Père Matignon Sur le Surnaturel. The Roman spring. Healthiness of Rome. "A pearl of great price." Perseverance in the means of grace. The preachers of the Mese di Maggio in Rome. Conclusion of his Roman business. Father Porter in Paris. The mortification and conquest of self-love implied in following certain rules necessary for attaining peace of mind. The devil's game in France.

Collegio Germanico, Nov. 20, 1880.

My dear Child,

P.C.

I think I wrote a hurried line to —— before I left England, so you will have known that I was very busy, and soon to be on the road. Father Morris has taken my place at Manresa. Flitting after a year's absence was no easy, no pleasant, no short task; leave-taking, paper-sorting, &c., terrible even to remember. I crossed the Channel to Boulogne on the 18th October, slept one night in Boulogne, another in Paris, another at Turin, two at Florence, and reached Rome on the 24th. The journey was not cheered by all I heard at Paris and Boulogne. The powers of darkness are making use of their hour in France. Pray it may be short. On the evening of the 24th I began my retreat; when that was ended, I found myself turned out of the German College (still send my letters there). I hope to regain my room there, but at present I am enjoying the hospitality of an old friend of the Society in Rome.

The business is now well *en train*, and the days are well filled.

I give you my impressions of the Passion Play.[1] I could write a long article on the subject, and I am not sure I will not do so. You must be content with some jottings and observations.

1. I don't think I gained one single idea about the Passion or Crucifixion. The sight may impress Protestants in this way. I do not understand a Catholic who has meditated the Gospels, learning anything.

2. The drama was essentially a religious act. The action itself was, and must be, religious; and the whole bearing of the actors was as grave as the bearing of the priest and choir in Holy Week. There was infinitesimally little which jarred with the earnestness and seriousness of the actors.

3. The acting of individual actors was nothing surprising. The Christ was very dignified; Judas exerted himself; Barabbas, St. Peter, were wonderfully in harmony with known artistic types; but acting, real stage acting, there was none. There was not in any one actor the slightest attempt at acting up to the audience, or looking for applause. This was as it ought to be;

---

[1] Father Porter went to Carlsbad for the month of August, and thence to Ober-Ammergau.

stage acting would have been little short of profanity, where the action is so Divine, and the words of Holy Scripture are so largely introduced.

4. The *mise en scène*, the management of the mob, the crowds, the soldiers, was very fine; artistic in the highest sense of the word. It could not be imagined more perfect than it was.

5. The introduction of the chorus was most happy. Their explanations, their singing, were admirable. They prevented monotony and weariness, and gave a wonderful life to the whole play.

6. The music was often very pleasing. It was not classical, nor was the singing wonderful. They were always bearable, and occasionally positively pleasing.

7. The *tableaux vivants* were perhaps the most marvellous part of the whole performance. The conception and the carrying out, were both eminently artistic. You have seen descriptions of them. I will not repeat what you know. Imagine a picture of two or three hundred figures (sometimes), with endless variety of grouping, colouring, dressing, &c., all thrown into a very fine representation of some well known painting; all the figures, down to the infants, living persons; and not a finger moved—all motionless as statues of marble. Certainly the training must have been great, and the teacher must have been no ordinary artist. I saw the play twice, and was well pleased with it. I am glad to have assisted at it.

I am running on too far. *Addio.* God bless you.

Rome, Nov. 1880.

You say you have not given the rule of life a fair trial. It is true you have not carried out the whole of it, but you have made a beginning, which I trust will encourage you to carry your attempts further.

Advice about Confession and Prayer. 67

As regards your confession, for the present be satisfied to avail yourself of Father ——'s help in examining your conscience. As to the contrition and purpose of amendment, if there has been any considerable fault, an outburst of temper, some gross negligence or omission of prayer, then you can always say with truth to God, "I wish I had not committed that sin of anger, wilful negligence, or what not." And in such cases, and even in cases where the faults committed were rather involuntary, or at least not very deliberate, you can say truly, "God has been so good to me, I must try and serve Him more faithfully and fervently. I must keep to my rule of life, to my prayers, &c. I must watch myself and not give way to ——." When you can say in truth and sincerity, even though the *feeling* be not very strong, "I wish I had not done it, I will try to love God better and to serve Him better," then have no fear about your dispositions. I always recommend this finishing to the confessions: "I accuse myself of all my other sins which I do not remember and of all the sins of my past life, especially of my sins of —— and ——. I am sorry for each and all of them. I purpose amendment, I ask absolution."

I am glad you begin to feel some satisfaction in vocal prayer. Continue to take pains with it, make an effort to pray with attention, say the prayers slowly and leisurely. Such vocal prayers are the best introduction to meditation.

I won't forget you on your birthday. May you see many happy returns, live to be older and live to be holier.

We are enjoying a rare Martinmas summer, with occasional showers and storms. At this moment we have a sun and a sky you would be glad of in the month of July.

Collegio Germanico, Nov. 16, 1880.

I think I have not written to you since I left England. It is time I should give you some account of my journey. You may remember I left London on the 18th of October for Boulogne: I slept at Boulogne and broke my journey again at Paris. The execution of the decrees was being then pushed forward; it was melancholy to witness this tyrannical proceeding: every one was on the *qui vive*, rumours were flying about in every direction. Obnoxious Fathers were sent to remote towns. In Boulogne there was something of a demonstration the very day of my arrival. The Government Inspector had gone with much display to our former College to weed out any Jesuit professors who might be there in the dress of secular priests (many of them were actually in the place), but the fishwomen of Boulogne had their ideas on the subject, and assembled round the College in such numbers and with such looks of mischief that the Inspector left without having weeded the College. Whether he returned to his task on a later day, I do not know. At Paris the same weeding was anticipated. Since that date how much woe the Ministry has brought on the country. There was no doubt much discontent, and some think it will break out into open resistance. The Republicans in France evidently look upon their tenure of office as a chance to do all the wrong in their power to those who differ from them in politics or religion. Unfortunately, Republicanism of this extreme kind has become a sort of religion. Italy threatens to follow suit in the system of persecution: there is talk of hunting down the scanty fugitives who escaped the first persecution. And last night I see that Portugal has taken up the same odious policy. Where will it end? Well may Leo XIII. complain that he is not free to rule the Church, that he has been and is hampered in every direction. Did you see his dignified *pronunciamento* to the " impiegati " of the Holy See on the 24th of October?

I went from Paris to Turin in twenty-two hours. I rested the night at Turin: then went to Florence, rested there two nights and gave a day to Fiesole; and finally reached Rome in the afternoon of the 24th. I found the General at Fiesole in good health and in good spirits, but somewhat feebler. Father Weld was very well.

The day after reaching Rome, I went into my retreat. When I finished it on the 3rd of November, the first news I heard was that my room at the German College was wanted. I am at present the guest of Miss Sherlock, an old Roman resident, but I hope to get back to my old quarters early in December. My letters still go to the German College.

There is some probability of our business being terminated quickly. A prelate who enjoys the confidence of the Pope said the other day that the decision would be given in December. I fear this anticipation will not be verified. Real work only commences this week.

It will not increase your affection for London weather if I tell you that our Martinmas summer is perfectly delightful. You would be glad to have it in July in England; such a blue sky and such genial air. . . . Have you read Freppel? I shall be glad to have your opinion upon his Conferences. . . . You are right in saying Ludolph of Saxony will help you in meditation: it is a book written from pure love of our Lord, without a thought of literary power, or the faintest trace of self-consciousness—a truly devout book, brimming over with the most genuine piety. . . . Have you ever used Lancisius' *Meditations for Advent*? I think you would like them.

Collegio Germanico, Dec. 20, 1880.

. . . This is dated from Coll. Germ. but I am still at Miss Sherlock's in a room with a fire, a wood-fire blazing away cosily, though we are still enjoying fine weather.

I must begin by wishing you a *buona festa* and many graces and blessings for Christmas and the New Year. We have no more *pfifferi* from the Abruzzi singing and piping novenas to "bambin Jesu," but the churches are well attended at early hours. At 5 a.m. there is a chorus of bells inviting pious souls to the novenas, at which they pray devoutly and sing lustily for a good half-hour, all winding up with Benediction and that inimitable Roman *Tantum ergo* by the whole congregation. Many of the churches are quite filled at these early services. . . .

The feeling which the Conferences of Freppel has awakened in you is in some respects right; but it may easily carry you too far. We believe that the one road to everlasting happiness made known in Revelation is the Church, Christ's Kingdom upon earth, which rests on faith in God and His Son Jesus Christ Whom He has sent into the world.

At the same time we believe that many will be saved who never gain admittance into the visible Church, and never become visible members of Christ's Kingdom on earth. Such souls do the best they can, in their circumstances; they avoid wrong and do good, up to the measure of light they have received, some as pagans, some as sincere heretics, some as unbelievers. It may be that some of these, rising to a certain level in their ignorance of anything higher, spend better lives than they would have done had they received the light of Revelation. But it would be wrong to suppose them incapable of taking in the fuller truth; every one who comes into this world, and reaches the use of reason, is capable of knowing and loving Jesus Christ. They may appear indifferent to the supernatural at any given time, or for a given time, but capable of better things they are, and possibly one fine day they will see and embrace the truth.

I am much more disposed to adopt the opinion that most persons who outwardly seem indifferent, often in their heart of hearts become conscious of the insufficiency of what they have, and feel a craving for something higher. Pilate I do not take to be a sample of the best of men who do not believe. Yet even Pilate asked our Lord, "What is truth?" The unfortunate fellow was too giddy to wait for the answer: had he waited, who can say which side he might have joined?

My inference is, that it is good to pray for the conversion of *all*. One must have infinite patience and not push the matter, where there is no apparent preparation for the faith; the grand art is to make the most of what one finds, and lead the inquirer to wish for further instruction. Conversions not unfrequently follow after years of patient waiting and praying. Wait and pray, watch and pray, and if you do not throw away obvious occasions, when you may speak with advantage, you will find your confidence in God's goodness strengthened. . . .

. . . I hope you have spent a good Advent, the beginning of the Church year, the preparation for Christmas, without an overdose of the blues. You must try to keep up the Christmas devotion through all the feasts which follow up to the Purification. It is not without reason the Church lingers on all the mysteries which are connected more immediately with the Incarnation and the Nativity. *Et Verbum caro factum est*—the biggest fact in the history of our world. . . .

. . . Our business came on to-day. I cannot say

as yet when it will be ended. It is very possible the end may come very quickly, much more quickly than people generally expect. Pray for a favourable issue. *Addio.* God bless you. Pray for me.

Collegio Germanico, Jan. 18, 1881.

... Last week I had to distribute a copy of a document to nine Cardinals; the document was to be given into their own hands. It is very difficult to find Cardinals; either they are *in congresso,* or *non riceve,* or *sta occupato.* My week was spent in the attempt. I succeeded in handing my document to seven; the eighth I found in the house after two or three calls; he was laid up with gout, and I was invited to return the same day week, as the attack was a sharp one; the ninth was Cardinal Nina, he lives at the Vatican. I paid four visits in vain, and in the end was obliged to give him up.

The Commission has ended its labours. The fifth and last session was held yesterday; the secretaries will draw up their report, which they will present to His Holiness within the week. No one can say when the Pope will publish his decision; he is in very good health now, and he will in all probability act promptly....

... If possible, I will get you more of St. Bernard's Sermons. They are very devout and very suggestive. It would be possible to string together a very beautiful selection of passages on our Lord and His Blessed Mother.

Your experience with the "antipatica" relative bears out one of my theories of life, viz., that bad people are the minority in the world, and that in every bad person there is more good than bad if you will only look for it. It comes very much to St. Thomas' rule of practical charity: fix your attention on the good side of your neighbour, and turn away your thoughts from the bad side; and do the contrary for yourself. Next time you try to make her life a misery to her, ask her if she owes any duty to God, over and above what He requires from her towards her neighbour. These matter-of-fact duty people, as a rule, overlook the First Commandment, and the obligation of knowing and serving God, of believing in Him and hoping in Him; to keep out of the hands of the police, and to play the lady bountiful is their standard of duty, and no place is left for the claims of the Creator, or the personal service with mind and heart.

You promise some remarks on what I said about every one being capable of taking in the truth; don't forget your promise, the subject interests me deeply. My principle is to take a soul *tel quel* just where it may be, and then try to carry it forward to something higher. Souls are in all stages, some are sunk very low, perhaps in vice, perhaps in darkness; the art is to "exploiter" just what you find, and make something of it. Not a few souls, if taken for what they are really worth, and not for what they ought to be, might be won to God; but more of this another time. . . .

Collegio Germanico, Jan. 29, 1881.

My dear Child,

You were not forgotten at my Mass this morning; and I shall give you a special memento again on the 2nd. When asking the Pope's blessing for others, I asked for a special one for you and all your children.

The business which brought me here, is now drawing to a close. The final word of His Holiness is all that is wanted, possibly we may have to wait a little time for it, but it cannot be long delayed. When that word is spoken, my steps will be turned once more to England. Pray hard for a good *finale*.

This letter is intended to be a very short one; but I must not close it without some spiritual suggestion. Take up that little prayer which has been indulgenced, "Jesus, meek and humble of Heart, make my heart like to Thine." The use of this ejaculation will confirm you in peace of soul—a gift most precious, and much to be prayed for.

I hope your mother keeps well during this severe season. Here we have had much rain, not much cold. I cannot complain. I am living in a private house, with a cheery wood-fire, when I want one. *Addio*. God bless you.

[No date].

I am sorry you have been disappointed in getting to Paris for your retreat: the change would have done you good. I saw the other day a book which you might read with advantage: the life and writings of Père Marquet, of our Society. The good man died last year just after the execution of the famous decrees. This volume contains some forty letters written by him to a nun who was left by God in great darkness for a number of years. Her case is not quite the same as yours, but much that he writes to her would suit you. The letters struck me very much. The book was only lent to me for a few days. It is not to be procured in Rome, otherwise I would buy a copy for you and send it to you. The rest of the little volume did not interest me much; it is all very Frenchy, excellent for French people, but not the best for solid, stolid, English people.

Meanwhile, plod away, as if everything was right, and all will be right. Lead a life of faith, and cease to trouble yourself whether you believe or not. Don't entertain the thought whether you believe or not. I will answer for you, you believe well enough. Pray that your faith may be strengthened, and then persevere in the life of faith.

Collegio Germanico, March 10, 1881.

On Ash Wednesday I left the Palazzo Calabrini for my old room in the Collegio Germanico; a fitting beginning of Lent! The weather was *un po rigido*, but a farce to last year, and I am very happy in my old quarters and in the midst of my old friends. . . . The business is not yet ended. Some say it will not be ended much before Easter: the matter at present is before the Pope himself.

This morning I propose to write you a long letter about faith; but before I enter on that very wide subject I may make a brief suggestion for Lent: a frequent remembrance of the Passion, and frequent acts of contrition for sins both of commission and of omission. This exercise will sanctify the preparation for Easter and lead you nearer to Jesus Christ, I hope.

In what I am about to say on faith I shall write rather generally, leaving you to make the application both to your own case and to those whose apparent incapacity for faith puzzles you.

The first point I insist on is that you must distinguish clearly and *resolutely* between the act of faith and what is outside it, whether the outside be a preparation for faith, or consequence of faith, or obstacles to believing, or obstacles in the workings of faith. Besides, distinguish between an act of faith and the habit of faith; the latter is a supernatural quality of the soul which disposes it and renders it able to make acts of faith. The act of faith is an act of the understanding (not of the will), in which I say, I believe, I confess to be true, not what I see or what I understand, still less *because* I see it or understand it. But what I do not see and do not understand and what seems difficult, mysterious, even incredible, because a witness who can neither deceive nor be deceived testifies to the truth in question. Several acts of the will go before the act of faith, several acts of the will ought to follow it and spring out of it, but the act of faith in itself is a pure act of the understanding, such as I have described. And if I may say so, I do not think Cardinal Newman has always insisted on this idea of the act of faith with sufficient resolution and pertinacity.

What is the preparation for faith? Sometimes, it may be a deep conviction that the Creator cannot have left His creature without saying something more to him than he gathered from the voice of nature; a conviction that the outward shell of human life without a special revelation is an unsatisfactory riddle. Or, it may be a rationally worked out conviction that man in his present state bears testimony to some great rebellion or upset in the moral world. Or, it may be a witness, say the Catholic Church, or some wonder-working apostle, or some plain homely priest, or, for the matter of that, some honest old Biddy says, God has spoken to man, you are bound to listen to His message, your first duty is to your Creator, it takes precedence of all duties to your fellow-men, to individuals, to society; you owe it to Him to inquire whether He has spoken, and to bow down your understanding if He speaks what is higher than your understanding. Under many forms the mind may arrive at the conclusion, "God has spoken as a fact; at least there is good reason for presuming He has spoken," or, "I cannot satisfy my reason, unless I discover a revelation has been made: I will go and see."

Thereupon the will enters in, with a simple, honest desire to discover the truth, to face it if it is hard or terrible, to accept it, even should it prove incomprehensible, even should it condemn one's present life, impose difficult obligations, &c. And here I may observe in the mysteries of revelation there presents itself a strange mixture of the intangible and the tangible: how tangible Christ on earth, the carpenter's Son, nailed to a Cross, how intangible His Divinity, how tangible the Eucharistic species, how intangible the Real Presence, how tangible the Church, Pope, Cardinals, Bishops, virtues, scandals, how intangible the abiding presence of the Holy Ghost! We see, we touch something, we believe far more than we see and touch. St. Thomas saw the form of a Man, he touched His wounds, but he confessed how much more, my Lord and my God.

The sixth chapter of St. John gives a good illustration of the progress of faith. *All* the disciples admitted that Jesus was no ordinary man. They followed Him, He propounds the mystery of the Eucharist; then the will of some broke down and they walked no more with Him, they recoiled from the act of faith. St. Peter understood no more of the mystery than those who went away, but he had believed and confessed that Christ was the Son of the living God, and so he believed all His teaching about the Real Presence.

The difficulties, therefore, which *precede* faith may be in the understanding or in the will; minds which don't reflect, which ask with Pilate perhaps, What is the truth? but with him do not stay to hear the answer, minds which never travel beyond, "This is a hard saying and who can bear it," which waste life in considering the difficulties and objections to revelation and allow no time or thought to the positive arguments in its favour, which turn away from the sun and complain they don't see it, minds, in one word, which do not go in quest of truth with honest simplicity, will not see it and will not believe the Church or Christ Himself or God in Heaven. You can easily comprehend how an indisposed will fails to require from the understanding the act of submission which is implied in, "I believe, O Lord, assist my unbelief." How pride of intellect, contempt of the Church or of God's ministers, the pride of life, the tumult of the passions, the inordinate desire of wealth, &c., harden the will and prevent it from accepting the yoke of faith.

I think one of your difficulties is how good-living people don't receive the faith. Sometimes they absolutely refuse to think; more frequently they think only of the difficulties and refuse to apply their minds to the consideration of the reasons for. Even in natural sciences this method would never lead to knowledge. If the student were to raise all the objections in his power and concentrate his attention on them, his progress would be miserably small. Or again, take an illustration from practical life. A competent physician tells his patient you have such and such a complaint, you must avoid such and such diet, &c., you must employ such and such remedies. What hope would there be for the patient who would insist on chapter and verse for everything, especially if the physician were not merely competent but infallible?

Will this dissertation clear up at all for you. I wonder how and why some reach the faith, some sooner, some later, some quickly, some slowly, some not at all, remembering that God leaves us to work out our own salvation, by the light of reason, with our right will, aided by His grace? Can you understand how early education, certain intellectual habits, even bodily ailments, irritability, provoking spines, congested liver or spleen, to say nothing of disordered brains, in fact, how past and present, how soul and body, how oneself and one's surroundings, all tell on the effort and acts of the mind, in what goes before faith? Can you understand how the will may not rise to the height of the act of faith?

And now observe, how after you have made the act of faith, even after you have received the habit of faith, the greater number of the difficulties which stood in the way before still remain, the habit of doubting, the habit of objecting, the infirmities of mind, the infirmities of body. Perhaps some of these increase with advancing years, bodily infirmities especially may supervene and with them say despondency, irritability, &c. How should the sincere believer act? He should make frequent acts of faith, he should often pray for faith. *Credo, Domine, adjuva incredulitatem meam. Credo, Domine, adauge mihi fidem. Dominus meus et Deus meus.* He should fight against any intellectual habits which he discovers in himself opposed to faith, he should break himself of the habit of doubting, questioning, objecting, these habits are strengthened by indulgence, they are destroyed or weakened by starving them out. Bodily miseries one contends against as well as one can, chiefly by regular habits, moderation in food, outdoor exercise, taking rest or nourishment as one requires it. Some neglect the body, especially invalids, and grumble against God because He won't work miracles and save them from the consequences of their own folly. However, there are many cases where neither doctors, nor care, nor good sense avail to keep down infirmities; then comes in the grand salve of patience, and the thought, how much soever I suffer, whatever my pains and aches, God remains unchanged in His Eternity, the truth is as it was, only my duties are changed and have become more difficult. *Credo, Domine,* &c.

This letter has run to great length, and there still remains much to be said on the conduct we are to observe during temptations against faith, **and much too on the** life of faith. Till that letter comes, exercise yourself in thinking about Jesus Christ, strive to love Him and to imitate Him. Think, were He in my place would He speak thus, act thus; but in applying this measure don't renounce your common sense.

Collegio Germanico, April 6, 1881.

... To go on with faith now. You ask whether an act of faith increases in strength with the understanding? Not exactly: by strength of the understanding you mean probably power of reasoning out a conclusion and holding to it. The act of faith rather partakes the character of seeing than of reasoning; the believer sees, not with his own eyes, but with the eyes of Him Whose word and revelation he accepts. The certainty of an act of faith, the power to drive away all fear of error in what we believe, is greater than the certainty of any merely natural act of the understanding.

The cultivation of the understanding may influence the acts which precede the acts of faith; simplicity and singleness in the understanding, the exclusion of all habits of doubting and indecision, a study of the grounds of faith, *i.e.*, the grounds for accepting the fact that God has made a revelation, all this tells in the act of faith, removes difficulties, makes faith easier, arms the believer against temptations, but it does not reach the act itself. Poor people have little time or inclination perhaps to make any deep study of the motives of their faith; but then as a rule they are not troubled with many doubts: they find a very short way to settle the question of the Divinity of the Church. It is the oldest Church; no other body calling itself a Church can show marks of a Divine origin, of sanctity, &c. In their own fashion, according to their lights, they arrive by a short but sound argument, to the conclusion that the Catholic Church is the Church of God. If temptations assail their faith, or if soupers try to pervert them, they devise answers for themselves or consult the priest. More learned people who see more difficulties, who are capable of profounder considerations, discover more numerous arguments for the Divinity of the Church, take in the relations of the several truths of revelation to each other, the beauty of the body of truths, and are led perhaps to elicit more frequent acts of faith, and if they are holy merit a great increase of faith.

What strengthens the *habit* of faith is to make frequent *acts* of faith. Acts of other virtues, of charity, of hope, of self-abasement, of self-denial, strengthen the habit of grace, or habitual grace, in the soul, and so indirectly strengthen the habit of faith. Prayer for faith obtains increase of faith. *Credo, Domine, adauge mihi fidem; credo, Domine, adjuva incredulitatem meam.* The stronger the habit of faith, the easier, the more perfect, the more meritorious the act of faith.

The best way to overcome temptations against faith is to perform the works of faith. A life of faith is the victory over doubt and unbelief. A life of faith, *i.e.*, keeping the Commandments, recognizing God in all authority, Jesus Christ in our neighbour, not stopping in the things which strike the senses, but going beyond to the eternal realities of life, &c.

An observation may find its place here. Habits of doubting, indecision, indirectness of mind, often leave in the soul tendencies which make faith more difficult and may even invite temptation.

You ask whether the manner of resisting temptations against faith will differ in different cases. Undoubtedly it will. Certain general principles may be laid down: for instance, it is not well to read works against religion while one is actually under temptation. Temptations against faith frequently create a panic, and panics don't help to clear perceptions. Again, no one can safely live long in an atmosphere of doubt or unbelief, without suffering serious injury, unless special precautions are taken and the foundations of faith be looked to occasionally and strengthened by prayer. Hence persons who always read infidel works, or seek infidel conversation, usually end as sceptics or downright unbelievers. Again, temptations against the faith, real difficulties ought to be discussed with a theologian or some one capable of giving an explanation.

There are some cases in which the study of the objections of unbelievers becomes a duty, the one way out. I don't much like the thought that one's faith is confirmed by reading all that can be said against it; but I am quite satisfied that most objections thoroughly sifted amount to very little. Sophisms only pass for arguments as long as they are not accurately examined.

Perhaps these remarks will help your further reflections on faith. As you seem interested in the theology of faith, do you know Père Matignon's *Sur le Surnaturel*? The volume is a small one; it only treats of faith incidentally and at no great length, but the question of the supernatural order ought to precede the study of faith. The subject is very interesting. The author treats it luminously, and if you read his explanation attentively you will learn much theology and understand faith more perfectly.

I have been very comfortable in the Germanico. The first few days of Lent (I moved in on Ash Wednesday, in a suit of sackcloth and ashes) were somewhat chilly, but since then we have enjoyed real Roman spring, than which I know nothing better. Under that sun, with the dry enlivening air, you live *au bout des ongles*. In April we have commenced summer heat, and reckless characters are throwing aside warm clothing, notwithstanding the proverb which advises even in Maggio, *va adagio*: as we say in England, "Doff not rag nor clout, till the month of May be out." This evening we have been kept indoors by a thunderstorm and heavy rain, and probably the thermometer will not stand so high to-morrow.

If you can get as far as Rome, you will find me here. Don't pay attention to the reports of Roman fever. Many have suffered from colds through their own imprudence, and probably some colds have run into fevers. But I imagine these reports are set afloat by the people in the northern cities of Italy; much in the same way as the Romans run down Naples, and tell you every case of fever at Rome is brought from Naples, which, they add, is so ill-drained. . . .

. . . When you arrived at the conclusion that it is a great mistake to mind things, you found a pearl of great price. Life is a school at which we learn our lessons slowly, if ever we learn some of them at all; this time you have learnt a precious truth.

You ought not to fast, and I doubt much whether you ought to abstain: you require your nourishment. I suppose you act on the opinion of some conscientious doctor. Those who are not able to fast or abstain commonly find abundant field for the exercise of their patience in the round of daily life, and the same cause which disables them from fasting and abstaining renders them more sensitive to worries. In the resurrection we may hope we shall have no back-bones, or they will be better than those which serve our turn in this world.

Rome, May 11, 1881.

In answer to your May letter, I am much pleased that you can give such a good account of the past month.

If you will only persevere in the use of the means you have employed with such happy results, you cannot fail to derive great benefits.

Regular and rather frequent use of the sacraments (never yield to the temptation of staying away from Holy Communion because you do not think yourself worthy), fidelity in your spiritual duties, prayer, and reading, only attend to these points and you will attain great peace with yourself and with your neighbour. In your case there is an additional duty, you must watch your health. I have no fear in asserting that your spiritual difficulties are much mixed up with the state of your health. You understand the points to which you must give your attention, and I need not return to them.

Father —— is not on his way home. I am happy to tell you that he was in my room this morning. It is even probable that I may reach home before him. You must not be surprised if my next communication is a post card, saying that I leave Rome on such and such a day. I expect to be in England before June, or at least early in June, but I have been so often disappointed before, perhaps this time too I may remain longer into the summer.

The weather has not been propitious. April was too hot, May has been too wet and too cold for Rome, and the weather prophets hold out small hopes of an improvement till the 25th or 26th, and some of the prophets have been unusually correct in their conjectures.

The *Catholic Times* comes very regularly, and I am much obliged to you for it. To my mind it is a more interesting paper than the *Tablet*. *Addio.* God bless you. Keep up your courage and battle away with yourself to become holy.

Collegio Germanico, May 17, 1881.

... The May weather came to us on Saturday, bright warm days, without any sultriness or *aria di terremoto*, of which the Romans were complaining before. Business took me this morning to the other side of the water. The Borgo, and the Tiber, and St. Peter, all looked very beautiful, bathed in the warm sunshine.

Father Gallerani continues to draw crowds to the Gesù. One of the rival preachers, who is not so great a favourite, congratulated his congregation that they did not allow themselves to be drawn away by certain preachers with *voce simpatica*, who carry with them a grand *sequito di code*—the *code* being the trains now in vogue. The other evening I went to a Capuchin who attracts many to San Carlo al Corso. His month of May is novel in its form: every evening he makes an imaginary pilgrimage to six or seven famous sanctuaries of the Madonna; as you may imagine, he cannot give much time to each, but he contrives to recount the history of the origin, sometimes add a *grazia* received in the sanctuary, and closes with a short application. He possesses a marvellously fine voice, which rings through the church and can be heard in every corner. He preaches with much dignity, *tanquam auctoritatem habens*, and denounces the vices of modern Rome with great freedom. He evidently pleases a large audience, for he is listened to with marked attention. The month of May is to close on the 26th, and then a course of *Esercizi* will be given for ten days, at least, this was the programme announced at the beginning of the month: but the Romans are not pleased that the Mese di Maggio should be interfered with: *vedremmo*.

Paris, Whit Sunday, 1881.

My dear Child,

The Roman business has come to an end at last, and the address will tell you that I am on my way to England. You have seen the Constitution in the *Tablet*, I make no doubt. I have great hope that we shall enter on a period of peace with the secular clergy, and work in good feeling together: there is so much to be done, all our combined forces will find an ample field. I feel every confidence that the many prayers offered to God by the religious and their friends, will draw down some signal blessing on our work.

I left Rome on the 25th May: stayed at Fiesole till the 31st: gave a long day to Livorno, and then came on straight to Paris. I go to Boulogne on Wednesday, and my plan is to cross the Channel on Thursday. When I reach England, and learn my destination, I will tell you where I may be found.

At first sight, the advice to aim at calm and peace, and not undertaking too much, and not going beyond one's strength, &c., suggests no difficulty: it seems like the wisdom of this world; and yet when one's month is looked over, it is not easy to human nature to be tied down to this rule of conduct. Fidelity here implies much real mortification and conquest of self-love, and entire dependence on Almighty God.

In the same way, beginners easily suspect the advice that they stand in need of encouragement, that they must strengthen the virtue of confidence in God, that they must often say, *Sursum corda.* They are apt to prefer the idea that terrifying would advance them, and much self-examination, and a stern director. The older we become, the better is our understanding of the workings of self-love; and experience teaches us that hope and confidence in God, and attending more to what we may do for God, takes much out of human nature, and most effectually brings us closer to God.

I won't give you any news from Paris. The devil is playing his game to the end, and very completely and very skilfully. Good people are powerless to offer any resistance. Very extreme measures of confiscation of property, of proscription of the clergy, in fact, the banishment of God out of France, are being studied and prepared. Where can we find comfort? All the world over, those who believe in Jesus Christ, are driven to the wall, and given up to their merciless persecutors. We must pray for the Church everywhere! most of all in France, which still directs the world to so great an extent.

God bless you. Pray for me.

CHAPTER IV.

LETTERS FROM FIESOLE.

Nov. 1881 *to May,* 1882.

Journey to Florence. Religious affairs in Paris. Scruples. Supernatural virtues. Comforting considerations when difficulties are suggested against revelation. On acquiring the virtue of faith. The Breviary for Advent. Tuscan religious customs. How devotions to the Blessed Sacrament and to the Holy Souls became united in Tuscany. The Nun of Kenmare. Answers to three questions. 1. Whether our Lady and the Apostles were baptized? 2. How is the Immaculate Conception proved? 3. What is the meaning of St. John x. 16? Why our Lady suffered from the effects of original sin. Whether Jesuits govern the Church. Feeling of lonesomeness. Meaning of the Immaculate Conception. The devil's interference in our daily life. On cherishing a desire for the spirit of prayer and for perfection. Evil of hurrying. Latin studies. Tuscan Christmas. Beauty of Fiesole. Mr. Spence. Cartier's *Life of Fra Angelico*. Cornoldi's Philosophy. Counsels—to be faithful in prayer, not to expect a sensible faith, and how to avoid being overwhelmed with business, &c. The death of a religious Superior. Despondency a bad adviser. A desolate sick-bed. Worries and prayer. The prayer of petitions. De Ponte's *Spiritual Guide*. Abbé Guthlin's *Doctrines Positivistes en France*. Tediousness and stupidity of positivists. Climacterics. Management of health. Simplicity in confession.

In the month of June, 1881, Father Porter returned to England. The few notes which follow, indicate some of his occupations that summer, and his appointment in September as Rector of Farm Street, London. Also the reason of the summons to Fiesole which so quickly followed.

111, Mount Street, July 16, 1881.

I am to give the retreat to the ladies at Roehampton. We begin on the 22nd. I don't know whether you can come, but send me word in case you are free.

St. Beuno's, Aug. 10, 1881.

I am giving the retreat here. I return to London on Saturday. Thank God your retreat was such a help to you. I hope the fruits of it may last for a long time, especially the improvement in your meditation. Do not forget the hint to vary it and to substitute at times litanies of petitions, praises of God, a Psalm, or some favourite vocal prayer recited slowly.

St. Stanislaus, Beaumont, Windsor,
Aug. 18, 1881.

The Provincial has sent me to Beaumont, that I may do some work he has given me in greater quiet than I could find in London. I hope you are keeping all the resolutions of your retreat. Not so easy to keep them in the world, as to make them out of the world! However, it is no small advantage to know what we ought to do. God bless you.

111, *Mount Street, Oct.* 7, 1881.

I thank you for your good wishes on my appointment as Rector of Farm Street. Give me also your help in your prayers. I shall want all the help I can get. . . .

For your comfort remember the rule; if you doubt whether you have consented (to a temptation) it is clear you did not consent. Consent is so plain and distinct an act, there can be no doubt about it.

Never trouble yourself whether any remarks you make may suggest wrong thoughts to others: hope your neighbours are not so prone to evil as to find it everywhere.

111, *Mount Street, Oct.* 27, 1881.

Prepare yourself for a surprise. I am leaving London and going to Fiesole! I start early next week.

Father Weld has been sent to Gibraltar, and Father General does not expect him back for a year. I am to fill Father Weld's place in his absence. This day week I shall have the valley of the Arno at my feet.

I remain Rector of Farm Street, though absent in Italy. Father General hopes I may return to my post after a year.

The Strozzini, Florence, Nov. 12, 1881.

It is 6.30 p.m. My first Saturday's work at the Strozzini is finished: there is a domestic exhortation at 7.30, and so I will devote the hour before me to letter-writing. The letter reached London about noon on Saturday, Nov. 5. I left Charing Cross, Sunday, 10 a.m., for Calais and Boulogne: spent a few hours at Boulogne; reached Paris 6 a.m. on Monday, and took my place for Florence by the 11.15 a.m. train on Tuesday. The railway authorities kept their time: we were in the Florence station before 9.30 p.m. on Wednesday. I slept at the Strozzini, and next morning, after breakfast, found my way up to Fiesole. I ought to have said that Paris was buried in a fog (a white, not a yellow fog) all Monday, and on Tuesday at noon the fog was very dense. But a few hours of our journey carried us away into sunshine and a cloudless sky, and a clear, dry atmosphere: it was almost intoxicating. The same weather I found all along the road, and we are still enjoying it at Fiesole and Florence. What a sunset I saw from my room on Thursday evening! The *tra montana* had been sharp during the day, and the sun left a deep border of gold and crimson all round the horizon, a perfect blaze of glorious warm light. But I am travelling too fast. The journey up to Fiesole was delightful: wild roses thick on both sides of the road; butterflies flitting about, and the valley a carpet of most beautiful colours. The hour passed quickly. When I reached Fiesole, I found my haste had been in vain: the one man I cared to have interviewed for an hour had left the same morning, three hours before my arrival, and he is as good as buried for a month, for to-morrow evening (the 13th) he begins his long retreat, and I shall not see him till the middle of December. To complete my sell, I found Father General and the whole house making their annual retreat of eight days, finishing it to-morrow morning. However, I consoled myself by the thought I had two days to place my room and its belongings in order. I find a small but very interesting library on my shelves: it remains to be seen whether I shall have much time to bestow upon it.

The state of religious affairs in Paris is not much changed: the seals of the Government are still on the Church of the Rue de Sévres: some constant sympathizer every day strews fresh flowers at the church door, and has never failed one single day, winter or summer, since the fatal decrees were put into execution. Every now and then the police make a display of energy and sweep the leaves away, but only to find them replaced within a brief space. The Fathers are scattered all about, in threes and fours, but they see a great deal of each other. The Cardinal Archbishop of Paris is all kindness for them: the clergy, too, are not afraid to show their sympathy; a great deal of work, preaching, retreats, &c., is pressed upon them. More, indeed, than they can get through. It was most edifying to see how resigned and cheerful the Fathers were, doing their best, yet quite prepared to be exiled on short notice.

To-day I had a commission, my first one in Florence; curiously enough it took me past your habitation of last spring. I was in quest of a shovel hat, and the religious of the Chiesa del Carmine have the monopoly of shovel hats in Florence. Unfortunately, the particular friar charged with the hats was in the country; so I left with the sacristan the number of inches round my head, and the statement that I carried a *testa ovale:* the result of this transaction I shall see some day next week at Fiesole. Time and paper ended, I conclude.

San Girolamo, Fiesole, Nov. 14, 1881.

This letter may be posted to-morrow, it may not be posted for several days. There is plenty of work to occupy me here.

Your account of yourself is satisfactory. I felt very sure Father —— would afford you real help. He is right enough in saying that you have fallen into a scrupulous state. It is not very difficult to explain the fact. You encouraged the scruples, then you allowed yourself to conceive a fear of the sacraments, especially Holy Communion. From bad one easily goes to worse, and perhaps for a time you did not make very serious efforts with your prayers. However, all that, I hope, is now changed for the better. Obey Father ——, and before long you will enjoy peace of mind, and be much happier, and make more real progress in virtue.

I have nothing new to add about the temptations; you must not be frightened by them. You find you have gained by the Particular Examen: with a little more patience and courage you will conquer yourself.

Many thanks for your prayers, and for the lamp before our Blessed Lady's statue. Some day I shall procure you a photo of Father General. He is very well. Please remember me very kindly to all.

San Girolama, Fiesole, Nov. 18, 1881.

. . . You raise a question, Is one meant to *have* virtues, or only to be always trying to get them? We are certainly meant to have virtues, but God in His Providence, *for our benefit*, often leaves us with our difficulties undiminished in number or strength, perhaps even increasing, so that it seems to us that we only try to obtain virtues, and never really acquire them. This manner of dealing with those who wish to serve God, I remark especially in the matter of meekness and patience; again in temptations against faith and hope, and in general, in temptations which attack us from without, caused either by our neighbour or by the devil. Irascible people, though very genuinely holy, are often allowed to remain irascible to the end, and they probably derive great benefit from their temper, while they provide their neighbours with an opportunity of practising patience.

A supernatural virtue is a habit, a quality of the soul, infused by God into the soul with habitual grace; forfeited only by grievous sin, and strengthened by every supernatural act we perform, especially by every act of the particular virtue of which there may be question. So long, therefore, as we continue in the grace of God and endeavour to lead a holy life, we are acquiring all virtues in a more perfect degree. Our continuing, however, in a state of grace and our efforts to become holy, don't prevent our neighbours from treading on our corns metaphysically, nor will they prevent agnostics from proposing very unwelcome difficulties against revelation, still less will they induce the enemy of our souls to relent in his attacks, and prevent us from enjoying the sensible effects of God's grace. One comfort we may draw from this never-ending struggle: it gives us an assurance that we are in the right way, and really in the friendship of God. How different are the thoughts and conduct of those who care nothing for God's grace! how different their temper, or their unbelief, or their despair!

You remark that sometimes we seem to make acts of virtue only with the understanding, whereas the will seems to hang back and not go with them. The understanding in the presence of truth must act. Liberty is not a quality of the understanding; it may not see a truth clearly, then it holds back. Liberty is the privilege of the will; difficulties are felt in the will; temptations attack the will principally, and hence it may come about that we seem to perform acts of the will only with half a heart. In fact, however, the act of virtue is truly the act of the will, and perhaps the will has a larger share in it when it seems to hang back. Your faith is never so strong as when the temptations to unbelief importune you most, provided you don't give up your faith, provided you lead a life of faith, provided you pray, *Credo, Domine, adjuva incredulitatem meam.* How pleasing to God must be the perseverance of a soul, incessantly molested with thoughts that there is no God, no Christ, no Church of God, no anything. How meritorious such a life must be!

Believe, therefore, that you have the virtue of faith, and God means you to have it, and to grow in it every day. Don't be discouraged if you are tempted violently to disbelieve anything. I sometimes console myself with the consideration I cannot, without abdicating my reason, say there is no God. I cannot say there is a God, and at the same time say Jesus Christ is not God. I cannot say Jesus Christ is God, and at the same time say the Roman Catholic Church is not His Church. Or again, if I am deceived in my faith in Christ and His Church, God has deceived me Himself.

Dec. 11, 1881.

. . . You must utilize the lessons in Latin. My idea is that you should read a great deal of *easy* Church

Latin, and make yourself familiar with it, *e.g.*, the New Testament, the Psalms, the *Imitation*, and the Breviary; above all, avoid the poets; read Cicero if you will, but the Church books you will find easier, and you will soon make a sensible progress, and see that you are advancing. The *Cœleste Palmetum*, or the *Paradisus animæ*, two excellent prayer-books, might be of use.

The plan of meditating in bed has its advantages, as long as you can keep awake: I think it is very possible to be very recollected, and very devout, only you must make more effort of mind in order to pray with advantage, in order to make the prayer a wrestling.

I hope your interruptions have not entirely prevented you from using your Breviary during Advent. The antiphons, responsories, &c., are all drawn from the depth of the mind and the heart of the Church: the liturgy of Advent is most rich and beautiful. By the way, I find the little Ristretto of Meditations for Advent eminently satisfactory.

I must tell you some of the peculiar religious customs of Tuscany. We don't fast during Advent, we fast on the vigils of the Apostles instead. The animal man can hardly be the gainer, what with the Ember days and the vigil of the Immaculate Conception (a fast in Florence, in discharge of a vow against the plague, and elsewhere a fast much observed through devotion). The Tuscans are rather famous for their devotion to the Blessed Sacrament and to the Holy Souls. In Rome a *De profundis* is said one hour after *Ave Maria*. In Tuscany the same custom prevails, and in addition the bell tolls one hour before *Ave Maria, alle venti-tre ore*, and good people say a *Credo* for the dead. I have not found out when this custom was introduced, nor do I know why a *Credo* is recited. The devotion to the Blessed Sacrament has come to be mixed up with devotion for the Holy Souls in a curious way. Leopold II., the Grand Duke, brother of Joseph II., was something of a sacristan. He disliked the funeral bell and the passing bell and much ceremony about the dead, and forbade many long established uses. The people eluded the laws by associating devotions to the Blessed Sacrament with prayers for the dead. The *Quarant 'Ore* is the usual function for a funeral, *i.e.*, exposition and the bells peal a joyous peal. *A giro di quarant 'ore* is the regular thing when any important personage dies. With all this devotion, however, it is to be wished a St. Bernardino of Siena could issue forth from Fiesole (he was ten years guardian of the convent which crowns our hill), and rouse the Italians to penance: they want a thorough reformation.

I have done no sight-seeing in Florence yet, my time is well filled up. I only go into Florence on Saturday morning, returning on Sunday. I have several hours of writing every day. Perhaps later I may find more leisure. The weather has been very fine. Yesterday and to-day the rain has fallen fast, almost the first since my arrival. The cold is not intense. I have not lighted my stove as yet. The valley is still beautiful. On two mornings it was filled down below with a dense white mist and presented a perfect image of a lake, with the small hills rising out of it like islands; it was quite a fairy scene.

San Girolamo, Nov. 28, 1881.

My dear Child,

It was no little relief to my mind to know that the lawn-tennis had reached the Countess safely. I am glad you are pleased with the game. I have never played at either lawn-tennis or croquet, but lawn-tennis looks much more inviting. I sent your money to the Nun of Kenmare. She is not an impostor, but has taken up the *rôle* of a political agitator, which ill becomes a Poor Clare, and she writes in a violent, unseemly way. Don't collect any more money for her. You must always be prepared for some little persecution from N.B. I could see that at T——, you will never be a favourite with her. A little cross! accept it patiently; it will not hurt you and ought not to rob you of your sleep, or appetite, or of your peace of mind. Please remember me most respectfully to her. I am so sorry to hear my dear friend has been so poorly; it is some consolation to know she is better. Remember me to her very kindly and tell her I will pray for her. I know she loves God, otherwise it would be sad to see her life, already so tried, cut short.

Keep me *au courant* of the Danish religious question. We do not know. The hour of grace for that noble people may have come. God grant it may be so.

Give my best love to my dear friend, Count S——. Any time he may wish to write to me on any point of religion, I hope he will do so. If you think it prudent, you may tell him this, if not keep silent. I will answer your questions. 1. Were our Blessed Lady and the Apostles baptized? Answer. Yes. You know the fact is not given in the Gospels. But in some of the old writers it is said that Christ baptized His Blessed Mother and St. Peter, and that St. Peter baptized the other Apostles. That our Blessed Lady should be baptized will not seem wonderful, for (1) Christ said of all, "Unless a man be born again," &c., there is no reason of excluding our Lady. (2) Her baptism would give good example. (3) Baptism is the Gate of the Kingdom of Heaven. It seems fitting our Lady should enter in. (4) Baptism renders us capable of the other sacraments. As our Lady received Holy Communion, she would be previously baptized.

2. How is the Immaculate Conception proved?

Answer. With weighty arguments from Holy Scripture, with weightier from tradition, beyond a doubt by the definition.

Scripture. The Catholic Church has always understood the woman who was to crush the serpent's head to be Blessed Mary. Now unless Mary was conceived Immaculate she was conceived in original sin, and she was therefore the slave of sin and of the devil, which jars with Genesis iii.

Tradition. Omitting other Scriptural arguments, we find these propositions clearly and frequently laid down by the Fathers. (1) Mary was never the slave of the devil, not even for one instant. (2) She was always at war with the devil, from the first moment of her existence. (3) She belongs to the new order, the old order was darkness, she ushers in the order of light, she is the dawn of a new day, her Divine Son is the glorious Sun of that day. (4) She is likened to to Eve as the Mother of the human race, as fair and holy as Eve was before her fall. (5) She is also contrasted with Eve. Eve listened to the devil, and brought *death* into the world. Mary listened to the Angel, and brought *life* into the world. Eve shared the sin of Adam. Mary stood by the Cross of Jesus Christ. Eve ruined her family. Mary gave her family salvation, &c. Now, if Mary was not conceived Immaculate, if she were conceived in original sin, none of these propositions would be true: they would all be false.

The definition. Pius IX., speaking as Lord of the Church of Christ, as Pastor of Pastors and Flocks, declared that the Church does believe and always had believed the Immaculate Conception, and in so defining he is not allowed to say what is false; otherwise the gates of Hell would have prevailed over the Church of Christ.

Let me add a word, stating what is meant by the Immaculate Conception. When God created Adam and Eve, He raised them to a supernatural state beyond their nature. Men naturally cannot see God in Himself, directly, but only in His creatures. God, when He created Adam and Eve, said, I will raise you to that happiness, you shall see Me face to face, as I am in Myself, if you keep My commandments. So He placed them in the supernatural state, in the state of justice, of original justice, in the state of grace. He robed them, as it were, in the robe of grace, of justice, which testified that they were His children, heirs to His Kingdom, dear to Him. And this robe Adam received for himself and for all his descendants, on the understanding, if he were to forfeit it by actual sin of disobedience he was to forfeit it for all his descendants. Adam disobeyed and forfeited this state, this grace for himself and for all his descendants. We are said to be born in original sin, because we are born without that robe of grace God intended us to have, because we are born without that friendship He intended us to have. When God decreed the redemption of man by the Incarnation of His Son, then He exempted the Mother of His Incarnate Son from the common law enforced on account of the sin of Adam. When Mary was created, her soul was robed with the robe of grace, with the state of justice, she was placed in the supernatural state, as Eve was at her creation, but with this difference, there was no law excluding Eve from such elevation; there did exist a law excluding all children of Adam, and Mary's Immaculate Conception, her immunity from original sin, her receiving the robe of grace and justice at her creation, was a singular privilege, and very suitable to the Divine Maternity God had reserved for her.

3. What is the meaning of John x. 16? Understand

our Lord to speak of the Gentiles, and the verse is quite easy. The other sheep are the Gentiles, who formed no part of God's chosen people in the Old Law. These answers are short, but you can fill in the explanations which may be necessary. Try to spend Advent holily. Make this your ejaculation, "Thy Kingdom come" (indulgenced prayer). Ask Jesus to give you the virtues He loves best, patience, submission to His will, love of your neighbour, love of God.

God bless you.

Yours very truly in Christ,

GEORGE PORTER.

San Girolamo, Jan. 19, 1882.

My dear Child,

Your letter reached me quite safely, with Minnie's note. I expected the cheque every day, and waited to answer the two letters by one—thank you for sending it. Before I go further I ought to thank you, and I do most sincerely, for your kind wishes for the New Year. You had my poor prayer that 1882 may prove a year of blessing for you and for those with whom you live. Your news about Père H—— is sad. But, my dear child, he has made you a present of a white elephant in giving you the four volumes of the *Somme* of St. Thomas. I shall be amazed if you ever read four pages of the book. I know you and I know something of St. Thomas; you will surprise me more than a little if you get beyond the first page and understand it.

In your letter you continue your theological questions. N. asks, why our Blessed Lady suffered from the effects of original sin, if she was Immaculate. She remembers that our Lady's Son, Who was not only Immaculate, but holiness itself, suffered.

But that does not answer the question. The answer is, that God was pleased to associate Mary with her Divine Son in the work of expiation for all sin. A woman, Eve, played a part in the fall of man: God wished that Mary should have her part in the work of man's redemption, hence Mary is called in tradition the second Eve, the second and better mother of the human race. This doctrine is nicely drawn out in a short work, *Mary the Co-redemptrix*, by a Père Janjacquet, S.J., written in French, and translated into English. What you quote from Father Faber, that Blessed Mary suffered much, because she loved much, explains how she suffered much, not why she suffered.

So the Count believes the Jesuits governed the Church in the time of Pius IX. No doubt the Jesuits had some influence by their books, their preaching, &c., but if he could know all we suffered during the reign of Pius, sometimes from the Pope himself, sometimes from those around him, he would not easily believe that we governed the Church. It is the fashion to say we govern the Church, as it used to be the fashion to say we governed kings and courts; that is not our business, our business is to work for the salvation of souls.

You say you missed your Père H—— *dreadfully*. I am not surprised. I rather wondered when you wrote that you liked the country so much. Paris is a dreadful place, but you have many helps to be good when you are there.

The old feeling of lonesomeness has come back. I pity you much, it is a sad feeling when it gets the upper hand, but you must meet the temptation (for such it is) in the right way. God has put you where you are and intends you to serve Him there, and to be detached and to give Him your heart. You might reflect too, that perhaps if you had a home of your own and been happy, you might have forgotten God. After all, you have many staunch friends; you are not quite alone in the world. Have courage. Please thank M—— for her good little note. Ask her how far she has got in her beads for the nine hundred victims of the Ring Theatre. Warn her against making rash promises.

Jan. 20.

A further statement of your question: When God created Adam and Eve, He gave them the robe of grace; they were His dear children, heirs to His Kingdom. He intended to do the same for all their descendants. Adam by his rebellion forfeited the robe of grace for himself and for all his descendants. The taint of his treason fell on all his offspring. Because the body of each was descended from the traitor, the soul created for it did not receive the robe of grace God intended for it. The absence of the robe of grace, where it ought to be found, is original sin. The Blessed Virgin Mary was truly the daughter of Adam. Her body descended from him as the bodies of all other men. And her soul by rights should not have received the robe of justice. But by a special privilege, in consideration of the merits of her Divine Son, that the Mother of God might never have been the slave of sin, she received the robe of justice when she was created, as Eve had received it at her creation. The Immaculate Conception was this. Note a difference between Mary and Eve. Eve received the robe; there was nothing to prevent her. If she had not received it, she would have been created in original sin. She was not bound to have it. Mary as child of Adam was bound to have it; we are all bound to have it. God intended it; and because we have not got what we ought to have, and that, through sin, we are conceived in original sin. Mary was preserved from original sin because she received the robe by a special privilege.

My respects to the family. Good-bye. God bless you.

Yours very truly in Christ,

GEORGE PORTER.

San Girolamo, Jan. 17, 1882.

. . . It looks like raising the dead to answer your questions in the letter of the 20th of December. Perhaps you don't remember them. However, I must help your memory, and not leave them unnoticed. You refer to Father Coleridge's account of the devil, and his interference in our daily life. He may be the cause of the many interruptions you had met with, and the author of the thought that it would be useless to attempt an account of your conscience. He probably had his finger in all this. What merits attention is, that most frequently he works through external objects—business, servants, tradespeople, &c., and still more through our natural character and temperament, *e.g.*, through your tendency to melancholy, especially in the morning before breakfast. All your morning inspirations and judgments are apt to be tinged with despondency, and the devil will act upon you to deepen the shade: hence always distrust the morning thoughts, and revise them after breakfast or lunch. We cannot always recognize the devil's action: sometimes he may be seen distinctly suggesting some evil thought, quite disconnected from any visible cause or occasion; more frequently his hand is not seen; we know he has been at work by the spirit left behind in us.

During the dreadful fit of irritability and despondency, which terrified you so much, lasting twenty-four hours, and preventing you from praying and from going to Holy Communion, if you could have knelt down and fought it out with half an hour's earnest vocal prayer, and then gone to Holy Communion, you would have achieved a precious victory. Such a fit does not show your usual temper to be an accident; but only that it will not carry you through a certain amount of provocation, and that you must pray still, "Jesus, meek and humble of Heart, make my heart like to Thine!" and especially that you must pray for special grace when you see the storm coming: special graces are granted to special prayers and petitions.

You ask, can I get the spirit of prayer I want to have, without more separation from the world than seems compatible with my state of life? First, beware of aspiring to a spirit of prayer which is not compatible with your state: I mean which would interfere with duties. Secondly, within that limit you may arrive at a great spirit of prayer. Cherish the desire for the spirit of prayer, and carefully remove any obstacle you may discover in yourself: your chief work lies in the removal of obstacles. Almighty God will do the rest. In the same way cherish the desire of perfection: understand what you are aiming at, and remove all known obstacles. Naturally, such desires seem to fade away amidst the wear and tear of every-day life; but they do not wear away, if you revive them in meditation, in Mass, and above all, in Holy Communion. Pray for perfection, and for the desire of perfection. We never know how much God has in store for us.

You are right, "there is nothing so unsatisfactory as spending one's life in a perpetual hurry." St. Francis de Sales calls *precipitation, la peste de la devotion*—and so it is, and calmness and leisureliness are great helps to devotion.

As to your Latin studies, I take it for granted you

wish to know Latin in order to be able to read ecclesiastical Latin, Breviary, and Missal, and Fathers, and later ascetical writers. The Latin of the poets is almost a different language, and it is difficult. I am in favour of the easiest books, *e.g.*, the Latin Vulgate of the New Testament, A Kempis; repeat often, and work out the parsing honestly. If you want the best Latin prose, and that not too difficult, read Cicero, *De Amicitia*, and *De Senectute*, and his *Orations*. I say this supposing that you are studying Latin for your own private use. . . .

. . . I was too busy at Christmas and the New Year to pick up much of the Tuscan customs of that delightful season. The bambin Gesù, swaddled up to his very chin, lay beneath the crucifix above the altar; on Holy Innocents', and some other days which I could not well understand, a veil was thrown over the figure; and it was taken away before the octave of the Epiphany. Epiphany is called a *Pasqua*, in some places the natives speak of the *Pasquelle*, or *Pasquette dell' Epifania*. Some call it the *Pasqua d'inverno*. Easter is the *Pasqua dei fiori;* Pentecost, the *Pasqua dei grani*. The system of Christmas boxes flourishes here. You may have noticed the small omnibus which runs between Fiesole and Florence. On Christmas Eve a card, on which the *mille felicitazioni* appropriate to the season were inscribed, was handed to me in a neat envelope by the conductor. I must own that they are satisfied with very little. My donation of fifty centesimi was gratefully acknowledged; and the nuns who go their rounds at this season are quite pleased with this small sum. . . .

How do you find Cornoldi's Philosophy? Intelligible enough? If he is too abstruse, I can send you easier volumes by Padre Liberatore, *Il comporto umano, La conoscenza intellettuale,* each in two vols.

I must close in order to catch the post. I have been

writing for four hours, my usual morning occupation from 7.45 to close upon 12, when I break off.

Our wonderful season still continues. I have never anywhere observed such a succession of beautiful visions as those which for more than two months have succeeded each other day after day. I feel so tempted to write out descriptions—perhaps it is well my time is better taken up. A better pen than mine would be taxed to give a small part of what I see from Fiesole.

San Girolamo, Feb. 15, 1882.

... I have not seen Mr. Spence again. I heard of him leading off a ball with his grandchild, not three weeks ago. He sent me up a photograph of an interesting painting Sir W. Drake had asked him to clean. It was a portrait of one of the Medici I fancy, and through the window in the painting Spence, as he cleaned, recognized his own villa and our San Girolamo, connected with it by a long steep flight of steps up to the door of our chapel. These steps no longer exist. Lorenzo de Medici substituted the present approach from the high-road, and built the porch which now protects the door of the chapel and looks down on Villa Spence.

By the way, do you know the *Vie de Fra Angelica da Fiesole*, par E. Cartier, Paris, 1857? Cartier was an admirer and a disciple of Père Lacordaire, a student of St. Thomas Aquinas, and an enthusiast for Christian art, even with its quaintness and imperfections. He discusses the questions of art, and the merits of Fra Angelico, with much power and discrimination.

Cornoldi seems to frighten you. Would you prefer Balmez, *Filosofia Elementale*, in an Italian translation? There is a Naples edition in one, handy volume, not well printed, but legible. I would rather recommend a forced and rapid march through Cornoldi, with enough attention to take in the distribution of the matter and general ideas; and afterwards a more careful study of the more important matters. I expect to-day two small, but highly recommended books on positivism; I will report on them, if they are worth anything.

As we are on the threshold of Lent, I must add one or two words on spiritual matters. You express a fear lest the duties of your state may interfere with the spirit of prayer you aspire to. The *duties* need not interfere with any prayer. The first point to clear up is whether God calls you to that form of prayer; and then, when you are satisfied He does, see whether society, pleasures, impatience, under crosses, &c., keep you back. Be very faithful in the prayer which lies within your reach, and leave yourself in God's hands. In the same way, don't suffer the desire of a vivid realization of the things of faith, or of a sensible faith in the Blessed Eucharist, to worry you. Do the best you can with such faith as you have, and wait God's good will to indulge you in a more sensible feeling of heavenly things. Lastly, when the feeling of hurry and being overwhelmed is upon you, break off your pressing work, and calm yourself with a quarter of an hour's slow attentive reading, a very deliberate meditative prayer.

TO A YOUNG MAN IN THE WORLD.

San Girolamo, March 9, 1882.

My dear ——

Your letter of 20th February was very welcome. I am always glad to hear that you are getting on well, and to join you in thanking God for all the blessings He has showered on you.

As you say, He sent you a great trial; but I much suspect the trial was a real blessing: you escaped a peril.

And how many advantages you have enjoyed! You can never be thankful enough.

You ask me how I keep my health. I am very well.

This Fiesole is an earthly paradise: we live in a good house, enjoy a beautiful scene, the air is most healthy, the work is constant without being too heavy; and a more tranquil, happy life could not be imagined.

You should come out to Florence for a holiday.

Good-bye. God bless you. I won't forget to pray for you. In return, do you pray for me.

I remain, yours very truly,

GEORGE PORTER.

San Girolamo, March 24, 1882.

Your letter of the 20th I received yesterday afternoon, and this morning I offered Mass for Sister Superior. R.I.P. Poor soul! she had worked nobly whilst her health lasted, and she has been sorely tried since she lost her health. I think she will have a grand crown in Heaven; she was very devoted and very self-denying. You owe her a great debt of gratitude; so far, you have not been wanting in gratitude, continue to pray for her, and she won't complain of you. You will miss her much. You begin now life anew, in a sort of a fashion. *Dieu seul.* You can manage now to get on without Sister Superior. Pray and labour for God, and in a few years you will join her in Heaven.—R.I.P.

Death has been busy of late amongst our friends. Father Noble, then good old Father Waterworth, both taken, the former very suddenly, the latter after a very short illness.—R.I.P.

I am sorry you have been giving in to a fit of despondency. Despondency is always a bad adviser. You have been getting out of the habit of looking at St. Ignatius' Rules for the Discernment of Spirits. It is all passed now: but just imagine that for two or three days you felt convinced that there was no hope for you, that your sins were not forgiven, and that it was impossible to get right. What an obvious fraud of the evil one! Had you shut your ears at the beginning of this temptation, it could never have run to such lengths. Now it is over, you must prepare yourself not to be caught in the same trap again.

You say you don't want to die with a lot of things on your mind. Of course die with a lot of things on your mind, with a lot of those fears and fancies which the devil causes in your mind. Tell him you leave yourself, and all your sins, and all your fears to the mercy of Jesus Christ, in Whom you believe, Whom you hope to see in Heaven, Whom you love above all things.

During your next retreat you will have to pray for hope and work hard to strengthen it. I think you would do well to read again the little book on *Holy Confidence*, by Rogacci, which I gave you. It is so natural and so easy to despond; our self-love tricks us into this temptation so cunningly, we must always be upon our guard and keep ourselves up to the mark in the love of Jesus Christ, and in confidence in His mercy.

As soon as I have a Mass free, I will say one for your blind girl ——. When good people die, death has no terrors. I trust the poor child sees God in Heaven now, and rejoices in the light of His face.

How desolate some sick-beds are! Yesterday I was called to a poor English nurse in a huge hospital in Florence. She cannot speak any Italian, and the Italians don't speak English, and not many of them can speak

French, which the girl understands somewhat. She was very glad to be able to make her confession in English. She is down with typhoid, and her head was beginning to show the effects of the fever. It was with some difficulty she collected her thoughts and found expression for them. The nuns seem to be very kind to her, but she looked forlorn and desolate, all alone amongst strangers, though I think myself most people when they are ill like to be left alone, and don't care to see company; at least, in fever and other sicknesses, though perhaps not in all.

Addio. God bless you. Let us try to spend the rest of our time well, and prepare to go when the Master calls us.

San Girolamo, March 28, 1882.

... Florence has suffered from the want of rain; but last week much rain fell, the Arno was swollen, and the streets were well washed. I hope everything will be bright when you come for your well-earned holiday. I don't believe in discomfort as the price of a short Purgatory. Enjoy the sunshine, orange-trees, and myrtles and beautiful scenes; only take care to raise mind and heart to the Author of all that is good and bright.

You have been troubling yourself, I fear, about many things, or allowing many things to trouble you; even Lent has not been satisfactory. Get your Holy Week book, and rest your soul in the services without, however, attempting too much: a thorough *sfogo* in the services, following them, entering into them, doing little else in the way of prayer or meditation may do you great good.

Have you ever tried, when you are worried, to make the worries the subject or occasion of your prayer? talk them over with our Lord, reason about them, about the trouble they cause, ask for counsel, for help; there is much reality about such prayer, and much help. I have faith also in the prayer of petitions for self and for others. Do you know Father Ramière's *Apostleship of Prayer?* he has some chapters on this prayer which are very encouraging: he draws out the teaching of our Lord, and it certainly recommends begging and importuning. However, in prayer, as in everything else, we must not tie ourselves down too rigidly to forms or to any one kind of prayer: we are not always in the same frame of mind, and our prayer should correspond to the actual state of the soul. The safest rule is that we do what we can, perhaps God will raise us and enable us to do more; this He commonly does, if we place no obstacle. I mentioned Father Ramière's *Apostolat de la Prière;* the most suggestive work on the whole subject is the *Dux Spiritualis* of Da Ponte, and if you are not sure that your Latin will carry you through, there is a French translation of *Le Guide Spirituel*, by Père Dupont (French dress of *Da Ponte*); he does not say so much on the higher states of prayer, but he is very full on the ordinary prayer, and the helps to it. I learnt more from *Da Ponte* than from any other.

To go to more mundane matters. I have been reading and have almost finished *Les Doctrines Positivistes en France*, par l'Abbé A. Guthlin. He deals with Comte, Littré, Renan, About, Taine, and all the modern leaders of French infidelity, quotes largely from their books, and refutes them very solidly, and as a matter of course in a Frenchman, very eloquently. The Positivists are tedious to any one who knows the Catechism and the elements of reasoning; they are poor adversaries for an able writer, and they rather provoke exclamations of wonder and indignation. Abbé Guthlin follows them up and down, and his modest 12mo of some four hundred pages ought to open the eyes of some who have been imposed upon by the audacity and charlatanism of the Comtist school. He will be at your service, if you have time to read him during your stay at Florence. I must not break into a second sheet; so *addio*, God bless you. A quiet Holy Week. Then Italy.

San Girolamo, April 14, 1882.

... You know the doctrine of the ancients about climacterics, every seven years or so a change takes place in the body and this is often accompanied by changes in the disposition. I think there must be some foundation in fact for this notion. I have often remarked trials of health, new temptations and difficulties make their appearance about mid-life and sometimes multiply in old age; other cases I have seen of persons, delicate in youth, becoming strong as they advance in years. My next-door neighbour suffered from dyspepsia when he was young, he is now verging on eighty and has no experiences of indigestion. When these trials make their appearance we can only do our best. I fancy it should be rather an aim not to allow the system to fall below par, never to go beyond one's strength, or call upon one's energies when there is a feeling of exhaustion.

Yes, Easter is very joyous, especially to those who have been following the Breviary and Missal of Holy Week. Both Breviary and Missal for Easter week are most happy, and the special Masses and Offices for the Apostles and Martyrs during Paschal time are very encouraging. I have been snatching a few readings from Ludolph on the Resurrection: he always helps me. ...

San Girolamo, May 6, 1882.

My dear Child,

Your letter of the 2nd reached me yesterday. My first duty is to thank you for your previous one of

19th of April, with all its good wishes for St. George, for which I am very grateful, as well as for your good prayers.

I wish you could get over your nervousness and fidgetiness in Confession. If you could follow the simple rule to believe you did not consent, whenever it is not clear to you that you consented; if you are quite certain that you did consent, then confess it so, if you are not quite clear, confess I am not quite clear, I confess as God sees me guilty, and don't worry your mind about it. Don't accumulate worries upon worries, by asking yourself whether you mean to deceive your confessor: let that dog slumber in peace.

I thank you for the *Standard* with the account of the royal wedding. Beaumont has distinguished itself and done very well on the occasion of the two royal visits.

I have found a Carlsbad, here in Italy, not very far from Florence, and I shall probably go there during some part of June; the Italian cure takes less time than the German one. The name of the place is Monte Catini. I trust you keep your health fairly well.

I see advertised in the *Catholic Times* which you kindly send me so regularly, at the Catholic Publishing Depôt, 50, Manchester Street, Liverpool, *Questions on Christian Doctrine*, and *Questions on Sacred History*, I think by an Inspector. They are small books. You will confer a favour on me if you make me a present of a copy of each of these books.

CHAPTER V.

LETTERS FROM FIESOLE.

June to Oct. 1882.

Beginning of summer. Engravings of Hieronymus Wierx. Arrival and speedy departure of Father Weld. Visit to the Bagni di Lucca. The *cicala*. Lessius, *De Divinis Perfectionibus*, and *De Divinis Nominibus*. How to teach English Composition and History. The Corpus Christi processions. The writings of Mr. Allies. Penitential cure at Monte Catini. Visit to Lucca. The *Sacro Volto*. Symond's Renaissance in Italy. Advice to a Sister of Charity. Pisa. Pistoia. The work of a retreat compared to that of an etcher. Anxiety to be avoided. God's action on the soul in retreat. Nothing equal in interest to a human soul. Liberalism and the *Univers*. Disquieting thoughts. Dissatisfaction with self, when good, when evil. Pleasure in life. Faith. Discouragement. Savonarola. What is necessary to constitute sin. Beauty of the vintage. Contrition. A wet September in Italy. On realizing truths. Connection between faith and hope. A conversion to Catholicism, what wonders of grace it implies. Hopes about Heaven and motives for encouragement.

TO A FRIEND WHO HAD JUST LEFT FLORENCE.

San Girolamo, May 31, 1882.

I must not allow the octave of Pentecost to close without sending you my wishes for a *Buona Pasqua*, in true Italian fashion. May you receive a good measure, running over, of the gifts and fruits of the Holy Ghost.

You left on Wednesday night. On Saturday we found ourselves in full summer, three weeks before the usual time. I do not know the highest reading of the thermometer, but on Monday, at 5 p.m., it stood at 29° Centigrade, about 84° Fahrenheit. The olives are out in flower: the grapes will follow in a day or so, and at night the fire-flies are darting about in thousands. Perhaps this summer heat may not continue, and indeed yesterday I thought I distinguished symptoms of a storm. Are you acquainted with the name or the works of Hieronymus Wierx? an engraver of considerable ability, who attached himself to the Society, and did much good work for our Fathers. I enclose a small picture of St. Ignatius, St. Francis Xavier, St. Stanislaus, and St. Aloysius: with a sweet Infant Jesus casting fire upon the earth. . . .

. . . I have done nothing as yet to continue the visits to the treasures of art in Florence: but the good intention survives. . . . Christian art in its earlier stages always helps me, whenever I can find the time and the opportunity of studying it. I fancy I derive spiritual benefit from it, besides much instruction and pleasure.

Father Weld was expected at Madrid on Sunday. He may reach Fiesole before the end of this week.

San Girolamo, June 26, 1882.

. . . Father Weld has flashed past, like a disturbing comet. He came to us on the 13th, left for Rome on the 15th, returned to Fiesole on the 21st, took me with him to the Bagni di Lucca on the 23rd, brought me back after my usual Saturday confessions about 8.30 p.m., and yesterday started for London by the 7.40 p.m. train, *via* Innsbruck and Brussels, hoping to be in London next Saturday, and leave it for the Cape of Good Hope on July 4, which means for me that I am to remain here till he comes back: he cannot come back before March. I shall not be surprised if I see the summer of 1883 at Fiesole. We rushed through Lucca, snatching a few minutes for San Michele and San Frediano, on the way from the station. The drive (fifteen miles) to the Bagni was a *vero incanto :* a beautiful road along the Sverchio,

I dare say you know it; the day, bright summer, not too hot. We went there on some business Father Weld had in hand. I found a large part of my Florence flock there, and I hope to pay them a clerical visit before long, and then I shall contrive to visit the *Duomo*, and see the *Sacro Volto*, for which I hope to have an order. The harvest in the Lucchese was a sight to remember; much of it was cut, and before SS. Peter and Paul the last sheaves will be gathered in. Both for quantity and quality it is said to be extraordinary. The summer made a false start at the beginning of the month, and the intense heat was followed by some very chilly days. About St. Aloysius, the 21st, the real summer began, the *cicala* opened their chorus, as if at a signal, and the heat and the *cicala* keep going on, and I suppose will go on. My dictionary condemns the *cicala*, saying *canta noiosamente*: to me this music is welcome, it tells of sunlight and sun heat.

You ask me whether Lessius' *De Divinis Perfectionibus* has been translated into Italian. Allow me to make a Paddy answer and say no, but Père Marcel Bouix (translator of St. Teresa and other valued works) has translated Lessius' *De Divinis Nominibus, Les Noms Divins*, (Paris, 1882). The latter work is the easier, and so devout. I recommend you to read it, with the help of Père Bouix's translation, before you attempt *De Perfectionibus*. It is safer as well as easier. *De Perfectionibus* contains some deep matter on predestination and kindred mysteries, not easily understood. When you do begin *De Perfectionibus*, get the very convenient edition by Father Roh, S.J., printed at Freiburg, Herder, 1861. The Latin of Lessius is clear and intelligible, and has a certain elegance. You ought to manage the *De Divinis Nominibus* without difficulty, especially if you have Bouix to fall back upon. . . .

... There are two things you may teach your boys besides religion: English composition and history. ... Look over what they write, point out to them ungrammatical English, insist on their writing clearly, and intelligibly, and in good taste; every now and then, point out to them in papers or elsewhere specimens of ungrammatical, bad English, specimens of bad taste: read sometimes purely for the style. When they are more advanced make them compare passages, *e.g.*, of Junius, Burke, Macaulay, Addison, &c. You might set them exercises, narratives of stories they have read or heard, descriptions of scenes from nature, letters about ordinary events: and leave out, or put off to the very last, essays on virtue, patriotism, &c. ... Within a few years Longmans (I think) has published one or two serviceable guides to composition. As to history, you have read the English history several times, make that always the *point de depart*. When you begin a new book, require them to fix their dates and to see what they know already about the period. With a little pains, they ought to get into their heads all the leading dates of our history, and refer back all their knowledge to that framework. Teach them to hate tyranny and tyrants; to hate the excesses and tyranny of demagogues; to love liberty as distinguished from license; to respect law and right; to be enthusiastic for what is noble and heroic. Then the cultivation of a taste for what is beautiful in art or nature completes and adorns the character, and finishes the education. In our day there arise two dangers, two extremes; out-and-out Toryism, and out-and-out Liberalism. It seems to me the excesses of both parties ought to be dwelt upon, the tyranny of democracy, as well as the tyranny of despots.

I mentioned some books in my last letter. I will add Bossuet's *Histoire Universelle*, Miss Drane's *St. Catherine of Siena.* Fenélon's *Telemaque* always pleased me, as a humanizing, elevating book. . . .

. . . Our Corpus Christi processions came off on the feast, on the Sunday, and on the octave. The rain interfered with the procession of the feast—at least, obliged the good people to shorten their walk. The Liberals wanted to create a disturbance. As a preliminary they sent young men to write *abasso i clericali, abasso i papisti,* at intervals on the large stones which form the open drains on either side of the road from Florence to Fiesole; but the *contadini* turned out in force with their stout sticks, and no disturbance took place. Latterly, in many of the large towns, the roughs have come forward unpleasantly; disturbing the congregations in the churches, smoking cigars, provoking priests and people. In some instances blood was shed. The recurrence of these unruly displays in several towns about the same time, points to a concerted action. Liberty covers a number of ugly consequences.

I am glad to hear you like Mr. Allies' *Church and State.* It is too true his books are not so much read as they deserve to be. Many do not know that he wrote the *Formation of Christendom.* Yet he is a very able writer, he has learning, sound doctrine, and a fair style.

Pensione Martinelli, Monte Catini,
July 16, 1882.

The above address is not meant to be used. Take it as a sign I have been to Monte Catini, and gone through the cure. The life is penitential, quite as much so as Carlsbad, and without the compensations, the reading-room, the endless variety of visitors, the really good music, the lovely scenery, and the walks in the pine woods. Monte Catini can only boast a small population (including, however, Cardinal Howard, the Verdi, Mustafa, the grand Roman *maestro*, Berti, the Minister of Agriculture, to say nothing of minor luminaries), drugged, and boiled, and broiled on a most fertile, but most uninteresting plain. I don't know whether I ought to quote it as in favour of Monte Catini; but the doctors here do not worry their patients on the subject of food, or generally try to make us miserable. The pension provides two full, hearty meals per day: 10 a.m. and 5 p.m., and no more. The cook does not lack talent, every now and then we get a pleasant surprise, but he is nearly always too salt, or he does not make allowance for our being so extensively salted, and he does not study his work as he ought to do. The heat is fierce: we are told that great heat favours the cure. Never shrink from laying down a principle. The grand consolation is the briefness of the purgatory. The doctor says ten days will do for me. I began on last Tuesday. I hope to leave this on Thursday for Leghorn, and return to Fiesole to-morrow week.

I have managed to see a great deal of Lucca since I last wrote. On the 8th, on my way up to the Bagni, I managed a hurried examination of the *Duomo;* and on the 13th I went from Monte Catini and met Father Tylee at Lucca. I had from 10 a.m. till 6.20 p.m., and *did* Lucca. I ventured to call on the Archbishop, hoping to have a glimpse of the *Volto Sacro*, but was quickly informed such favours were not for the likes of me, no one under a prelate need apply. So I missed the *Sacro Volto*, and the brother who might have shown me the body of the glorious servant of God, St. Zita (a maid of all work), was asleep, and I lost that privilege. Otherwise I saw nearly everything, and very leisurely, and very enjoyably. The sculptures of the Pisani (father and son), of Jacopo della Quercia, and above all, Matteo Civitali, many marvellous paintings; and last, not least, the architectural triumphs of the *Duomo*, S. Michele, S. Frediano (the Irish Bishop of Lucca), &c, Then I stumbled on a treasure of an old book shop. I wanted some book on the *Sacro Volto*, the centenary. Some centenary takes place next September, and so men's minds are busy about the *Volto Sacro*. If the book is worth reading, I will send it on to you. Besides this, I bought some precious theological works, and a fine copy of an Italian translation of St. Augustine *On the City of God*. This I reserve for you, if you have not got a copy already. Next week I have set my heart on visiting Pisa and Pistoia, the latter is near Monte Catini, the former I shall bring into my Leghorn journey. Do you know John Addington Symonds' *Renaissance in Italy?* Much of what he writes is very distasteful, but he interests me, and sets me thinking. . . . I hope you will have a good retreat. Refuse to be disquieted. Go over old ground, and strengthen principles and resolutions already made. If God suggests new ones, when they come, then consider them, but don't worry: *non in commotione Dominus.* . . .

TO A RELIGIOUS SUPERIOR, A SISTER OF CHARITY.

San Girolamo, July 4, 1882.

Your letter of the 29th of June pleased me. So you have found out at last that Father —— is not all stone, that he has some feeling and that he can give you good help. Why did you not make this discovery sooner? If you had not made up your mind that you could not get on with him, and if you had studied him a little at first, you might have received much valuable help during the past two years. Perhaps this experience may teach you not to be so easily carried away by first impressions, not to take matters just as you find them, but to try and make them as you want them to be. I am very glad that even so late you have recognized in Father —— a sympathizing confessor.

You are quite right not to overdo the visiting of the poor. You are not as well able to bear the fatigue of walking and standing about all day as you were fifteen years ago. Besides it is very possible to attempt more external work than is good for the soul. Fatigue of the body does not help prayer, and it does not help you to govern and guide your community. I am a firm believer in the importance, I might go as far as to say the necessity, of some quiet time every day for Superiors. There is much good left undone outside, very true, but the same may be said when you have gone about far and wide and wearied yourself—there is always more to do; but in the long run most is done when a fair amount of work is attempted and when it is honestly carried out, and when the home life for self and for community is religiously attended to. You particularly must guard against over-fatigue if you don't want to be drawn into despondency and melancholy.

Might it not answer to allow the Sister who is not strong to go out for a short time, two hours or one hour? her visiting would relieve you somewhat, and she would get into the work, which requires an apprenticeship, and learn by degrees how to deal with the poor.

Then you must make good use of the help you find now with Father ——; lay up for the evil day. I wonder whether you can read now St. Ignatius' Rules for the Discernment of Spirits, which instruct us how to derive most profit from consolation and how to prepare for desolation. You may apply the doctrine to your present sunshine with your confessor.

I am glad you are able to give so good an account of your resolution not to say anything unkind of any one.

I have always thought we may merit graces from God by attending to that point. Show mercy and you will receive mercy.

You say you don't get on very well with your meditation. Try the effect of a change, as I have taught you to do before; use the second method of prayer, or even vocal prayer, for a part if not for the whole of your meditation. Or read a little, then meditate and pray a little. Then read again and meditate on your second reading. Introduce change and variety into your meditation, till you feel you can make a regular meditation properly....

You ask me when I am coming back. Not for a year, I think. Father Weld sails to-day for the Cape of Good Hope. He will hardly return to Italy before this time twelvemonth, and as long as he is away I occupy his place, unless something unforeseen happens. My life here is so quiet, so regular, and you cannot imagine how beautiful the spot is we live in. I sometimes think it was a merciful providence which took me out of the racket of Farm Street.

Addio. God bless you. Pray away and work away for the poor; it won't last very long, and after all comes the long reward.

San Girolamo, August 13, 1882.

... I have returned once more to Lucca, and found much that was interesting. The *Sacro Volto* has a very respectable history; later on I will send you Canonico Guerra's volume. I have some idea of making an article on this very ancient crucifix. Having gone through my penitential course at Monte Catini, I went to Leghorn for three days, and from there made an excursion to Pisa. The heat this summer has been moderate so far, with few exceptions, and that day in Pisa was one of the excep-

tions. It was broiling hot; but the Cathedral, the
baptistery, and the Campo Santo abundantly compensated for the suffering. Besides, we examined very
carefully the gem of Santa Maria della Spina (on the
Arno), which has been thoroughly restored. I hope to
revisit Pisa more than once before my return to London.
From Monte Catini I made a *scappata* to Pistoia, and
there too saw much that I hope never to forget: the
altar of St. James in the Cathedral, much of Luca della
Robbia's work, sundry pulpits by the Pisani. I saw the
Seven Works of Mercy by Luca della Robbia. Within
the building in a *cortile* had been an Entombment by
him. The medical students threw stones at it, till it was
broken in several places, and it was then taken down
and left as old crockery in a corner. The figure of
Christ was uninjured, and a second-hand bookseller
offered two hundred and fifty francs for the pieces. The
official at the Spedale asked the central authority at
Florence leave to accept the offer. Four wiseacres were
sent down from Florence to report, and they reported in
favour of the sale; but the Spedale official fell ill and his
successor refused to complete the sale. What a history!
I had it from the bookseller, a shrewd, interesting old
fellow. . . .

. . . I was sorry to hear that the retreat was a time
of suffering; however, it was some consolation to know
that you found you were the better for it when it was all
over. Do you worry yourself beforehand, hoping to
make a very good one, or to receive very special consolations? All this anxiety stands in the way of the
retreat and its fruit. It is well to desire, even ardently,
to get much fruit: it is not wrong to desire consolations
and encouragement; but these desires should never
interfere with perfect peace and self-possession. Before
the retreat, or during the first meditation, try to see

clearly the answer to the question, What do I want from God? what faults have I to correct, what virtues must I aim at, what temptations and trials must I prepare against? Then, go through each week of the Exercises and each meditation, trying to revive and engrave more deeply in your mind and heart the thoughts, the principles, the convictions, the likes and dislikes you have gathered in previous retreats, not refusing any new ones which may present themselves. I sometimes imagine the process to resemble that of the etcher who touches up an old plate, improving the old lines and now and then adding a new one. Sometimes a retreat passes in this process: the sense of guilt, sorrow, shame, purposes, renunciation of the world, of self, &c., are renounced in the first week; the love of Jesus Christ, the knowledge of His teachings and counsels, the familiarity with His virtues, &c., in the second week, and so on. Sometimes God grants quite a new glimpse into spiritual life: a truth, a principle, a desire finds its way into the soul, which changes life for us and opens up a new world. Such glimpses are very precious, both for the retreat itself and for the time which follows. They may be compared to an electric light concentrated on an object which had previously been lost in darkness. Side by side with the labour on the worn plate, is the tale of desolation or consolation, which follows its course. I am much in favour of always studying the Rules for the Discernment of Spirits, both the first series and the second series. They keep the soul alive and watchful not to neglect the action of Almighty God.

I have known the fruit of a retreat lost in part by too much anxiety to ascertain what God requires of the soul. He may enlighten her on this point, previously to the retreat; more commonly He does so while the process of renewing the plate is being continued, and He does it so clearly and so distinctly that the soul in a state of quiet cannot be mistaken. Then He does not always favour the soul with new and special illuminations, and in that case the time of the retreat is spent, and very profitably, on the plate. You say you passed through a long fit of desolation and hope to forget it. I beg you not to forget it, study it, how it began and how it went on; you may extract some wisdom from the history.

I am interested in your joyless friend who has begun to like Mr. Allies' book. Follow her up. You will be rewarded. Nothing is comparable to a human soul when you can get near it, when you break through the shell of conventionalities and reserve, and reach the soul. Marble and canvas and metal are uninteresting in comparison, and God's dealings with souls are so wonderful, and there is so much to be done with a soul, once you can establish any intimacy. Think how your own life has grown to its present fulness, the words, the thoughts, the examples which one time or another have influenced you strongly. Do what you can for your friend. Perhaps she is joyless because she has never found cause of joy, and there are so many. I own I have never had to do with a soul which did not interest me deeply. God's hand I see in each, in the wondrous capacity for goodness; and then the romances of spirits, of guilt, of conversion, of holiness. One day you will send me word that the joyless face has been lighted up and that you have assisted at her First Communion. *Speriamo.*

San Girolamo, Sept. 14, 1882.

I had planned a visit to Lucca for to-day, to see the *Santo Volto* and witness the splendid ceremonies for the centenary of the arrival of the *Santo Volto*. A violent storm kept me at home, and I give you some of the benefit of my enforced leisure.

You ask me whether I have read the fourth volume of Bougaud (*Le Christianisme et les Temps présents*). I have not. Perhaps you will remember to bring it to Florence next spring. Though I have not read the book, I have read a series of articles against it in the *Univers* by a certain Abbé Morel. Bougaud was Vicar-General of Dupanloup, and openly confesses himself to be a Liberal. The *Univers*, and in a special manner the Abbé Morel, won't hear of Liberalism; and volume four is denounced for its open contradiction with the Syllabus teaching of Pius IX. and Leo XIII.'s Pastoral as Archbishop of Perugia on the Church and Civilization. On the merits of the quarrel I won't attempt to decide. With much inclination to be liberal, I think most liberties, liberty of the Press, liberty of conscience, &c., are apt to degenerate into license, if not resolutely limited. Modern Liberalism is to me a hateful form of tyranny.

To come to spiritual matters. Try to carry into daily life the directions I suggested for your retreat. Don't aim at too much, don't expect too much, *e.g.*, don't hope to escape all worries, don't ask to find prayer always easy and delightful, and take what comes with as good a grace as possible. You have your order of the day. Be faithful to it, as far as other duties or calls allow you. By spiritual reading, by varying the form of prayer, by sometimes substituting vocal prayer, try to keep the meditation up to the mark. Overcome yourself when with others, putting up with their peculiarities, striving to please them or interest them or benefit them. Disregard all suggestions which tend to disquiet. You may be quite certain that all *disquieting* thoughts come from the evil spirit, as long as you are endeavouring to serve God, even though you may commit many faults. I will not say as much of the feeling of dissatisfaction with yourself. How much reason you have to be dissatisfied with yourself! If this leads you to confess your weakness, your sins, and to humble yourself before God, then it is a right feeling and it will draw you to God, and it will bring deep peace to your soul. But if the dissatisfaction makes you vexed with yourself, as if it were a wonder you could be so weak, so unfaithful to God, then the feeling does not come from God and it will not lead to Him. It is an artful expression of self-love.

You are exercised about happiness, pleasure in life. Does your good Angel seek to prevent you from taking pleasure in life? If pleasure in life meant resting in creatures and forgetting the Creator, then our good Angel in mercy might break in on our lying dream. But if pleasure in life means enjoying what is good, beautiful, &c., and referring all to God, and thanking Him for His gifts and wishing to love Him and serve Him, that enjoyment will not be disturbed by the good Angel. We may encounter pain and sorrow and sin. They will remind us we have no abiding home here. They will warn us not to give up our hearts to creatures. They won't make us exactly unhappy.

You surprise me when you say the Rules for the Discernment of Spirits don't help you much. The descriptions of consolation and desolation (I speak of the first set of rules), and the directions for one and the other state, are invaluable to enable you to see how your spiritual life is progressing. Some day take them up for a spiritual lecture and study them.

Among your four maladies you place in the first rank want of faith. Don't you attach too much importance, pay too much attention to the current difficulties of the day? After all, you could not give up the fact of the existence of Jesus Christ or His Divinity, without knowing you had gone against your reason. "Thou art the Christ, the Son of the living God." What is all the rest? To come back to old rules, continue to lead the life of faith and your faith is amply strong to carry you happily into port. You have plenty of faith. Don't fear for it.

The continual discouragement was written, I suspect, in a gloomy moment. We are always going to sink, but we don't, especially if we call out at the sorest pinch, Lord save me or I perish. The remedy against discouragement is analogous to the remedy against doubt. Lead a life of faith, act as you would do if you knew your faith were perfect before God, and it will be so. So, lead a life of hope, act as if you had a revelation that your soul is at peace with God and on the right way, and it will be on the right way. Act as if all were right and all will be right.

I have been continuing my readings about Savonarola. My respect for him is on the wane. The last biography was by a Rev. Clark, prebendary of Taunton and Wells, I think. He champions Savonarola, but even on his showing, Savonarola by degrees became more and more the tribune of the people, a political monk, and he was the victim of a faction. I found a good review on Villari's Life in the *Etudes*, by Brucker, S.J. He sums up clearly in this sense, and I don't see how a Catholic, or indeed any impartial reader, can do otherwise. My next book must be Villari, and then I will try to read Savonarola's own works, especially his sermons.

I have not put pen to paper on the *Santo Volto* as yet. I don't know whether I may not abandon my project of writing. Such an article ought to have preceded the centenary. In any case, sooner or later, I will send you the book by Canonico Guerra. It is a most interesting and a most readable volume.

Did I procure for you Father Spinola's *Compendium of Meditations*, a small volume, one page for each day? I picked up a nice copy in parchment for one franc. I have a copy which I use myself. His meditations please me. You remember Bart. Ricci's *Meditations on the Life of our Lord*, with engravings. The other day I came upon Vivaldi, S.J., another series of meditations and another series of engravings by the brothers Wierx and other famous artists. The book should contain 149 engravings, 3 are wanting. The others are all there, and fine impressions, folio size. I got this prize for four florins. . . .

San Girolamo, Sept. 5, 1882.

Before answering your letter of the 1st inst., I must thank you for your letters of the last month, and in a special manner for your good wishes and prayers on the 27th.

I thank God you have been able to send a brighter report, and can say you are less bothered and less discouraged. Only persevere in the way you have begun, and you will enjoy greater peace, and come even to feel happy in the service of God. Do you remember my ever giving you a short rule, "Go on as if you had received a revelation that all is right, and all will be right," recall it to your memory, and *never be afraid* to act upon it. You allow yourself to be too easily scared by certain temptations; violent temptations, involuntary sensations and involuntary pleasure, you do not sufficiently distinguish from deliberate, wilful and voluntary consent. The former ought to make you cautious, they ought not to make you miserable as if you had consented. The consent necessary to a mortal sin is a broad, unmistakeable fact, not less clear and distinct than the full moon in a cloudless sky at midnight. Be brave, and trust in our Lord and His Blessed Mother. The account you give of your health does not please me: some of the symptoms are ugly ones. I hope Dr. ——'s visit to-morrow will enable him to form a more favourable opinion. Don't play pranks with his remedies and prescriptions. I suspect you will be obliged to observe much care for some time. You must take special precautions not to catch cold. No doubt the cold damp weather you have had in England has increased the evil. Do what the doctor tells you, and wait patiently to see the effect of his treatment.

Our summer has not been *very* warm. At least, I can say I have not found the heat inconvenient on any occasion. Perhaps the mid-day in September may yet be very hot. Our nights are long already. The sun goes down about 6.30, and the daylight does not break much before 6.30.

You can form no idea how beautiful the country looks with the rich vintage, the vines hanging in festoons between the trees, or trained into arbours, or against the walls. The vintage this year is very abundant. We have great variety of good fruit: grapes, peaches, apricots, plums, figs, pears; and so cheap, you buy twelve magnificent figs for one penny. Last week I found myself in a poor village, where there was no sort of inn even in which I cared to be seen. I made a capital lunch in the tramway, with 1d. of bread and ½d. of figs. There seems to be no end to the figs; thousands and thousands are dried, over and above those which are eaten. With all this fertility, Italy is a wretchedly poor country; nowhere have I met so much misery and want, such utter destitution, and so much wealth of buildings and arts side by side.

I shall hope that your next letter will be the bearer of better news about your health. *Addio.* God bless you.

San Girolamo, Oct. 11, 1882.

Try not to be unhappy about the temptations which still return from time to time. I am persuaded they do not return through any fault of yours, and I am persuaded you do not consent to them, beyond perhaps a certain want of promptness and energy in sending the thoughts away and in fixing the attention on some distracting object. Persevere as you are doing in your manner of confessing. I promise you all will be right.

Regarding your contrition, you tell me you do not grieve so much for having offended God, as on account of what will happen to me; and you ask, Can that be a right disposition? True contrition for sin may be conceived thus in its simplest form: "I wish I had not offended God, I will try not to offend Him again." The motives may be various, the highest is, because God is infinitely worthy to be loved and served, for His own sake, on account of His goodness; the next, because He is worthy to be loved and served in return for His goodness to us; another, because by offending Him, we have forfeited Heaven; lower still, but a good motive and sufficient for confession, because by offending Him I have deserved Hell. So the answer to your question must be that the disposition is a right one, though not the most perfect one.

Father Weld by this time has reached India. He may be back here about May, but nothing certain can be fixed.

We have passed through a dreary September, not unworthy of a rainy Lancashire month, which is saying a good deal. The fall of rain has been something extraordinary. In the north of Italy the inundations have covered a huge tract of country with desolation; no one can say how much misery the people have borne, and how much is in store for them during this winter.

Our beautiful vintage was much injured by the heavy and continuous rains; the promise of olives is good, but we have suffered from the rain not a little this month. I am writing 9.30 a.m., and a dense fog covers everything within a few feet of my windows.

Good-bye. God bless you. Say everything most kind to all from me.

San Girolamo, Oct. 20, 1882.

Your two letters are waiting for an answer. I am glad you like Spinola. You must know it is a compendium of three volumes, in which the meditations are expanded to a considerable length. If you would like the fuller edition, pray let me know. Did you remark the pretty incident in the meditation for this morning, quite new to me: our Lord appearing to St. Martha, when she was near death, with the pleasant invitation, *Veni hospita mea dilectissima.*

In your second letter you revert to the subject of your difficulties about faith. You say they are not intellectual; you are conscious of an utter inability to realize that the truths *are* true. I am tempted to ask you what you mean by realizing that truths are true? how do you realize natural truths, I should have said truths in the natural order? *e.g.*, that we are a law to ourselves, that we are immortal, that truth is a duty, that selfishness is mean, that theft is wicked, &c. Perhaps you will say, you do not realize that some of these are true. Some at least you will admit you realize, but they are those truths which bring us into contact with our fellow-men, and the social consequences of certain acts. I imagine it is not easy to realize that **truths** are truths, except in the cases of truths which are self-evident (*e.g.*, 2 and 2 make 4; the whole is greater than its part, &c.), and which we cannot reject if we would, or practical truths which reach our relations with our fellow-men. Or to put my idea in another shape: we cannot realize that truths are truths, all in the same way or degree; different classes of truths act upon our feelings in different ways. Besides, different classes of truths are open to doubts and difficulties in different ways, and persons who do not appear to be otherwise particularly good, are believed to have a strong and simple faith, in great measure because doubts have never been suggested to them, or because they have been resolutely excluded when in the first instance suggested.

Again, I am not sure that your troubles about faith may not be rather against hope. Faith and hope overlap each other, and cover much ground that is common; hope presupposes faith. Your quotation from Father Coleridge leads me to think you may not have distinguished the two virtues; you wish you had the absolute clearness with which our Lord knew He was always doing the will of His Father. Certainly part of the trial of life consists in the darkness which overhangs our path; we don't see clearly, we don't see God, faith is the argument of things not seen, we are not sure of the way nor of the end of our journey. We can only follow the guidance of faith, do what we can, and hope firmly that if we are not wanting to God, He will not be wanting to us, and He will not fail to lead us to eternal life, though He may try us and let us be tried sorely before we reach the happy term. Perhaps your troubles about faith go off into discouragement, precisely because in reality the weak point is the hope. Yes! discouragement does come from self-love; we are vexed that we cannot feel sure of ourselves and of our salvation.

We rebel against fully and unequivocally admitting that of ourselves we can do nothing; that we depend entirely on God; and rejoicing in our inability and weakness, and in our dependence, costs poor self-love a great deal, obvious and plain as our nothingness is even to ourselves. . . .

. . . Since the beginning of September we have had dreary weather till yesterday, rain, scirocco wind, damp. Yesterday a fresh tramontana cleared the sky, and we have enjoyed two beautiful sunny days, so welcome after six weeks of rain. S. Gallo, the 16th, is an anxious day to Florentines; a rainy S. Gallo means one hundred days of rain; happily, no rain fell. The comet this morning at 4.30 was a magnificent sight.

San Girolamo, Oct. 30, 1882.

My dear Child,

This will be an answer to your two letters, that of the 23rd and that of the 24th. God be praised for the grace He has given my dear friend the Count. Yesterday I said Mass for him, and I shall make a memento every day for him at the Holy Sacrifice for a long time to come. Your other intention I will not forget; we must have patience, and pray hard. I shall write to him to-day or to-morrow. Is it not wonderful how slowly God prepares the soul for the gift of faith? The prejudices of early education, and the mistakes and misunderstandings which rise from ignorance have to be cleared away; then the conviction that Christ is really God, and has established a Church on earth, His witness to mankind, the startling revelation, I can call it nothing less, " If I hope for salvation I must join the Catholic Church," an agony, sometimes shorter, sometimes longer, the struggle between truth and all the many enemies of the truth for the possession of an immortal soul, and the ineffable happiness of possessing the truth, and knowing you are safe. *Addio.* Everything most kind, with my congratulations to the Countess, &c. My blessing to M—— and yourself.

I remain, yours very truly,
GEORGE PORTER.

San Girolamo, Nov. 14, 1882.

Your letter of the 29th of October has remained a long time unanswered, because I was making my own retreat. I enjoyed it very much. I scarcely opened my mouth the whole time. I find this week such a relief to the daily round of business, and every year I find more and more to be done during retreat.

You say age does not make you more sure of getting to Heaven. I should be sorry for you if you were ever to write to me that you had reached the point of feeling sure. I hope every day you are growing more hopeful of getting there in the end. I heard a story the other day which may help you. A distinguished theologian of our Society was on his death-bed. He was as merry as possible, and full of fun. The Rector was alarmed at this joyousness. At last he said to him, "Father, I must tell you that you are nearing your end, there is no chance of your recovering; death is a very serious matter, you ought not to make so light of it." The sick man said to the Rector, "Father, do you believe in the Real Presence?" "Yes, certainly." "You believe when the priest says, 'This is My Body,' Christ becomes really present?" "Yes, certainly." "Well, the same Christ Whom you believe present, has promised me, 'You who have followed Me, and left all things, shall receive eternal life,' &c. Can you wonder that I am full of joy, and hardly know how to contain myself, now that I see the hour of my happiness drawing near?"

Yes, we have so much reason to hope that we shall be saved, notwithstanding our many faults. If you were free to-morrow, you would again leave the world, and perhaps try to make better use of the graces of religious life. You wish to love God, and you strive to serve Him. When you commit a sin or an imperfection, you are sorry for it; you purpose to do better.

Some fine day, you will reach the point when you will not be easily put out, and when you will feel amused if you are snubbed and put upon. I suppose you won't be at that point just yet awhile; still keep your eye upon it and hope to reach it.

Naturally, the bazaar makes you nervous and more irritable. You must see that you secure the full time for your spiritual duties night and morning, and keep that time free for God and your soul. Every day resolve not to allow yourself to be worried or hurried, and pray at Mass for the grace to keep this resolution.

CHAPTER VI.

LAST LETTERS FROM FIESOLE.

Nov. 1882 to Aug. 1883.

Instance of a truth *believed* but *realized* in various degrees, sometimes very imperfectly. The Florentine painters and their realization of the Divinity of Jesus Christ. Degeneration of Modern Art. What to do when uncertain about our duty. How to acquire a habit of decision. Palmer's Notes of a Visit to the Russian Church. Life not wasted because spent in attending to prosy duties. St. Jerome's Letters. Mgr. Freppel. Samuel Wilberforce. Life of Bishop Mazerod and privations of missionaries. Translations of the Fathers by the early Tractarians. Evil of vagueness in spiritual matters. New Year's note of encouragement. Devotions for Lent. Helps for the memory, Gibbon's plan. Life of Mgr. de Ségur. Father Weld's movements. Illness of Mgr. Rogerson. Holy deaths. Bougaud's works. The Immaculate Conception. Hettinger's *Apologetik*. Temptations. Necessity of rest. Sunshine after storms. Reliquaries in the Baptistery of Florence. Advice to a Superior. Reopening of the Duomo at Fiesole. Procession of *Corpus Domini* at Careggi. The facciata of the Duomo at Florence. Death of the architect. Visit to the Convent of St. Domenico. Balmez and Cornoldi. A Retreat, the Exercises of the First Week, their importance. Return of Father Weld. Siena. How to measure progress in our spiritual life. The Sisters of Charity at Siena.

San Girolamo, Nov. 17, 1882.

I hope when you receive this, you will have got through the Slough of Despond, quite to the other side. These fits of depression with you are often natural, and are not the work of the evil spirit. Still they may be prescribed for as for desolations which he has caused: and the Rules for the Discernment of Spirits, which don't help you, you say, recommend a change in our prayers, in penances, and I may add in occupations.

Realizing the truths of faith has engaged my attention

since I last wrote to you. I can furnish an excellent instance of a truth, on which we may make an act of faith, for it has been revealed; which we know, however, from other sources besides revelation. We shall all die. This truth we hold with perfect certainty; on various grounds which we need not stay to consider. Some foolish people keep it out of their minds as much as possible, and their doctors help to keep up the delusion. One of our Georges left the world, asking, "Is this death?" Many others have realized the fact of their mortality much in the same way. There are infinite gradations in the realization. Very sensible people make all their arrangements as if they might die at any moment and then pursue their life as if they were to live always. Very holy people shape their thoughts so that the thief in the night may never take them unawares, and at the same time attend to their duties, enjoy the pleasures of life. This is truly realizing death: yet it is very different from the realization of which we become conscious when we hear of a very sudden death, or a very painful death, or an impenitent death. In such circumstances the impression is most vivid; as a rule it is transient, and we soon relapse into our ordinary mood. Follow out this comparison, and if I am not mistaken you will convince yourself that it is possible to hold a truth and to realize it without experiencing any very decided emotions. We realize death best when we prepare for it: we realize the truths of faith best when we do the works of faith. You will not find it difficult to improve on these suggestions and extend the application.

Another thought came to me from the religious painters of Florence and their Nativities, Annunciations, Entombments, Adorations of the Magi. How those men realized the Divinity of Christ, in all the scenes of His Life and Death! Even Overbeck and the most religious artists of our century are poor, thin, feeble in comparison. The atmosphere was full of Christ: nobody denied Him. His Divinity was assumed to be true from morning to night, in every phase of the daily life, and so many of the clergy and laity led lives of faith, shaped on the life of Christ: whereas now, all these conditions are reversed; the atmosphere is charged with doubt, with unbelief, with blasphemy: His Divinity is almost entirely ignored in daily life, unless it be assailed: the number of faithful worshippers is smaller and they necessarily conceal themselves. No wonder the lustre of faith disappears, no wonder much which ought to follow from faith is lost nowadays even to those who believe very firmly. No wonder pen and pencil have lost the ancient cunning and have fallen on landscape and mere natural life, and even within those departments betray some feebleness. And no wonder if believers pay some of the penalty for the unbelief of the age in the loss of some of the unction and joy and soaring of faith. At your conversion, you had gone through something like an agony, or like death; you were prepared for stronger impressions; and I believe as a rule God favours converts with extraordinary sensible graces, to carry them through their trials and to prepare them for what is to follow, as the glory of the Transfiguration was revealed to the three to prepare them for Gethsemani and Calvary.

So much for realizing the truths of faith. Your last letter contains a remark, that you will always think the greatest trial of life is the not knowing what one ought to do, when one only wants to do right, and in consequence so often doing the wrong thing and then worrying about it. I could write a whole homily on this text; but I will only give the heads. If you are in doubt what line of conduct you are to follow in a given instance, don't aspire to be infallible in your decision: be satisfied and contented that you may decide wrongly; but give your problem what thought you can, and then decide for the best. On important matters it is not amiss to employ the rules for election given by St. Ignatius: generally, talk over any important decision with our Lord; always ask for a blessing on your conclusion. Should the event show you had not decided wisely, see where your previous consideration of the case had failed: perhaps you had not taken into account all the conditions: perhaps the failure ought not to be attributed to you at all. Deny your self-love the luxury of a worry.

If your doubt concerns the manner in which you are to spend your day, what time you are to give to study, to visits, &c., remember every decision is a good one which transgresses no law of God or His Church. Often, one line of conduct is quite as good as any other: the great point is to decide on something and then stand to your resolution, for better or for worse, unless some sufficient reason arises to induce you to change. When you can foresee the course of a day and map out your occupations, you gain the advantage of acting in obedience to a law, which you have given to yourself indeed, but on the guidance of reason. Following out a prearranged plan gains some of the merit of obedience. Obedience, premeditated plans, laws, are all so many extensions of reason; they supply us with clear reasons for acting in a given way. The habit of decision, like all other habits, natural habits, may be acquired, by multiplying acts of decision. Every morning, after breakfast say, map out your day; you will soon discover that you reduce your worries.

The weather with us is very dreary: rain, wind, cold.

I don't see it on account of fogs and cloud, but there must be snow on some of the higher ranges of hills.

I have just finished my annual retreat, a quiet happy time. Fiesole is perfectly adapted for a retreat, though I should prefer the summer to the autumn.

I am glad you paid a visit to the École Apostolique. That is a really good work. You would be delighted and edified if you could see some of the youths I have known prepared in that hardy way: so virtuous, so manly, so courageous.

William Palmer's *Notes of a Visit to the Russian Church*, edited by Cardinal Newman, has just come into my hands: it promises to be most interesting. The Preface by Cardinal Newman, though very short, contains some choice bits. How completely he has identified himself with the Church!

San Girolamo, Dec. 5, 1882.

My dear Child,

In your letter of the 26th you lament your life as wasted. I do not think you ought to consider it wasted. God has assigned to you a peaceful existence, what the world would call an unimportant existence. You have spent many years at home under the roof of your father's house, attending to very prosy duties, for many years taking care of your brothers and of your mother and of your father. These duties must be discharged by some one: you can deserve Heaven (I hoped you have deserved it) in this home life, and you can please God.

Barring some scruples you have indulged in, and a perverted way in looking upon the frequentation of the sacraments, you have done fairly well. I do not say that you could not have done better: of course you might, and it is a pity you did not, but the life is far from having been a wasted life, and I trust if God were to take you now, you would hear the words, "Well done, thou good and faithful servant," &c. Discharge your house duties faithfully, strive to make every one around you happy and contented, and make diligent use of the graces and opportunities within your reach, and you may become a great saint.

Thank God, I keep very well.

Addio. God bless you. Pray for

Yours very truly in Christ,

GEORGE PORTER, S.J.

San Girolamo, Dec. 20, 1882.

Christmas Day must not find me behindhand with Christmas greetings. I wish you a merry Christmas and a *buon capo d'anno,* many graces and blessings and many joys and consolations—and fine weather. . . . I sent you a few days ago St. Jerome's letters in Italian: the copy fell in my way by chance. Some of the letters you will find instructive and also interesting. St. Jerome stands out as one of the grand old rugged figures of antiquity; you will be pleased to see him almost in the original. . . . Palmer's *Notes* are indeed most interesting: the editing may be called perfect. What a genuine photography of a beautiful character and a beautiful mind. I have not enjoyed any reading so much for a long time. . . . Occasionally I see some of Mgr. Freppel's speeches in the French Chamber, they always delight me; he has remarkable talents, and his industry is unceasing. He has conquered for himself a commanding position in that very odious assembly of legislators.

San Girolamo, Jan. 10, 1883.

... S. Wilberforce never attracted me. The revelations of the biography increase my dislike for him: a fussy, restless, shrewd man, with not much high natural principle, and much want of any Christian standard; a man to whom Jesus Christ represented a faint reality, if any; a man whose hatred of the Church was deep and bitter. I am glad a near relative has taken the pains to make him appear what he really was.

I fancy Father Cooke's *Life of Bishop Mazerod* can hardly exaggerate the hardships and privations of the missionaries among the American Indians. I know what many of our Fathers are doing at this moment. The preparation of Littlehampton is none too rude. I have often wished I had the time to put together a volume I should call Tales of the Missions from the histories of our Fathers in Paraguay, Brazil, Canada, and the Indies; the world never secured the services of such heroes. There is a volume of the history of the Canada Mission. I have seen it in Italian, perhaps some day it may fall into my hands.

I am glad you were pleased to have St. Jerome. Would you like the Homilies of St. Gregory? they are very beautiful. If I am not mistaken, the Italian translation was made by Cavalca, the tre-cento translator of St. Bernard, some of whose homilies I sent you from Rome. If I fall in with St. Gregory or St. John Chrysostom, I will secure them for you. Both authors furnish beautiful spiritual reading. You know, I presume, that the early Tractarians published translations of several of the Fathers. I think lay persons have not availed themselves sufficiently of them; they contain rare treasures. ...

You say Father —— makes you dreadfully low-spirited. I suspect the reason is that he leaves you under a vague sort of impression that there is something wanting, without giving you a clear idea what the want may be. In spiritual matters beware of vagueness; aim at least at forming clear definite ideas and definite wishes. If your conscience reproaches you with any infidelity, strive at once to atone for it; if you see clearly that God demands a sacrifice, pray for strength and encourage yourself to make it; lastly, pray that you may be preserved from self-deception and that you may never be lulled into a false security. Beyond these precautions, aim at high thoughts in the service of God, persuade yourself you can never do enough or do anything well enough, at the same time do the best you can and wish it were more. Wage war against gloomy thoughts. . . . Keep hope alive.

San Girolamo, Jan. 9, 1883.

My dear Child,

    I am rather behind time in wishing you a happy New Year. I count on your faith in me that the wishes travelled to you over land and sea in due time. May 1883 bring you an increase of peace of mind and heart, and many blessings temporal and spiritual.

Accept my thanks for your Christmas card and your good wishes and prayers.

Our weather has been pretty much what you describe yours to have been. Father Purbrick has just been here, and the rain and snow might have led him to believe himself in dear Lancashire. He reached Florence on Saturday night and left it yesterday night, a hurried visit, but I hope a pleasant one for him. Father General was glad to see him again after an interval of sixteen years.

The depressing, desponding thoughts are connected

with your health. You do not give way to them. Try not to be frightened by them. Omit none of your duties, above all, none of your spiritual duties. At such times say your prayers with more than usual attention and deliberation, slowly and faithfully, thoughtfully.

Good-bye. God bless you.

I remain, yours very truly in Christ,

GEORGE PORTER.

San Girolamo, Feb. 10, 1883.

Our winter has not been particularly cold, but it has been very changeable and uncertain. Barometers and thermometers, sunsets and sunrises, and the other aids to weather clerks, fail us utterly this season. Still primroses and violets and anemones begin to show, and we hope the spring is near. . . .

Shall you have the courage to try some of the " First Week" exercises during Lent, the Penitential Psalms, the responsories and antiphons of the Breviary, and the Masses for Lent? My experience bears out the utility of these penitential prayers and thoughts. They drive away every thought of pride, and hence bring peace and a feeling of dependence on God.

You find your memory not so retentive as it used to be. Worrying and fussing blur the memory. I have found help in Gibbon's plan. Before beginning any new book, he considered what he already knew about its subject, fixed his dates, the period, contemporaries, &c. Besides, at the close of a chapter, he thought over what he had read. This habit of reflecting and repeating, and placing facts and persons in their relative places with what we already know, I find a real help.

You say you will be glad to have Italian translations of some of the Fathers. I once had the forty Homilies of St. Gregory the Great, translated by the tre-cento Dominican Cavalca. Perhaps I shall fall in with a copy. You would read them with advantage. In the Breviary you have seen specimens. . . . Latterly I have not been able to find much time for reading. I take up at odd moments Mgr. de Ségur—*Souvenirs et recit d'un frère*, par le Marquis de Ségur: a good Life of a good specimen of a Frenchman.

Father Weld writes that he will be in Calcutta by March 1st. From there he goes to Singapore. Perhaps he will sail from Singapore to London. He can scarcely return before May is well advanced. If you come to Florence, as I hope you will, you will find me here still. I count on nothing as certain in my future: the present affords me plenty of work; I give myself to it and leave the future to bring its tale for better or for worse.

When the weather clears up, I promise myself a day in Prato, where St. Catherine of Ricci lived, and where our Lady's girdle is kept. I shall get myself up in Prato history before you come.

March, 1883.

. . . The Passion has two sides, you must remember: the savage war and triumph of the unjust over the Just One, and on the other side, the charity, the virtues of our Saviour, and the deep mystery of the reconciliation of man with God. How much there lies concealed in the Passion to excite our gratitude and love for our King. *Dilexit me et tradidit semetipsum propter me.*

I am glad to hear you are satisfied with Holy Week and Easter. I agree with you that it is good to be roused on great *festas*, and on Easter Sunday above all *festas*. I detest orchestra music in the church and I am not devoted to Mozart's Masses, but I should be ready to hear the *Gloria* of his No. 12, with full band, every

Easter Day of my life, and a grand *Alleluia* at the end of the Mass. I never assisted at this Mass on Easter Day without feeling myself the better for it.

WRITTEN TO A YOUNG MAN IN THE WORLD.

San Girolamo, Feb. 28, 1883.

My dear ——,

Accept my best wishes for the ——, after date. I hope you may be spared to see many returns of the day, and to do much good in the world, especially to your own family.

I agree most cordially in your estimate of Father John Etheridge. His charity was truly admirable. Who ever heard from his lips an unkind word? How often he spoke to defend or excuse the absent, or to put a favourable construction on the conduct or words of others.—R.I.P.

I agree with you, too, in your veneration for Father ——, he will bring a blessing on the home and the parish.

The news about the spire is cheering. I hope it will be adorned with a fine clock. As the bells already exist, the expense will not be very great. The clear-story must wait for some first-class engineer. I have the conviction a clear-story can be put in, and ought not to cost very much. You see I still cherish some interest in St. Francis Xavier's, notwithstanding years of absence and my exile in a foreign land.

I read your account of yourself with much pleasure God has taken good care of you. You are left, as you say, alone in the world, but you have escaped many cares and anxieties, you are more free to serve God and attend to your own soul, and you have been able to assist others. Make the most of the graces placed within your reach: you never know what God may ask of you.

All your family with good constitutions have still a weak place somewhere, I suspect it is the liver. You all require a good deal of support, and fasting does not suit you, and sometimes abstinence is more than you can manage.

You ought all to eat good meals. Say your grace devoutly, and make up for penance by prayer and alms-deeds.

Good-bye, my dear ———. God bless you. Thanks for your daily memento in your prayers; don't leave it off.

Believe me, your sincere friend,

GEORGE PORTER.

San Girolamo, March 3, 1883.

My dear Child,

I had hoped to send you a *buona Pasqua* and an Easter letter, but Holy Week and Easter Week brought me so much business, I was obliged to push all my correspondence aside. I send you my *buona Pasqua* at the foot of the altar. Many thanks for your news of M. Rogerson, I hope he may still be spared to do some work for God's honour and glory, but if he is called away, I am glad he meets the end with courage and cheerfulness. After all death generally reaches us as a friend. We dread him till he comes. At the last most people are glad when he knocks at the door. Give him my affectionate remembrance, that is M. Rogerson, not the grim friend, the latter will take good care not to forget me.

I congratulate you about the good news you have had about dear Hedvige and your cousin. Please give my cordial congratulations to Hedvige. I shall pray for her every day at Mass that she may enter on her married life with great graces.

You do well to leave the white elephant in his cage. Sister Emmerich and *La Perfection Chretienne* are much better for you. A book I should like you to have would be *La Vie de Jesus Christ*, par Ludolph of Saxe; that would last you all your life, and it is so devout. When you look for Rio, at the same time look for Ludolph. His name in English is Ludolph of Saxony. He was a Carthusian and wrote in Latin. I try always to have him near me and often to dip into his pages.

Macaulay was a conceited, shallow, shrewd man. Lord Melbourne said of him, I wish I was as sure of any one thing, as Tom Macaulay is of everything.

Addio. God bless you.

Yours very truly in Christ,
GEORGE PORTER.

San Girolamo, Fiesole, April 5, 1883.

. . . The account of the little angel whom you have sent to Heaven, gave me endless pleasure and edification. A sick-bed and a death such as hers tell us more about the value of suffering than many pages of holy books, and they draw us nearer to God than anything I know. I trust she sang her *Alleluia* on Easter Sunday with the angels in Heaven.

Yesterday I received news of the death of a spiritual acquaintance of mine, whom I had never seen, an invalid and sufferer for long years. About two years ago, she was carried, more dead than alive, into a convent, leaving a wealthy home and parents who adored her. She took her vows, edified all by her heroic patience. For three years she prayed she might die on Good Friday, and quite unexpectedly her prayer was answered.

I had recommended her to say every day the service of Extreme Unction. In one of the last letters she dictated, she sent me word that her daily Extreme Unction had been a great comfort and help to her.—R.I.P.

Everything most kind to ——. I won't dispute her accusation, that her last letter remains unanswered. Possibly I may enclose a wee note to-day if time permits. Time is the one luxury which fails me here, so much to be done, and the days only seven to the week, and only twenty-four hours each. Before I close my letter, I may say the spring seems to have commenced in earnest. This is the third beautiful day we have had. The winter has been very long and cheerless. *Addio.* God bless you.

Do you know Abbé Bougaud, *Le Christianisme les temps présents?* It is to be finished in five vols., four have been published. He does not carry me with him always, but he says many beautiful things. He suggests very much. He is the author of the well-known Life of St. Jane de Chantal, and another, not so well known, of Blessed Margaret Mary Alacoque. Sometimes, when I am at my wits' ends, and despair of ever getting through my writings, I put it on one side, and read Bougaud, or some other eloquent writer. I gain time by this proceeding.

San Girolamo, April 30, 1883.

My dear Child,

I thank you for your good wishes on my patron's day, and still more for the Holy Communion you offered for me.

The books arrived safely: *L'Art Cretien* and the *Conferences* of Père Monsabré. Your letter I received late on Saturday. It had been sent on to me to Florence from Fiesole. If you let me know the day of Hedvige's marriage, I will say Mass for her. The news that she is to be married to a good Christian gives me no end of consolation. She has been a dutiful, devoted child. I pray she may be blessed and rewarded in her new home. I am interested to hear that Count S—— is so fervent. He is a man who may do much for many souls. I should be so glad to meet him, and to talk over matters with him. As you know, a soul that has passed out of the cold into the sunshine, and stepped over the threshold of the Church into an entirely new life, sees what had not been visible before.

I will pray much for your Count. He is too good a man to be left out in the cold. You ask me for him how we prove the Immaculate Conception. By any chance have you the letter I wrote to you for Count S—— on that subject?[1] It would answer much of your question. The great point is to understand what is meant by the Immaculate Conception. It means that the soul of the Mother of Jesus, when it was created by God, to be united to her body born of Joachim and Anna, as the bodies of other children, did not contract the taint of original sin, as the souls of all who are descended from Adam in the ordinary way, and as she ought to have contracted it, being about to be united to a body descended from Adam in the ordinary way; but by a special privilege, in consideration of the merits of her Divine Son, that she might be a worthier temple of this Divine Child, she was preserved from the taint, and at her creation received from God the robe of grace, just as Eve received it when she was created before Adam had sinned. We prove the Immaculate Conception from the tradition of the Church, which has always taught that the Blessed Virgin Mary was never for *one instant* the slave of sin and the devil, that she from *the*

[1] Letters, Nov. 28th, 1881, and Jan. 19th, 1882.

first instant of her existence waged war against the devil and that she overcame him through her Divine Son. This truth we read in Genesis, c. iii. v. 15. This is, in short, our proof. You should get Hettinger's *Apologetik*, three vols.; costs about £1. In that book you have a special treatise on the Immaculate Conception, and the best book of controversy and instruction which exists. I understand Prince George of Saxony reads it through every year. Your "white elephant" cannot be understood on the Immaculate Conception without much explanation. But St. Thomas did not deny this privilege to Mary. There was no irregularity in the last Council. Hettinger has an excellent treatise on the Infallibility too.

Get the short Ludolph of Saxony. It will do you great good. Everything kind and affectionate to you all. God bless you.

Very truly yours in Christ,

GEORGE PORTER.

San Girolamo, May 23, 1883.

Your letter of the 2nd has remained a long time without its answer. I have been more busy than usual. I had to go to Rome for a week, and this absence, together with visitors at Fiesole and sick people at Florence, has thrown my correspondence into confusion.

I do not like your abstaining from Holy Communion. "The feeling of not being determined coming upon you" is not a reason for abstaining. In all that matter of temptation, remember that which displeases God is the part which is voluntary and deliberate. What is involuntary and what you cannot help does not displease Him, and ought not to keep you from Holy Communion. You must do all you can to resist this growing fear of Holy Communion and these worries about your spiritual exercises.

Your intention has not been overlooked by me. I shall continue to pray. You must do the same, and ask Almighty God to guide everything for the best for your soul's salvation and your happiness in this world. You must not despair.

I shall not be in England before the end of June. Father Weld has postponed his return by one or two weeks. I do not think he can leave Bombay before the 1st of June.

The weather here is perfection now. I suppose you are still under the rule of easterly winds.

Good-bye. God bless you. Say everything kind to all from me.

San Girolamo, May 29, 1883.

I must not allow May to pass away without sending you some sort of a letter. Since Easter I have been very busy. A fever case of sixty days' duration called me nearly every day to Florence; then I had a visitor here in Fiesole, to whom I was obliged to devote much time; lastly, I was absent in Rome for a week. You can easily imagine how all my correspondence has been thrown into confusion.

From both your last letters I conclude that you have been working beyond your strength. That over-taxing of the strength always betrays itself in the symptoms, which you describe;—everything seems to require such an effort, you feel so lazy, so incapable of fixing your thoughts in meditation, so sleepy, so filled with distractions.

I am afraid you have not learnt as yet how to deal with this state of things. Extra sleep for two or three days. A little extra food or support. A little less work for a few days. Then in prayer, substitute vocal prayer for meditation, or even read instead of meditating. You may be sure of one thing: in one way or another, the body and the brain must have rest and some change. You may regulate it and finish the rest in two or three days, or you may struggle on and spread it over many days or weeks, sleeping at all manner of times, plodding through your spiritual exercises very wearily, dragging yourself through your work; but rest you must have, and nature will take it, if you do not take it yourself. I shall not be surprised if you sleep quite half the time of your next retreat.

Your account of —— is a sad one. I am afraid he is not a strong man, and he will wear himself out; that is the way, the best die first and the inferior men live longest. . . .

TO A FRIEND WHO HAD LATELY LEFT FLORENCE.

San Girolamo, June 25, 1883.

. . . Your description of the St. Gothard route creates the wish to travel home that way; if Father Weld ever turns up and I cross the Alps again, I may go from Florence to Calais, breaking my journey rather oftener than you did.

We have not had good weather since you left; rain fell on most days, the winds were high and the air more than *freschetta*, positively chilly. On Friday last a violent storm broke over the valley, with a diluvio of rain and very angry thunder and lightning. I hope the bad weather closed with that storm. Yesterday was a perfect day: the sky cloudless, the air light and bright and sweet, the sun glorious, the heat tempered by a gentle breeze. Yesterday followed in the same style, the breeze rather stronger in the *dopo pranzo,* yet not a cloud above the horizon. On Friday after the storm the wind seemed to carry everything like a cloud right away to the sea. How completely one fine day blots out the recollection of weeks of cloudy, cheerless weather. I suppose one moment of Heaven will swallow up a lifetime of sorrow and trouble.

The Duomo at Florence and the Duomo at Fiesole are to be reopened for public worship next Sunday afternoon. What will be done in Florence I cannot say. At Fiesole a pretty programme has been drawn up, the concluding feature being a procession of the Blessed Sacrament from St. Maria Primerana (the little chapel used during the repairs of the cathedral) across the Piazza to the Cathedral, followed by grand *Te Deum*. . . .

On Saturday I went into the baptistery, and saw the grand *tabernacolo* in silver and some very beautiful reliquaries, which contained, I dare say, precious relics; but I had no guide to tell me what they were. The forms of the reliquaries struck me much. . . .

TO A RELIGIOUS SUPERIOR.

San Girolamo, July 10, 1883.

I am sorry to hear my good friend —— is on her death-bed. If she is still living when you receive this, will you tell her she has my most fervent prayers that she may make a good end. When she dies I will say Mass for her. Ask her not to forget to pray for me when she is safe on her throne in Heaven. The prayers of many poor people will follow her.

Father ——'s visit must have been a great consolation to you. With his knowledge of you since you began a spiritual life, and with his experience and with his holiness, you can satisfy your conscience more completely in accepting my word that you are going on all right and that your chief danger lies in the neglect of your strength. The strongest have a limit to their strength, and break down unless they observe some moderation. You are not very strong, and you require a great deal of rest for your brain. If you could always sleep full eight hours in every twenty-four, you would pray better, you would be less impatient, and I believe you would get through more work and do it better.

I will make a little confession to you. I think if I had always eight, or at least seven and a half hours' sleep, I should be a better religious: my brain needs much repose.

Even putting the sleep on one side, those who are in authority especially, easily fall into the snare of standing about or running about all the day: they can with difficulty preserve that calm, that self-possession, that amount of attention which subjects have a right to look for when they address themselves to their Superiors. So I conclude, less running about, more sleep, more quietness, and so, more time to think.

San Girolamo, July 11, 1883.

... We have been keeping high *festa* at Fiesole. The Cathedral, after being closed for many years, was reopened with some solemnity. On July 1st the Blessed Sacrament was carried in procession from St. Maria Primerana, the little chapel on the Piazza, to the Cathedral. There was a sermon and Benediction and *Te Deum*. The Cathedral looks well; simple and grand. I don't quite like the new altar, which is more Gothic than the building permits. The organ has been placed more out of sight, and some new stops have been introduced. In the campanile the old bells still hang, but the clock is a new one, and it strikes more vigorously and with better effect than the old one. The outside of the Cathedral has been finished very well and in excellent taste. The great *festa* was Friday the 7th, St. Romolo, disciple of St. Peter, first Bishop. We had even a *dispensa* from *magro*. Great doings in the church, crowds from Florence, *diligenza* both ways every half hour; fireworks and illuminations on the Sunday and the Friday, very pretty in the beautiful, cool, deep blue night. We were good for one hundred *fiaccole*—great extravagance!

Sunday, July 1st, I spent at Careggi with old Mrs. Sloane. On that day the *Corpus Domini* procession goes from Careggi Church to her villa, walks through the grounds, the Benediction is given in her little chapel, and the procession leaves through the second entrance and winds along the hill back to the parish church. A very fierce-looking band, in magnificent uniform, nodding plumes, every man wearing his sword, happily not drawn, trumpeted and tromboned without much intermission; the men, women, and children, who walked with torches, made a poor figure. The *baldachino* and the priests round the Blessed Sacrament looked as they ought to do, and the procession as it moved through the grounds and followed the road under the hill, was very beautiful : the candles and torches twinkled like stars. The grounds were thrown open all the evening, and thousands availed themselves of the opportunity: a happy, quiet, well-conducted crowd. Mrs. Sloane entertained as many of her neighbours and friends as chose to accept her hospitality. When I retired soon after ten, some of the company still lingered behind. The illuminations were very effective. Mrs. Sloane allowed herself to be agitated about the weather the evening before—quite a gratuitous piece of self-torture. On the Saturday evening, between nine and ten, after a cloudless glorious day I went with her into the garden. Thousands of fireflies were darting about: the *cicale* were practising for the opening of their summer concert on the following day. There was every promise of a beautiful day, and the day was equal to the promise. What a pretty neighbourhood surrounds Careggi!

The weather has been delicious. Cloudless mornings, a breeze in the afternoon, with some clouds and scirocco. The thermometer has not been so high with us as in London. We have never got beyond 85 Fahr., which is very endurable. I believe the promise of grapes and olives is good. Both showed themselves very late, and the harvest, which ought to be gathered now, will be at least a fortnight behind the usual time.

Florence has lost Emilio de Fabris, the architect of the *facciata* of the Duomo. He died about the 25th of June, leaving the work very far advanced. He was seventy-four years old, a grand architect, a good Christian, for whom every one has a kindly word. There is some dispute as to the finishing of the *facciata*. Some are for the simple basilica style, others want an ornamental arch, such as you have over the side doors. I went into the Duomo about 8 a.m. last Saturday, and there I saw on the ground what looked like a wooden model of the proposed ornamental finish. The eastern sun shone full into the Duomo and lighted it up into a new existence, pleasing as a change on its usual gloom.

Some little time back I paid a pleasant visit to the Dominican Convent at S. Domenico. I wanted to see Père Berthier, who is writing a monograph on S. Sabina on the Aventine at Rome. He was out. I saw instead Père Hyacinthe Bayonne, who wrote the Life of St. Catherine of Ricci, and is now preparing the Life of

S. Antoninus of Florence, brother of Father Emmanuel Ceslas Bayonne (twenty years junior), who has published an *Étude* on Savonarola, and is now preparing his Life, hoping to whitewash his memory and promote the cause of his canonization. Père Hyacinthe was very pleasant company, but he was called to the parlour and he handed me over to the Prior, whose name I failed to catch, a lame, halting Frenchman, very genial and very chatty. He showed me the Crucifixion by Fra Angelico, lately discovered in their chapter-room, or as much of it as they still hold. A very fine fresco. Only one figure, the Christ, with a curious foreshortening of the head, throwing it down on the chest. When the director of the Louvre heard of the discovery, he made the journey from Paris to S. Domenico on purpose to see the picture. He and the critics pronounce this crucifixion a fine specimen of Fra Angelico. I venture to agree in this verdict. The convent is a very pleasing building. One corridor is built like those of S. Marco, the rooms having a ceiling under a roof which covers the whole corridor. The Prior told me this corridor suggested the idea for S. Marco. Another corridor, added in the seventeenth or eighteenth century, has a series of portraits over each cell by a painter, Muti, whose name I had never heard and have not yet found in my books. He painted well. The portrait of Fra Angelico is a very good one. So is that of St. Dominic. . The monks have a fine garden and a noble cortile. By degrees they are putting the place in order. At present they have few novices, but they hope soon to put in a number of promising youths. I hope they will succeed.

A word on Balmez. By all means read the *El Criterio*. Then the Metaphysics. Then the Psychology. The Ethics if you like. Don't waste time now on his Fundamental Philosophy. After the *Criterio* and the Metaphysics, go as soon as you please to Cornoldi. He is closer reading, but immeasurably superior to Balmez, indeed, he is a good, if not the best course of philosophy you can read. He is a scholastic. Master him and you can read the *Summa* of St. Thomas, the grandest book ever put together by human genius.

Only imagine a swarm of bees alighted last week in the smaller cortile of the Strozzini. Made a terrible havoc of a lay-brother who tried to house them. Fled away and came back. I have not heard the sequel of the story.

San Girolamo, August 14, 1883.

I had intended to post this letter (write, I should have said) so that you might receive it on the Assumption, with my wishes for a happy feast. My wishes must travel from the foot of the altar on the feast itself and the letter will tell you afterwards.

Your account of the retreat pleased me very much. You have found out a weak place in your spiritual life, and I have been waiting a long time for this discovery to come. To avoid the great truths, the malice of sin, its punishments here and hereafter, is a mistake. What spiritual writers call the Exercises of the First Week ought to play a great part in our spiritual *régime*. We ought to fall back upon them every now and then. The deeper we enter into the knowledge of sin, of our own sinfulness and nothingness and weakness and misery, of God's holiness and justice, the stronger do we render the foundations of our edifice, the stronger the humility, the stronger our docility to learn any lesson God may be pleased to teach us, the stronger our capacity to soar to any height to which He may call us. I think I once gave you a list of affections for the different weeks of the Exercises. You would be well repaid for your trouble if you wrote out, from Da Ponte for instance, a number of texts from the Scriptures expressing such affections. When the facility acquired during a retreat begins to wear away, a course of three or four days of the meditations of the first week will often give courage and secure the gain of the retreat for a longer time. Do all you can not to part with this really solid fruit from your retreat of 1883. You allude to the difficulties you meet with when you begin to aim at any particular virtue. Help yourself by studying the true character of the virtue, its motives, its acts. Then map it out into a number of degrees, rising easily from the lowest to the highest. You will find this preliminary study no small help and no small encouragement.

Father Weld has returned at last. He reached Brindisi on July 21st. The authorities refused to let the steamer enter the inner port, whereupon the captain turned her head round and made for Trieste. Trieste was gained on the 23rd. Ten days' quarantine had to be passed in the harbour on board, though there was no single case of sickness, and the steamer had simply passed through the canal, without once touching land. His Reverence came to Fiesole on August 4, left again for Rome on the 6th, and returns to us to-morrow. I shall not be free to leave quite at once, as it remains to be seen whether Father Weld will settle down. I cannot complain. July and August have been beautiful months. The thermometer scarcely ever above 90°, seldom above 80°, and a breeze most days. The farmers want rain. The sun and the breeze have parched up the earth. That is the price we pay for a cloudless sky and for wonderful evenings.

Last week I had a great treat. On the 5th I went to Siena, and enjoyed two clear days. About a dozen of my Florentine flock, summering there, wanted benefit of clergy, and thus I had a reason for my journey. The Siena paintings alone would have repaid me. They link on to the Florentine school and almost equal them. But I enjoyed the scene of the life and many miracles of St. Catherine of Siena. Also the Osservanza, where St. Bernardine of Siena laid the beginnings of the Friar Minors Observantines, to say nothing of the Duomo (happily the pavement was uncovered), the frescoes of Pinturrichio and the oratory of S. Bernardino. The weather was glorious even for Italy. Siena has taken possession of my imagination ever since. I am always stealing back to one or other of its sights or memories. On the Wednesday, before starting, I said Mass for you in St. Catherine's chapel in the fine Church of San Domenico. I shall not be sorry to repeat my visit to Siena. I was on my feet most of the two days, but some things I could not see at all, many I could not see leisurely, and most I would gladly see again.

I have picked up some additions for your Italian library. A neat copy of *Fiori dei Morali di S. Gregori, Lettere di S. Bernardo, Oposcoli di S. Giovanni Grisostomo, Sermoni volgari di S. Bernardino,* &c.

Next week business will take me to Turin, to see Don Bosco. In my next letter I will tell you of my journey, and also of an expedition which I made to the Franciscans at Quaracchi. The clock warns me I must bring this long story to a close.

San Girolamo, August 28, 1883.

I thank you for your July letter and the good wishes and prayers you offered for me on St. Ignatius' day. I suppose your retreat is ended and you have got back from ——. I am sure the quiet, the country air, the change and the absence from your daily anxieties all helped you to make a good retreat.

It seems to me you are too anxious for some sudden, striking advance in holiness. As a rule, God leads His servants onward very slowly, almost imperceptibly, and He leaves them with old faults, or enables them to discover new ones, just to keep them in humility; and He does not always succeed, for it is wonderful how easily we give way to conceit or vanity, notwithstanding our many defects.

If you want to know your true state before God, you must go back to distant states, your entrance into religion, your vows, your removal to ——, your last retreat, or the one before it. Examine quietly whether you have corrected, wholly or in part, some leading fault, *e.g.* uncharitableness, impatience, whether you have renounced the world more completely; whether you are more entirely devoted to your duties, to prayer, to service of the poor, &c.; whether you have improved in the use of the sacraments, of Holy Mass, of prayer, of reading, &c.; whether from retreat to retreat you have made a step forward. Such examination cannot be made in a minute: it is rather tedious and requires time; but I am convinced it would show you that, though creeping along, you have still made progress, and it would enable you to find where your efforts must be directed for next year.

Oh! you may thank God for many graces and mercies and blessings. Never weary of asking pardon for sins and negligences and offences and omissions, yet at the same time never weary of thanking and loving God. As you get older in religion, make it more a point to secure some quiet time every day to think about your own soul and about those entrusted to your care.

Father Weld has come back from India. He is in the house now, and is likely to remain. Still I do not go back to London for the present. Perhaps Father General has not quite made up his mind whether Father Weld is to be sent off again. He looks none the worse, but rather much the better, for his long journey.

I hope your difficulties with —— have been smoothed away. Don't be too anxious on that head. Better that cross than many others which might be imagined. I see from the papers there has been an awfully sudden death at Ince Blundell. I knew the Archbishop of Sydney very well, having once spent a week with him at Belmont: he has done a good work during the few years of his episcopate.

A few weeks ago I paid a visit to Siena. Your Sisters have a house there, and take charge in part at least of the famous hospital La Scala. Among others I found an English Sister, a convert. She has lived seven or eight years in Siena, and has got into Italian ways very completely, without however ceasing to be thoroughly English. She seems very happy. The hospital, which used to be the richest in the world, was commenced by a shoemaker, so the story runs. Much of its wealth has been made away with. It still remains a noble monument of Christian charity, facing the splendid Cathedral.

Addio. God bless you. If you don't write within a fortnight, wait till you hear from me, and I will give you my address.

CHAPTER VII.

LETTERS FROM VARIOUS PLACES.

From Oct. 1883 to Dec. 1886.

Work at Rome. Announcement of speedy return to England. Hints for meditation. Commentaries on the Psalms. The Third Order. Happiness of a convert. The Last Judgment. London. Devotion to the Holy Souls. Obedience. Opening of the New Oratory, London. Dr. Wace's Preface to Luther's primary works. Maclear's evidential value of the Holy Eucharist. Short notes of counsel. Plans for Sept. 1886. Pusey and Meyrick on our Lady. Prayer of petitions. The Scotch Synod. Journey to Florence. Turin. San Girolamo again. Storm on the Lac du Bourget. Return to Paris. Caro's books on Positivism. St. Bernard, depth and devotion of his writings. Montmartre. Notre Dame. Works of Father Franco.

In the autumn of 1883, Father Porter went from Fiesole to Rome, having been chosen as one of the representatives of the English Province in the General Congregation of the Society held that year. He then returned to England, where he remained till Sept. 1886, when he again went to Fiesole for a few weeks as Procurator of the Province, at the Triennial meeting of Procurators.

Collegio Germanico, Via del Seminario,
Rome, Oct. 8, 1883.

Your letter of Sept. 11th has remained too long unanswered. You will have guessed from the papers what has occupied me. I came to Rome on Sept. 14th, and I have been very closely occupied ever since. Thank God, we have got through the important part of our work without any disturbance from the Government or from the violent party. We avoided making much noise about our meeting, and reached Rome in small parties.

The pilgrimage of the Italian priests coincided with our arrival, and our comparatively small number escaped observation. The result has been highly satisfactory. You may wish to know how I am personally affected by the change. Unless some unforeseen and improbable combination is made, I shall be back in London next month. When I see you, I will tell you more about the Congregation. Also about my visit to Bologna and to Orvieto, and to Cortona, always supposing I can contrive to return to Florence *viâ* Cortona. . . .

The plan you propose of introducing the thoughts and affections of the first week into meditations on the Life of our Lord, His Passion, even His Resurrection, is the right one. Set meditations of the first week may be made sometimes, but it is wiser not to dwell long on them, unless you feel specially drawn to do so. The essential point not to be lost sight of, is the strengthening the ideas and principles and affections of the first week and making them run as a sort of groundwork through the whole spiritual formation of the soul. A choice of verses from the Psalms, sayings of the saints, and above all, maxims of our Blessed Lord, will render these first week digressions very useful and very pleasant.

Yes, the reflection is very useful, especially if you make it not merely as an examination, but also as a repetition, a *resumé* of the thoughts and affections of the meditation.

What you call your disasters in prayer may be turned to your advantage, if you examine closely into their causes and history, and if you can discover to what extent they were brought about by your own negligence or by faults against charity, &c. . . .

The cold has been keen in Rome these last few days, the mornings and evenings especially. Walking, however, is pleasant. Yesterday Rome, Catholic Rome, kept *festa*. I did not see anything of it, as I was obliged to remain indoors nearly all day. I think we shall not get away much before the end of October.

Collegio Germanico, Oct. 10, 1883.

My dear Child,

Your letter was forwarded to me here. I have been in Rome since the 14th of September, and do not expect to get away before the end of this month. I hope to be in London, at my work in Farm Street, before the middle of November.

You know from the papers the business which brings me here. We have chosen our Vicar-General, with right of succession, to Father Beckx; and we have chosen the Assistants and Admonitor, an event for which we feel very thankful to God.

The Italian papers happily take little notice of us and our doings. On the other hand, we are very peaceable and live very quietly, and a large pilgrimage of priests from the north of Italy occupied the public attention. We have not encountered the smallest annoyance that I hear of. Have you any commentary on the Psalms? Bossuet wrote an edition of the Psalms for his priests. Père Berthier has a longer work, *Sur les Psaumes*. Get to the meaning of those Psalms which you have in your Office, and understand how they apply to our Blessed Lady, to the Church, to the soul in the possession of God's grace. And then pick out some verses which take your fancy and use them as ejaculations. The recitation of the Office will become your consolation and your strength.

The mornings and evenings in Rome are now cold, the days beautiful, and the air marvellously clear.

Addio. God bless you.

San Girolamo, Oct. 29, 1883.

My dear Child,

I answer your letter of the 27th without delay. By all means join the Third Order, if you see you can observe the rules. I have not yet studied the new rules, but I say without hesitation, if you can live up to them, you gain immense advantages and graces by joining the Third Order. You enter into closer communion of merits and good works with a large number of holy souls, and your own prayers and good works acquire an additional merit in the sight of God. I am glad to hear of the Count's growing sympathy and attraction for the Church. We must all pray that he may receive the gift of faith. What a gift it is, what a blessing! The same post which brought me your letter, brought me one from a Russian lady whom I received into the Church about Easter. She says, "If you knew how happy I am as a Catholic, you would perhaps be quite astonished. I think so often of what you said before the abjuration, 'Only take the step, and you will feel quite different.' And how afraid I was." Now she is so satisfied. She took a long time before the final step. Thanks for Casimir's card. It shall go into my breviary. I wrote to the Countess. I expect to return very soon to London. Perhaps to-morrow night. Perhaps a week later. In any case I shall leave Italy soon. I shall stay one or two days in Paris. Mgr. R—— does not get any better, and he asks me to give him some help to get ready for death. I must also break my journey at Boulogne for a little work of charity. I fear you will be at Glouys, when I am in Paris. This morning I received Miss G—— into the Church, in our little chapel of S. Girolamo, and she was confirmed afterwards by the Bishop of Fiesole in the chapel of his seminary. Write her a line. I think she will do well.

As to the permission to keep the Blessed Sacrament, speak to the Curé of F——. The rules may be special for the northern countries. If he does not know how to set about it, write to me, and I will manage for the Countess at Rome. But you must tell her such permissions always pay a tax. I do not know the amount, but it might easily run up to £12 or £15 sterling. The officials of many of the Congregations are paid out of these taxes.

I know Père Olivaint's *Journal des Retraites*, and thank you for offering to send it to me; but give it to some one who has not read it.

You ask me about the Judgment. Every one will be judged according to his conscience and the law of God. God will take everything into account: temptations, circumstances, education, friends, the age men live in, their health, their passions, everything. Those who have received better education will be judged more severely than those who enjoyed fewer advantages of instructions. "To whom much was given, from him shall more be required." God will be immeasurably more considerate than the best of men, at the same time He will be more just. Your other questions I must answer in my next letter. Kindest remembrances to all. *Addio.* God bless you and your charge.

I remain yours very truly in Christ,
GEORGE PORTER.

111, Mount Street, London,
Nov. 7, 1883.

My dear Child,

I must begin my London life well, so I send you a few lines in answer to your letter of welcome. I reached Mount Street on Sunday evening. The passage from Boulogne was a very rough one, and London as foggy, rainy, and dirty as possible. Such a contrast to an unusually fine October which I left behind me at Fiesole. However, Fiesole, Florence, blue sky, and the rest, are all things of the past. I must set my teeth and face the grim realities of London. The journey in your direction must remain in the remote future, I fancy; though I have found that very unlikely things have a knack of coming to pass.

Try the Devotion to the Holy Souls. When I was in Italy, I heard some cases in which they had obtained very signal graces for their clients, and I will say these cases made a great impression on me. Who can say? Perhaps they will do something for you, if you pray for them and to them, with much fervour.

You have still much to do for Almighty God before you join the Holy Souls. That will come in time—sooner than you imagine.

Kindest remembrances to all friends. Tell —— that Père Rubillon leaves Italy and returns to France. He will be stationed in Paris. I left him in excellent health and spirits yesterday week.

111, *Mount Street, Grosvenor Square, W.,*
Nov. 26, 1883.

My dear Child,

I have only time to write you a short note. I fear I cannot give you much encouragement. If you take the management of your spiritual affairs into your own hands you must come to grief and go from bad to worse, there is no help for it. If you obey your director, you may and you probably will suffer much, but you can never come to grief. These are two certain truths to be dealt with, not very palatable to a wilful person, but quite certain. It seems to me you go through as much suffering now as if you were a model of obedience, perhaps more. You gain nothing by your half sort of obedience. And you forfeit very certain advantages.

Give the line of perfect obedience a trial for a time: do exactly what Father —— tells you, no matter what repugnance you feel. See what will be the result after six months.

You show one symptom which tells your director at once, that the black gentleman has gained a hearing with you. You ask now and you have asked before, May not my director be deceived? You could not easily give a stronger proof that the devil has put wrong and false ideas into your head. *Addio.* God bless you. Try to behave sensibly.

111, *Mount Street, Feb.* 20, 1884.

My dear Child,

I certainly cannot refuse to write an answer to your letter of the 17th, and to an earlier one of last month, Jan. 13th. You may imagine that the account you sent me grieved me much.

I am afflicted beyond measure to know that your long struggle has ended in such a complete overthrow. However, we must not lose courage. You must break the spell as quickly as possible and very resolutely. Shall I tell you what you must do? You must do what you ought to have done from the beginning: you must obey Father —— quite simply and exactly. Your obstinate self-will in the past always filled me with terror: I have remarked that disposition is the ordinary forerunner of a fall. Hence the first condition for regaining the ground you have lost must be humble and simple obedience. Father —— will give you more particular instructions.

I will only repeat what I have said to you long ago: take a reasonable care of your health. You know by this time the points you ought to attend to, and I think you have learnt the lesson that troubles of the soul often depend on the state of our bodily health. Above all, don't yield to despondency. The evil may be arrested. You have a good will. Employ the means pointed out to you: pray earnestly for strength, and then resume your battle. If you fall, rise as quickly as you can, and resume the fight once more.

I will join my prayers to yours. By the way, take up the prayer, "My Queen and my Mother." I have known signal graces granted to the daily recital of it. Good-bye. Keep up your courage. God bless you.

111, *Mount Street, London,*
May 7, 1884.

I have just finished a triduum at Harley House, which crowded the last few days. . . . The weather has been unusually severe in London, the cold bitter and piercing, and on Monday a violent thunder-storm startled us. You will see from the *Times* how alarmed we were. You noticed, of course, the earthquake on the 22nd. See the *Times* of this morning, Mr. Chancellor's letter on the mischief it did. I went down to New Hall that day: the house was shaken, and the nuns all noticed the shock.

The opening of the new Oratory Church was a grand ceremony. The account in the *Times* I consider a very exact and a very complete one. The report of the sermon of His Eminence did ample justice: the sermon lasted three quarters of an hour. The whole ceremony took quite three hours. The procession and the High Mass were beautifully arranged: perfect order was observed, and I could not detect a single hitch. The music obtained the praises of outside professionals, and therefore I conclude it must have been good. The ceremony was followed by a grand luncheon. I could not wait for it, and I speak on report. The donations were liberal: I have heard that upwards of £1,100 was received during the day. The offertory at the Mass amounted to £600. The Church looks well. I don't like all the details, but the general effect is good; the proportions are noble. At the Mass some two thousand assisted, all admitted by special tickets. At the evening service three thousand persons are supposed to have been present. Few preachers will fill the building, unless the authorities contrive a very clever pulpit, with a very good sounding-board. I am told that the Fathers intend to adopt the American sounding-board, which is parabolic, and covers the preacher much as a huge shell might be supposed to do.

. . . I have just read Dr. Wace's Preface to (three of) Luther's Primary Works. I do not know when I have seen such a thorough-going piece of Protestantism. I was surprised to find such a sound man, as I believed Dr. Wace to be, an uncompromising adherent and admirer of that arch-impostor Martin Luther. . . .

Lady Georgiana Fullerton is pronounced to be somewhat better. Since May began her friends have combined novenas and prayers for her: she has certainly gained ground. Lady Londonderry went to Eastbourne. I fear she is much worse; she is expected back in town on Friday.

I have been reading a book by a Protestant which has pleased me—*The Evidential Value of the Holy Eucharist,* by the Rev. George Frederick MacLear, late Head Master of King's College School, London. The title is strange, the treatment of the subject is strange, the style is strange, the book altogether is strange; yet it contains many excellent thoughts, and brings out certain points in the Gospels with much force. I should call MacLear a thoughtful and a devout writer: I might have added, an interesting writer. I think you would read this volume with pleasure and profit.

Sacred Heart Convent, West Brighton,
June 18, 1884.

My dear Child,

I have two of your letters waiting for an answer; the first one I cannot put my hand on at the moment, so I will answer that of the 11th. It was in my intention to have answered the older one long ago. I do not know how it came to be put aside.

I came here on Monday to give the nuns a Triduum previous to the ladies' retreat. I wish you could have come; I dare say you would have derived much benefit from the retreat and from the change to the South. Your account of your spiritual condition is not very brilliant; still you must not lose courage. Remain with Father ——, and try to follow out his instructions. And I will add, take every care of your health: your troubles depend on causes which demand the greatest attention. Much of your present suffering comes, I fear, from past recklessness in the matter of health. And if you are ever to get right, you must observe constant watchfulness and care. Your misery is as much a bodily ailment as an ailment of the soul. I shall be very happy when you can tell me that your misery has abated still more. I will pray for you. Keep up your hope.

The summer has commenced in a curious way. The sun shines brightly and warmly, but we are seldom without a keen cold wind, sometimes very cold. Many people keep up their fires, and I must say that delicate people have need of them. If you have the same sort of weather, you must be careful.

Good-bye. God bless you.

I remain, yours very truly,

GEORGE PORTER.

31, *Farm Street, April* 25, 1885.

My dear Child,

I thank you for your letter of the 22nd, which I received on St. George's day, and for all your good prayers and wishes.

The accounts I receive from various sources lead me to think that your health is not what we could wish it to be. Do you see any prospect of a complete change? I have much faith in change of air and scene. I am sure you do what you can by taking plenty of food and by following the directions of the doctor to regain your strength. I put some faith in the summer.

I am very thankful to know that spiritual matters are more satisfactory. I feel sure they will come quite right in the end. Obey F. —— with the fullest confidence. The more perfectly you follow out his directions, the sooner you will attain the point you desire. You have my best prayers. Keep up your courage. Pray yourself and make certain your prayers will be heard. Good-bye. God bless you.

I remain, yours very truly,

GEORGE PORTER.

31, *Farm Street, July* 7, 1885.

My dear Child,

I am truly sorry that you are disappointed about your retreat. However, you see yourself, you give it up for excellent reasons; so you must make a sacrifice of your wishes and try to get up your health.

You must make up for your temptations to despondency by implicit obedience to your confessor. In the end you will triumph, though you will pass through many a hard battle. At the same time, pray often and earnestly for the grace of which you stand in need. I date this 31, Farm Street; in reality I am writing at 48, Great Ormond Street, where I am giving the Sisters of Mercy their annual retreat. Father Wilson returned quite recently from Jamaica. He says he left Father Thomas in splendid health. Good-bye. God bless you.

31, *Farm Street, June* 7, 1886.

I have written by this post to —— and asked —— to send you to the retreat. You say your life with others has been somewhat brighter, and you add that counts for little. I am very pleased to hear of the improvement, very pleased indeed. I do not think it counts for little, on the contrary, I am sure it counts for much. Your troubles I trace back surely to neglect of matters of health, &c., which you thought unimportant; and your cure will depend much more on similar causes. Do your best to establish your health; do your best to be cheerful with others; do your best to have a succession of reasonable amusements and occupations. You will soon become an altered being. God bless you.

Aug. 15, 1886.

I want to tell you my plans. I am going to Italy on Sept. 3, for an absence of four to six weeks. My destination will be Fiesole. The meeting at Stonyhurst ended soon after noon on Saturday. I lingered in the North to escape a Sunday at Farm Street. To-morrow I return to town. On Tuesday I go to Arundel for a rest and a change till the 23rd or 24th. On that day I hope to be in London, and I remain till Sept. 1st. Sept. 1st to Wellingborough to preach two sermons on the 2nd for the opening of a new church. Sept. 3rd back to London by an early train. Start in the evening for Italy.

I have been reading some of Pusey and Meyrick on our Lady. Dreadfully unpleasant reading; showing a state of mind quite phenomenal and to be feared.

Aug. 15, 1886.

My dear Child,

I wish you a happy feast and a store of graces through our Lady.

Your letter did find me at Stonyhurst. We spent a chilly week there till the Saturday, when our work came to an end, and more genial weather commenced.

Your account of your retreat reads well. I think you have passed a useful week. I was not surprised to hear that F. —— took well with the community. I suggest one addition to the resolutions, viz., frequent and earnest petitions for grace and help. The Pope in one of his Encyclicals quotes a beautiful idea from St. John Chrysostom: "As God sent us into the world with hands and brains to provide for our bodily wants, so He gave us prayer as the grand means by which we may supply our needs in the spiritual order." We don't pray enough. We ought to weary God by incessant petitions.

My recollection of Sister —— is only a vague one. I am sorry to hear of her illness. I dare say she has done her life's work, and is found to be ready for Heaven.

I hope much from the Scotch Synod. I trust a new epoch will date from its assembling. So much capability for good, and so many opportunities abound in Scotland.

The Councils of Baltimore and Australia fill me with hopes for the coming one in Scotland.

On Sept. 3rd I start for Italy. I do not expect to be absent for more than six weeks. I may come back sooner. This week I devote to quiet and rest at Arundel. Then I return to town to prepare for my journey.

Take care of yourself while I am away. Pray for my speedy and safe return. God bless you.

I remain, yours very truly in Christ,

GEORGE PORTER.

San Girolamo, Sept. 13, 1886.

I reached San Girolamo this day week, about 9 p.m. The work and the weather together have crippled my letter-writing. The heat is excessive. Day and night one lives in a bath. The air is heavy and depressing. The temptation to go out is easily overcome, and one would be better with a stimulus to work, or rather with an irresistible push to work. I have seen little of Florence, little of Fiesole, and I am ashamed to say I have not written much since I came. The journey out was a rapid one. Leaving Victoria Station on Friday, 3rd, at 8 a.m., I only stopped at Chambery about 7 a.m., said Mass in our old church of Notre Dame, breakfasted, took a walk round the city, and continued my route to Turin by the 10 a.m. train. We reached Turin about 6.30 p.m. After a short rest I went to look up Don Bosco, but he was out of town. Then I tried to get into the Cottolengo Instituto. There again I was disappointed. The establishment was assembled for Benediction and my time was limited. I asked the portress (a nun) how many inmates the place contained; about 4,000, with seven or eight communities to look after the invalids and afflicted, all under the direction of the Lazarist Fathers.

I slept at one of our residences, formerly a convent of the Visitation in which St. Frances Chantal had lived for a time. Our Fathers have opened a college, and their school is well attended. They have more than 200 scholars, day scholars.

From Turin I travelled to Leghorn by the Sunday train. I was anxious to make inquiries about a statue of Our Lady of Lourdes, to be made at Carrara. The result of my inquiries is satisfactory. I can have a first-class copy of the grotto statue for little more than £50. I did not leave Leghorn till 5.15 p.m. on Monday.

The valley of the Arno looks lovely as ever. The quantity of uva is enormous, and you may imagine the heavy clusters of purple and green hanging in great profusion in all possible and impossible places. The olives, too, promise well. Pears, peaches, *pomi d'oro*, everything seems to abound.

A steam tramway now runs from San Domenico to the *barriera* every fifty minutes (an Italian arrangement), for 25 cents on ordinary days and 35 cents on *festas*. The tramway has not interfered with the old *diligenza* from Fiesole.

The Archbishop of Florence is very poorly. Said to be dying of a cancer in the tongue, though on Saturday Father Charnley heard a report that the doctors think they can save him. The Bishop of Fiesole I found looking older, but gracious and pleasant as ever.

The uncovering of the *facciata* of the Duomo has been deferred till April. Florence is empty. Neither Italians nor strangers would attend the ceremony. The cholera scares away the multitude. I hear the highest praise given to the work. If the heat subsides, I mean to try and get a peep at what has been done.

Matters look as if I may be back in England before Oct. 1st, but I will not be so rash as to promise.

Paris, Sept. 23, 1886.

This address looks very like reaching London before Oct. 1st. The work was accomplished with great expedition, and I was able to leave Fiesole on Saturday last. I have come away from Italy without seeing either Ravenna or the Certosa of Pavia. I was obliged to sacrifice these projects in order to take care of one of the Fathers as far as Paris. Thank God, I have landed him at his destination, no worse than when he started.

The sultry weather only broke at Turin. There we met the autumn chill. On our way through France we were accompanied by a great downpour of rain, and we witnessed a terrible storm on the Lac du Bourget. You can picture to yourself the clouds on the hillside, the green waters of the lake, the thunder and the lightning; the sight was grand. The stations were all under water for many a mile.

Paris looks and feels autumnal. When I see you, I will tell you the state of matters in our houses here. . . . On my way I have been reading *Le Materialisme et le Science*, par E. Caro, in which the weakness of Positivism is well shown. The same author has a volume, *Littré et le Positivisme*, which I have in store, to follow the work I am now engaged upon.

Yes. St. Bernard is very deep, very Scriptural, and very devotional. He gives an idea of the endless riches contained in revelation, which are to be dug out by private study and prayer. He is very much at his best on the Canticle of Canticles, if we except the direct sermons on our Lady.

31, *Farm Street, Sept.* 29, 1886.

You see I have kept to my programme, home by Oct. 1st. In fact, I reached Farm Street on Monday afternoon. I should have written yesterday, had not endless visitors and a regiment of friends taken up the whole day.

I gave myself a day in Paris, a day in Boulogne, and Sunday in Walmer. In Paris I paid my first visit to Montmartre. The Church of the Sacred Heart is rising slowly. The proportions are not *very* grand. They are good, however. The foundations would carry a citadel. The crypt forms a church in itself, and the position exceeds all my imaginations. The whole of Paris lies before you as you look out from the porch. Altogether this Church of the Sacred Heart will stand a not unworthy monument of French piety and devotion.

My commissions took me to the neighbourhood of Notre Dame. My visit fell in with Vespers. The singing of the choir seemed to me admirable. I thought it quite up to the mark even for Notre Dame. There was more soul in it than in the best I have heard either at Westminster Abbey or at St. Paul's. The Cathedral itself always pleased me, though it lacks the air of vastness, which one looks for in a Cathedral. I liked it better than ever last Thursday afternoon.

When you come here next, you will see some nice books I have brought from Italy and from Paris. Father Secondo Franco has begun a collected edition of all his works. If you will allow me, I will ask you to accept *Il Sopra naturale, ossia Le Richezze Interiori del Christiano*, by him, and also *Le Vie della Perfezione cavato da uno scritto di S. Catterina da Siena.* Both works have had a great *incontro* in Italy. A box will cross the sea containing other treasures, but I arm myself with patience and dare not fix a day when I may expect its arrival.

Manresa House, Dec. 11, 1886.

My dear Child,

Your letters of Nov. 25 and Nov. 30 have remained too long unanswered. I have been dreadfully busy, more so than usual.

I am very thankful to hear that your spiritual troubles have diminished, and that you have more hope for the future.

You must resist discouragement. With God's grace you will come off victorious in the struggle. You must trust your confessor implicitly and obey him with perfect simplicity. You must also take great care of your health. I am persuaded that much of what you have suffered may be attributed to negligence on this head. The punishments of nature follow slowly but very certainly. Do take a lesson from the past, and for the future be reasonable about your health. I hope you won't worry about the past. The best reparation for the past will be obedience, hope, and vigilance in the present and the future.

Be very devout to our Lady. She will surely help you if you do what lies in your power.

Remember me very kindly to all. I wish you each and all a very happy Christmas. Good-bye. God bless you.

CHAPTER VIII.

LETTERS ON RELIGIOUS VOCATION.

First Series. Importance of forming a high idea of the religious state. Rules for the examination of conscience, for Communions, for times of depression. *Christian Perfection.* Evil of over-doing self-examination. Fidelity to inspirations. Prayer for guidance. Acts of Love. Evidence of God's education of the soul. How to prepare for the sacrifices of religious life. Craving for affection. Consolations and desolations. Fidelity the great virtue necessary in times of desolation. Congratulations on the vocation being given. Certainty that trials will come. Happiness of being called to the religious life even at the eleventh hour. What God really asks. Regular soldiers as distinguished from the militia. On the death of a young nun. Encouragement to perseverance.

Second Series. Calmness indispensable for forming a decision. Holiness of the married state, but superiority of the religious state. No one should embrace the religious state without a call. Different forms a call may take. Indications of a true vocation. A vocation may be genuine, though imposing a very hard sacrifice. Mistake of assuming that nuns must be narrow-minded, scrupulous, and ignorant. Natural affections implanted by God. True love of relatives helps true love of God. Scruples. Encouragement to aspire to religious life. Use of time. Devotion to the Sacred Heart. Vocation distinctly manifested. Abundance and variety of work to be found in the Order of the Sacred Heart.

This chapter contains two series of letters on Religious Vocation, the first addressed to a lady who had seen much of the world and who, on being left a widow, formed Father Porter's acquaintance at the retreat he gave in 1881, at the Convent of the Sacred Heart, Roehampton.

The Second Series is written to a young lady just beginning life.

111, *Mount Street, Aug.* 12, 1881.

By all means encourage the thought that you are not intended to stay in the world. Form a high idea of the religious state, and pray God to give you the grace of a vocation. Meanwhile, live up to the good resolutions you have formed, and endeavour to make yourself more and more worthy of such a privilege. God will form and educate your soul for such a life, and He will make known His will to you, when He sees you are prepared for His call. It is a grace to have this higher life before you, if only as the object of your desires.

For the dreadful examination of conscience ask yourself: (1) Did I offer my heart to God on rising, and make an act of love of God? (2) Did I say all my prayers slowly, with attention, with devotion? (3) Did I make my meditation well? (4) Did I keep my order of the day as well as I could? (5) Did I say anything unkind to any one, or of any one? (6) Have I done any kindness to anybody this day? (7) Have I been quite dissipated and forgotten God during my amusements? (8) Fix on some fault, say vanity, say impatience, or any one you find most salient in yourself, and see every day whether you have curbed it. (9) Also fix upon some virtue, say the thought of God's presence, say doing good to your neighbour spiritually, say anything else, and see how often you have exercised it during the day. The big defects proclaim themselves.

Thank God He has inspired you to love Him, and every day make many acts of the love of God. You may adopt the little prayer: "Heart of Jesus, Thou lovest, Thou art not loved; would that Thou wert loved!" The love of God and the love of Jesus Christ are the mightiest forces to make us good.

St. Gertrude's House, Alexandra Park,
Manchester, Sept. 21, 1881.

As to your Communions, ask no questions, but follow this rule. Go to confession once a week, and go to

Holy Communion as often as you have the opportunity to do so, and if any confessor asks you the question how often you receive Communion, tell him you are often changing from place to place, and that your director gave you this rule.

Be faithful to God in times of depression as well as in times of joy. Whatever you feel, He is always the same. Try to love Him more and more; keep His commandments, praise Him and pray to Him in all weathers, and trust to Him unreservedly.

Every day ask to know His will about your entering religion, and be quite sure He will make His will known to you. Never mind your imperfections and shortcomings and limited qualifications: leave all that to Him. You seek to know His holy will and to accomplish it.

Take care of your health. From something Reverend Mother said to me, I fear you have fasted too long. Don't fall into this mistake. Keep your health for God. You may have very fair health, and you do not require much food; but you must never allow yourself to fall below par. If you do that often, your health will soon become worth very little.

As you are a wanderer on the face of the earth, keep God your friend everywhere, and always take your sorrows and troubles to Him.

111, *Mount Street, Oct.* 23, 1881.

Christian Perfection contains a perfect mine of wisdom and good sense. Read it very leisurely, and go back from time to time to refresh your memory on what you have seen. At the end of a chapter, again at the end of a treatise, it is useful to lay down your book and think over what it contains, and get it into your head.

Beware of being drawn too much by Father Faber's

chapter on Self-Deceit. In all of us that element enters in too largely, but you may overdo the self-examination. When you catch yourself in a little piece of self-seeking, or vanity, or imperfect intention, pounce down upon it and draw your lesson for the future. But overdoing self-examination is calculated to foster self-consciousness, too much attention to what passes within us, too subtle a balancing of whys and wherefores: and this is a hindrance to advancement in holiness. Live out of yourself, in your duties, in your occupations; throw yourself into them and give each one in its turn your best attention. As I said before, if by chance, casually, coming round a corner, as it were, you surprise some wretched little piece of vanity or pride, collar it and proceed to judgment; but for the rest, go on rather roundly and *bonnement*, as the French say, with as much love of our Lord as you can call up in your heart, and a strong desire to love Him more and more.

Don't be in a hurry to decide upon the convent. Be very faithful to God's inspirations, and take note of all your likes and dislikes, your attractions and repulsions. In due time it will all shake down into its right place, and you will see pretty distinctly where God wants you to serve Him. Pray very much to be guided.

I have already answered your difficulty about the examination of conscience. Avoid the searching: at the end of it all you find yourself only. Expedite the examination and hurry on to the purposes for the future, and encourage desires to do more for God and to do it better.

San Girolamo, Dec. 19, 1881.

. . . I am glad you are getting into the way of making your examination of conscience. Some few culprits may elude your vigilance. Never mind: they won't be the biggest ones, and by degrees you will become sharper in putting your hands upon them and the smaller fry too.

Par rapport au couvent, when I say don't think about it, you must not understand me to mean that you are to keep the thought out of your mind: that was not exactly my meaning. What I meant was this: don't think of it to come to any decision; avoid making any decision. You may think and pray to be guided by God, and pray that you may have a vocation. In the meanwhile, aim at sanctifying your soul, so that later, when you do come to form your decision, you may form it under the Divine blessing.

Brush away the mist of doubt when it arises in your mind, and do this by making acts of the love of Jesus Christ. "My Lord Jesus Christ, I love Thee with my whole heart, with my whole soul, with my whole strength, above all things, and I wish to love Thee more and more." The love of Jesus Christ, in words, and still more in deeds, in the observance of His commandments, in attentive, devout prayer, is the great answer to doubt.

Whatever the past has been, love Him now and in the future, as though you had always loved Him and never offended Him. The way to make your soul as nearly as possible what it would have been had you always been true to Him and never offended Him, is to live now as you would have done had you the certainty of having always been true. Be sorry for the past, atone for it by loving your Saviour now and during the rest of your days.

San Girolamo, Feb. 8, 1882.

In your spiritual life, first take care you don't fall back and lose the grace God has given you; and secondly, don't be in too great a hurry to decide the future. You are very capable of enjoying innocent amusement. There is no harm in that, if when you return to your prayers, you say to God, you have enjoyed yourself, you hope without offending Him, but that your heart is empty, that He alone can satisfy the cravings of your soul. Watch and see that no creature gets into your heart. Pray you may keep it wholly for God, and never admit *any wilful fault*, without repenting of it as quickly as possible.

God is plainly educating your soul. You are right in judging that your new-born desire to lead others to know Him and love Him is a proof of this. Follow up the desire and try your hand at gaining souls from heresy or from the world.

The alternations of dryness and consolations also point to the same education. The time of dryness may be very trying to you, yet this dryness is most useful to your soul. While it lasts be most exact in all your prayers. Don't shorten the time, don't hurry through them, but battle as you best can, and extort from God by your importunity the return of His consolations, or at least an abundance of grace. Consolations, with your excitable disposition, are apt to call you away from the solid virtues God requires of you. Always receive them with a certain fear and diffidence, and pray that you may never forfeit the friendship of God, or think too much of His consolations, or come to care for them more than you do for Him.

The unrest and the turmoil in your brain may be due to natural causes. They may come from the heart or from the brain. In any case resist them as much as you can. When they are upon you, get to prayer and pray very leisurely and very deliberately. Read or write again with all possible deliberation. Above all, don't give way to the excitement or encourage it.

Don't trouble yourself as to what is the biggest defect you have to cope with. Take any one in hand. You cannot be far out with what you know of yourself. For instance, wage a little war on your craving for human affection. When you catch yourself dwelling with satisfaction on the thought that you are liked, chide yourself and say: What business have I to seek the love of creatures? The love of God ought to be enough for me, &c. If you feel a shudder at the thought of the lonesomeness of religious life, offer yourself to God for that state, with all its sacrifices, if He is pleased to call you. Beg Him to call you and take your heart entirely for Himself.

Rodriguez is the very best book for you. No *exalté* ideas there, no wild flights of the imagination, but sound sense and sound piety and love of Jesus Christ.

Persevere, and God will make known His will to you before long.

San Girolamo, March 7, 1882.

The craving for affection still torments you. Have patience. Some serpents take a great deal of killing. Meanwhile, you must try to grow in the knowledge and love of our Blessed Saviour crucified for us. This love will absorb all love of creatures and either destroy it or hallow it. You see the Church in Lent plays on two strings: sorrow and penance for sins which nailed Christ to His Cross, and love for Him Who loved us and gave Himself up for us.

I think you might now read and meditate with much fruit St. Ignatius' Rules for the Discernment of Spirits, the first series. Those, he says, are more fitted for persons in the first week of the Exercises. They will teach you how to receive consolation and desolation, and derive the greatest fruit from them. That is one of the most valuable lessons of spiritual life. Go on patiently. God takes time in the education of the soul. Let Him do His work. Don't put any obstacle in His way. Aim at what you see within reach, and love Him and trust Him for the rest.

San Girolamo, March 21, 1882.

In answer to your two letters of the 16th and 17th, I say in one word, I approve. I approve very much, without any reserve of your obedience to Father ——. And as far as I can form an opinion upon your letters, I approve your offering yourself to Rev. Mother. I assume Father —— finds your spiritual education has reached the point at which you thoroughly understand the meaning of leaving all things to follow Christ and give yourself up to Him calmly, deliberately, and unreservedly. I have only encouragement to give you and my best prayers, that you may become a worthy child of the Sacred Heart, a chosen spouse of our Blessed Lord. Don't trouble yourself to observe whether you have consolations or desolations. You have made the offering of yourself. Stand to it and pray you may be accepted, and for the rest make the most of the graces which each day brings to you.

You ask me whether I think you ought to pray that consolations should be taken from you. No. Follow the rule given by St. Ignatius. Thank God for the consolations He gives you, make the best of the happy time, prepare for the dark days, which will certainly come, and strengthen yourself to meet them.

It is all very well to pray that you may do the will of

God, but I recommend you to say nothing about His leaving you in the world. Pray with all your heart that you may not be left. It will be time to think of resigning yourself when you find the convent will not receive you.

San Girolamo, April 27, 1882.

I thank God for the grace He has given you, and you must thank Him all the days of your life. How tenderly and yet how surely He has shaped everything for this crowning favour, the vocation to the Sacred Heart. You may make a wholesome meditation by following out the history of the last twelve months especially, and observing how the seed was cast into the ground, and how the ground was prepared, and how rain and sun brought the plant to its present happy proportions.

You enter on a beautiful feast, the day of the Sacred Heart, in your great month and the anniversary of ——'s flight to Heaven. There is a little invocation of the Sacred Heart which you may adopt and often use: "Sacred Heart of Jesus! Thou lovest! Thou art not loved! Would Thou wert loved!" It contains all the essence of the devotion to the Sacred Heart, love, gratitude, and reparation for the ingratitude shown to the Sacred Heart by so many.

The desolation will certainly come. Prepare for it, not only by laying up a store of comfort, but also by laying up a store of strength to carry you through the dark hours of the storm. Train yourself now to a rule of life, to exactness in prayer, to good methods of performing your several duties, to patience and charity, so that when the storm breaks, you may gather in all your sails, pull your ship together and hold on *bravely and faithfully* through darkness and dryness and disgust and despair. *Fidelity* is the great virtue of the time of desolation; fidelity to God, fidelity in faith, fidelity in hope, fidelity in charity, fidelity to your good resolutions of the time of consolation, and fidelity to prayer, the sacraments, and all the outward helps of a holy life.

At present you may not find that you have a great sacrifice to make. The sacrifice begins the day you set foot in the convent and fall under the care of your guardian angel. The noblest sacrifice we can offer to God is the sacrifice of our whole being. Every day in religion, how long soever you live, that sacrifice is renewed. We are privileged and happy in being allowed to make it, yet it will always be a sacrifice to the very end.

San Girolamo, July 5, 1882.

I am sending a "God speed you" to your companion in arms, Sister ———, so I add another "God speed you" to Sister ———. I pray you may both persevere in your glorious vocation and prove worthy children of the Sacred Heart.

My last word is, make ready for trials and desolations. Don't be surprised when they come. Confess to God that you deserve to be treated with severity, and pray for patience and courage. Fidelity to all spiritual exercises and to all the purposes of your calmer, happier hours, is the virtue God asks from you in the time of desolation.

San Girolamo, Sept. 6, 1882.

Here is my "God speed" and my "God bless you," for the first day of the next *étape d'une conversion et d'une vocation.* I wanted to send it yesterday, but could not. I hope it will reach you on the 8th. I shall give you and Sister ——— a special memento on the 8th. On that day I offer Mass for a perfect regiment of candidates, young novices, and novices taking their vows. What a happy day is our Lady's Nativity for them, for the Church on earth, and the Church in Heaven.

Don't be uneasy because you have met with no trials as yet. Thomas à Kempis says that some have their trials in the beginning, some later on, some at the end of their life. Be quite certain they will come, and never let the day pass without strengthening yourself to meet them. This you do, persuading yourself that you deserve to be tried, that you have no strength to bear them, that you need much grace from God, and you must pray for it, pray daily and pray very earnestly. Prepare and thank God for His exceeding great mercy to you. Try to pay the debt of gratitude and service you owe.

San Girolamo, July 25, 1883.

You wrote in April. I am answering you in July. Have mercy on me.

So you can report yourself "very happy." *Deo gratias.* The dark hours are not known as yet. I am glad to hear that. If you keep them at a distance by fighting all your spiritual enemies bravely and taking up the many little crosses which are always lying about in noviceships, by praying earnestly for all the graces you require, by telling our Blessed Lord all your troubles and difficulties, dark hours can be changed into happy ones by a good will, honest self-denial, and the grace of God. As you have no dark days, I shall hope you escape them by keeping to the shady road of the Cross. You have great reason to thank God for giving you your vocation to religious life at the eleventh hour even. What a grace it is! and what a privilege to spend the few years of our weary life in doing some good to ourselves and others, and in helping our Blessed Lord in establishing His

Kingdom in the souls He has redeemed. Let us not degenerate from the high thoughts of the children of God. In such a life we ought to be self-sacrificing, to be generous, to attempt great things, and to wish to attempt even greater.

And the great things are often not very great nor very lofty. However, such as they are, let us go about them with grand intentions.

Stonyhurst, Sept. 6, 1884.

I do wish you "God speed" on your vow-day. May you consecrate yourself unreservedly to your King on that happy day, and may He grant you the grace to persevere to your last breath and to grow daily in His love and in the spirit of your holy vocation.

Look a little closely, and you may discover some things God does really ask from you. Don't resolve never to give way to a distraction (though you might promise you never will do so deliberately); but do resolve to aim at greater attention of mind and heart in prayer. Do resolve to recollect yourself going to prayer, and think whither you are going and what ought to be your dispositions.

Perhaps it is no use to say you never will give way to nature, but it is useful to say: "I will not seek the esteem or praise of others; I will not fish for compliments; I will not yield to sadness when I do not get them."

You need not anticipate being cast out as a leper or becoming a bye-word to the whole world, nor need you wish it. But you may think it would be a great privilege, and you may resolve not to be sullen and discontented when you are snubbed or reprimanded; you may resolve to bear it patiently, to bear it cheerfully and to try to rejoice.

I exercise my powers of plenipotentiary. You must

not swerve. You must make your oblation of self and your brave resolutions.

I will give you a special memento on the 8th, and to the two novices who take their vows, and to the postulant.

Addio. God bless you. Take your place with the regular soldiers, not amongst the militia. Don't hang about the baggage, but go under fire.

Fort Chapel, Bombay, July 9, 1888.

I am much obliged to you for your letter giving me what you knew of the beautiful and edifying death of Sister B———.—R.I.P.

God has taken her to an early crown—perhaps not so easily won, though so early. She was a child of predestination.

As you say truly, such a death has nothing sad about it. We who are left behind ought to feel encouraged and cheered to love God more and do more for Him, seeing this young religious so well prepared to meet death. I cannot tell you how much happiness the perusal of your letter afforded me. I thank God that He used me as His instrument to lead this chosen soul to her true vocation.

One feature in her religious life struck me very much : the sensible strength she found in her vows. They seem to have lifted her up to a higher life and to a nearer union with God which was sensible.

I join you in your prayer. May our last end be like unto hers.

How are you getting on yourself? Have the troubles ever shown themselves as yet? Never mind if they have not. Plod away, with some failings and faults, with many high desires and generous resolutions (seldom carried out to the full perhaps), always striking your breast and accusing yourself *quia peccavi nimis cogitatione, verbo, et opere, mea culpa,* &c., always wishing to do your best and better than your best. In the end all will come right, and you will join Sister B—— when your turn comes.

The following letters belong to the Second Series of those on Religious Vocation, mentioned above.

San Girolamo, Feb. 20, 1883.

My answer to your letter will take the form of a series of statements. I do not propose to follow you paragraph by paragraph. Before I begin I wish to impress on you the fact that you are not in a calm state of mind, and the very turmoil of your mind prevents you from seeing much, which under other circumstances would be clear to you.

1. You would like to be convinced that the state of virginity is better than the married state. By "better" you mean higher, more perfect in itself, because for some, nay, for many, the married state is better.

The married state is a holy state, and many sanctify themselves in it. But it is in accordance with nature. There is no heroism in marrying. The state of virginity voluntarily chosen is a triumph over nature. It places the spiritual half of our being above our material being. Again, married persons by the duties of their state are unable to devote themselves specially to the service of God. Unmarried persons are free to devote their whole life and energy to God.

2. The religious state goes beyond the state of virginity. The religious leaves the world, marriage, earthly goods, everything, to follow Christ.

3. Although the state of virginity is higher than the

married state, and though the religious state is higher than either, no one should embrace it unless called.

4. I need not tell you all the forms that calls may take. It may be the fear of being lost in the world. It may be some disappointment revealing the emptiness of the world. It may be the desire to give God the best one can give Him. It may be the desire to imitate Jesus Christ in His poor obedient life. However it comes, there is always in it something of a call, an invitation to a higher life.

5. If you felt a very strong personal love for our Lord and the wish (a call) to live for Him alone, and if that love continued, and you saw that it saved you from sin, and led you on to holiness, and if your director, watching you for some time, were to say it comes from God, then you might conclude you had a true vocation to leave the world and become a religious.

6. To marry against such a call would be an infidelity to Jesus Christ, and the marriage would put an end to the religious vocation. In the same way, to fall in love seriously would be an infidelity; but the vocation might come back, or even never be lost.

7. Such love for Jesus Christ you may call a sentiment. But if that sentiment comes from Him it may be a vocation. Such love for Him may have been a girlish fancy. It may have been a great gift from Heaven. (How many of the saints felt this great gift in their early years!) It may have been somewhat of both, somewhat girlish, somewhat heavenly.

8. You incline to think your love was merely sentimental and therefore silly, because you did not try to be good. Perhaps you did not follow the good inspirations you received. Further, without that love of our Lord, might you not have been much worse?

9. Several reasons adduced by you prove too much.

Either that every one should marry or that every one should become a nun. That all nuns are narrow-minded; that married women never are so. That all nuns are ignorant; that married women never are, &c.

10. If you feel a great craving for love and admiration, if you believe you cannot be happy without them; if you like to dwell on the thought of your own home, of the affection of husband and children, certainly this contrasts with the hard and cheerless life: "Go, sell all thou hast and give it to the poor and come and follow Me," and shows there is no vocation.

11. On the other hand, the vocation may be a genuine one and the sacrifice it imposes may be very hard. Life with Jesus Christ may appear hard and cheerless, but it has its own special consolations, very different from what the life in the world can offer.

12. One observation of yours I cordially endorse: "Convents are bad places for scrupulous people," though the reason you assign does not correspond with the facts, "Nuns live in an atmosphere of scruples." I have known nuns who lost their vocations through scruples, and through scruples alone.

You will never settle your vocation satisfactorily till you free yourself from your agitation of mind, which is half-sister to scruples.

13. It is possible being a nun not to be narrow-minded, not to be scrupulous, not to be ostentatiously pious, not to be ignorant, not to be useless, &c.

To conclude. Pray that you may become more calm. Do not attend so much to the thousand and one wild ideas which crowd in upon your busy brain. Look quietly over these few observations, and after a day or two write me what you think of your vocation. Please don't destroy this letter, but bring it with you the next time you come to talk with me on the matter, for I have no second copy, and it may be useful to refer to it. Within the short compass of a letter it is not easy to say all that you wish said.

Pray God to guide you. If you can only become calm, I promise you God will let you know His will quite clearly. You must have a little patience. But I hope before you leave Florence you will see your way and know what God asks of you.

San Girolamo, March 2, 1883.

Your letter leads me to hope that your ideas are falling into order. The process, remember, is a slow one, especially on such a subject and under your peculiar circumstances. I hope you will see your way clearly, long before the end of a year; if you don't, then by all means wait a year, or longer even if necessary. You must not act till your mind is made up. Do what you can while you remain here, and we shall see what point you reach. I don't despair of your knowing exactly what you ought to do, and where and how.

Your ideas of natural affection require a reformation. Such affections are implanted in us by God: if we don't cultivate them, we become selfish, and to some extent pagans, who, as St. Paul says, were without affection, without mercy. The affections have their proper sphere. We must not look to find what cannot be found. Husbands and wives, parents and children, friends love each other, partly through natural impulse, partly hoping to receive a return of affection, partly because they see qualities which merit affection. In true affection there will be true happiness, but not perfect happiness; such happiness we may not find in this life. People may marry for money or for a home; they have no reason to complain if they get nothing else. You don't blame them. I hope you don't admire them: they have their price, and it is not a great one. Perhaps it won't content them.

Your *principle* of not caring for any one does not recommend itself to me, I confess. If you cared for people in a right way, your soul would be very much the better for it. Love those you ought to love, because you ought to love them, and for what is loveable in them: love them in God, don't make gods of any of them, and perhaps you will not be so often disappointed. You seem to me to look too much to happiness in your estimate of life: look more to what is right, to duty. Happiness will always follow, such as you can find in this world.

You ask, Is it possible to love God just as much when one loves brothers, sisters, &c., as if one loved God alone? I think it is: true love of relatives helps true love of God, and true love of God fosters true love of relatives. But I should add, true love of relatives clings to their presence; true love of God in a religious vocation tears us from their presence. The religious continues to love home, &c., but sacrifices its joys to follow the call of Christ. And certainly such a sacrifice of legitimate natural affection is a great act of Divine love, and will strengthen the love of God in the soul.

You are afraid you don't know enough of the two terms between which you must make your choice—the world and religious life. You know something of the world, you know nothing about religious life. But observe: knowing the world you know enough. The question is, Am I called to leave the world? When Christ said to St. Peter, "Leave all things and follow Me," St. Peter did not ask where He would lead him to. When Christ called the young man, He only said, "Sell all thou hast and come and follow Me." Our Lord did not explain where he was to go. You may follow Christ without knowing beforehand all that is before you.

I suspect you say truly that after you left school you fell into worldly ways of looking at things, and talking against what in your heart you loved and esteemed. I should like you to reform in this respect: renounce the love of paradox, talk seriously of serious things, and have much patience with yourself and with me.

San Girolamo, June 16, 1883.

I won't call you very obstinate for pressing your question about the General Confession. You desire peace of mind, and you are quite right to desire it and to strive after it. I have hopes I shall satisfy you that you have no reason to worry yourself, that you may leave the past in perfect confidence to the mercy of God, and turn all your anxiety to the correction of faults and to advancement in virtue.

1. As to the confessions you have made since you came to Florence. (*a*) You say your preparation has been short and not always careful. That I can easily believe; but your preparation has not been so far defective as to render your confessions invalid. By listening to your scruples and worries you have deprived yourself of some of the grace, and perhaps all the peace of mind, which you might have found in confessions prepared quietly and devoutly. (*b*) You fear you do not explain your scruples clearly. To this I will say I find no obscurity in what you tell me: your meaning is quite clear. I fear you fall into the error of giving too much attention to your scruples every time they come to you, so that you imagine there must be something new about them. You wish to be understood;

you take ordinary pains to be understood; take it for granted you have been understood, unless you are asked to give explanations. (c) You say you put off thinking out your difficulties and speaking of them, to escape trouble. This way of acting may not always conduce to peace of mind: it will interfere with Confession and Communion, and your preparation for those sacraments; but it does not render the confession invalid. You are not bound to speak of your difficulties; you are not bound to think them out and put them into an intelligible form. Making up your mind, as a rule, ought to strengthen the authority of conscience, and this would be a gain. But you are not bound to clear up your mind at all times, and the effort to decide yes or no, right or wrong, may interfere with matters of clear duty. In confession you are bound to confess all recognized grievous sins. It is well to confess some venial sins, those especially which were more deliberate. You are bound to be in the disposition to say, " I wish I had not offended God by those sins, and I will try to avoid them in future." So much is required for the validity of your confession. In order to receive more abundant graces from the sacrament, hope, peace, joy in the service of God, avoid worries, and endeavour to conceive a more lively sorrow and a more fervent desire to serve God well, and make Him a better return for all He has done for you.

2. In your case, you should confine yourself to the accusation of three or four more serious venial sins, those in which there was most will.

3. Scruples exercise a fascination over your mind. You know the dwelling on them injures you and makes you miserable: still you fall back on them as keenly as if somehow your happiness was dependent on them. Convince your reason that you can derive no benefit

from them: they are a malady, they darken the understanding, they trouble the heart. You will make great progress in the service of God when you can despise them. When you are tormented about the past, about past confessions, never go back, never mention any sin older than your last confession unless you see clearly that (*a*) it was a mortal sin, and (*b*) that you never confessed it. When you are tormented as to your duty of putting others right on matters of fasting, abstinence, *magro stretto*, &c., know that you are not bound to speak, and that you have a dispensation to eat what is provided for the family. When you are tormented as to whether it is a sin to do this or that, note the first word of your common sense: if you see plainly there is a sin, be sure there is; but if common sense says there is no sin, and you begin to worry and fear there is some sin, you may rest satisfied there is none. When mamma asks you, Is to-day a fasting-day, or an abstinence-day, or a *magro stretto* day: if you know how the case stands, say what you know; if you don't, say you don't know, and eat what is put on the table for you.

4. You ought not to try to find out whether you committed many mortal sins in the past: leave the past to the mercy of God, often make acts of sorrow for all your past sins, and rather insist on this penitential spirit.

Take my word that the past should never exclude you from religious life; the present and the future call for your attention, and for all of it. Conquer the scruples; tame your temper; learn to love Jesus Christ better, and you will see your way clearly before very long.

5. You dare not count upon yourself, if a very bright future in the world were offered you. Nor would I count on you, if you allow the tyranny of the scruples

to continue: but I should have good hopes if you break that tyranny. You have enough perception of the emptiness and nothingness of the brightest future in the world, and a sufficient glimmering of the dignity and happiness of living and battling for Jesus Christ, and striving with Him to save immortal souls. You have gifts and capacities that ought to sustain you and carry you forward in such a life. Only remember, you must sweep away all this untrue false life which you have allowed to cover up and bury your real self.

You will never know what your real nature is, nor what you are capable of, until you can say sincerely *Sursum corda*, and begin to love God in earnest. Your worries fetter you and bind you down to the earth for which you are not made and hinder you from rising to God for Whom you are made.

6. Lastly. Have patience about your vocation. Deal first with the scruples and worries, then soften the temper, regulate your outer life, your studies, your amusements, and last (not least), your devotions. *Orientez vous*, as the French say, and you will see all things will fall into their places; you will see your way clear before you; you will know, without any misgiving, whether God calls you, and you will know whither He calls you, to what Order, and you will see the road before you, with more or fewer obstacles, to be surmounted as God may think best for you.

I attach more importance than you do to regular systematic study or use of your time. The best thing would be to divide your time: take so much for yourself, and beyond that (if she will submit), seriously and earnestly direct the studies of your sister in some one or more branches. Teaching does so much to form the teacher, as long as there is room for formation; and I fancy, in your case, some margin is still left.

As to penance for past sins. At present content yourself with the discipline of your temper and the yoke of study and the privation of the luxury of scruples: here is a wide field for penance and mortification.

I shall conclude with three short prayers to the Sacred Heart.

1. *Jesu, mitis et humilis corde, fac cor meum sicut cor tuum*—"Jesus, meek and humble of Heart, make my heart like unto Thine." Indulgence, 300 days, once a day.

2. *Cor sanctissimum Jesu amas, non amaris, utinam ameris*—"Sacred Heart of Jesus, Thou lovest, Thou art not loved; would Thou wert loved."

3. *Cor Jesu flagrans amore nostri
Inflamma cor nostrum amore tui*—
"Heart of Jesus, burning with love for us,
Set our hearts on fire with love for Thee."

In the devotion to the Sacred Heart you possess the most effectual remedy against the depression which weighs you down. Scruples disturb the reason and unsettle the heart: then succeeds depression; and in a moment of depression the soul is capable of abandoning its nobler aspirations and falling into very ordinary and ignoble ways. The love of the Sacred Heart should raise us to a higher world.

111, *Mount Street, May* 5, 1884.

I congratulate you on the improvement you have made in the management of your temper. You have become the meekest of correspondents, and you have submitted to my long silence with admirable good humour. All the same, I must ask your pardon for taxing your forbearance. My only defence must be the dog's life I lead, with two days' work staring me in the face every twenty-four hours.

However, to-day I have shut out everything and everybody, and attacked my Italian debts, yours among the first.

In answer to your questions, I say without hesitation, you have a vocation to leave the world and to serve God in religion. I will not trouble you with my reasons. You only care to know the conclusion. On this point, I will only add, you must not distress yourself about the thought that your great reason for entering religion is to escape the worries of your daily life. Doubtless you are much exercised by many worries and they keep you in a state of irritation, and as the worries are ever present, you give them more of the credit of your decision than they deserve. In the same way your appetite for worldly goods, for admiration, and for pleasure, exists more in your imagination than in your heart. I am quite satisfied that the deepest feeling of your soul is the wish to leave all for Jesus Christ and follow Him as nearly as you can. So I say, in God's name arise, take up your cross and follow Him.

I rejoice to hear that the scruples and conscience troubles don't disturb you so much, and that practically you need not take any account of them.

111, *Mount Street, July 22, 1884.*

... You express some doubt whether you will have plenty of work in the Sacred Heart. On that point make your mind at rest. You will have plenty to do and something more serious than mending rosaries. Teaching, and teaching of the upper classes, forms the chief work, but not the only one of the Order. The Nuns of the Sacred Heart give retreats, instruct converts and ignorant people; keep orphanages, poor-schools; in fact, make themselves generally useful spiritually as aids to the clergy. You wonder why it is a good work to teach the upper ten. St. Ignatius lays down a sound principle. A good thing becomes a better thing when it takes in a greater number. A sermon to one thousand is better than a sermon to one hundred. A child of the upper ten becoming a good Christian ought to influence more people for good than the child of a tradesman. Nuns sometimes teach indifferently well, not because they are nuns, but because they are wanting (the particular individuals) in common sense and are not effectually controlled by Church authorities or by the public. Nuns, like other people, do their work better if they are well looked after. If you take into religious life sound common sense, you may do a great deal of good. Only *do* the good. Don't set up for a prophet or a reformer.

CHAPTER IX.

SPIRITUAL COUNSELS. NOTES OF A SERMON PREACHED AT A PROFESSION.

Spiritual Counsels on the way to cure scrupulous fidgets. On the frequentation of the sacraments. Holy Purity. To one troubled with scruples. Confession. Patience with temptations. Despondency. On how to distinguish between temptations and sins.

As a sequel to the preceding letters on Religious Vocation it will not be out of place to insert here some notes of a sermon preached by Father Porter at a Profession of nuns, though this sermon belongs to a much earlier period—the time between 1860 and 1863, when he was at St. Beuno's College, North Wales.

Taking for his text the words from St. Paul's Epistle to the Romans—" Know ye not that all you who are baptized in Christ Jesus are baptized in His Death. For we are buried together with Him by Baptism unto death, that as He is risen from the dead by the glory of the Father, so we also may walk in the newness of life. For if we have been planted together in the likeness of His Death, so shall we be also in the likeness of His Resurrection,"—Father Porter said that the death of which St. Paul spoke was the death of the soul to sin—to the captivity of Satan and to the exile which had closed the gate of Paradise against us. Our Lord, by His cruel agony upon the Cross, loosened the bonds of sin, rescued us from the thraldom of death, opened to us for a second time the way into Paradise. And we died with Him—were planted in the likeness of His Death in holy Baptism when we renounced the devil with his pomps, the world with its works, and the flesh with its temptations. To the Resurrection of Christ and the likeness of the Resurrection, there were various degrees: for one was the glory of the sun, and another the glory of the moon, and another the glory of the stars—for star differeth from star. So in the likeness of the Death of Jesus Christ there were various degrees. There was the death to mortal sin, which was essential to salvation; there was the death of the devout Christian living in the world but not of the world, who used the world as though he used it not. But higher than these and higher than all was the death of the religious state, which aimed at true, absolute, perfect, entire, uncompromising death in order to be planted in perfect likeness to the Death of Jesus Christ. They must not conceive of the Death of our Blessed Lord as included merely in His Passion and in the brief moment of the separation of His Body and His Soul. His Death began from the instant when He was conceived in the womb of Mary, ever immaculate. From that instant He was poor, He knew none of the pleasures that the world might offer, He knew not the satisfaction, the delight that there is in the use of one's own will and one's own power, for He knew only the will of His Heavenly Father. Through the whole of that Life there was not a symptom or sign of repose, or of rest or of honour; but they read of sleepless nights—all honours fled, all glory shunned—they read that that Life, from the first until the last, resembled not in any particular the life to which our nature aspires. He was poor as the corpse which had been given to its native dust, he knew no more of pleasure than the corpse; He knew no more of its own will than the corpse that was carried hither and

o

thither. And this perfect Death of Jesus Christ was the model which had always stood out before the Church. It might be that the vocation to the religious life was decided by the terror of God's judgment upon sinners; it might be from a deep insight into the nothingness of the things of this world; it might be that a bitter disappointment had dispelled the charm that had bound them to the world—these might be the motives in the first instance, but sooner or later, all aspirations, all feelings, were merged and lost in the contemplation of that picture of the living Death of Christ. Well might the Fathers of the Church say that human language failed to tell the dignity, the excellence, the glory of a religious life; well might they say that a religious life was the sun, the essence, the perfection of Christianity; well might they compare its merits to the merits of martyrdom, with only this difference, that the death was more lingering, though it might not at any one moment be so painful; well might they call it the second Baptism, for if the first Baptism had planted them in the likeness and the death of Christians, the vows of religion planted in them a true likeness of the perfect Death of Jesus Christ. No wonder that St. Thomas laid it down that those who took the vows of religion, in the act, received the same cleansing of their souls that they received in their first Baptism; no wonder that it was looked upon as a precious pearl for which all else might be given up and left aside; no wonder those were called blessed, and were happy, who were privileged to enjoy this grace—for many were called, but few were chosen—many invited, but few had the courage and fidelity to correspond to the invitation. "Devout Sisters," said the Reverend Father, addressing the candidates, "you to-day, with the grace of God, are going to seal this second death—this second Baptism.

For a long time you have expected this day, you have looked forward to it—for a long time in your hearts you have given up all; it is your happy privilege that God will seal and accept your gift. As the waters of Baptism cleanse the soul that has already, by an act of its will, freed itself from the shackles of sin and of the devil, so your vows will in the sight of Heaven, and in the sight of Holy Church, free you from those bonds to a less perfect life which are in your hearts. It is not for me to say on such an occasion what must be the feelings which animate your hearts after so long an expectation; it is not for me to say with what awe you will utter those vows which are to bind you to poverty, to chastity, to obedience, and to the humble service of the poor and the ignorant. It is not for me to say the admiration and wonder you feel that you should have been chosen above so many others, that to you should be reserved the privilege of ranking among the princes of God's people. No words of mine can tell the gratitude that you feel, and the gratitude that you ought to feel, in the presence of such a boundless grace. But without offence to you, I may say a few words to encourage you to feel a brave and cheerful trust in the mercy of God. You have not taken this important step in a moment of youthful, unreflecting enthusiasm. Like the wise man in the Gospel, you have sat down and have reckoned up the cost. You know that in the life to which you pledge yourselves there are difficulties, and toils, and trials, trials of mind, trials of heart, trials of body, trials of health; but these have not dismayed you; they have rather urged you to take them, to accept the religious life with all its trials and all its sufferings as the Cross of Christ, and because it is the Cross of Christ. In the spirit of St. Catherine of Siena, who was placed by our Lord between the crown of thorns and the wreath of roses, you have grasped the thorns, pressed them to your brows and to your hearts, that you might more perfectly resemble Him Who is the copy that is set before you for the rest of your lives. It is a great gift, a great responsibility; but fear not, tremble not. Christ, Who invited you to the banquet, will clothe you with a wedding garment; Christ, Who has bidden you, and Who has said, "Come, follow Me," will give you grace to follow Him to the end up the steps of Calvary, to be planted in the perfect likeness of His Death, that you may be planted in the perfect likeness of His Resurrection. He will enable you to say, "Here is my inheritance, here is my portion. Whom shall I fear?"

Devout brethren, you who with me are the witnesses of this sacrifice offered to God, to the great Giver of life and Creator of mankind, you especially who have part in this sacrifice which is now being made, join with me in praying that God will deign to accept and to bless the offering thus laid at His feet, that He will grant His faithful servants long to labour profitably for the salvation of souls, and to their dying day to cherish the dispositions in which they now make their profession.

The counsels on spiritual subjects which follow, fragments from various letters, some undated, which have been sent us, may be read with interest and profit by many who have experienced the difficulties and temptations of which they treat.

San Girolamo, March 5, 1883.

You tell me you fidget terribly about all your actions, and you cannot understand how you have got into this state. I think I can throw some light upon the subject. You have by degrees *trained* yourself to listen to almost every doubt which arises in your mind. You have formed a habit of examining such doubts, and you are now at the point that you cannot disregard them easily. What is to be done? You must break the habit. How? by resolutely dismissing the doubts. At first you will not succeed without an effort. By degrees less effort will be necessary. When you see *clearly* that you ought to act in some particular way, then act. When you see *clearly* that such an act is a sin, omit it. When you discover doubts arising in your mind, refuse to listen, follow the light which at first pointed clearly in one direction. You may encourage yourself by asking sometimes, how should I like to propose my doubts to any sensible person, say to Father ——. As a rule you will answer, he would laugh at them. Do you laugh at them.

As to the frequentation of the sacraments, I won't put you under any obedience, but I do advise you strongly to persevere. The less frequently you go, the more difficult you will find it and the more scrupulous you will become. Long examinations of conscience are not good for you. Make very short ones.

You must not expect to receive great consolations when you go to the sacraments. Your neglect in the past, and your present scruples, are quite enough to prevent you from receiving consolations. Persevere, prepare shortly, and leave God to console you when He thinks fit. He will do it one day.

As to thoughts against holy purity, you do not sin grievously if you do not banish them instantly. Perhaps there is no sin at all. If there is negligence on your part, if you are slow in putting them away, that is a venial sin. Confess in this way: " I have been tempted with thoughts and feelings contrary to purity. I hope I did not wilfully consent to them, but I accuse myself as far as God sees me guilty," or "I have been slow in repelling them," as the case may be. Don't spend much time in examination. You can quickly decide whether you have wilfully consented, or been negligent, or repelled the temptation promptly. The less you think about it the better. You may take my word for it, the devil is at your elbow advising you about the sacraments. Read the *Imitation*, book iv. chap. x.

TO ONE TROUBLED WITH SCRUPLES.

As regards confession, spend some time in meditating on the grievousness of sin and its punishments, then say an act of contrition; last of all examine your conscience for a few minutes and go to confession as quickly as you can, resolutely despising all scruples and bothers. In the same way after confession approach Holy Communion, disregard all temptations, troubles, &c., as if they never existed, and go to Holy Communion. Don't trouble to make up your mind. It is by going that you must triumph over this misery.

San Girolamo, July 30, 1882.

Referring to your letter of the 12th, I cannot help thinking that you rather give in to what is plainly a temptation. It is no affair of yours whether your confessor understands you or not. As long as you do not intend to tell him an untruth, as long as you make yourself known to him honestly, however imperfectly, you have nothing to answer for before God. You wish to serve God and lead a good life, but you picture to yourself an imaginary standard of goodness, you confuse your ideas on many points, and then you become miserable, you get disgusted and you relapse into what you call perfect indifference. All this is temptation and the work of the devil. Read the *Imitation*, book iv. chap. x. Indeed you may read the whole of the Fourth Book with advantage. Remember the devil is opposed to frequent Confession and Communion. The Spirit of God draws the soul to the sacraments, when there is a serious effort to avoid mortal sin and a serious effort to please God by leading a good life. You are not so much scrupulous or timid, as muddled. You don't see clearly.

When you examine your conscience, see whether you have violated a commandment. If you did not, say nothing. If you did, confess your sin. If you are not certain that you did, say you are not certain, and you wish to accuse yourself as far as you are guilty in the sight of God. When you are not certain, you worry yourself to attain certainty. You might as well try to get the moon. When you don't see that you have sinned, you worry yourself to see that you have sinned. All waste of powder. For the contrition: if you have deliberately offended God, you can say truly, I wish I had not done it. You can always say, God has been good to me. I will love Him and make Him a return of gratitude. I will try to serve Him better.

When you can bring youself to worry less about sins, and especially about doubtful sins, when you can make frequent acts of love of Jesus Christ, you will be able to pray with fewer distractions, and you will find peace and happiness in the sacraments. You have still to discover the simple truth, that you create your own troubles. The remedy for them is in your own hands. If you will make a little effort, your spiritual life would be entirely changed, and for the better.

You must not lose courage about yourself. The case is not a desperate one. Don't give any thought to the past, beyond always accusing yourself in confession under the sweeping formula: "I accuse myself of these sins and all the sins I have forgotten, and all the sins of my past life, especially sins of . . ." Do what you can in the service of God. Be sorry when you offend Him, and begin again. Think more of loving God and less of how you have offended Him.

San Girolamo, August 15, 1883.

In answer to your letter of the 4th, I will tell you that you must have a little patience with yourself and with your temptations; you would gladly be free from them, you do not bring them on, you do not encourage them, you must not ask yourself, "Am I in the disposition to resist these temptations?" Your one question will be, "Did I deliberately and fully yield to the temptation in thought or in deed?" If you are sure that you yielded fully, confess the sin and the number of times. If you are not sure that you yielded, yet you fear there was some negligence, say so. "I cannot say certainly that I yielded, but I fear there was some negligence, some partial consent." After that let the confessor decide whether you ought to receive absolution and whether you ought to go to Holy Communion. You have nothing to say to these points, unless you wish to create for yourself a very serious responsibility. A penitent who dictates to the confessor really does incur a very serious responsibility. As long as you recount to your confessor what you have said and thought and done as simply, as truly as you can, and then obey him, you cannot go astray. Once you take it upon yourself to say, I won't do that, I can't do that, I know that is wrong, I feel it is wrong, my confessor does not understand me, &c., then you quite unnecessarily place yourself under a heavy burden, and you run great risk of coming to grief. And as a rule you make your temptations become more frequent and more violent. As an experiment, try one whole month of simple and entire obedience to see what will come of it.

ON DESPONDENCY.

The strong point of your spiritual life is constancy in Confession and Communion. When you fall away from one or the other, or both, then your soul is falling away. Pay no attention to discouragement. Ignore it and it will not hurt you. Your temptations always come back to the same point, discouragement. They require the same remedy, fidelity.

I wonder whether you realize all the harm the temptation to despondency has done you. I believe that temptation has kept you from becoming a saint. On account of desponding thoughts how often have you stayed from Confession and Holy Communion and Mass, and shortened or omitted your prayers!

If only you could surmount your repugnance to prayer! Without prayer you are like a man trying to lift a weight while his hands are tied behind him. If your hands were free, if you could only talk to God, even to grumble to Him, your condition would be improved. You would soon find yourself a changed person.

Your last letters have been rather desponding. I hope you are now in better health and better spirits. You have a lesson to learn. The state of the mind depends much on the state of our health. When you find yourself low-spirited, discontented, imagining all sorts of miserable things about yourself and your friends, you may be sure much of this mind-sickness is connected with health. A good walk in the park, even by yourself (better if you have a companion), or an expedition on the river in a penny steamer, would do you good.

It is our duty to contend against our spiritual enemies, and it is also our duty to contend against our bodily infirmities. Now you will get into a small rage on reading this, and deny what I have written, and say it is of no use to walk in the park or sail on the Thames. Well, get into a rage, and then cool down and try the experiment. Always be on your guard against your imagination. How many lions it creates in our paths, and so easily! And we suffer so much if we do not turn a deaf ear to its tales and suggestions.

You must pray for courage and strive on your part to keep it up. I feel very much the great difficulties you have to contend with, and for this reason I want you to be more constant and fervent and regular in your prayers. If you could understand the power of prayer, your life would be changed.

———

Nov. 6, 1882.

You still make yourself unhappy about the temptations. They are very trying that is certain. Have patience with them. You may take my word for it, you do not sin as often or as seriously as you imagine. Father ——— says very truly you exaggerate. You do not understand that the greater part of these annoyances are natural and come from natural causes, and you must not hope to escape all occasions. That is impossible. You guard your senses, your imagination and your affections in a reasonable way, and you go through the world like other people, and if temptations come to you, that is no sin on your part; the sin would be if you *wilfully* encouraged them and *wilfully* did what they suggest to you.

Distinguish also between pleasure that is involuntary and pleasure that is voluntary and is sought deliberately and deliberately encouraged. Certain sensations necessarily bring with them pleasure. No effort of your will can prevent the feeling of pleasure. Even though you are miserable about the matter and really torment yourself, the pleasure remains. This is an involuntary pleasure. There is no sin in it, nay, you merit in the sight of God, if you keep your will from *wilfully* and *deliberately* encouraging the feeling of pleasure. Were you to consent deliberately, you would know the fact with as much certainty that you know you go into town or sit down to write a letter. The devil seeks to keep you from Confession and Communion. Your own experience has taught you that you serve God better when you frequent the sacraments, provided at the same time that you obey your confessor. You are somewhat inclined to prefer your own ideas to those of your director, and a perfectly simple obedience is a virtue you have still to learn.

Let me come back to the point of health. Pay much attention to your health. I dare not promise you that you will be free from temptation if you keep very well; but you will experience fewer temptations and you will resist them more easily and you will be worried less than you are at present. In your case a sensible care of your health is most important.

Addio. God bless you. Pray for, yours very truly,

GEORGE PORTER.

CHAPTER X.

FROM LONDON TO BOMBAY.

January to March, 1887.

Nomination to the See of Bombay. Farewell Notes. Journey by Lourdes to Fiesole. A word of consolation. Peacefulness of Fiesole. Arrival at Loreto. Impressions of Lourdes. Last Mass in Farm Street. Partings are not separations. On board the *Assam*. Fidelity to rules in times of trial. Description of the Santa Casa. The Church's work in Bombay. From Alexandria to Suez. A night at Suez. The Suez Canal. On board the *Peshawur*. From Aden to Bombay. Uneventful voyage. Arrival in Bombay. Welcome. Celebration of the Queen's Jubilee. Sermon at the Cathedral. The Jesuit Colleges. Feeling of bewilderment. Population of Bombay. Hindoo cemetery.

31, Farm Street, December 29, 1886.

Yesterday's post brought me a very terrible letter from Propaganda. The Holy Father has named me Archbishop of Bombay. You may imagine my grief and consternation. Pray much for me: I need great grace to carry me through the trial and responsibility before me. I shall go to Bombay to receive my consecration there at the hands of the Apostolic Delegate.

31, Farm Street, January 9, 1887.

My dear Child,

The news is only too true. I sail on the 20th. The consecration will take place in Bombay. I don't altogether cease to be a Jesuit; I hope to live in a Jesuit house, community life, under Jesuit rule as far as possible. Thank God for the little piece of good news. May I offer my congratulations? The secret shall never pass my front teeth. I go on Saturday to Swansea. Now, good-bye. God bless you. I have endless letters to write. Pray much for me and for the souls for whom I become responsible.

I remain, yours very truly in Christ,

GEORGE PORTER.

31, *Farm Street, January* 9, 1887.

My dear Child,

I fear I cannot pay you a visit, I wish I could. I must say good-bye by letter. I sail on the 20th.

Keep up your courage, you are going to surmount your difficulty. You have those near you whose guidance you may trust implicitly; try to obey them simply and perseveringly.

Then you know Bombay is within reach of a letter. I am very hopeful that the new year will bring you peace and happiness.

Kindly say good-bye to each and all the members of your family. God bless you.

I remain, yours very truly in Christ,

GEORGE PORTER.

31, *Farm Street, January* 9, 1887.

My dear ——

I thank you for all the kind things you say to me in your letter of the 2nd. Indeed the nomination did come to me as a blow; I have not recovered from it. I have no choice. I must say, " Lord, I am Thy servant, send me where Thou wilt." I am sure I shall always have the help of your good prayers in the great work to which I have been sent.

I will not say good-bye by letter, because I hope to

say it in person. I will write to you and say on what day I can go down to S——. I sail from London on the 20th in the *Peshawur*, due at Bombay on February 15th.

Pray for me, and believe me, yours very truly in Christ,

GEORGE PORTER.

31, *Farm Street*, *January* 9, 1887.

My dear ——

Many thanks for your letter. I trust our friendliness will never be broken or forgotten.

I am not going to Rome. Later I may be able to help on your business, and shall not fail to do so when the occasion offers.

I sail from London on the 20th. Good-bye. God bless you.

I remain, yours very truly,
GEORGE PORTER.

San Girolamo, Fiesole, January 27, 1887.

... I was in great good fortune at Lourdes. The Fathers of the Mission received me, gave me supper, took me in for the night, and gave me every facility to satisfy my devotion in the morning. This little pilgrimage afforded me great consolation, and I shall dwell with pleasure on the thought that I have placed my future work under the special care of Our Lady of Lourdes. The air of the place is holy. Everything about it, except the omnibus people and the traffickers in holy objects, breathed holiness. I carried away with me great peace of mind and great trust in our Lady.

A day was taken up in the railway from Lourdes to Marseilles. A few hours' rest at Marseilles; then ticket for Pisa. But a *contretemps* spoiled my plan—the train from Marseilles reached Ventimiglia (the frontier) so late, that the Italian train had started. Finally, I reached Fiesole 9 p.m. yesterday, and here I am at home, almost too much so; my last resting-place before facing the new life of the East, a spot where I have spent many blessed, peaceful hours.

You ask me for a word of consolation. *Sursum corda. Gratias agamus Domino Deo nostro.* Love God with all your heart, love your neighbour for His sake, do some good to others, and wish to do more; seek your consolation in this way, and God will give you peace and strength.

Santa Casa, Loreto, January 29, 1887.

I asked —— to tell you I would answer your letter from the steamer. I find myself with some leisure, under the very shadow of the sanctuary, in the house of a worthy priest, so I propose to write before going on board.

I received your letter at Fiesole, as you intended I should do. Going there, and joining in the peaceful round of duties was very much like going home; the only drawback was the frequent reminder of the impending mitre and the deference of my Superiors and Brothers. I arrived late on Wednesday night, 9 p.m., and left late on Friday, about 6.15 p.m. The visit was a very happy time, as happy as it could be under the circumstances; from Father Vicar, and from all the Fathers, I received so much sympathy and charity.

The sky was cloudless for those two days; the sun was more the sun of April than of January; the country smiled as in the early spring, and on the long walk from the upper gate to San Girolamo the rose-buds in the hedge looked very resolute, and determined on breaking forth. The weather has been of all descriptions on the road—Paris very cold, Pau very warm, Lourdes bright but cold, the Pyrenees snow-clad, glistening under a glorious sun, rain about Narbonne, San Remo quite pleasant in the open air at 10 p.m., Fiesole sunny, Loreto bitterly cold, without a cloud in sight.

My pilgrimage to Lourdes was a hurried one, but most satisfactory. I arrived late on the evening of the 23rd, was hospitably received by the missionaries of Lourdes (some fifty to sixty of them were beginning their retreat that same evening under one of our Fathers), said my Mass in the crypt next morning, visited the Basilica and the Grotto, and left at 8 a.m. in great peace, and I trust strengthened for the work before me. Everything about Lourdes delighted me, once I had got clear away from the railway station. The Grotto, the Basilica, the new immense Church of the Rosary, which is rising fast above the ground, the chalet of the Bishop (I occupied his apartment for the Sunday night), the roads, everything looked holy and peaceful and solid. I shall ever retain a happy recollection of Lourdes, and my visit there. In my Mass you and your intentions were remembered, you may be sure; as again this morning in the Casa Santa.

I sleep here to-night, and go on to Brindisi to-morrow, so I shall say Mass a second time at the shrine.

I have not rested long anywhere on the road, but I do feel rested and greatly recovered from the rush of those three last weeks in London. Thank God we all got through it without any breakdown!

The last Mass in Farm Street reminded me, as it did you, of St. Paul's parting; many contrasts between the two partings might easily be found, but not a few resemblances also struck me. Partings, not a few, must enter into the apostolic life, the messenger knows not what is in store for him, save that crosses await him; there is the pain of parting, and yet they are partings without separation; the work of the Master pushes on, perhaps even more vigorously, and the communion of charity and prayers grows closer. So you will find, I hope, that your activity increases, and that you can do more for God and for souls. These partings ought to bear that good result, and drive us nearer to God, nearer in spirit. You must tell me how you succeed with the souls in whom you are interested. . . . *Une aide dans la douleur* has never fallen in my way. All His ways lead up to the Cross, I suppose—there the sorrowing have always comfort and strength. Good-bye, and God bless you. I thank God I have been able to brighten your life, and teach you that you can do some good in the world. I cherish the hope you will discover before long, that you can do a great deal of good.

Ship "Assam," January 31, 1887.

My dear ——

In my hurried visit, I thanked you for the beautiful rochets you had contributed to my outfit. I did not know then that I was indebted to you for my *mitra pretiosa*, so I write now to thank you for this beautiful gift, and to tell you how deeply I feel the great kindness you have shown me in my migration to India. I can never forget what you have done, and I shall ever place your name and your intentions in my *memento* at Holy Mass. You will in return pray for me and all my needs, and all the needs of the Bombay Mission. I have reached this steamer in very good health, thank God, quite recovered from the fatigue of my last weeks in London.

On my journey I had some consolations. A visit to Father Vicar and the community at Fiesole, where I was received with all possible sympathy and charity. Then a pilgrimage to Lourdes, and a second pilgrimage to the the Santa Casa at Loreto. In both sanctuaries I was able to say Mass, and I trust our Lady has taken me and my work and my friends under her special protection. Under her wings I shall feel strong, whatever difficulties arise.

You will be pleased to know that I found Father W—— at Fiesole, nearly quite recovered from his erisypelas. The attack had never been a very serious one; confinement to his room seemed the chief inconvenience it had brought with it.

I am writing this note about mid-day on Monday, 31st. The sea, so far, has been very calm. All the passengers put in an appearance at breakfast; we are a large number on board.

And now, thanking you once more, I say good-bye, and God bless you. Pray for, yours very truly,

GEORGE PORTER.

S.S. "Assam," February 2, 1887.

. . . Now for yourself. Continue to be faithful to your rule of life; be regular in approaching the sacraments. The point on which you should insist most is regularity. Let your rule be a law to you. Do not heed times of desolation or discouragement; persevere as you would have done in consolation. When you are tempted to despond, say: "The good time will come back again if I hold out resolutely." And when the good time comes, then pray for strength to carry you through the next trial. Life is always and must always be a trial in one way or another. Make up your mind that you will be tried, and make it the chief object of your life to get ready to meet your trials, and not be overcome by them.

P. and O. Steam Co. S.S. "Assam,"
February 2, 1887.

I am not quite clear where my last letter was posted. I fancy it must have been from Loreto; but I do not remember how much I told you about my pilgrimage to the Santa Casa. I carried with me a letter of introduction to Canonico Carozza, the Archdeacon. He found me a respectable lodging with a certain Aldegonda Cenerelli, housekeeper to her brother, a priest, who has an apartment within one minute of the church. And he made everything very smooth for my devotions. I had the happiness to say Mass twice in the Santa Casa.

An American conventual, the Penitentiary for the English language, soon found me out, and became my guide and companion for the day.

In old times, Loreto was one of the strong places of the Society, and at the Suppression the conventuals were put in our place in both sanctuaries. At Loreto, the house, the rooms, the library remain much as they were when our Fathers were turned out.

The Casa Santa interested me far more than I had expected. I don't mean for the great events which took place within its walls, but for its form, its accessories, and its history. The history was by no means new to me, and what I knew, supplemented by the fresher and fuller information of the American conventual, who is meditating a book in English for English-speaking pilgrims, enabled me to examine very minutely all the salient points. The statue of the Madonna, the altar, two cells, and three small dishes went with the house in its wanderings. The dishes are placed in a rich gold setting, the very first gold brought from America. The statue you must know from the pictures, which are common enough. On the wall can be distinctly traced a crucifixion of a most ancient type. Remains of another painting representing St. Lewis of France and our Lady (?) can still be traced; his Dominican biographer mentions that the holy King caused this painting to be made when he went on his Crusade. The original window remains where it always was. Doors have been made for the convenience of the faithful, but the one door which served in our Lady's time has been so filled up with the materials removed from our modern doorways that you see the lines easily. A *prie-dieu* occupies the place where our Lady is said to have been kneeling when the Angel appeared to her. The window in the centre of the end wall, the Angel and our Lady would have been nearly in a line, as well as I could fill up the picture. What thoughts that sanctuary calls up! Meditation did not seem difficult there.

The voyage has been quiet, no rough sea, no incidents, a most restful monotony. I have made the acquaintance of one or two Bombay residents, all Church of England men. They agree in representing the work of the Catholic Church in Bombay as immense. Anglicanism has been left quite behind. The College is a power. Our work among the natives is the only real work done; we do make converts, no one else does. Pray all the more that I may become an instrument to advance the interests of God and souls.

Thanks for the beautiful extract from St. Mary Magdalen of Pazzi. I will read it often.

The " Peshawur," February 5, 1887.

I begin this letter about 2 p.m. on the 5th; it will be posted next Tuesday at Adeu, if all goes well.

My chapter of accidents began with the last stage of my Italian journey. I think I told you that on my arrival at Brindisi my Gladstone bag, which I had registered at Foggia, only two stations before Brindisi, did not make its appearance. The sail from Brindisi to Alexandria was all that could be wished; three days of a most prosperous voyage. We left Alexandria about 11 a.m. by the Egyptian train; the ten hours' rail seemed dreadful in anticipation, but the first half proved most interesting. A smart shower of rain laid the dust, and saved us from one of the plagues of Egypt. Then the fertility of the first half of the distance surprised one not a little. The land of the Pharaohs was the land of the palm-tree, of bright verdure, of plenty. The people formed a constant subject of wonder; no roads, no conveyances, no carts; only tracks, paths through the soft soil. Small caravans with camels and asses, and men-servants and maid-servants. Numbers of solitary passengers, for the most part on foot (the ship vibrates a little, so I must leave some task to your ingenuity to make out an occasional word), every one with much covering to their heads, and the slightest of covering for the rest of their bodies, often only a long shirt. The homes of the peasants were the most wretched huts: mud, and something to hold it together, a door, a window, and a hole in the flat ceiling. The whole scene took one back to Genesis and the Patriarchs; it at least furnished an easy "composition of place" for Old Scripture scenes.

The railway seemed an utter anachronism, and it too was unlike most railways; not one tunnel in one hundred miles, the stoppages not frequent, and without any presentable reason. About 4 p.m. we drew up at Zazagi, and dined; dinner very so so, and dear at the price. After Zazagi, the only point of interest was the station Tel El Kebir; we made no halt. I could just distinguish a small remain of outworks, and the outline of more;

and on the right, soon after leaving the station, we passed a neatly kept little churchyard where our soldiers rest.

Suez we reached about 8.30 p.m. Before we got into the station, a number of Arabs and Egyptians boarded the train to tell us that the canal was blocked, and that the *Peshawur* could not get out. Too true! the worse for the passengers, and the worse for the P. and O., which was bound to look after us. We fared not so badly after all; at the hotel at Suez, with an Oriental courtyard, and a staring clock on its outside wall, we found a tolerable supper, and some sort of a shake-down. I had sheets, &c., on a sofa in one corner of a very large drawing-room; three others filled the other corners, and I was able to sleep well. I rose in time to see the sun rise on the Gulf of Suez, heard that the *Peshawur* was through the canal, breakfasted, and got on board about 10 a.m. We steamed down the gulf at 11.30, and in the next twenty-four hours made three hundred and fourteen miles.

On the *Peshawur* I find my portable altar. Alas, I cannot say Mass; the altar-stone had not been consecrated. On my way through Italy I had feared such might be the case, and I provided myself with an altar-stone in Florence, but that stone is locked up in my Gladstone bag, and so I must satisfy myself with a small modicum of outward Christianity till I reach Bombay.

Otherwise the voyage has not many discomforts. We are only 60 passengers on board, 34 first class, 16 second. I have a large cabin all to myself. We have a German vice-consul for Zanzibar on board, a gentleman. The rest of the company are mostly Anglo-Indians, not in a very good humour, returning to Bombay, and not very sociable.

One of the sights on board is the post office. We took on board at Suez 373 bags (the average is 350:

the Christmas and New Year's Day mail ran to 460 bags), and three officials who, with their blacks, spend long days in sorting this mountain of letters, papers, and parcels.

The Suez Canal becomes an immense fact out here. The charge to the *Peshawur* for going through amounts nearly to £1,250 sterling, 8 frs. for every ton; 10 frs. for every stranger: rather a large disbursement.

February 7th, 2 p.m.—We shall reach Aden to-morrow afternoon, so I will close my letter. The sea has been very smooth, and continues to be so. Nothing special has broken the quiet monotony of this sea-life. I forgot to say we met Stanley at Suez, with Dr. Junker, the companion of Emin Bey. They will follow us to Aden, and there change for Zanzibar. We have a Mr. Jamieson on board, who goes with the relieving expedition; he is a young married man, but fond of adventure, and has contributed £1,000 to the expenses fund.

February 8th.—Last evening the wind changed to a head-wind, and at times blew rather stiffly. The oldest Indians on board say they never remember such a passage, so smooth, so calm, so pleasant. The thermometer in the companion has never risen above 80°. I wonder what is the thermometer at London!

Five days and a half, perhaps six days, to Bombay, my huge pagan world.

The Indian Ocean, February 10, 1887.

We have entered on the last stage of our journey. We reached Aden on Tuesday about 8.30 p.m.; landed the mail, four passengers, and a certain amount of cargo. We took on board three Europeans, Colonel Spring, with his assistant and servant, and nine deck passengers, all Mahommedans. These men pay twenty rupees from Aden to Bombay, but find their own food and cook it; they brought on board poultry, a sheep, with *et ceteras*.

The food question has its difficulties on these ships. The Mahommedans insist on killing their own meat; they allow an infidel butcher to divide the carcass, but they must have their own cook. We carry two native cooks, one for the Lascar crew, the other for the Mahommedans, and these cooks have their separate kitchen. All the men belonging to the engine-room are Mahommedans, a superior set to the Lascars.

The sail to Bombay does not promise many incidents; the weather is less bright and the sea is less smooth than in the Red Sea. Old Indian travellers look for a rather stiff head-wind when they get within two days of Bombay. We met a head-wind as soon as we left Aden, and it has continued to blow ever since, and rather stiffly.

I shall give you our log on the last page; it will give you an idea of what you will have to go through when you make the trip to Bombay. I cannot imagine more complete rest than we have had since we left Brindisi, excluding of course the railway from Alexandria to Suez, which by the way will be omitted from Feb. 1, 1888, as all the ships will take passengers from Brindisi right through the canal. Whether you stay in your cabin, or the saloon, or go on deck, with the soothing sea, more or less of a breeze, and a bright sun from which you are screened by a double awning, talking to a friend, or with a book, or with one's thoughts, or in vacancy of thought, you have the most perfect rest I can imagine. You live in the air and in the sunshine.

At Aden I received a telegram from the Pro-Vicar Apostolic, our Father Willy, warning me to expect a deputation on board, on our arrival in port. We ought to reach Bombay on Monday afternoon. But as the postal authorities claimed their right of detaining us six hours at Aden, we only got away at 2.30 a.m. yesterday morning. This delay, with the head-wind, may prolong our sea-voyage till Tuesday the 15th. We are bound by the contract to reach Bombay before noon on the 15th.

From the Bombay papers of January 28th, I gather that Monsignor Agliardi has not yet reached Bombay. On the 25th he had a great function at Bangalore. Probably I shall reach Bombay before he does. I shall be glad to get a week for my retreat before the consecration takes place.

Sunday, 13th.—The last entire day on board. At our present rate, we ought to land to-morrow about 3 p.m. In referring to the log, remember it is always from noon till noon. The Indian Ocean has disappointed the sailors: they promised us bright, warm days on leaving Aden; we have had somewhat cloudy, rather cool days. The wind was to be with us till within two days of Bombay; it has been a head-wind all the way. The voyage has been most uneventful. We passed through a vast shoal of porpoises on the first day. A young lady on board took them to be flying-fish, but the same evening, as she was reading in her cabin by candle-light, a real flying-fish jumped in at the open window, and gave her the opportunity of examining him closely. A few flying-fish have been seen. Three steamers have been sighted within the week. For the rest we have the sea around us, the sky above us, and the *Peshawur* our narrow, uninteresting world. My letters from Bombay will be more interesting, I trust; at least, I shall have more to write about. The first post leaves on Friday, and I shall not close this till Thursday.

Bombay time is nearly five hours before Greenwich time (4 hours, 51 minutes exactly). We have had to advance our clocks and watches about 20 minutes every day.

We dropped anchor in the Bay of Bombay 2.35 p.m. by Bombay time, a quarter of an hour in advance of the noon of the 14th in my log.

Our arrival was not expected; even the launch of the P. and O. was found wanting. In about an hour a deputation of the clergy and laity came on board, told me they were glad to see me, promised me no end of work, and hoped I might live through a lot of it. Then we went ashore, and after further introductions and a rest, drove round Bombay, supped and rested.

The weather had been cold two days before, the thermometer stood as low as 56° Fahr.; but yesterday the sun showed himself master of the situation. I did not examine the thermometer, but I feel satisfied the heat had passed 85°. The mosquitoes raged outside the mosquito-curtains all night, but I contrived some good sleep in the morning. I had the unspeakable joy of saying Mass this morning, after a long fast. Since breakfast I have been hard at work at my desk. At present, I am to go to Allahabad. A Council will be held on the 24th. The consecration is fixed for the 27th. I think the latter part of the programme will be changed.

The "Peshawur," February 13, 1887.

Dear Reverend Mother,
     P.C.

Your letter of January 25th only reached me at Suez. It was kind to write me those words of farewell and God-speed, and to add the photos of dear Mary Vale and its sanctuaries. I value them deeply, and I thank you for the promise of prayers.

You ask me for my photo. Some day you shall receive

Arrival in Bombay. 235

one. I have not got one with me that I can send you, but I will try to remember to order one from the photographer in London. A photo taken in Bombay would tell you nothing of Father George Porter who used to visit —— some years ago.

The voyage has been favourable beyond all expectations. Sailors and travellers both agree that such a pleasant voyage at this time of the year was never known. We have had no rough weather, no sea-sickness, no great heat, no accidents. Day succeeds day, one more pleasant than the other. The voyage has been a complete rest of body and mind. To-morrow afternoon, probably about 3 p.m., we shall land in Bombay, and then farewell to rest, my new life and work commences.

Pray very much for me, that I may be the instrument in God's hands of doing some good in this vast city, with its 600,000 pagans and Mahommedans. Bombay is the second city in the British Empire, but the Christians are little more than 20,000, and all these are not Catholics or saints. I have a great burden laid on my soul, and I need all the prayers I can get.

Please to remember me very kindly to all the Sisters, especially to those who remember me. Tell them I count on their zeal for the Mission of Bombay. God bless you.

I remain, yours very truly in Christ,

GEORGE PORTER.

Bombay, February 17, 1887.

The *Peshawur* reached Bombay on the 14th, about 2.30 p.m. (Bombay time, 4 hrs. 51 min. before Greenwich), three hours sooner than we were expected. The passage was most favourable. My confidence in prayer for temporal blessings has been strengthened. The officers of the ship, and the oldest Indians aboard, all testified that they had never made such a favourable run at this time of the year. *No* rough weather, sea only enough ruffled to give us a welcome breeze, heat never distressing; only thirty-four first-class passengers, a fore first-class cabin all to myself; company, though not interesting, very good-tempered. . . .

Everybody has been most kind in welcoming me. Many regret the removal of Dr. Meurin, but to myself they have shown every mark of indulgence and good-will.

Bombay had been chilly, the thermometer had actually gone down to 58° Fahrenheit; people were looking for wraps. On the 14th the change came. We found the sun fierce in Bombay harbour, and he continues to be fierce. This morning, 10 a.m., the thermometer stood at 82° in my room in the shade; yesterday, in the afternoon, it stood at 98°.

My arrival coincided with the celebration of the Jubilee of our Queen-Empress. Yesterday, the 16th, Bombay and all India was in gala. Great affair by the Governor, parade of troops, church and religious celebrations. I preached my first sermon for the occasion, at the Cathedral in Kalbadevie Road, to a very large congregation, and a curious congregation, mostly Europeans—some dressed sensibly, others very fantastically—then a great number of natives, among them several Christian Hindoo women, wrapped in a white sheet, and squatting on the floor. Our Christians like long services, whatever the thermometer may say—High Mass, sermon, *Te Deum*, and thanksgiving, took from 10 a.m. to 12.15.

I have been running round, as the Americans say. We (S.J.) have two NOBLE establishments here, St. Xavier's College and St. Mary's, the former for day-scholars, the latter for boarders. But much remains to be done; I see work for many Archbishops a-head. I have not yet passed the limits of bewilderment; the variety of races, faces, costumes, languages, makes up a Babylon of heathendom and a Babel of tongues. Pray I may benefit some of this mass of humanity.

Fort Chapel, Bombay, February 20, 1887.

Dear Rev. Mother,

I reached Bombay on the 14th, after a most pleasant passage. Bombay was getting ready for the celebration of the Queen's Jubilee, and the week has been taken up with festivities.

It was only yesterday that my large box was delivered to me, and then I saw for the first time the beautiful present you sent me. I fear I did not write to thank you. Allow me now to supply this omission, and thank you from my heart for this present, which will often remind me of your community, with which I have been united in bonds of charity for so many years.

You must pray for me and for Bombay and its heathen world. I will give you a place in my daily *memento* at Mass.

Bombay has a population little short of 800,000 inhabitants. The Christians are said not to be more than 20,000; all the rest Mahommedans or heathens—300,000 Mahommedans, 125,000 Hindoos, 115,000 Parsees, &c. The Hindoos burn their dead. I passed the cemetery yesterday evening, and at sunset a volume of flame and smoke was rising to heaven. The Parsees leave their dead to the vultures on the summit of their Towers of Silence—a ghastly ending to what should be God's temple.

This huge heathen world bewilders me. How can it be reached? how reclaimed from the darkness of sin and error? I see no answer as yet. For the present I pray, and invite you to join your prayers to mine.

This evening at 6 p.m. (it will be about 1 p.m. with you—we are almost five hours before Greenwich) I start for Allahabad, 844 miles to the north-west. A Council will be held there by the Apostolic Delegate on the 24th, and he will consecrate me on the 27th, with another Jesuit, Father Beiderlinden, who is to be Bishop of Poona. In the present arrangements, I am to make my entrance into Bombay on Sunday, March the 6th. And then my real work will begin.

The great heat commenced the very day of my arrival. The thermometer varies from 80° to 90° Fahr. between sunrise and sunset. So far I stand it well, and like it rather than otherwise, but a week does not make a very reliable experience.

Please remember me most affectionately to all my old friends at ——

Yours very truly in Christ,

GEORGE PORTER.

CHAPTER XI.

ALLAHABAD AND THE ARCHBISHOP'S SERMON.

March, 1887.

Journey to Allahabad. The Council and the Consecration. Garden party. Vegetation of India. Fort Chapel. Work. Minor crosses and patience.
Sermon on the Catholic Hierarchy in India. The Church, Christ's Kingdom upon earth. How it differs from the kingdoms of the world. Its independence. Its form. Its vicissitudes. The normal organization of the Church. The Episcopate in communion with the Apostolic See. How the Pope provides for the government of countries where for various reasons a regularly constituted diocese cannot exist. Difference between Bishops and Vicars Apostolic. Substitution by Leo XIII. of twenty-five regular sees for the vicariates previously existing in India. Review of the past history of the Church in India. Advantages which will ensue from the establishment of the Hierarchy.

Fort Chapel, Medows Street, Bombay,
March 10, 1887.

To put our correspondence in order, I begin by acknowledging your two letters of Feb. 11th and Feb. 18th. I sent a telegram to Europe, announcing the date of my consecration. Did it ever get about? I also tried to utilize Reuter. How far the attempt succeeded I do not know. The 844 miles of rail to Allahabad made a wearisome journey: miles and miles of plain, miles and miles of corn glaring at the traveller. How welcome was the sight of the Ganges, which is joined by the Jumna, just at Allahabad. I felt indulgently towards all who hold its waters to be sacred. Allahabad is known for its dry, fierce heat. The Council and the consecration and a sermon on the Hierarchy filled my time. Happily I was lodged sumptuously in a room 20 feet square, 25 feet high, without a window, all light and air supplied by a door and an opening (20 feet from the ground), into a magnificent verandah running all round the building; no superfluous furniture, and only whitewash on the walls and ceiling. My room belonged to the College. This was reserved for Bishops, actual and future. The minor clergy, the Fathers of the place (Capuchins), and the servants, had to put up with living under canvas or sleeping on a mattress in the verandah. When you travel anywhere in India you always take bedding with you, more or less, as you prefer it. A man undoes his bundle and soon arranges a shake-down. The nights are often downright cold. The company at Allahabad was very delightful. Our meetings at meals and afterwards passed most pleasantly. Of the Council and the consecration I won't say anything. You will receive a paper telling all. The paper contains a short paragraph on a garden-party held in the "Compound" the day of the Council. It began at 7 p.m. and went on till 10 p.m. The Compound is the land belonging to the church and its dependencies, forty acres in the present instance. The Cathedral, the College, the Bishop's house, and all the chief roads and walks were illuminated. All Allahabad, Catholic, Protestant, Pagan, &c., flocked into the Compound. Tents had been set up and refreshments were given to all. The scene was magical. In Europe, such a gathering (thousands) would hardly be possible. In Allahabad everything was as happy as possible, and I am confident the garden-party brought many people together in a kindly spirit, who otherwise might always have remained strangers, if not enemies. I won't say much about my feelings. Sometimes the country, the people, the business, all seemed a dream in a picture; then at other times the whole reality comes home with great force. Every now and again the heat or the mosquitoes drive away every other thought, and now, thank God, the work fills my time and my thoughts. I am afraid to count the souls for whom I am to answer. A Bishop at Allahabad told me he had fifty-eight millions in his diocese! The thought takes away one's breath. And then how to reach this crowd? or how to reach one single mind amongst them? Perhaps in time the eye may grow accustomed to the darkness and discover some way out.

The vegetation would delight you. The mango-tree almost repays one for the journey. The mere mass of foliage and the colours of the leaves make a restful picture to the eye. The fruit will soon show itself. The roses of Allahabad for size, form, and colour, surpass all the roses I have ever seen. The lilies, too, are most graceful, pendant, bell downwards. I cannot enumerate trees or plants all new to me. Imagine the sensation of finding great big monkeys dancing about in perfect freedom, or peacocks wild, or to be told as we rowed through two miles of Marble Rock at Tubbalpur, "Here I shot an alligator last year;" or as you are walking in a garden in the dusk, "Come down this walk: I hear the ruffle of a cobra." All very novel. A few weeks will make one very much at home with it. Of the natives I must not speak in this letter: there a long chapter begins. I am very well and do not find Bombay heat as yet unpleasant. The house I live in is cramped and small. Every one tells me to get away and find a new home. The Delegate urges a move with great vigour. The Fort Chapel forms a part of the building. It is small and insignificant. Fort Chapel stands in the fort, in the centre of the business quarter. The Cathedral, Kalbadavie Road, is in the native town, in the midst of

Hindoo temples and a Hindoo population, which is often very noisy.

You are good enough to offer to send me any book. A modern, handy Portuguese dictionary, especially if it contains a *short* grammar, would be useful. I am glad to hear the tonics are helping you. The doctor is right in forbidding abstinence. Take food and air and exercise, and supply all deficiencies of penance by patience and kindliness and some work for souls by pen or speech. . . .

Fort Chapel, March 18, 1887.

The Gladstone bag reached Bombay just one week after its owner. The contents were uninjured, and my *capella* I find is pretty complete. I hope you have received the *Bombay Catholic Examiner* for the last few weeks. You will learn about my doings and sufferings from its pages. I have promised the Allahabad sermon on the Hierarchy to the printer, and I fear I cannot escape publishing a panegyric on St. Patrick, a theme on which I have been holding forth for the last five-and-twenty years. I will send you what I do print.

My work has fairly begun. The small part, sitting for photos, being interviewed by endless visitors, taking part in public meetings, presiding at distribution of prizes in schools, &c. A great field of patience opens up before me. Perhaps great meekness under all these minor crosses may draw a blessing on one's work with the Pagans. As yet I am groping about, trying to find a door or window to enter by. This Eastern life is profoundly mysterious and fascinating. I will send you a pamphlet on child-widows, which will open up quite a new world to your mind.

Go on praying for your brother. I hope the hour of

grace will soon strike for him. At any rate, continue to hope and to pray. You can do no more.

I like to think of Edward Dean's children at Rome, noticed so kindly by the Holy Father. . . . The mail is just leaving, so I must say good-bye and God bless you.

The sermon preached by Archbishop Porter in the Cathedral of Allahabad on the evening of February 27, 1887, to which reference is made in the preceding letters, was printed at the *Examiner* Press, Bombay, with the title—*The Catholic Hierarchy in India.*

All power is given to Me in Heaven and on earth. Going therefore teach ye all nations, baptizing them in the name of the Father and of the Son and of the Holy Ghost, teaching them to observe all things whatsoever I have commanded you (St. Matt. xxviii. 18, 19, 20).

Dearly beloved Brethren in Jesus Christ,

On Thursday the establishment of the Catholic Hierarchy in India was proclaimed by the Apostolic Delegate to the North-Western Provinces in this Cathedral. What is meant by the establishment of the Catholic Hierarchy in India? My discourse this evening will contain the answer to the question. Allow me to begin from the beginning.

The Catholic Church is the Kingdom of Christ upon earth. Christ received a commission from His Heavenly Father to found His Kingdom. Its establishment was the great work of His Public Life. The last touches were given during the forty days which preceded the Ascension. This Kingdom, composed of mortal frail men, ruled over by men not exempt from the infirmities of human nature, will never crumble to ruin, as do the works of man. The gates of Hell will never prevail against it till the end of time.

The world is divided into many kingdoms. Human society cannot subsist without government, and since

God created man to live in society, we infer that He created him to live under government. In this sense every legitimate government comes from God and derives its claim to obedience from God. "He that resisteth the power resisteth the ordinance of God."[1]

Earthly kingdoms exist for the attainment of objects which belong to our life on this earth, for the protection of the individual, of the family, and of the kingdom itself; for the protection of life and limb, of property, of good name, of liberty and of all rights. Whatever attributes or powers are necessary for the preservation and well-being of the State and its subjects, those the State rightfully claims. The State may lawfully repel aggression from without. It may repress rebellion at home. It may enforce obedience even by pains and penalties. It may levy taxes. It may raise armies. It may equip fleets. It may make laws. It may appoint tribunals to administer them. It may secure their observance by punishments. It may regulate commerce. In a word, the power of the earthly kingdom reaches to every part of man's life in this world. The State may be said to be omnipotent, and in the heathen world and under those governments which have repudiated Christianity, the State is in matter of fact omnipotent and often wields its power tyrannically.

Jesus Christ assigned a limit to the authority of the State. He withdrew from the domain of the State and reserved to His own Kingdom the consciences of men, their faith, their obedience to His law. The High Priest in the Sanhedrim spoke to the Apostles: "Commanding, we commanded you, that you should not teach in this Name. . . . Peter then answering, and the Apostles said, We ought to obey God rather than men."[2] The Church and the State were brought face to face.

---

[1] Romans xiii. 2.   [2] Acts v. 28, 29.

The Kingdom of Christ in many essential points differs from the kingdoms of this world. The Kingdom of Christ knows no limits of space. It claims the whole world as its territory. It is not confined to any race or nationality. It would embrace the entire human family. Every subject of every kingdom on earth should become its subject. The kingdoms of the world rise and fall and leave only ruins to tell of their greatness. The Kingdom of Christ has witnessed the vicissitudes of nearly two thousand years, and full of vitality, she still believes in her Founder's promise that she will be found standing erect when this visible world comes to an end.

The kingdoms of this world derive their power from God, but not immediately. Some rest on popular election; others were inherited; others were received as a gift; others were won by the sword. The Kingdom of Christ derives its origin, its rights, immediately and directly from God. God constituted Christ King over all men, and Christ Himself entrusted His Kingdom to St. Peter and the successors of St. Peter.

The kingdoms of the world exact obedience from all who are born within their territory. The Kingdom of Christ admits only willing subjects, those who from conviction with their own free-will believe in Him.

The kingdoms of the world pursue the good things of this world. The Kingdom of Christ seeks only the eternal salvation of men in the life to come, through faith in God and faith in His only Son, Jesus Christ.

The kingdoms of the world wield the weapons of the world: power, riches, genius, learning. The Kingdom of Christ has no sword save the Word, the testimony of faith; no buckler save the patience of the martyr; no wisdom save the weakness of the lowly, chosen by God to confound the mighty.

At the same time, the Kingdom of Christ claims

every attribute which is necessary for her existence and well-being, and for the accomplishment of her mission in the world. She claims the right to preach the Gospel of Jesus Christ, to administer His sacraments, to continue His priesthood. She makes her laws, she establishes her tribunals, she enforces her laws by spiritual sanctions; she claims the right to hold churches and schools and universities, and to administer them. She possesses her own Hierarchy of jurisdiction and of order. She supports the kingdoms of the world by inculcating a rational obedience. She gratefully accepts the protection of the State; but she refuses to become the slave of the State, a mere department of the civil framework of society.

Such being the Church, Christ's Kingdom upon earth, and its mission being to gain all men to the faith of her Divine Master, what form does its life assume? You have Popes, Patriarchs, Primates, Archbishops, Bishops, Vicars Apostolic, Prefects Apostolic, Parish Priests, Vicars, Curates—what do all these distinctions imply? How much is essential? How much non-essential? How much normal, how much provisional, how much exceptional? Remember that Christ came not to send peace, but the sword.[3] His Kingdom is an aggressive kingdom. He is the armed warrior who contends with Satan for the souls of men. He wishes all men to be saved through His Precious Blood, in the Church which He redeemed in that Blood. The war between the Kingdom of Jesus Christ and the kingdom of Satan never relents. Its tide rolls, now here, now there. Success here follows Jesus Christ; there His adversary gains the advantage. In one age territory is gained by the Church, in another age territory lost by her.

What a glorious province of the Kingdom of Christ once flourished on the northern coast of Africa. Ter-

[3] St. Matt. x. 34.

tullian, Cyprian, Augustine, belong to the inheritance of ages. Vandal and Goth and Mahommedan buried the land in silence and gloom, in desolation and darkness, for fourteen centuries. Here and there in our day the ancient fire has been rekindled.

The East, the home of Chrysostom, of the two Gregorys, of Basil, the pulpits once vocal with such rich eloquence, the schools once thronged by crowds of eager students, the Holy Land so lovingly visited by the pilgrim, Egypt, with its world of monks and hermits, have all passed out of the life of the Church of Christ; the barren life of schism is barely tolerated by the victorious Moslem.

In the West how many souls perished in the apostasy of the sixteenth century! To our day their children wander in darkness, sheep without a shepherd, or fall to a lower depth in the abyss of unbelief.

In former ages the conversion of the conquerors of the Roman Empire more than compensated for the losses sustained in Africa and in the East. During the last three centuries the Catholic Church has won more in the continents of America and Australia than she lost in Europe.

Now she sends her message of redemption to the teeming world of India! Oh, that India may respond to the call!

You must distinguish, therefore, between that portion of the Kingdom of Christ which has been and remains completely incorporated, and which enjoys the blessing of a perfect, normal organization, and the other outlying portion, which has not been as yet so incorporated, or which has been wrested from her.

The answer with regard to the perfectly organized portion is quickly given. The unit in the Kingdom of Christ on earth is the diocese, with its Bishop at its head. The Bishop, in virtue of his consecration, validly administers all the seven sacraments, and hence is said to possess the fulness of the priesthood: he continues the succession of the clergy; he watches over their education, he alone consecrates churches and altars, he alone consecrates the chrism and holy oils used in the administration of the sacraments, he alone consecrates the chalices and patens required for the Sacrifice of the Mass. In virtue of his appointment or mission, he exercises jurisdiction in his diocese; the extent of his powers being regulated partly by law and usage, partly by delegation from the Holy See: the sphere of his jurisdiction being partly sacramental, appertaining to the tribunal of penance, partly extra-sacramental, embracing causes to be dealt with in open court. The Bishop, as pastor in his diocese, may make laws for the welfare of his flock and the advancement of God's service. As pastor, again, he names one or more Vicars-General, Rural Deans, Parish Priests, Missionary Rectors; he portions out the work of his clergy. Within his diocese he judges and decides ecclesiastical cases: always with dependence on the Holy See. He inquires into abuses and misdeeds. To him the goods, the property of the Church are entrusted; he is responsible for them. On him in a special manner devolves the duty of watching over the property and the revenues of the charitable institutions of the diocese. The Church requires him to live in his diocese, to visit every part of it frequently, to meet his clergy in Synod. He owes a special duty to the poor, to the widow, and the orphan, to the suffering, and the defenceless. Every few years he visits the Tomb of the Apostles, pays his homage to the successor of St. Peter, and confers with him on the affairs of his diocese. When the Bishops of his province or nation assemble in Provincial or National Councils, he takes his place amongst them. When the Bishops of the world are convened by the Pope to an Œcumenical Council, he witnesses to the faith he has received, and he has a voice in its deliberations and in its decisions. The whole spiritual life of the diocese centres in the Bishop, and through the Bishop the diocese enters into communion of life and action with the Church Universal.

Among the Bishops of the world the Bishop of Rome enjoys a pre-eminence of honour and of jurisdiction. To him, as the successor of St. Peter, the care of the whole world has been committed. To him all the other Bishops of the Catholic Church look up as to the Bishop of Bishops. To him the faithful in every other diocese turn as to the supreme Pastor of all, as to the father of each. He is more completely Bishop in every diocese in the world than the Bishop who takes his title from the diocese; he is more completely parish priest in every parish than the parish priest at its head.

The Bishops of the world, presided over by the Bishop of Rome, form the Catholic Hierarchy of the world.

Where, then, have Patriarchs, Primates, Metropolitans, Archbishops, and others their place in the Kingdom of Christ on earth? I answer: these titles point to various groupings of dioceses, introduced at different times, principally to facilitate the government of the Church. These gradations of rank in no way affect the essential organization of the Church.

But the parish priest! he at least enters as an essential element into the life of the Church. No: the parish cannot be traced to Divine institution. During four centuries, parishes were unknown to the early Church, even in rural districts. In cities which were governed by Bishops they were not introduced till many centuries later. The parish priest takes a part of the Bishop's duty; he cannot confer Orders, he cannot confirm without a special delegation from the Holy See; the other sacraments he may administer within a defined portion of the diocese. He is responsible for the instruction and spiritual care of its inhabitants; he enjoys certain rights and privileges; he himself, his duties, his rights, and his privileges, are recognized by the law of the Church.

In countries inhabited by savage tribes, in countries where the Catholic Church is persecuted by the civil power, in countries where Catholics constitute an inconsiderable minority, a regularly constituted diocese could not exist: its essential elements would be wanting. Such countries fall to the Universal Bishop, the Bishop of Rome; he is, in the words of St. Paul, a debtor to all. "To the Greeks, and to the barbarians, to the wise, and to the unwise, I am a debtor."[4] He does not shrink from his duty. "A necessity lieth upon me; for woe is unto me if I preach not the Gospel."[5] The successor of St. Peter will answer to God for all, for Jew and Gentile, for pagan and infidel, for Hindoo and Mahommedan, as well as for the few Catholics scattered amongst them.

So long as a regularly constituted diocese remains impossible, the successor of St. Peter governs such countries by his Vicars. In our days the Vicars are called Prefects Apostolic or Vicars Apostolic: more commonly they are Bishops, occasionally they are only priests. Even if Bishops, they do not govern the territory confided to them in their own name, but in the name of the Pope. They do not exercise a jurisdiction defined in law, for the law does not know them, but only such jurisdiction as the Pope delegates to them. They have no cathedral, no chapter, no staff of diocesan officials, such as are supposed in the law. The law cannot be carried out: the life of the Church is

[4] Romans i. 14.   [5] 1 Cor. ix. 16.

Establishment of the Hierarchy in India.

struggling into form. The powers of the Vicar Apostolic are limited by the terms of his appointment, and may and do vary in different circumstances. Each carries his own special instructions; he receives exceptional powers; much, necessarily, is left to his discretion. Each stands alone: he is not the member of any ecclesiastical province; he may hold a meeting with other Vicars Apostolic, but they cannot form a Synod. Each Vicar Apostolic is personally responsible to the Holy Father, and his delegation as Vicar Apostolic may cease any moment at the will of the Holy Father.

Catholics, the children of the household, rightfully claim the first place in the thoughts of the Vicar Apostolic. His second duty he owes to those who sit in darkness. Lastly, his labours should advance the Kingdom of Christ, so that the vicariate may be expanded into a perfectly constituted diocese of the Church.

When the Bishop of Rome erects several vicariates in any country into regular dioceses, and groups them together in a province or provinces, he is said to have established the Hierarchy in that country.

Our Holy Father, Leo XIII., has substituted for the vicariate which previously existed in India, twenty-five regular sees, grouped in eight provinces, under the primacy of the Archbishop of Goa, with the title of Patriarch of the Indies; and thus has completed that establishment of the Hierarchy in India, which was promulgated in the Council of Allahabad on Thursday last.

The establishment of the present Hierarchy in India closes a remarkable chapter in the history of the Church. The Portuguese landed in India at the very close of the fifteenth century. Portugal at that time ranked as a first-class power. She was ruled by high-minded Christian princes; a long list of great names might be framed from the soldiers and statesmen who upheld the Portuguese flag in India. A succession of Apostolic missionaries carried on the work of St. Francis Xavier, and the Kings of Portugal, with truly royal munificence, seconded their labours. Portugal began a great work of civilization in India, chiefly through the preaching of her missionaries. In 1534 the see of Goa was founded as a suffragan bishopric to that of Funchal. Later it was raised to the dignity of metropolitan see over all the territories which Portugal might conquer. In 1557 it was established as an independent see and made an archbishopric. Suffragan sees were given to it, that of Cochin in the same year, that of Malacca in 1558, that of Macao in 1575, that of Cranganore in 1600, and that of Meliapur in 1606.

Here was the nucleus of a vast and grand Hierarchy. Alas! its growth was destined to be checked for nearly three centuries. Portugal did not maintain her place among the States of Europe; she could no longer send to India the troops and the treasures she had previously so lavishly given; the Dutch wrested many of her conquests from her, and needless to add, the conversion of the heathen ceased where the influence of Portugal was felt no longer.

At the same time British India was growing up. Year by year her rule became more widely extended, more firmly established. In the armies and navies of England Catholics fought and died; among her civil servants not a few professed the old faith. England had been an exclusively Protestant power; by degrees the persecuting enactments in her statute-books were repealed; Catholics recovered their rights as citizens, and their numbers in India continued to increase.

Many causes combined to prevent the Archbishop of Goa from sending to the Catholics in British India the priests they needed. Hence the Pope, the Universal Bishop, sent Vicars Apostolic to supply the want; and Vicars Apostolic were multiplied till the day arrived when Leo XIII. decided that this provisional form of government should give way to the normal organization of the Church, and the vicariates should be replaced by regular dioceses. Much, how much remains to be done in India! We have to create cathedrals, chapters, seminaries for many of the new dioceses; but our increasing numbers, the multiplication of priests, secular and regular, the rapid growth of our colleges, convents, and works of charity, influenced the Holy Father to organize the Church in India and rank her as a province among the older provinces of the Church.

Outwardly the change will appear to be one of name. Those who before guided you as Vicars Apostolic will for the most part continue to do so as your own Bishops. Your churches, your colleges, your schools, your orphanages will prosper as in the past. Your priests, your nuns will not relent in their devotedness. But as time rolls on, the fuller sap of Catholic life, the closer union with the other portions of the Church, the vitality of the organization of the Church will produce yet grander results. Your children, and your children's children, happy in their more favoured day, will bless the memory of our great Pontiff, Leo XIII., and will recount with grateful hearts the humble beginnings, the difficulties, the sacrifices, the devotedness of priests and people who prepared the way for the establishment of the Hierarchy in India.

In conclusion, I invite you, beloved brethren, to give glory to God, and to thank Him for the mercy He has vouchsafed to His Church in this country.

Unite in prayer to our King, Jesus Christ, on behalf of His Kingdom on earth, on behalf of His Vicar, on behalf of the Apostolic Delegate, finally on behalf of the Church in India and her newly appointed Bishops.

With greater zeal than ever, devote yourselves, your intelligence, your time, your worldly goods, in union with your pastors, to extend the good work you have commenced so well under their guidance.

CHAPTER XII.

FIRST MONTHS OF THE EPISCOPATE.

March to July, 1887.

The order of the day. Reminiscences of the last weeks in London and of the journey. Account of the Hindoos. Description of Fort Chapel, of the Archbishop's residence and commissariat. Hindoo ideas about the Blessed Eucharist. Arrival of the "precious mitre." Embarrassing variety of languages. Colleges and charitable institutions. On guarding against despondency. Description of Bombay and its inhabitants. Khandala. The gift of tongues. The Hindoo religion. Rukmabai. Child-marriages. Mahommedan women. Parsee women, their emancipation. Parsee persecution of converts to Christianity. Novelty of Bombay life. Pectoral cross. Hindoo marriages. Miss Martineau. The clergy. The native Christians. Graces that come in sickness. The rainy season. Excessive moisture. Indian customs. Feast of Corpus Christi. Proposed volume on Marriage. Portugal and India. The first Pastoral. Consecration of the Archdiocese to the Sacred Heart.

Fort Chapel, March 16, 1887.

. . . You ask for the order of the day. I rise between 4 and 5 a.m. I say Mass at 6.30. Dine at 12.30. Supper 7.30. Take *siesta* from 2 to 3 p.m. So far I am very well. The summer has delayed its visit; we are never without a breeze, and sometimes the breeze has force enough to set papers flying across the room. In Bombay, one grand object seems to be to get all the air possible. I am writing in a room provided with two doors and three good-sized windows, all more or less opened day and night. I have been fortunate in getting at least fair sleep every night. I find sleep not less important than food. The food is well cooked, and we cannot complain of short allowance.

I pretend to walk out for an hour every evening about sunset. Alas! I am often defrauded of this enjoyable exercise—a meeting to attend, visitors to be received, &c., &c. The days are already crowded with occupations which require time. As yet I have not done much preaching, nor have I heard a single confession. The church-life is gone through early at morning, or late, about sunset. The churches are none of them large, except the Cathedral, which stands in the native town, in the midst of a number of Hindoo temples. The congregation is motley—English-speaking, Portugese-speaking, Mahratti-speaking. Next week I take part in a public retreat, preached in all these languages, confining myself to English—*cela va sans dire*.

. . . .

The trip to Lourdes has my very cordial approval: you have certainly earned your holiday. Lourdes ought to benefit you body and soul; if you cannot walk about much, you can creep about in the neighbourhood of the Grotto. Remember Bombay and its pastor when you are there.

. . . .

As regards your visit to the Blessed Sacrament, try to get it in quite early or quite late, outside of business hours. Keep the time of business for business; otherwise you are apt to worry yourself all day about some devotion, to the serious detriment of the work, and to the detriment, too, of spiritual life, which thrives in peace and tranquillity.

Bombay, April 5, 1887.

Yours of March 15th reached me April 4th. I have been long in your debt; at any rate, I wish to begin well from Bombay.

You may imagine my surprise and horror at the

news of my nomination. I was perfectly helpless; I could not help myself, and no one else could help me. You can imagine what "flitting" from London involved. I do not remember ever to have passed through three such weeks, as the three first of last January. Thank God, I got through them. My overland journey to Brindisi was very fatiguing, but it was not without its consolations: a visit to Lourdes, a day at Loreto, and a talk with Father Anderledy at Fiesole. The rest of the journey was a delightful rest. Since my landing, I have not known much rest. The Queen's Jubilee commenced the day after. Within the week, a journey of 844 miles to Allahabad, where the Council was held, and where I was to be consecrated. The journey home, receptions, distributions of prizes, General Communions (two lasted an hour each), visits, dinners, parties—the day is too short for all; the lightest part being the sermons and Church work.

My flock—Europeans, good, not many; Eurasians, less good, more numerous; lastly, native Christians, good in their way, but trying. A grand work lies before me, and I am nibbled down by mosquitoes, metaphorically speaking. An empty treasury, a long list of debts and obligations. You see I have my cross. Happily my health is excellent, and I try not to let worries interfere with sleep or meals. God will help me in His own time.

Pray for me and my flock.

✠ GEORGE, Archbishop of Bombay.

Fort Chapel, April 7, 1887.

By this post I send you the pamphlet I promised you on the Hindoo child-widow. Perhaps you have seen in the *Times* a leader and some letters on what we know as the Rukmabai case. The lady has been sentenced to live with a man she was married to when she was eleven years old, or go to prison for six months. I won't go over the case, as I think you must be acquainted with the particulars. Much excitement prevails through India, especially in Bombay. The much wider question has been touched, viz., the position of woman in these Eastern populations. The position is a sad one, and the Church has a grand work to accomplish in the emancipation of woman. How much the West owes to the Blessed Mother of God! In this letter I must tell you a little of my observations on the Hindoos. They form the vast majority of our population in Bombay city. Physically they are very unequal. Many of the lower castes especially are very lean, slender-limbed specimens; among the Brahmins you meet finely-built men; and up-country sends us sturdy, well-made soldiers and policemen. They are of all shades, from a sickly olive to deep bronze. Some of the darker shades take my fancy much. The tailor's bill is kept down, as a rule, amongst the Hindoos. The children go quite naked till they are six or seven. After that age they put something round their loins. I have seen small urchins with just a thread, and what looks like a medal, enough to assert the principle of clothing. This dress round the loins grows till it assumes the importance of a cloth from two to three feet wide: the *dhoti*, it is called. This is wrapped round the waist, passed between the legs in a clever fashion, so that with some it assumes the appearance of a pair of drawers, reaching to the knee; with others it will fall to the ankles. When the *dhoti* is ample, the dress is most picturesque. The working men often wear nothing above the waist: the better class indulge their humour in jackets, and exhibit much taste. The men wear a white *dhoti*. The women who go about in the streets wear usually a red *dhoti*, always below the knee, and cover the upper part of their bodies with a green cloth which falls into all manner of shapes, generally, I may say always, leaving the arms free to carry burdens and work. The Christian Hindoos cover their arms, and a Hindoo Pagan is distinguished at once by the bare arm and silver armlets. All the Hindoo women dress modestly: the Christian Hindoos go through the streets wrapped in what looks like a sheet covering the head, but not curtailing the opportunity of observation. When the sheet flies open, you often see an immense display of pearls, chains, and jewels. All Hindoos love jewellery: they invest their money in ornaments, and call wearing them "enjoying their money." Both Christians and Pagans wear a ring, carrying pearls or stones, through one nostril: to our ideas this appendage does not improve their appearance. The Hindoos are very fond of their children: they frequently remind me of the Romans in this respect. They carry their babies and small people in a strange way; not on their backs or before them, but straddle-wise, on their side. Perhaps the load is less felt. The great number lead hard lives: they work early and late; they go about with heavy burdens; they live on very little and very simple food. Thousands sleep in the open air. The other night, returning late from a Parsee gathering, I saw hundreds and hundreds, stretched on the flags, generally with a mat or a cloth under them, many without any covering beyond their working suit, such as it might be, and many quite covered from head to foot with a sheet. A fine, nice sight met me as I went to an early Mass. Numbers of men, some very old, squatted on their haunches like monkeys, cleaning their teeth with brushes extemporized from bruised wood.

I stop for the present. I keep excellent health. I never felt better in my life. I wonder at myself. To-day I sang my first High Mass. I wish you a happy Easter, and send you my blessing.

Fort Chapel, April 8, 1887.

You express a wish to know something of my surroundings and mode of life. I write from Fort Chapel, you observe; it is situated within what was the fort (the walls of said fort were thrown down in 1863) in Medows Street; Sir William Medows was Governor of Bombay in 1790. The Archbishop of Goa, the Portuguese priests, and the Jesuits, were accused by the English of treasonable designs about 1718, and were banished from Bombay without any ceremony. The Carmelites were at the time in charge of the vicariate of the Great Mogul, who held his Court, I think, at Delhi. To them the English Government applied for Catholic priests, and with leave from Rome they accepted the mission, and the first Vicars Apostolic were Carmelites. The East Indian Company gave the Carmelites the ground on which Fort Chapel stands, and the chapel still keeps the name of Our Lady of Mount Carmel, and the figure of our Lady holding the scapular occupies a niche in the reredos. The chapel, which was enlarged by Bishop Meurin, my predecessor, at a pinch, might hold three hundred persons. I speak of a reredos. It is a considerable structure which nearly fills the wall at the altar end, by no means inelegant, mostly gilt on vermilion ground, the columns of *lapis lazuli*, blue and white. The little sanctuary looks very devotional. The chapel consists of what I may call a nave, one aisle on the Epistle side, the end of which screened off by a curtain serves for sacristy, and a side chapel on the Gospel side, a continuation of the sanctuary, with an altar at the far end. You enter Fort Chapel at No. 39. You find yourself in a porch the width of the sacristy aisle, the nave and a part of the side chapel; large doors open into the aisle and nave, and the door beyond the nave leads into our tiny, too tiny garden. A staircase on left-hand, facing the entrance from the street, leads to first floor. To the left of the porch lie coachyard, stables, and far behind kitchen, &c. When you have *climbed* the staircase, on your left you see a verandah, which has three entrances to first floor. Before you is a small ante-room which leads into a small dining-room (six fill it, eight would crowd it), and this leads into a private room. Every room in Bombay has at least two doors and two windows; the chief aim of Bombay life is to get air. Let us go back to the head of the stairs, and turn your back on the suite of small rooms. On your left the stairs take a turn to the upper regions; beyond them, as you move on, on your left is a door which leads to a gallery, a choir gallery for the chapel. Avoiding this door, and walking straight on, you enter a fair-sized parlour or reception-room, with a window on Medows Street, and a door giving on to the verandah, above described. On your left, as you face Medows Street, a curtain separates this room from a room which ought to be called a gallery; it runs over the aisle, the length of the chapel, and opens into the nave by a series of large windows. At the end, above the sacristy, is a private room. The first floor is lofty, so when you ascend the stairs you will see they break off, half-way up the wall. You turn right and gain the next storey by a steep step-ladder, which lands you on a verandah. From this verandah doors open into half a dozen small but well-ventilated rooms. Three of these I occupy more or less, my secretary has two others, and one we reserve for visitors. This suite of rooms runs over the entrance porch and a little beyond; for I did not tell you there is a room beyond the staircase on ground floor. If my description is intelligible, you will understand that I look through my windows across the garden towards the side chapel. You may puzzle out this picture as well as you can. The fort is rather closely built upon. Beside the fort, we have modern Bombay, which is magnificent and beautiful, with many striking buildings and fine open spaces; and the native city, which satisfies neither the sense of sight or smell. Bombay is an island, and hence the sea meets you wherever you turn for a walk or a drive.

Our commissariat is good enough for any one: those who are not satisfied ought to be sent to the work-house. The bread is fairly good, not equal to best London bread, but good. We have a novelty on London bread, in the shape of small brown loaves made from Indian corn. The coffee is good, if your cook knows how to deal with it. The milk, whether cow-milk or buffalo-milk, fails to convey the idea of green meadows; knowing people say buffalo-milk is bilious. The butter most people make at home: it is as white as snow, and cannot boast of much flavour. The eggs are good as far as they go; they don't go far, as they are much smaller than the eggs of English poultry. I hear that Persian hens produce a larger and a better egg; as yet I have not fallen in with them. Breakfast winds up with the inevitable banana, of which one never tires here. The mutton supply deserves all praise. Bombay cooks, however, incline to rubbishy dishes, brains, tongues, &c. We have some beautiful fish. Dinner is not complete without curry, and I accept the position without difficulty. The cook makes his own curry, and he has a long list of varieties; nor is he limited to one kind of chutney.

I think curry a very wholesome dish here. We have a great variety of very good fruit. The drink is soda-water, with whiskey or claret; the wines from Europe are dear, and on the whole rather unsatisfactory.

Bombay, April 15, 1887.

You say the Forty Hours with their soothing influence answers one's doubts about the Mystery of Faith. Very true; but add to this influence a series of meditations on the *Pange lingua*. See what we don't believe, as well as what we do. Don't go beyond that limit, and then you will find yourself saying with St. Peter, "To whom shall we go?" These Hindoos talk of the Blessed Sacrament as the God of the Christians; they are struck by the procession, the lights, flowers, &c., and they join in and burn incense as the Blessed Sacrament passes. I don't like this. These heathens have a great jumble of ideas; if possible, I would enforce the *disciplina arcani*, the old rule of the secret, and only admit well-seasoned Christians to the knowledge of the Blessed Eucharist, or to Mass, or to Holy Communion. The primary end of the institution, "Take ye and *eat*: this is My Body," is lost sight of to some extent in the more modern development of adoration, provoked by the denial of the Real Presence. As you know, Benediction is a modern practice. And reservation in the early ages was much tolerated, with a view to Holy Communion.

I should like to have heard Father Coleridge's sermons on the martyrs. Most theologians admit their special crown. Our Lady, however, reigns as Queen of Martyrs; her not dying with her Son being taken as the hardest part of her martyrdom.

. . . I hold the opinion, at least I am inclined to hold it, that the position of woman offers the most vulnerable point in Hindoo heathendom. In the old Pagan world, the Christian idea of marriage changed the lot of woman; the same idea ought to do as much again. My account of the Hindoos must be resumed in my next letter.

Fort Chapel, Bombay, April 21, 1887.

My dear ——

The "precious mitre" arrived in Bombay a fortnight ago, but it was detained more than a week in the Customs, for no particular reason that I can discover. I thank you with all my heart for this beautiful and costly gift. I confess to some feeling of awkwardness with so much splendour upon me; but I console myself, it is your offering to the worship of God. I showed it to Monsignor Agliardi, the Delegate, the very day he left India for Rome; he admired it much, and said he had not seen a finer one, even in Rome.

I have not written to you since I came out. I have sent you, however, several papers which will have told you, if you had the patience to read them, the principal events of my public life in Bombay. I was called upon to preach for the Empress-Queen's Jubilee the very day after I landed. I must not go over the history again for you; I will only add that you ought to have received a copy of a sermon I preached on the Hierarchy in India at Allahabad, on the evening of the day I was consecrated.

I am by way of being at work now; but the work is of a novel kind, and I find it rather bewildering. Bombay contains three distinct Catholic communities: the Europeans, the Goanese, and the native Christians who are not Goanese. The Goanese are native Christians, born in Goa, and brought up always under Goanese priests. The native Christians are descended from the converts of St. Francis Xavier and those who followed him. They are looked to by native priests; they retain much of the Hindoo dress; they observe the castes rigorously; they are good people after their own way, but would be better if they received more instruction. The language, or languages, rather stand in our way. The Marathi is the language most needed in our part, then Hindustanee is indispensable; Gujerati is wanted for the Parsees. Oh! if that Babel-building Co. had never started their wretched tower! A Brahmin takes me in hand every morning for half an hour, and torments me with strange letters and stranger sounds; my throat and nose attempt performances never before known to them. In the end I hope to learn my prayers and catechism in Marathi. With Hindustanee I hope to advance a little further.

Our native Christians have a turn for getting up rows, and they have a great ambition to administer the Church property.

We have in most churches an institution called the "Fabrica," which administers the income of the church, is answerable for the building, &c. Unpleasant quarrels and lawsuits not unfrequently arise.

Bombay can boast of a first-class College, St. Francis Xavier's, attended by 1,300 students, of whom 400 are non-Christian; St. Mary's, a Christian College, having 150 boarders, and perhaps 60 non-Christian day-scholars; two convents held by most devoted and holy nuns, who have between them perhaps 120 children; and we have various institutions: Deaf-Mutes, Foundlings Home, Lepers' Home, Widows' Home.

In another letter, I will tell you about the huge Pagan world which surrounds us, which, to some extent, is giving up their idolatry, but only to become quite materialistic. Some of the Protestant professors make no secret of their disbelief in Jesus Christ. Imagine the effect on half-educated Pagans! God bless you.

Yours very faithfully in Christ,
✠ GEORGE, Archbishop of Bombay.

Bombay, April 22, 1887.

... At the same time guard against discouragement. To all who wish to serve God it is a danger: in your case it is a special danger. "Even if He shall kill me I will hope in Him," was the hope of holy Job; you may take it and repeat it often.

Your tendency to despond forms the chief hindrance to your becoming a saint. Triumph over that tendency and work on patiently, and you will soon become a saint.

Fort Chapel, Bombay, April 27, 1887.

My dear Child,—

I am really writing from Khandala, a place up in the mountains somewhat less than one hundred miles from Bombay. I came up by the mail train last night, and return to Bombay by the mail on Friday morning. The native priests are making their retreat up here. The spot is very wild, abounds with snakes, occasionally a tiger is seen. The air is considered an improvement on Bombay air. The actual heat is greater, but it is drier and the house can be kept cool even during the day.

Bombay is a magnificent city. The European portion would bear comparison with almost any port in the world. I have met travellers who place Bombay A 1. No one in their senses could think of comparing Bombay with a little outlandish island like Jamaica. As Bombay is built on several islands, you are never very far away from the sea. The public buildings are on a scale of much magnificence. We had a railway station (I cannot say I think such magnificence in place), which most people take for a cathedral.

The native city does not please Europeans so much, it is crowded, ill-smelling, unsightly; but the people, their life, their shops, are most interesting.

Our population must be near on a million; certain vain Bombayites call Bombay the second city of the Empire. The Hindoos are the most numerous, next come the Mahommedans, then the Parsees, the Europeans form a mere handful. The greater part of our Christians are natives of India, descendants of those converted by St. Francis Xavier and his successors. Many of them very dark coloured. They dress like the Hindoos, only more modestly. In the native town nearly all the children run about quite naked till they are seven years old. After that the boys and men keep down their tailor's bill very conscientiously. The Pagan women (Hindoos) have their arms bare, and the dress does not descend much below the knee. The Christian women are known by the modesty of their dress. When they go to church, they wrap themselves up in what looks like a sheet (white). The native Christians are fervent in their way. Two or three times already I have given Holy Communion which lasted fully an hour.

I am answering your letters of February 28th and April 4th. I must thank you for your good wishes on St. George's day; also for the paper which comes regularly and is very welcome. Keep me *au courant* of all your news; I can never cease to feel an interest in the "fishing village," or to remember my old, old friends there. Keep up your courage about your own spiritual affairs, they are mending, and will mend still more. Only be faithful in using the means. Don't fail to let me know how you get on.

Khandala, April 28, 1887.

This is an answer to yours of April 1st. I came here on Tuesday night, and return to Bombay on Friday. The native priests are making their retreat, and I want to be near them. Khandala is about 70 miles from Bombay, about 30 from Poona in the Ghanta, 2,000 feet above the sea. Our Fathers have two large places here, a *sanatorium* and a *villegiatura* for themselves and their scholars. The heat is great during the day, but the mornings and evenings are deliciously cool. Mosquitoes don't worry one, and mosquito-curtains are not required. There is a native village of Khandala, distant half a mile. Otherwise the solitude is perfect; we are close to the jungle. Some of your aunt's Anglican Sisters, from Poona, with a party of their scholars, have pitched their tents on a hill, not half a mile away. This tent-life (the tents are double) is in fashion in India. In Bombay itself, on the beach, gentlemen and families go under canvas for a time. The tents are not expensive. Everything has been reduced to system. Perhaps £1 is claimed by the municipality for the ground; a good tent can be had for £1 per week; the man who lets the tent sets it up, and your commissariat you contract for or manage through the Goanese butler.

Tell —— that the Anglicans have a Bishop of Bombay, Dr. Mylne; he came out as a Cowley Brother, but shocked Bombay by taking a wife, and saying he did so by the advice of his confessor. He is a good man and a learned man, but he is not popular in Bombay. Tell —— I consider him a wolf in sheep's clothing, an intruder.

The Cowley Brothers and Sisters devote themselves with much zeal to various good works, in Bombay and up country. They have opened communications with the Hindoos, give them lectures, discuss with them, but they get no farther. They have no mission.

I sent you a Railway Guide and occasional papers, and my Allahabad sermon; they may occupy a leisure hour, and give you some notion of Bombay and Indian life.

I have not yet received the Portuguese books you sent by Parcels Post on March 30th. . . . The gift of tongues will only be given after long and hard study. The Marathi alphabet has given me a week's work. A clever, nice Hindoo teaches me for half an hour every day except Sunday. He comes every day with his two strokes of red paint on his forehead ; by these he declares himself a worshipper of some special deity. I have not yet learnt the mysteries of all these signs which the Hindoos carry on their foreheads ; some day I hope to be initiated. A word now about the Hindoo religion. The Brahmins count in their number some really learned men, learned in their philosophy, and in their literature. They keep their followers completely in the dark, or mystify those who have come in contact with Western life by denying that they are idolaters, and giving a symbolical meaning to their idols and worship. The fact is, Hindooism consists in gross idolatry, carried on with endless lights, tom-toming, *i.e.* drumming, and unmeaning cries. It is a most impure religion, and much obscenity and indecency is mixed up with their festivals. Some of their worship has come to light in the courts. The very temples and idols scarcely attempt to veil the wickedness. One sees the depth to which the devil has degraded his victims. The result is, in their language, in their quarrels, they say what Christians, even bad ones, could hardly imagine. The better class of Hindoos are ashamed to talk to Christians about their practices.

Fort Chapel, Medows Street, May 5, 1887.

Yesterday evening I received the *pacco postale* containing the Portuguese dictionary and the two grammars. I have just turned over the pages of all three vols., and I think they contain what I want; the dictionary has a modern look about it, as if it were not a mere reprint. Accept my best thanks.

I have your letter of April 14th. I hope you received a lecture on child-marriages by Sir W. W. Hunter, which I posted to you perhaps four weeks ago. He will tell you more about the matter than Rukmabai's letter (bai is a feminine termination, and tells Rukma had never been a boy). Some of the Hindoo ideas are very strange. No man can be saved in the next world unless he has a son to look after him. Hence an insane craving for boy babies. Every woman must be married, under great penalties in this world and in the next. Hence the dread of parents, lest their daughters be left unmarried. The practical miseries to which this system of baby-marriages give rise are innumerable. Even in my short experience I come upon them, viz., a young Christian girl wants to marry a Christian; as a child she was married to a man who has gone to some other part of the world, and left no word of his whereabouts. The girl before the law is the wife of this wanderer, and may not marry; she never lived with the man. In Madras a Christian woman who married a Christian man, though as a Pagan she had been married to a Hindoo, has been condemned for bigamy, and the priest who assisted at the marriage for abetting. I am not sure that the Judge in the Madras case did not lay much stress on the omission of some formality, the omission to have the first marriage declared null and void. I trust the Rukmabai agitation will give a blow to these Hindoo baby-marriages. As far as I understand, Christianity brought about the emancipation of women by insisting on the laws of marriage, and by the example of those who kept the Counsels. This morning I saw a lady who has had exceptional opportunities of studying Mahommedan life. She had the *entrée* into the zenana of one of the native princes, and became very friendly with the ladies. She says, with one or two exceptions, they are most ignorant, show no mind, and she wound up, " They are little better than animals." A sad picture which, I fear, does no injustice to the Mahommedan women of India and elsewhere.

The Parsee women have emancipated themselves or been emancipated by their husbands and fathers. They appear in public, in carriage, walking, sometimes driving; they visit foreign lands; they learn and speak modern languages; but on the question of religion they are held in great restraint. Some are brought up, as day-scholars, in convents. They remain much attached to the nuns, visit them, send them presents, but never, or very seldom, will speak on religion. The Parsees live in great awe of their Punchayet, a committee or ruling body, chosen in some way amongst themselves, which forbids all conversions to Christianity. I know two Parsee gentlemen who have become Catholics; one is driven out of Bombay, the other staves off his fate by keeping as quiet as possible. I fear he will soon be forced to declare himself, and then have to brave a sad persecution.

You see here some of the problems of my new life. Pray that I may do some good before I die.

Fort Chapel, May 5, 1887.

Your letter of April 12th reached me on May 2nd. The mail from London takes seventeen or eighteen days to Bombay. I thank you for all your good wishes and prayers. My letter will reach you before Pentecost. May the Holy Ghost enrich you with a large measure of His gifts, and bless your undertakings. I won't forget to pray for you and your retreat. . . . What you tell me of the services and the sermons, &c., . . . interests me much. Only it all seems a very long way off, as if it belonged to another world, which I had left. This Bombay life is very strange, and very unlike anything I have known before. I seldom hear a confession, preach very rarely, not for want of will, but for want of a church and of a congregation that can understand me. I preached in the Cathedral the day after my arrival, for the Queen's Jubilee; at Allahabad the day of my consecration; three or four mission sermons in the Cathedral during Passion Week; at some Confirmations, *voila tout*. I sit at my desk from 8 a.m. till 12; again from 3 p.m. till 6 p.m. I have plenty of writing to get through.

The languages form a great difficulty. I ought to know at least Hindustani and Marathi. I am learning Marathi. The alphabet is a very strange one. I find it hard. I take lessons every day from a Pagan, a nice fellow enough, but a real idolater.

Unfortunately neither the Government nor our Church authorities encouraged English. Some silly people actually make it a point to keep up Portuguese. The English spoken here, and the English the natives print in English papers, is not what would pass muster in London or even in Liverpool. Then we live in the midst of a Pagan world, worshippers of idols, worshippers of the sun, of the rain, Mahommedans, anything but

Christians, and no way of getting at them. Why don't your Sisters come to India? Have you any rule against it? The other day an old Parsee offered me a large sum of money to found a blind asylum. What do you say to coming out here and ending your days in the East? I sometimes think the conversion of India will be brought about by nuns. The great obstacle to conversion is the position of woman in the East, and her terrible degradation. Nothing very lasting can be accomplished till this evil is remedied. Pray for India and for the millions of poor Indian women. . . .

Perhaps A—— and B—— will now revive the tradition of the last generation, and make a retreat every year. This example would do great good to many. Did I tell you that A—— gave me my pectoral cross. He had bought it at Rome to keep it out of the hands of the Jews. A—— thought he would present it to the first of his friends who should be made Bishop. Little did he think I was to be that unfortunate friend. I keep well, thank God. Thermometer about 90°.

Sursum corda! and keep up your courage. God bless you.

Fort Chapel, May 22, 1887.

. . . We have entered on monsoon arrangements, viz., the mail leaves Bombay on Tuesday instead of Friday. Last week the telegraph told us that the monsoon had broken at Colombo on the 18th; it takes about twelve or fourteen days on its way along the coast to Bombay. Of the monsoon I will tell you more when it comes to us, now I can only say it is our rainy season. The steamers from Bombay are obliged to go south, and then they try to catch the monsoon wind, and run before it to Aden. Their contract allows them three days longer for the transport of the mail; hence the earlier start.

Hindoo marriages. These poor people pay a great penalty for their institutions. It is believed that the much larger number of Hindoo families are always in debt on account of the extravagant expenses entailed by these marriages. A family in very moderate circumstances must spend between three and four thousand rupees, roundly £300 to £400.

Instances of cruelty to wives are very common. The ordinary punishment is to disfigure the face by cutting off the nose, or to brand the poor creature with a hot iron on different parts of the body. One consequence to Bombay has been that the making of fresh noses is well known here! Our wise people in Europe forget how much they owe to the Church, and that she has raised them out of the depths of paganism. So much for Hindoos. . . .

. . . My hands are rather full. I am contemplating a Pastoral on the Sacred Heart. Then I am tempted to write a book on Marriage. I would like to try my idolaters and infidels with tracts on the Existence of God and the Divinity of Jesus Christ. Mountains of projects rise before my eyes; in fact, my time is short, and much goes in worrying *minutiæ* and trifles. . . .

Fort Chapel, May 27, 1887.

This is my answer to your two letters of the 23rd of April and the 5th of May. The volume, *Men of the Time*, arrived by the last mail. I thank you for it very much: it will be useful to the *Examiner*. I want, if possible, to raise the *Examiner*. A first-class paper might do much good in India; but here, as in other departments, we want hands, or rather brains. Don't give yourself any more trouble to find *How to Observe*. Miss Martineau never won my admiration. She was a weak, credulous, odious atheist. If you chance to meet a copy, well; but don't trouble to hunt it any further. My dream of making great use of the Press has commenced to vanish: the ground which I thought was unoccupied is not so free as I had imagined.

You ask about my clergy. Two live with me at the fort. Father McDonough, an Irishman, edits the *Examiner*. Father ——, my secretary, is a German. Bombay belongs to the German Province, S.J., and I suppose between Fathers and Brothers they reach the number of 50, mostly employed in the two large Colleges of St. Xavier, with 1,300 students, of whom 400 are non-Christians, and St. Mary's, a boarding-school, with 150 boarders, all Christian, and perhaps 100 day scholars, in part non-Christians. Some of the Fathers take care of the Boys' Orphanage at Bandora, which remains under my jurisdiction, although in the diocese of Damaô, under Goa.

The native clergy are about twenty—four at the Cathedral, the others in single missions as a rule—real natives, all descended from Hindoos converted under the Portuguese. The ever-changing plans of our Indian Administration has lessened the European, much to our loss, and, I think, to the loss of English influence. The natives, clergy and laity, are a peculiar race, not at all easy to manage. Some day I will send you a native paper, from which you will be able to form an idea of the native mind, its infirmities, and its aspirations. So far I keep very well with the native clergy, and hope to continue on good terms: they work well according to their lights. One drawback is the want of a fine church in the European quarter. The Cathedral is a fairly good-sized church, but stands in the midst of the native town. The other churches are miserably small.

Bombay society does not strike me favourably: it

may improve on a closer acquaintance. There are some very nice people, a few of them Catholics. Bombay society is a very changing element. At present the Catholics are not well represented; time was they were strong in numbers and position. I have no heavy commissions this mail: I send a light one. Ask B. and O. if they have not all the Encyclicals, &c., of Leo XIII. in one small handy volume? If so, I should be glad to have a copy.

Fort Chapel, Medows Street, Bombay,
May 31, 1887.

My dear Child,

Yesterday's mail brought me a packet—Père Monsabré's *Sermons* and Père Ravignan's *De l'Institut des Jésuites*. The address was written in a handwriting not quite like your usual one; but I know you either sent it or induced some one to send it for you. Accept my very grateful thanks. Both books will be very useful to me.

This Bombay life resembles nothing of my previous experiences. The heat has touched its highest point, pretty nearly 93° Fahr. out of the sun. In my verandah at night it falls to 85°. It is not so unbearable, I assure you, but it must sound very dreadful to you. We enjoy a constant, or almost constant breeze. I eat, sleep, and work pretty much as I did in Europe. I keep my health.

The work is quite different from London work. Not much preaching, scarcely any confessions; a great deal of writing; many functions; receptions, addresses, bouquets, garlands thrown over one's neck, &c. Before long I trust I shall get into the way of doing something suited to the climate and to the people. These native Christians are curious in their ideas and ways. They are not very well instructed; they are impressionable;

easily fall the victims of designing people; delight in tremendously tall talk, in violent speeches, in long letters. They are not always reasonable. As yet I have not got to be quite at home with my work: that will come in time. Pray for me. I sent you a sermon which I preached at Allahabad, in the evening of the day on which I was consecrated. Let me know in case it did not reach you. When you write, I shall expect some account how your spiritual affairs are going on. I hope Pentecost has been a feast of peace, joy, and courage. Have you managed a retreat yet? God bless you. Good-bye.

I remain, yours very truly in Christ,

✠ GEORGE, Archbishop of Bombay.

Fort Chapel, June 6, 1887.

I added my *Deo gratias* to yours very cordially when I read your letter of May 20th, announcing that your brother had been received into the Church. God is good, and His ways are very wonderful. I trust you have been able to visit him before now, and pray with him and give him courage. One effect of his malady is often to render the sufferer very desponding and lifeless and dead to everything. Perhaps God in His mercy has spared him this trial, and given him great peace and joy. Meanwhile, the grand point has been secured, and he now belongs to the true Church, and will have the help of the sacraments. To-morrow I will offer the Holy Sacrifice in thanksgiving for this wonder of grace. . . .

Death has been busy of late in your circle. . . . You must not be surprised if these sudden deaths do not make a deep impression on you: that sort of insensibility goes rather with the state of bodily health. One is too much beaten down sometimes to feel anything. Do not consider this a bad sign, as if it implied something wrong spiritually. The soul may be quite right with God, notwithstanding this numbness of feeling. As long as you keep the commandments, and wish to love and serve God, and wish to serve Him perfectly, make your mind easy. The rest at —— ought to do more for you than a retreat. Let your rest be as complete as possible. Go to the church; kneel there or sit down, and without any effort to pray, remain quiet before God. Pray when you feel disposed and as you feel disposed. And if the day is fine and nature smiles upon you, do the same in some quiet cheerful spot, or roam through a pretty glade, or join in easy talk with some genial companion. The least easy practice at such times is to accept the state of deadness with patience, and to believe that by so doing you are offering a good act of homage to your Creator. Take all from His hands, and try to believe that there is good in all He permits, even though we don't see it. When your health has been somewhat set up, then a retreat taken very quietly will do you much good.

You ask after my native priests. I suppose I have about twenty in the archdiocese. They are real natives, of a decidedly dark hue: true Hindoos, the descendants of the converts won over by the labours of St. Francis Xavier and his successors under the Portuguese. Hence the majority bear Portuguese names—Albuquerque, Almeida, Lima, Rosario, Gomez, &c. This leads to much confusion, as the same name has been taken by different families, very probably from their godfathers. The caste system lingers among our Christians to a considerable extent. Most are from the lower castes, and those who are Brahmins are not a little conscious of their superiority. Several of the Bishops in the last century were Brahmins. One of our difficulties is to extirpate Hindoo superstitions at marriages, in sickness, &c., among our native Christians; and only the other day I heard of worse—Christians keeping two or three wives, and not seeing the evil in it. . . .

Fort Chapel, June 28, 1887.

. . . I have been much interested in all you tell me about Y——. He has received a great grace, for which we ought to be for ever thankful. A long, tiresome sickness seems very dreadful to a person in health. I believe the invalid does not feel all that the looker-on imagines he does; he suffers, but not as we fancy. Who knows these days and nights when Y—— could not rest, may have been among the most precious moments of his whole life? Grace comes at such times to remind us whose we are, what we ought to have done and have not done, that we must cry to God for pardon and help. The long lingering end is part of the trial: don't be uneasy about it. God rules every moment of our course for His wise ends. I dare say you have already made the discovery that oftentimes the best way of helping the sufferer is to remain quiet, to read, write, work without talking, unless spoken to. Silence is such a comfort very often to a sick person; to be left alone, not to be petted or sympathized with in words; to know some one is near, ready at a moment to render a service, to answer a question—that satisfies the sufferer. Then at times to repeat some *very short* ejaculation, some familiar prayer, some reminder of the Passion of our Lord. Long prayers weary the enfeebled capacity for attention. I believe the soul gains and merits immensely during all the seeming confusion and unspiritual appearance of the surroundings. I will continue my prayers for Y—— till the end.

By this time you will have made your retreat. A private one would help you much, if you can make it quietly, taking what God sends and not worrying for something else. I dare say you would be more helped by a private retreat than by a public one.

You are in fear about your faith and your hope, because you *feel* (often it is only feeling) as if you could not stand persecution, or illness, or this or the other, as if all were on the point of giving way once and for ever. This feeling is a trial, but it adds to your merit if you don't give way, if you struggle on. Remark, you always seem to be giving way, and you don't give way. Fidelity ought to be the answer to these desponding thoughts. St. Francis Xavier wrote that he could not go on; but he did go on, and I suppose that his life appeared more meritorious to God because he had to contend with such thoughts. I sometimes think the prayer of petitions helps one at such moments—*Deus in adjutorium meum intende,* and the hundred and one forms in which David calls upon God: "Even if Thou shalt slay me, yet will I hope in Thee." ...

I have no news to add to the *Bombay Examiner*. My health keeps up, thank God. The heat between the showers of the rainy season is, if anything, more melting than that of the dry season. But what a luxuriance of green!

July 10, 1887.

Such showers! The rain beats in everywhere. You are flooded in a room before you have time to get out of your chair, when the storm bursts without warning. The dampness of the air cannot be described. Clothes, linen, shoes, every article of dress, is damp; envelopes are all closed for you before you use them; books in my drawer are mildewed; libraries have a bad time of it. What shall I say about vestments, gilding, &c.? Your imagination must fill up the picture. And this will last till the end of September, with more or fewer breaks. The result is a certain sense of discomfort. The thermometer still keeps near 80°, and, what seems impossible, one may feel chilly in that temperature. . . .

The household here offers a wide field for an observer. Cook, butler, hamal, malee, lamp-man, coachman—each tempts one to make a portrait. Then nearly every class of the natives, every shopkeeper, almost every individual, deserves a separate page. And what faces, what attitudes. How often have I wished I had an instantaneous photographic apparatus to fix a face or group that I see in the streets; or a side of the street in the early morning, when the inhabitants in their scanty attire may be seen washing their teeth, or doing the barber to each other, all before the whole world; or the benevolent Hindoo devoutly strewing sugar near the trees on the Esplanade, for the ants; or the holy cow, very sleek and fat, which goes from house to house on its own account, having no earthly master or owner. Not long since a devout Hindoo gave a live bull to one of his gods, and turned the animal loose. A less worshipful mortal collared the bull and yoked him in his cart. Thereupon followed a lawsuit; the devout man claimed the bull, but the Judge decided the bull was not his, he had given it to his god, and he implied that the deity had not looked after his property. Giving bulls as offerings to the gods will drop out as a common practice; the holy cow may survive longer, as it is harmless, and seems more than content with its lot.

Fort Chapel, July 12, 1887.

The mail will start very soon; I do not know how far I shall get in my letter. I begin with my begging. Will you kindly send me two copies of Freppel's *Conferences*, and two of Bougaud's *Argument for the Divinity of Jesus Christ*? One of the professors of the University invited me to his house; I spent two days with him. He accepts Prop. I.: There exists a God. He will accept Prop. III.; If Jesus Christ was God, the Roman Catholic Church is Divine in its origin. He hesitates at Prop. II.: The Man Jesus Christ was truly God. He is honest, and though his wife thinks he gives in too much, I hope he and she and four nice children will receive the gift of faith. Freppel and Bougaud would help him.

Many thanks for the account of Wimbledon Church and the Corpus Christi at Manresa. All delightful to read about, and much in contrast with my present surroundings. Corpus Christi falls during the rainy season. This year the rain did not prevent our procession. But such a procession! by lamp-light, in the Cathedral Compound; clergy and people enough for a fine procession; two altars in the Compound; Benediction at each; a Gospel from St. John, sung as at High Mass, at both altars. I could not help recalling Corpus Christi as I had seen it at Stonyhurst, Beaumont, and Manresa. . . .

. . . If leisure for writing comes to me—it has not come yet—I will write a volume on Marriage. Since I have come out here my ideas have taken a much wider range; I see farther than I did before and more clearly, and I flatter myself I can put together many thoughts which will waken an echo in right-minded readers, of whom the world is full. I shall begin at once to jot down notes. The conviction grows upon me that conversion on any great scale must be preceded by the emancipation of woman. . . .

Fort Chapel, Bombay, July 18, 1887.

God is very good, granting a reprieve to Y——; patience in sickness and resignation to the omnipotent will of God, and some prayer and an occasional Communion make up for many delays and omissions. I would suggest the Psalms, or even only verses from them, as generally welcome to the sick and suffering. Psalm cii. (Douay) soothes beyond measure, and so does the *De profundis.*

I shall be glad to see the notes of my three retreats. They will come like ghosts from the land of the past; I shall be curious to look them through. I always found no two retreats were alike (save in the general character), and it was a question for me what influences worked on me whilst I was preaching them. I was sometimes inclined to think that the good angels of my audience suggested many things.

Before you receive this, you ought to receive my first Pastoral, which treated on the devotion to the Sacred Heart. You must tell me if you do not get a copy.

On Wednesday I go up to Kirkee, about five hours' rail, to make my retreat. I want it so much after the revolution in my life; you can easily imagine how I look forward to it. A rest in some sense it will be, but it must be a preparation for very serious work. Signs are not wanting that I may have to face great opposition.

I never explained to you the state of India. In old times, when Portugal was great and Catholic, the Popes gave to the Archbishops of Goa a most extraordinary jurisdiction, extending over all the East. When Portugal fell into insignificance, she clung to this jurisdiction, and refused to surrender it or any portion of it to the Pope himself. The old Goan clergy were learned and good, but their successors were too often neither learned nor good. The native Christians are sincerely attached to Portugal, or rather to the native clergy of Goa, who are clever enough to identify themselves with Portugal. Portuguese is encouraged, much to the injury of our Christians, who would gain by learning English. The natives (I mean the descendants of Hindoos converted by St. Francis Xavier and his successors), Christian or not Christian, don't like the foreigner; and the name of a Propagandist priest rouses the native Christian easily. Leo XIII. has made great concessions to Portugal, but he has laid the foundation of a new and a better order of things. The designing men who lead the native Christians won't give up their game without a struggle. They talk of building an opposition cathedral and seminary in Bombay. So far, I have maintained a masterly inactivity, and my ignoring their intrigues and themselves has somewhat paralyzed them. But the time is near when they must do something or die; I look out for a lively time. At all times and everywhere, a Bishop's life is made up of small worries. What does it matter whether they come in this form or that? We can only do our best, and leave God to guide all things and us too.

Good-bye. God bless you. I pray for you and your intentions every day at Mass.

GEORGE,

By the Grace of God and the favour of the Apostolic See,

ARCHBISHOP OF BOMBAY,

TO

Our Reverend Brethren the Clergy, Secular and Regular, and our Beloved Children, the Faithful Laity of the said Archdiocese.

Health and Benediction in the Lord!

"And this is life everlasting, that they may know Thee, the only true God, and Jesus Christ, Whom Thou hast sent."[1] To know and to confess the only true God, to know and confess His only Son made Man, Jesus Christ—this is life everlasting. Thus preached St. Peter to the Jews after the descent of the Holy Ghost: "Ye men of Israel, hear these words: Jesus of Nazareth, a Man approved of God among you, by miracles, and wonders, and signs, which God did by Him in the midst of you, as you also know. This same, being delivered up by the determinate counsel and foreknowledge of God, you have crucified and put to death by the hands of wicked men; Whom God hath raised up, having loosed the sorrows of Hell, as it was impossible that He should be detained by it. This Jesus hath God raised up again, whereof we all are witnesses."[2] And later, before the High Priest and the Council: "The God of our Father hath raised up Jesus, Whom you put to death, hanging Him upon a tree. This Prince and Saviour God hath exalted with His right hand to give penitence to Israel and remission of sins. And we are witnesses of these things, and the Holy

[1] St. John xvii. 3. [2] Acts ii. 22, 23, 24, 32.

Ghost Whom God hath given to all those that obey Him."[3] Not otherwise Philip, going down to the city of Samaria, preached Christ to them.[4] And when the gift of salvation was extended to the Gentiles, St. Peter thus delivered his message before the devout centurion, Cornelius: "In truth I perceive that God is no respecter of persons. But in every nation He that feareth Him and worketh justice, is acceptable to Him. God sent the word to the children of Israel, preaching peace through Jesus Christ: (He is the Lord of all). You know the word which hath been published through all Judea: for it began from Galilee, after the baptism which John preached; Jesus of Nazareth, how God anointed Him with the Holy Ghost and with power: Who went about doing good, and healing all that were oppressed by the devil: for God was with Him. And we are witnesses of all things which He did in the land of the Jews and in Jerusalem; Whom they killed, hanging Him upon a tree. Him God raised up the third day and gave Him to be made manifest. Not to all the people, but to witnesses preordained of God; even to us, who ate and drank with Him after He rose again from the dead. And He commanded us to preach to the people, and to testify that it is He Who hath been appointed by God to be the judge of the living and the dead. To Him all the Prophets give testimony, that, through His name all receive remission of sins who believe in Him."[5] The same message St. Paul delivered to Jew and Gentile; the same message the other Apostles preached to the uttermost ends of the earth; the same message the Catholic Church repeats, and to the end of time will continue to repeat to succeeding generations. This is life everlasting, to believe in one God and in His only Son made Man, Jesus Christ. "No one cometh

---

[3] Acts v. 30, 31, 32.   [4] Acts viii. 5.   [5] Acts x. 34—43.

to the Father but by Me."[6] "He is Antichrist who denieth the Father and the Son. Whosoever denieth the Son, neither hath he the Father. He that confesseth the Son, hath the Father also."[7] "Nor is there salvation in any other; for there is no other name under heaven given to men, whereby we must be saved."[8]

Christ loved us and gave Himself up for us. The Church throughout all time dwells on this wondrous love of her Redeemer and her King. Her thoughts soar ever to the contemplation of the mysteries of this love; her memory loves to dwell on its endless manifestations, on the Incarnation, on the Passion and bitter Crucifixion, on the Blessed Eucharist, on the Priesthood, on the Sacraments, on her eternal espousals with her Divine Lord; her heart yearns to repay love with love, to grow in the love of Jesus Christ, to spread the knowledge and love of Him. Deepest love, most devoted loyalty to the Person of Jesus Christ, must ever be the soul of the life of the Church. Personal love of Him explains the holiness of the saints, the heroism of the martyrs, the zeal of the Apostles and confessors, the heavenly lives of the virgins.

The love of the Church has found many expressions, in the burning words of her Liturgy, in fervent worship, in tender veneration of the very image of Christ crucified. To-day we invite you, dearly beloved Brethren, to consider the love of the Church for Jesus Christ manifested in the devotion to His Sacred Heart.

How naturally the mind turns to the heart, the heart of flesh, that centre of a part of our life, from which the living blood flows, to which it returns; the heart of flesh, which answers so promptly to our changing affections, which expands in joy and hope, which contracts in fear

---

[6] St. John xiv. 6.   [7] 1 St. John ii. 22, 23.   [8] Acts iv. 12.

and sadness. In every language the heart is synonymous with love, it is the universal symbol of love.

The material Heart of Jesus Christ was the centre of His Divine-human life. It responded to all the affections of His soul. It was as the battlefield on which His immense love for our salvation contended and strove and suffered and conquered. Were that Divine Heart cold in death, what a treasure It would be accounted! What shrine could be imagined worthy to receive It? What gems sufficiently bright, what jewels sufficiently costly to have place in its adornment? Even in death that Sacred Heart would claim Divine adoration, as the dead Body of Jesus Christ in the tomb received Divine honours from the Angels. Death separated the Soul of Jesus Christ from His Body; its power did not, could not reach the Hypostatic Union, by which the Second Person of the Blessed Trinity assumed to Himself once and for ever the Sacred Humanity and all its essential parts.

The triumph of death quickly came to an end. The Soul of Jesus Christ on the third day rejoined His Body in the tomb, and the Sacred Humanity rose to a new and a glorified life, in which the Sacred Heart bears Its share. The Heart of Jesus in Heaven partakes of the whole of His glorified life. The sufferings of His Infancy, His Public Life, His Crucifixion, are graven there, though the wound opened by the spear is resplendent with beauty. The love which prompted the Incarnation, which crowned that mystery of self-abasement with that other Mystery of self-abasement, the Blessed Eucharist, glows in the Sacred Heart, and the desires for the salvation of men, the pleadings for the remission of their sins, the longings to set on fire the hearts of men with the love of His Father have grown yet more intense on His throne of glory. His parting gift to the world, reconciled with its offended God, the Sacrament of the Altar, brings that Heart to every heart which in truth and justice confesses and loves the only Son of the living God.

You make no division in Jesus Christ, when you honour His Divine Heart. You do not, even in thought, separate it from His Sacred Humanity. You worship It, throbbing in His breast with the life of His Blessed Body, answering to all the affections of His Soul, and sanctified as the very sanctuary of the living temple of the Divinity.

You understand what reason teaches and what the Church inculcates, viz., that all honour tends ultimately to the person, and never stops short of the person. The devout woman hoping to be healed, touched the hem of the garment of Jesus; her faith, her adoration reaches His Divine Person. The courtier kisses the sceptre of his sovereign, the act of homage he directs to the royal person. The orphan clasps to her bosom the image of the mother she has lost; this outpouring of love is intended for the loved person, torn away by death. Thus when you honour and adore the Sacred Heart, you adore the Person of Jesus Christ, the Person of the Son made Man. "I adore Thee, O Heart of my Saviour," only expresses in another form, "I adore Thee, my Saviour, in thy Sacred Heart."

Prayer and invocation take their place among the expressions of veneration and worship. When you offer your petitions, your praises, your thanksgivings to God, to Jesus Christ, to the saints, you honour the Creator or His creature each according to his majesty and dignity. Your petitions, your praises are addressed to the person. "Have mercy on me, O Heart of Jesus!" only cries in another form, "Jesus, by Thy Heart, have mercy on me!" Or, "By the love of Thy Heart, have

S

mercy on me." Human thought and human language seek expression of the deeper feelings by personifying the heart, the eyes, the lips. Heart of Jesus! is a loving, fervent personification, prompted by the thought of that Heart, and all its past and present love. The representation of the Heart of Jesus encircled by the crown of thorns, surmounted by the Cross, in the midst of light and flames, in language which all can understand, recalls the wonderful love of Jesus Christ which nailed Him to the Cross, and prompted that invention of love, the institution of the Blessed Eucharist as a remembrance of His Death.

This language of the Heart was understood by the Church from its birth. The privilege of St. John has ever been appreciated in every age. "Now there was leaning on Jesus' bosom one of His disciples whom Jesus loved."[9] The wounded side, the bleeding Heart of the dying Redeemer, fixed the wonder and devotion of the earliest ages. Jesus dead on the Cross recalled Adam in his mysterious sleep. Eve built from one of the ribs taken out of the side of Adam in this sleep, was the type of Mother Church, built out of the Sacred Heart, stilled in the sleep of death; the blood and the water which gushed forth signifying the Sacrament of Baptism and the treasures of the Precious Blood. Later, as the devotion of the faithful to the Passion of our Lord grew more intensified during the wars for the Holy Sepulchre, what was the favourite image? The Five Wounds, the wounded Hands, the wounded Feet, the wounded Heart in the centre, from which the Precious Blood flows into a chalice; or from which rise the Divine plants, faith, hope, and charity, justly called in an ancient English picture the Well of Life. When in the lapse of ages, heresies and divisions multiplied, many saints, each in

[9] St. John xiii. 23.

his own way, turned to the Sacred Heart as to the very centre of their spiritual life; their aspirations, their words, their writings breathed this devotion to the love of Jesus in His Sacred Heart, repeating the same tale of love, in all the varied and endless language of love. The limits of a Pastoral exclude the list of the many holy names which in the history of the devotion to the Sacred Heart of Jesus prepared the way for the revelation of that devotion by our Blessed Lord to His humble servant Blessed Margaret Mary, a little more than two hundred years ago. To her He made known His wish that a festival should be instituted in honour of His Sacred Heart; that the Friday following the octave of Corpus Christi should be set apart for the festival; that the devotion, founded always on the love of the Sacred Heart of Jesus which has loved man so well, should undertake the work of reparation to the Sacred Heart for the ingratitude with which Its love has been repaid, especially in the Blessed Eucharist and the further work of spreading the knowledge and the love of the Sacred Heart of Jesus amongst men. In this revelation Jesus Christ gave a more definite form to the devotion which had existed in the Church from the beginning.

The devotion to the Sacred Heart is not unknown to you, dearly beloved brethren. You have adopted it eagerly, and you cherish it lovingly. But in the beginning the enemies of Jesus Christ resisted its progress by all the means in their power: misrepresentation, ridicule, blasphemy, open violence were employed. Something of the kind delayed the institution of the feast of Corpus Christi. A similar opposition awaited the efforts of St. Bernardine of Siena in spreading the devotion to the Holy Name of Jesus.

Within our time only has the devotion completely triumphed within the Church, outside the Church it cannot be understood. The Church possesses a literature of the Sacred Heart: theological treatises, historical records, collections in verse and prose. The arts have contributed their homage; the sculptor, the painter, have multiplied statues and pictures of the Sacred Heart. Churches raised in honour of the Sacred Heart are found in every land.

Who can enumerate the pilgrimages, the associations, the confraternities to which this devotion has given rise? You have amongst you the Apostleship of Prayer, that vast organization of suppliants before the throne of mercy, under the standard of the Sacred Heart; the Living Rosary, continuing and extending this mighty intercession; the Communion of Reparation, the homage to the love of Jesus Christ so characteristic of this devotion.

Within the last fifty years the devotion to the Sacred Heart has affected the outward life of the Church in such a degree that even strangers and enemies have taken note of the fact. The members of the Church, the faithful laity and their devoted pastors, witness the deeper change it has produced in the inward life of the Church; in keeping alive, in intensifying, in spreading love and loyalty to the Person of Jesus Christ; in encouraging and animating those faithful souls who have thrown in their lot with Jesus Christ, as their King, their Captain, in the war against unbelief and lawlessness and worldliness, in building up what a century of impiety and revolution had overthrown.

In the year 1875, Pope Pius IX. sanctioned the petitions from all parts of the world, that individuals, families, associations, communities, and orders, dioceses, and archdioceses, might be allowed to consecrate themselves publicly and solemnly to the Sacred Heart. On the feast of the Sacred Heart that year, Archbishops and

The Diocese consecrated to the Sacred Heart. 293

Bishops, Generals of Religious Orders, communities of men and women, and thousands of the faithful, knelt before the Blessed Sacrament and consecrated themselves, their dioceses, their subjects, with all their good works and sufferings, to the Sacred Heart of Jesus.

On the 17th of this month the feast of the Sacred Heart will be kept for the first time since the proclamation of the Hierarchy in India and the institution of the archdiocese of Bombay. From many of our clergy and laity, beloved Brethren in Jesus Christ, we have learnt that the body of the faithful would hail with joy a solemn consecration of the archdiocese to the Sacred Heart of our Blessed Lord. This devout suggestion we gladly adopt; the thought that this archdiocese with all its spiritual wants, with its vast population of Hindoos, Parsees, Mahommedans, with its many votaries of business and pleasure, with its thousands of believing Catholics, has by a public act been consecrated to the Sacred Heart of our Blessed Lord, will be a motive of hope, an endless encouragement to us in the midst of our labours. O Sacred Heart of my Redeemer, from this forward enrich the archdiocese of Bombay with Thy treasures and riches, copious redemption from sin, abundance of Divine grace, and all Thy choicest blessings.

The festival itself would have been the most fitting day for this act, if the faithful could have taken part in the ceremony; but as very many will be hindered from assisting in the Cathedral on the Friday, we propose to make the consecration on Sunday, the 19th, at 5.30 p.m.

The service will commence with a sermon. Exposition of the Blessed Sacrament will follow. A hymn to the Sacred Heart will be sung by the choir and people, and the Blessed Sacrament will be exposed. After the *O Salutaris*, an Act of Reparation will be read, and then the consecration of the diocese. The *Tantum ergo* and Benediction of the Most Blessed Sacrament will close the service.

We invite all the clergy and laity to assemble in the Cathedral and take part in this homage to the Sacred Heart of Jesus.

Let not the day pass without leaving its mark in our lives. May all advance and grow in the love of Jesus Christ; may all renew the resolution to practise and to extend the devotion to His Sacred Heart; may all members of the Confraternity of the Sacred Heart redouble their fervour for their own sanctification and the gaining of souls to the knowledge and love of their Divine Master; may those excellent works, the Apostleship of Prayer, the Living Rosary, and the Communion of Reparation, be extended through the archdiocese, and contribute to the advancement of the glory of God and the salvation of many souls; to the enlightenment of those who sit in darkness and error, and to the perfection of all who enjoy the privilege of being members of the true Church.

May the grace and peace of God abide with you for ever. Amen.

We direct all parish priests and chaplains to read this Pastoral Letter at the chief Mass on the first Sunday after they receive it.

Given at our residence, Fort Chapel, Bombay, on the feast of Corpus Christi, June 9, 1887.

✠ GEORGE, Archbishop of Bombay.

CHAPTER XIII.

LETTERS FROM BOMBAY.

July to Nov. 1887.

Retreat at Kirkee. The responsibilities of a Bishop. *The Eternal Truths*, by Father Pergmahr. Description of house at Kirkee. Proposed work on Marriage. French Mission in Madura. Magnificence of Bombay: some account of its inhabitants. The crozier. The spiritual work of advancing life. Commissions for books. Galliffet's *Adorable Heart of Jesus. Was ist Christus,* by Father Roh. *The Throne of the Fisherman.* Faith strengthened by familiarity with the History of the Church. The Indian *Messenger.* More commissions for books. Hints for a private retreat. The writings of Mr. Allies. Unconsoling aspect of Bombay. Argument for Christianity derived from the spectacle of the non-Christian world. Patience under spiritual distresses. Meditation on the Divine Perfections. Mahommed's description of God. Consolations in a sudden death. Secret of contending with despondency. First moments after death. Father Humphrey on Christian Marriage. The Freemasons' persistent attacks on Marriage. Advice for a proposed treatise on the Divine Perfections. Projected visit to Karachi. Reminiscences of Lourdes. The Foundlings' Home and the cholera. The weather.

Kirkee, July 29, 1887.

I am writing at Kirkee, about five miles from Poona. The letter will not leave till Tuesday, August 2. I have not yet seen the mail of last Monday, the 25th, and the mail of August 1st may require a word, so I will not close the letter before Tuesday.

I finished my retreat this morning. Two years within two days have elapsed since my last retreat ended. I don't think I could possibly have contrived eight days since July, 1886. How I longed to reach this time of quiet! My nomination, my departure from London, my consecration, succeeded each other so rapidly, there was little time to think, and yet so much to think about. My seclusion has not reconciled me to my charge; the more I look at it, and consider it, and the more I read in holy writers about my responsibilities, the more terrified I become. The greatest Saints and Doctors of the Church dreaded the Episcopate: how much more ought I to tremble. The Council of Trent, and the various Congregations to which all the business of the Church must be carried, sing the same song, and thunder the same obligations and the same threats. Altogether I have had a good frightening. Still I am very thankful to have had it. The knowledge of the truth must always help one in the long run. With the whole of my task before me, I must resolve to do my best, always wish to do better, and pray God to supply all that my weakness fails to accomplish. Pray for me very much.

Much of my reading concerned my own duties: a very goodly quarto on *Il Buon Pastore*, made up largely from the Fathers; and even more useful, more practical, and more actual, I think, have been many instructions issued by the Popes, especially since the Reformation. The wisdom, the strength of these writings, are beyond description—a living, tangible proof of the presence of the Holy Ghost in the Church. For my considerations, I used a Retreat by an old Jesuit, Pergmahr (the name is not always written in the same way). Some years ago the book was sent to me from Germany, in German. I had never gone through the whole book. This time I fastened on the Considerations: they pleased me very much. A translation of the volume appeared in English, *The Eternal Truths*, by Father Pergmahr. I do not know whether the Considerations were included. Try to see the book.

My home during the past week was all I could wish—six hours from Bombay, quite in the country. Imagine a house twenty feet wide, sixty feet long, running north and south, one storey, divided into three rooms, each twenty feet every way, opening into each other, each having three doors and three windows, surrounded by a verandah ten feet wide, with creepers to shut out the glare, but admitting the breeze, running round the east, south, and west sides. Father Bridges lives in the south room, I in the north room, and we meet in the middle room for meals. The cook-house, servants' quarters, are all at a little distance from the house. Complete the picture by a good-sized church, capable of holding six hundred soldiers, connected with the verandah by a short passage on the west side of the house. No, the picture is not complete. Read the thermometer, never above 75°, almost, not quite, chilly. The silence and solitude were complete. I shall look back to this last week of July with a grateful recollection.

This morning I went over to Poona; saw its really fine church, its college, its convent. To-night I am to dine with Lord Reay, at Ganesh Khind; to-morrow at noon I return to Bombay. . . .

August 2.

I have received your letter of the 15th. I am glad you liked the Pastoral; it was my first—the topic was a happy one. One of my hopes and consolations is the existence of a very great devotion to the Sacred Heart. . . . My future work on Marriage, if it ever sees the light, will deal with some of the questions which perplex your thoughts. No doubt the religious state is a more perfect and a happier state than the state of marriage, but sound Catholic teaching will go great lengths in extolling the sanctity of marriage. I do not know Father Humphrey's book on Christian Marriage. Would it reach my heathendom out here?

In the present generation, the Catholics have not

addressed the natives in their own languages, beyond in catechisms and translations of the Gospels. The old missionaries created a literature, which is not altogether forgotten.

My progress in Marathi and Hindoostani has not been great; I can spare so little time for them. I live in the hope of more leisure later on.

Fort Chapel, Bombay, August 9, 1887.

... One of the Fathers from the French Mission in Madura is with me. He has been forty-one years working there. The mission, under an S.J. Bishop of Trichinopoly (eighty-three years of age! I am terrified by the great age many of our people reach out here), is divided into three districts. They have begun, latterly especially, to make notable progress among the Pagans. The annual Communions were 15,000 when he joined the mission; they are now more than 100,000. Whole villages come over. Most of the Fathers have constantly large batches of converts under instruction. He told me many curious facts about the power of the devil among the Pagans. ... The devil is a terrible reality to these benighted peoples; and no wonder, for in some temples he is openly worshipped.

Fort Chapel, Bombay, August 16, 1887.

My dear Child,

I find two of your letters waiting for an answer, one of May 19th, the other of July 24th. Allow me to thank you for them, also for the paper, which comes very regularly, and I believe I am indebted to you for a copy of the Jubilee *Graphic*, which was most interesting, for which also I thank you, and lastly, I thank you for your kind wishes on my birthday.

The rainy season continues, and will go on for another five or six weeks, but we ought not to have so much rain. So far the rain has continued from June 6th, when the rainy season opened with a tremendous storm, up to the present, without any interruption worth speaking of—at the most we may have had one or two days without rain. Already some seventy inches of rain have fallen. The thermometer stands ten degrees lower, but the heat of the rainy season is more oppressive and more vapoury than the higher temperature of May. The rainy season has brought also a sharp attack of prickly heat, which can be very annoying. And then it induces a feeling of lassitude which does not help work, and draws its victim powerfully to the easy chairs which abound in India. Otherwise, I keep very well.

Bombay is a magnificent city. The modern European part would compare very favourably with most cities of Europe. Splendid roads and streets, large open places, noble public buildings. The private houses, or bungalows, are of all descriptions—some deserve to be called palaces, some look no better than cottages, but as a rule they are built to invite the greatest amount of breeze. They are not comfortable, or rather, cosy, as you understand houses; but they serve their purposes. People here drag beds and furniture about as they please, the one principle being fresh air. The Europeans out here, as a rule, are very hard-working men; they are most assiduous in their attendance to business. In the season they give parties, and seem to enjoy themselves, but not to the neglect of work.

By far the greater number of Europeans are Protestants. There are few English-speaking Catholics whom I can visit. The time was when the Catholic element in Bombay was very strong, but the population is always changing; some day Catholics may come to the front again. Our congregation is made up almost entirely of the descendants of converts from Hindoostan, a dark-skinned race not wanting in intelligence, but easily misled, speaking two or three impossible languages, but not English; all knowing how to serve Mass, but not at all well instructed in their religion, all musical, and able, with one or two fiddles, to knock up a High Mass or a Benediction. The native Christians here are drawn from the lower castes. In the south they make converts, and in numbers, even among the Brahmins, who are the best blood of the country.

Good-bye. God bless you. Everything most kind to everybody.

I remain, yours very truly in Christ,

✠ GEORGE, Archbishop of Bombay.

August 21, 1887.

I am writing to Father Clarke for four dozen of Galliffet's *Adorable Heart of Jesus*, and four dozen of *Pontifical Zouave*. I have asked him not to have the parcel made up till he hears from you. I want you to spend £10 on prizes for convent girls. Use your discretion, avoid mere novels; prefer history, biography, saints' lives. Nice cloth binding with some gilding about it. And, lastly, don't buy expensive books; that is, as a rule, let them be not more than 2s. per vol., all the better if they are less. (At this point your letter arrives of August 3rd, and the photos, for which accept my best thanks). I am not in a great hurry. If the parcel reaches Bombay in November it will be time enough. Ask whether such a parcel may not be sent as "goods" rather than as a parcel. As you plainly see, I left London under the idea that I had given you one of the photos. My ideas were pretty well mixed by the time I took my departure. You must be generous and accept this lame excuse for a grievous omission.

I am very sorry you did not see the crozier, it is truly a magnificent work, artistic and costly. Some one wrote to me that it was exhibited in Hunt and Roskell's shop before it was sent out, and I thought you might have heard of it and had the wish to see it.

Father Coleridge has done so much good work with his pen, I don't like to think it is going to be laid aside.

I must not forget to thank you for the *Priest's Manual*, *How to Speak*, and I do not know how many other useful vols. you have put by for me. I am always afraid of not acknowledging what you have so thoughtfully put together. Believe me, I want not to be ungrateful.

We are still in the rainy season; a week or so ago the prickly heat took hold of me and rather disabled me. The torment can be considerable, and it has left me less disposed and less able for work, otherwise I keep well. Bombay life is monotonous just now.

I hope you are going to have a holiday out of London.

Bombay, August 21, 1887.

Your letter from the convent, July 29th, reached me by last mail; I see you have passed through a suffering retreat, no good thoughts, no good desires, not much encouragement, though the longing to feel more zeal for souls and to pray more for souls should be set down as some working of the Holy Spirit. There will remain some profit to you if you can accept with conformity to God's will the "stupid" state, the utter inability to do more than say *fiat*; if you can acquiesce in it and rest satisfied, waiting for a better time. Certainly the spiritual work of advancing life must consist in preparation of physical suffering, loss of spirits, numbness of intellectual power, and the feeling that life is slipping away from one. This is a time when the perusal of the Rules for the Discernment of Spirits for the First Week would do good,—taking desolation in its widest sense, as every condition of mind and soul drawing the soul earthwards and making prayer and the thought of Heaven distasteful. Fidelity during such times brings great graces and great merit to the soul: it is all service of God, nothing is left for self, save deep humiliation. . . .

. . . There are persons in Bombay who are exercised by the religious question; but they fear meeting me, and I have no pulpit in which I can meet them. Europeans won't come to the Cathedral, it is too *native* for them; the Fort Chapel is too small, and too far from Malabar Hill, the chief quarter of the Europeans. . . .

. . . I keep well, but the prickly heat has punished me very severely and made me more disposed to rest and do nothing.

August 30, 1887.

My last letter told you I am not in any hurry for the books. Now let me add you may get the *Baptism of the King*, the *Return of the King*, the *Mother of the King*, and vols. v. vii. of *Training of the Apostles*, at half-price. My ideas did not go beyond the 6d. (I thought it was 1s.) *Post Office Guide*. You need not get the fat *Post Office Directory* as yet. Please put into the parcel half a dozen copies each of *The Rights and Dignity of Labour*, by Cardinal Manning, and of *What is a Church?* by Bishop Hedley.

Thanks for the careful directions about the ironing of collars. I dare not tell the *dhobie* what he would have to do. In all probability he would never make the attempt; if he were rash enough to venture, I fear he would soon be added to the catalogue of Hindoos burnt out down by the sea in the cool of the evening.

I do not see any chance of going to Europe for a year or two. What may turn up, who can tell? ... Perhaps the chaos before me may take some shape within a year or two. At present chaos has the upper hand. My brother, the Vicar Apostolic of Jamaica, goes to England next year.

A copy of the *Notes of my Retreats* is on the high sea, if it is not already in the Bombay Post Office. The compiler thought I might like to see the ghost of some old work raised up from the dead. The notes travel in company with copies of Bougaud's *Argument for the Divinity of Jesus Christ*, and Freppel's *Conferences* on the same subject. There are some agnostics here who seem in earnest in their desire to reach the truth. Perhaps later I may charm the ears of Pagans and Mahommedans to listen to the arguments for the Divinity of Jesus Christ.

The *Manual of Prayers* in both forms will be very useful to me; the demy quarto is a real luxury. Don't send me any more bound copies of the *Banquet of the Angels* for the present. Here there are *very* few persons who appreciate such a book.

As to Galliffet, the whole book was prepared by me and printed, and waited during some years for my Preface, which I have in my drawer, not yet finished. Possibly the Preface may see the light some day as a separate essay on the history of the devotion to the Sacred Heart.

Going into collapse is an objectionable performance spiritually and every way. Never go to the end of your tether.

Fort Chapel, Bombay, Sept. 6, 1887.

... Since my arrival in Bombay I have met with two articles by Father Roh, "Was ist Christus," in the *Stimmen aus Maria-Laach*, vol. ii. for 1872, pp. 1 and 93. They are very well written, not so Frenchy as Freppel or

Bougaud, and better suited to the English mind. I feel much tempted to translate them. You would read these articles with delight. I won't ask you to translate them. I think you ought to give yourself complete rest from all severe head-work for a time. Quiet reading, a little composition, verse or prose, or perhaps a short translation, what will amount to occupation and not go as far as hard labour, is what you need. . . .

. . . Have you ventured on the *Throne of the Fisherman, founded by the Carpenter's Son*? It is rather stiff reading, but the matter repays the attention. Mr. Allies has taken a firm hold of the Primacy of St. Peter, and he sees well how Rome is the foundation of the Church and the bond of Unity. He has contributed a short paper to *Leo XIII.* by John Oldcastle. In your letter you say that nothing fortifies your faith so much as the lives of the saints, their realization of the supernatural world, of God and Christ and the devil. If you will make yourself familiar with the greater outlines of the history of the Church, her trials, her dangers, her enemies, her seemingly weak defenders on earth, the raging of the Gentiles as if they were on the point of sweeping the world clear of Christ and His Church, and lastly the utterly unequal means by which God saves His own, you will have there a still stronger argument for faith, "looking up to the Author and Finisher of our faith." Your life-long difficulty in faith will give you a great crown. Always to seem on the point of going down, daily to repeat the cry of distress, "Lord save me, I am lost," and to try to serve God faithfully—this is the best service we can give Him. And if physical weakness is superadded, the merit of fidelity will be much increased.

Wait, . . . some field will open up; you won't arrange it beforehand, it will be arranged for you, only you will do your best, when the work presents itself. . . . Nothing very new in my strange world, but I am always within distance of volcanoes and catastrophes in the spiritual world. Good-bye. God bless you.

Bombay, Sept. 12, 1887.

Many thanks for your letter of Aug. 24th. News from —— is always interesting to me.

I won't forget Reverend Mother's silver jubilee on Oct. 30th.

You have not been without your crosses, I see, this year, and you have others before you: the loss of your true father, Dr. Ullathorne, and the progressing illness of your brother. "Through many tribulations," the old road remains unchanged.

You were fortunate in having Father —— to give the retreat. You had known him before and learnt how well he can lead a community.

Last week's mail brought a letter from Sister ——, Eureka, Humboldt Bay, N. California. I did not know whether she was dead or alive. She enjoys excellent health and seems happy in her vocation. She says they have a nice convent and plenty of work.

If I do not forget it, I will send you the next number of the Indian *Messenger of the Sacred Heart*. It contains the history of the conversion of a soldier, Ward, before his execution. His real name was ——. I will send his mother's address: she lives in your neighbourhood. I suspect the old lady would be all the better for being looked up. The history is a consoling one.

I keep good health, thank God. We are just reaching the end of the rainy season. On Saturday seven inches of rain fell. Bombay was mostly under water. The thermometer has remained in the neighbourhood of 80°. It will soon creep nearer to 90°.

T

As yet no signs of life among the dead bones. Pray much for me and for my poor flock.

Everything very kind to Rev. Mother, —— and ——, to each and every one. God bless you all.

Bombay, Sept. 13, 1887.

... With your letter of Aug. 23rd I received (1) box of safety-pins, (2) three packages of books. Many thanks for both. I shall not want any more safety-pins, I have enough now for my wants. My ideal safety-pin does not exist, I fear, not more than ½ inch long and as strong as the strongest you sent. As I mentioned in a recent letter, I am very seldom in a hurry about books, cheapness is the chief aim. Are you aware that Catholic books (Father Coleridge's, too) are sometimes in Mudie's surplus catalogue? Edwards, High Street, Marylebone, always has a number on hand. Tell him it is hardly worth while to send me his catalogue, six weeks is a long interval for second-hand books. If he likes to send the catalogue, however, he can do so and take chances. If you happen to fall in with a complete set of Cardinal Newman's works, *cheap*, I should be glad to buy them. Burns and Oates advertise full set, thirty-six vols. half-bound, £14. That I don't call cheap, but anything under £7 I should be willing to pay. DON'T HURRY this commission. I was very glad to find you had extracted Leo XIIIth's *Acta* from Burns and Oates. Remember me to Mr. Leslie next time you see him. He is very obliging.

For the present I will not ask you for more *Manuals of Prayers*. The same with *Banquet of the Angels*.

The buckles have not arrived, they will probably follow by next mail.

For our *Messenger* we go to press about the 22nd or 23rd. Neale's translation, which last mail brought, will go into the October number. If you will allow me, I will send you sometimes a second or a third number, and ask you to forward them. Will you forward one of October to Sister M. Evangelist, Convent of Mercy, Handsworth, Birmingham.

By all means pay a visit to Walmer. The Superioress is worth knowing personally. As to the retreat, do you know Pergmahr's *Eternal Truths*? If you can get a copy, go right through with him, three meditations a day and one consideration. The considerations, at least in the German edition which I have, are at the end of the volume; they are excellent. I think in a private retreat there is no plan so satisfactory as to take a certain book and follow it from cover to cover. All the parts will not be of equal merit, but you carry away something more definite at the end.

I am glad you go to Lourdes and to France. Lourdes is very beautiful.

The monsoon has done its worst, and is nearly over. In three days we had ten inches of rain, on one day alone seven inches.

Sept. 13, 1887.

. . . I fancy you will do well to give your head a good deal of rest for some time to come. Those distressing symptoms which showed themselves towards the end of last year often indicate a sort of crisis or phase which may pass away. While it lasts, one precaution consists in not overtaxing the brain, in taking plenty of rest, and in not allowing your strength to fall below par. I trust you will get through this crisis, and get back all your old power of work. How we are made to feel our littleness and our dependence at such times: the soul hangs on to the body very closely. . . .

Before long I hope to publish another Pastoral on my Seminary. A poor little affair, which the financial commission threatens to impoverish, by stopping my ₨150 per month, an allowance which has gone on since 1828—a miserable economy! You shall have a copy when it appears.

I have just finished Allies' *Throne of the Fisherman*. The reading of that volume was one of the greatest treats I have had since I came out here. Mr. Allies takes a high position, and always writes up to his theme, which is invariably a noble one. These wide historical surveys of the history of the Church always attract me. You find the Lives of the Saints strengthen your faith. I find the history of the Church a still more powerful help. The finger of God is seen so plainly, and such grand results are obtained from such unequal instruments.

Our monsoon is coming to an end. We had a grand storm on Friday night. Ten inches of rain fell in three days—seven on Saturday alone, if the rain gauges tell the truth. A boy was swept away in a drain and drowned, and a boy nine or ten years old.

I have some other letters to write. I must say good-bye. God bless you.

Fort Chapel, Sept. 21, 1887.

Your letter of Aug. 31 reached me by the last mail on Sept. 18. I am glad to find you are still alive, still grumbling all round, still trying to do better. Life will be a scramble till the end; let us hope to scramble safely past St. Peter.

When you make your next retreat be satisfied with one meditation before breakfast, one before dinner, one before supper (half an hour each), and half an hour's consideration during the afternoon. Divide the rest of the time between quiet vocal prayer, reading, and musing or thinking. You will derive much greater fruit from such a retreat, and you will be spared endless running about. . . . I fear you have fallen back into your old fault, and attempt too much for your strength. It is so difficult not to work beyond one's strength, and over-work is so hurtful spiritually.

Many thanks for your news about my friends ———. I am always glad to hear that they are doing good work and becoming saints.

You want to know about my mission. It is unlike anything I have seen or imagined, and is most unconsoling work. Bombay is the chief port in India, so we have a population of sailors and people about the docks. Only add that they are of all nations, and many of them Indians and negroes. Then the bulk of the priests (mission priests) are natives, Hindoos, descendants of converts; the people, the same. Few of the priests speak English well, or write it correctly. Of the people, the greater part does not speak or understand one word. They talk Marathi, or Tamul, or Hindoostani. I must try my hand at Hindoostani, the most generally understood and happily the easiest to learn. I have not much time to study. I have much writing to attend to. After six hours' work here I do not find myself equal to any more. The heat is great: the thermometer has varied from 80° to 95° since I came out; for six weeks it stood 90° to 95°. Then the air is full of moisture; one lives in a bath, night and day. The heat I can manage. I found the rainy season (June—September, more or less, inclusive) far more trying. I had a severe bout of prickly heat, followed by three or four days of great prostration .of strength; otherwise I have been quite well, and on the whole like Bombay. We have no good churches. The Cathedral is large, but stands in a nasty quarter, in the midst of a Pagan population, surrounded by their temples, and disturbed by their endless drumming and most monotonous dreary chanting. The Fort Chapel is pretty, but small and so hot. The others (except the German St. Anne's) small, very tawdry, not very clean, and generally ill-placed. Little preaching, no confessions, no chance at all of reaching the Pagans, very little more of reaching Protestants. On the whole I must thank God for a very big cross. I do what I can, and hope for better times. The English or Irish Catholics at present in Bombay are few. You must pray for me and for my work. I keep my old practice of a daily *memento* in my Mass for you. God bless you.

Fort Chapel, Bombay, Sept. 23, 1887.

My dear ——,

Your letter of August 17 was a welcome surprise. I know how much you have to attend to, and what an extensive correspondence you are obliged to maintain, so I hardly expected to hear from you.

You have been passing through an unusually hot summer in England, while we have been doing our rainy season. It began on June 7 with a terrific storm; since that day up to date more than ninety-two inches of rain have fallen in Bombay (in some places in India the fall is nearly three hundred inches). On one day seven inches fell. What a deluge!

The rainy season I have found more trying than the great heat. I had a severe visitation of the "prickly heat," followed by some days of extreme prostration. Complete rest and a short course of good port wine soon restored me. With that exception I have been very well, and quite equal to six or seven hours' desk-work per diem.

The greatest heat preceded the rainy season. For five or six weeks the thermometer stood at 90°—95°, which is not much for India, however. Bombay heat tells more on account of the great moisture in the air; the result is that we live in a bath of perspiration, day and night. Generally we have the blessing of a breeze, and we live with windows and doors open, day and night.

The non-Christian world presents a sad spectacle of error, superstition, and degradation. In Bombay we see three large bodies—the Hindoos, nearly 500,000; Mahommedans, 150,000; Parsees, 70,000—each keeping apart from the others, herding together, and with endless divisions of castes and cliques among themselves.

The Christian world is very sick, and falls sadly short of the Gospel. Still, nineteen centuries of generations saying "Our Father," with all their sins, have left a mark which these poor people sadly want. I cannot tell you how one misses in their life—moral, social, and political—Jesus Christ, His Blessed Mother, St. Joseph, the Holy Family, and the Church. To me the spectacle of non-Christians offers such a strong argument for the Divinity of Jesus Christ and His Church. To what a depth man sinks when left to himself! As yet, these people will not look at the Gospel—the terror of caste, and excommunication, prevents them. I pray the day may dawn when they will turn to Jesus Christ. Pray very much for them. The place of woman in their world is sad beyond description.

The report of my visiting England arises from a confusion of my name with that of my brother, Father Thomas, Vicar Apostolic of Jamaica. He visits England next year.

You speak of spiritual distresses. Your great virtue must be patience — patience under your many trials, patience under the infirmities of advancing years, and patience with yourself. Go to Holy Communion as often as you can; there you partake of the Food which makes the weak strong. Often confess your shortcomings and ask for forgiveness. God is good. I am sorry that you were troubled by the Principal of the Deaf-Mutes. I could not well tell him not to write; but you must turn a deaf ear to Bombay beggars (unless I beg myself!). You have enough to do at home.

My life here is a very curious one, but I will tell you of that in some future letter. Good-bye. God bless you and yours.

I remain, yours very truly in Christ,

✠ GEORGE, Archbishop of Bombay.

Fort Chapel, Bombay, Sept. 21, 1887.

. . . In my last I ventured to suggest much rest for some time. I think your "indolent inclination" in reality comes from physical causes. It is not always wise to draw the unwilling and unable body up a steep hill. Patience and rest in time may restore tone to the brain.

I quite agree with you, meditation on the Divine Perfections has a special effect in soothing and strengthening the soul. Those exercises in the *Paradise of the Christian Soul* are new to me. I do not remember ever reading them. Lessius I know, and Da Ponte's Meditations, at the end of his book. If you have not read these, refer to them in your Italian edition, and compare them with Lessius.

A good book on God and His Perfections would suit the Mahommedan mind. During my stay at Allahabad I read *Notes on Mahommedanism,* by Rev. T. P. Hughes (London: Allen and Co., Waterloo Place, 1877). There he gives us from the Koran Mahommed's description of

God. That description brought to my mind Lessius' book. The Mahommedans must be taken up at the point of their monotheism. Their hatred of idolatry places them far above the superstitious Hindoos. In many other respects they are superior to them. They dress properly. Their children don't run naked. They have respect for truth. Though polygamists, they are outwardly more decent. Their weak points are their fanaticism and their aversion to education of any kind. Any advance with them must begin with God. I think you might very well write a book on the Divine Perfections. Make out a list of them. Then read Lessius, Da Ponte, and the *Paradise of the Christian Soul*. Omit what seems redundant, put in what strikes you as best. Make the chapters short, rather than long, break them into moderate paragraphs, and see how you succeed with one or two chapters. I think you will find you can manage it and take an interest in it. The matter in part you borrow, but the arrangement will be all your own. You might throw the book into the form of dialogues, if that form attracts you; my own preference would be for short paragraphs. Do you know the *Elevations de l'ame à Dieu*, by Bossuet? His pages always have a charm for me. Remember me to Mrs. W. very kindly. If I were at O—— I should feel tempted to teaze her about the definition of the Church lately elaborated by Convocation.

I shall be very glad to have Father Humphrey's book on Marriage.

My next Pastoral ought to appear soon. I cannot explain to myself why I delay commencing it; the matter has been in my head for some time.

I am sorry M—— has found such a poor biographer. I do not think biography is a strong chapter in Irish literature. The Irish mind fails to take in proportions.

Our rainy season is coming to an end, though we had a very heavy shower this morning. The mail arrangement has reverted to the normal order; the mail leaves Bombay on Fridays, till the next monsoon—this gives more time for answering by return. . . .

Oct. 5, 1887.

The news of your brother's sudden death did not surprise me much. Your letters had told me that the doctors had no hope of his recovery, and I have known his illness terminate suddenly in many instances. Perhaps this quick ending was in his case a mercy. Though no priest was at his side, we have every reason to hope he was well prepared. His conversion I look upon as a signal grace, I might also say a sign of predestination. I said Mass for him this morning, and will give him a *memento* for many a long day.—R.I.P. His death will leave a large blank in your life. But how much you will find to console you in the last year of his life. And how much consolation in praying for him.

I thank you for Father ——'s book, which the last mail brought me. As yet I have not had time to look at it. He always writes what is worth reading. As you say, he possesses a rare gift of explaining difficult theological points clearly. I quarrel with him for so entirely neglecting to adorn his explanations and set them forth with art. He professedly scorns art, and his sermons and writings have something of the effect of a pelting shower rather than of gentle rain stealing into the earth. He is a fine man; I am very glad you have made his acquaintance. . . .

Bombay, Oct. 21, 1887.

I look to your next letter to tell me how spiritual matters are with you. Have you yet discovered the secret of contending with despondency, of doing the best you can, and not getting vexed with yourself when you don't do very well?

Life, after all, is one continued battle. We shall never be able to lay down our weapons till we are carried out to the cemetery.

Bombay, Oct. 19, 1887.

I have left you undisturbed for some weeks. Your letter of Sept. 28th reminds me I must not prolong my silence. Now E—— has left, you will be very lonesome.

Your difficulty in moving about and in exerting yourself may not be old age and it may not be laziness. You know the doctrine of the climacterics: that in our lives there are periods of seven years, more or less, at which the constitution undergoes a change; while the change is being worked out, there is a feeling of *malaise*, lassitude, &c. All this ends in due time and one may resume renewed health, or one may fall into impaired health, but it will be settled one way or the other. One can only wait and see, and meanwhile avoid overtaxing mind and body. Doing less and doing it less well does not depend on our own will. Laziness may certainly be numbered among the temptations of such a time. One is inclined to do nothing at all, to vegetate or to suffer, when it is possible to do a little and to exert oneself gently. You seem to retain power to read and write. Do these when you can, but stop when you feel wearied. Change of occupation, of scene, even of order, helps through these phases of life.

Resist the thought of all worries about Z——. Under any circumstances you would see matters might have been better arranged; forget all the less satisfactory parts in the overwhelming grace. Beside that, how insignificant the disappointments ought to seem.

The first moments after death! Yes, it must be a surprise, a totally new existence, no longer dependent on the senses, no longer tied to their limits, to exist, to act as a mere spirit, with the memory of the embodied existence very vivid. I always liked Shakespeare's "shuffling off this mortal coil," stepping out into a spiritual world. In the first moment, how much we shall know and truly! things as they are really, in themselves, not as seen through our spectacles.

Father Humphrey's little book on Marriage I read with unmixed pleasure and satisfaction. He has formed his style of thought and diction, and this little volume may be taken as a very good specimen. It is very exact, very concise, very condensed. If only the men who rule the world could be made to meditate upon it!

Have you ever remarked the persistency of the Continental Freemasons in their attacks on the Sacrament and institution of Marriage. Since the middle of the last century the war has never relented, almost every Pope since Benedict XIV. has defended the sacrament, and one immense advantage the Church has gained from the warfare, the theology on the subject, which had been in some points obscure and even uncertain, has taken a complete development. Many of the difficulties came from within the Church, from those who sought to exalt the State and enslave the Church. The end aimed at by the sect was to take the whole domain of marriage from the jurisdiction of the Church. What wonderful pages the history of the Church contains! how plainly the finger of God may be seen, even in the periods of worst confusion.

. . . *Sursum corda.* Keep up your courage and keep yourself ready to do your share. Good-bye. God bless you.

Fort Chapel, Bombay, Oct. 28, 1887.

Yours of the 7th reached me on the 22nd, by the new P. and O. S.S. *Victoria*. I hope you have been able to take some rest and recover from all your fatigues and anxieties. You don't say how you take to the suggestion of compiling a treatise on the Divine Perfections. A book of that sort does not alarm by its magnitude. Each chapter forms an essay by itself, not necessarily much connected with any other chapter. It may be long or short as the materials in your hand suggest. You may take up a chapter, and lay it down if you don't feel inclined to go on with it. You can turn to another which tempts you more at the moment. You can add, you can take out, you can touch up passages, in fact you can do what you like, or if you like you can do nothing, the alternative, I fear, most attractive to your diffidence in your own powers.

I have not been reading much of late, business has been too pressing. I have several things I want to get at.

Early next month I ought to go to Sind, to Karachi. I shall leave Bombay in a British India steamer on Monday, Nov. 7th. I ought to land on Friday, and return by the steamer of the 13th. There is a fine church at Karachi, and a congregation of more than two thousand Catholics. I see from the papers that the Viceroy will be at Karachi on the 11th, 12th, and 13th.

There are rumours that Sind and Beluchistan are to be separated from the archdiocese of Bombay. I shall not be sorry to lose those countries. I cannot look after them properly, and I cannot help them. I shall then be left with Bombay and Gujerat and Cutch, where there are very few stations.

Fort Chapel, Bombay, Oct. 28, 1887.

... The account of your visit to Lourdes and Toulouse interested me much. Your pilgrimage was not like mine. I arrived in the evening, after dark, in January, went to the Mission House, met with the kindest reception, was lodged at the Châlet des Evêques. Did my devotions in the morning, saw everything in the church. Then drove down to the Grotto by the river. I can never forget the vision of beauty and peace which met my eyes on that clear, crisp January morning. My prayer was not a long one, I hope it was a fervent one. Twenty minutes later the railway demon was carrying me along under the snow-covered Pyrenees. You came in for the pilgrims and the life of Lourdes. I thank God for my visit. . . .

I am scarcely out of a great anxiety. The Foundlings' Home accepted a little Hindoo child. The Sisters did not know the mother had died from cholera, the infant was removed from the dead body. Cholera appeared in the home, seven foundlings died and one stout African nurse. Fortunately for her, she had been instructed, and she was baptized before she died. Eight souls went to Heaven, but a world of trouble and anxiety remained for those left behind. No death has occurred the last three days, and we hope we have passed the worst. The municipality did the work of disinfection energetically. Two or three hundred men were turned in, who washed and scoured and whitewashed the whole establishment. Cholera is a dreaded visitor here. Bombay has passed through several terrible visitations, and the lessons have not been thrown away. What sanitation can do to keep the enemy at a distance, it does with a will here.

The Rainy Season.

Fort Chapel, Bombay, Nov. 5, 1887.

My dear Child,

I have not much to say, but as I shall be away in Sind for the next fortnight, I write half a sheet. I am very well and have been very well since the end of August. We thought we had ended our rainy season. The covering had been removed from the splendid marble statue of the Queen (a sure sign that rain is not expected before next June), and lo! to-day it has rained continuously. We fear the extraordinary phenomenon may be the forerunner of a cyclone. The moon has looked greasy and green for the last two nights, and the sailors dread that appearance. We must hope the cyclone won't come. I shall look with some eagerness for your next letter. . . . But what is life but a succession of trials. The wise are those who accept them patiently, do the best they can, and remember the better and the longer life which is to follow.

Send me news, too, of ———. I am glad your health is improved and things go more pleasantly. Have patience and pray very hard, and things will go better still.

Many thanks for the newspaper, which comes regularly. I have plenty of papers, but not plenty of time to read them.

Good-bye. God bless you. I keep your name in my daily Mass.

I remain, yours very truly,

✠ GEORGE, Archbishop of Bombay.

CHAPTER XIV.

KARACHI.   BHAUNAGAR.   AHMADABAD.

Nov. 1887 to Feb. 1888.

Extent of the diocese of Bombay. The Archbishop of Goa's Pastoral. Decree from Rome. Visit to Karachi. Meeting with Lord and Lady Dufferin. St. Thomas of Aquin and the Missal and Breviary for Corpus Christi. Piranesi's prints of Rome. Purgatory. Worshippers of idols. Mahommedan hatred of idolatry and of learning. Mahommedan preachers. M. le Play's writings on social questions. Simple rule for those who wish for consolation. Prize-books. Visit to Bhaunagar. Gaorishanker. His present mode of life. Ahmadabad and its interesting remains. The grace of patience. Visit to the monastery and temple of the Swami-Naryan sect at Ahmadabad. Anniversary of appointment to Bombay. Celebration of Christmas. The climate. Words of encouragement. Two communities of nuns. Numerous conversions in the diocese of Calcutta and in Madura. Darwin's autobiography. Journey to Goa given up. Further account of the Hindoo monastery at Ahmadabad. The Epiphany. Benefit that may be derived from spiritual privations. Life of the Foundress of the Filles de la Croix. Father Baur, miracle related by him. His experiences as a missioner. St. Bernard's Homilies. Promise of the statue of Our Lady of Lourdes from Farm Street. Expedition to Juvem and Tara. Celebration of the Pope's Jubilee. Mosquitoes. The worse torments of Africa. Advice to an invalid. Few opportunities of preaching in Bombay. Sermon at St. Anne's. Remedy for discouragement. Darwin. Life of Père Liebermann. Account of work and diocese. Mahommedans. How and when to measure spiritual progress. The Archbishop's experience of the preceding twelve months. A religious of the Filles de la Croix. Her adventures in a jungle. "A Brahmin of the highest caste." An Anglican clergyman and the light of the Gospel.

Bombay, Nov. 6, 1887.

I am writing on Sunday evening. The English mail has not come in and is not expected before eight o'clock to-morrow morning. At 10 a.m. I leave to go on board the steamer for Karachi. We ought to reach that port about noon on Wednesday. I do not propose making a long stay. I hope to take the return Bombay steamer on the 14th, and ought to arrive in Bombay on Wednesday. If the steamer calls at the smaller ports on the coast we shall only arrive on Friday.

The Viceroy will be at Karachi when I am there. The coincidence of our visits was quite accidental. I have made the acquaintance of the Chief Commissioner of Sind, and he has been very civil and kind.

The diocese of Bombay is described as containing Sind and Beluchistan up to Cabul. Look at a map of India and you will be dismayed by the extent of territory. We have, besides Karachi, only a series of military stations along the railway up to Quetta inclusive, with small congregations. Karachi is more than a mere military station. It boasts of a splendid church, a good boys' school, a convent which does a great deal of good, a second small chapel at the port for the sailors, and a resident Catholic population of between two or three thousand. By every mail I expect a document from Rome erecting Sind and Beluchistan into a bishopric or a Prefecture Apostolic. My burden will then be considerably lessened. Quite enough will be left even then, Cutch and Gujerat, besides the island of Bombay and my stray stations on the other islands.

In my diocesan work I have little new to record. You may have noticed in supplements of the *Examiner* a translation of a Pastoral from the Archbishop of Goa and a decree from Rome in answer to some queries of mine. The Pastoral was an event. The Padroadists dislike it. Their paper did not so much as name it or notice it at all. The offence is that the Archbishop said so much about the Pope and so little about the King of Portugal. And yet the occasion and subject of the Pastoral was the Jubilee of Leo XIII. Then the Archbishop ordered a collection of Peter Pence, a step never heard of before. I thought the Pastoral a very fine document. The Archbishop is a good man, a true child of the Church and loyal to the Holy See, at the same time that he is a fervent Portuguese patriot. These Padroadists are ignorant, passionate people. The Padroado is dead, and has been buried with honour. And yet numbers of these people give up their religion and die without the sacraments, rather than give up what they call the Padroado. A leading man died of cholera the other day, and refused the last sacraments because he could not have what he called a Padroado priest. Ignorance and passion! It is not easy to say which plays the greater part.

The decree will become important later. As occasions present themselves the application must cause some friction. Pray for its having a blessing.

I have been and am very well. The weather has been pleasant, though slightly warm. Yesterday quite unexpectedly we had a day of rain—a very ominous sign. This evening the sky looks threatening. A rainy day out of the rainy season often precedes a cyclone or violent storm. I hope our steamer to Karachi will not cross its path.

Fort Chapel, Bombay, Nov. 25, 1887.

I forget whether I wrote to you from Karachi. I left Bombay on the 7th, reached K. on the 9th, after two days of a delightful voyage. Got through my visitation, took some part in the public reception of the Viceroy, left on the 16th, enjoyed another two days at sea (with 138 horses on board, from the Persian Gulf. It sounds dreadful, but the annoyance was very slight; though in a rough sea it might have been serious), and got back to Bombay on the 18th.

In Sind you are in a sandy desert. Karachi is a large

place thrown down in the sand. Most desolate at first sight, but interesting and habitable enough when you know it better. Still you are always in the desert. Camels are almost as common as cabs or horses.

The Catholics have a fine church and a fine convent. They number over 2,000, and the European element is not altogether swamped by the native.

Lord Dufferin showed much activity and desire to see and judge for himself. I was put next to Lady Dufferin at dinner. She takes a great interest in all charitable works, and questioned me much about our charities in Bombay. In her way she must be religious. She went to church twice on the Sunday. The morning preacher appealed on behalf of her fund, but took the wrong text and floundered about most hopelessly, to the horror of his congregation. I met Sir Frederick Roberts and Lady Roberts at dinner. They are zealous in the cause of temperance, especially in the army, but I had little opportunity of talking with either. Sir Frederick spoke a little in admiration of the work of St. Francis Xavier in South India.

The visit to Karachi was on the whole a pleasant change and consoled me by the evidence of good solid work doing there. On my return I found an accumulation of letters. Indeed, I have three mails to answer this week, among others your letters of Oct. 20th and Nov. 3rd. . . .

. . . I agree with your appreciation of the French "images." Many of them suggest pious thoughts about the Blessed Eucharist. My favourite aid to that devotion, however, I find in the Missal and Breviary for Corpus Christi and its octave, all the work of St. Thomas of Aquin. I like to think of him called to Orvieto by Pope Urban IV. after the great miracle of Bolsena, and told to prepare the Mass and Office.

St. Bonaventure, they say, had also prepared one, but tore it up leaf by leaf as St. Thomas went on reading what he had written. St. Bonaventure's would have been worth having.

Piranesi's prints of Rome cheer you in your sick room. The one ornament of this house is a complete set, nicely mounted in Oxford frames of oak. They are a feast to look upon, so full of the air and spirit of Rome, as it was when I first knew it.

The terror of Purgatory still haunts you. Why not take a note-book and set down all the consoling thoughts which centre round that place of love and fiery probation?

You speak of looking up Lacordaire on Mahommedanism. Get a small volume, *Notes on Mahommedanism*, by Rev. T. P. Hughes. Second Edition (London, Allen and Co., 1877). It puts all the strong points very fairly. And when you have read it, I shall be glad to have the volume. I have looked for it here in vain. A priest lent me his copy when I was staying at Allahabad last February.

Worshippers of idols, I believe, worship very little. Their acts of worship seem the merest dumb mechanical show, the farthest possible from "adoration in spirit and truth." I think the Mahommedan daily prayer nothing more than a mechanical repetition. They have a fanatical hatred for idolatry. India is covered with the fragments of idols they have thrown down and the wreckage of shrines and temples they have destroyed. To my mind they are much to be preferred to the Hindoos. I wish they did not hate books and learning so much. They have their preachers. I often see them holding forth in Bombay. I saw at Karachi the Peer of Rohree, a man of ancient family who is honoured as a saint and a prophet. A sallow, unpleasant looking individual, said to have been a great scamp, now claiming to have a mission from Heaven and to found a new Mahommedanism, a sort of rationalistic form of that belief. He was grandly dressed. I am told he counts his followers by tens of thousands. He trains disciples to continue his mission. Every one showed him the most marked veneration. If only we could make a beginning with the Mahommedans, a great harvest of souls would be gathered in.

E —— has decided wisely to go in for history and political economy. They are the studies for which he has most inclination and talent. At the same time, too many of the best known writers are free-thinkers. Take an opportunity to bring under his notice some of the writings of the late M. le Play. He was and is an authority on social questions, on the rights of the poor, on capital and labour, &c. He was a thorough Christian. I like very much the speeches of Count Albert le Mun. He goes over the same ground.

Bombay, Nov. 22, 1887.

. . . You ask me how you may get consolation and encouragement when you go to confession. I will give you a simple rule: don't think about it. Try not to be anxious for consolation. Give all your care and anxiety to making a good confession and a good Communion, and leave the consolation to Almighty God. You will find by experience that you enjoy greater peace of mind and receive from time to time moments of comfort and joy. You tell me you have been passing through a time of desolation. Those are the times when you ought to be most exact and regular at Mass and Communion and most earnest in prayer. At such times prolong your prayers and pray with all your heart.

Nov. 25, 1887.

From all you tell me I conclude that you are beginning well, and that you have really found your vocation. How strange are the ways of God, that He should send you this great grace when you are no longer young, and have been so long waiting to know what was before you. *Gratias agamus Deo nostro.*

Your chief temptation will be self-worry. Stand up against it. Don't worry about doing your very best. Do as well as you can, quietly and rationally. When you discover any faults, be sorry for them, make an act of sorrow, and resolve to avoid those faults next time. Get into the way, if you can, of thinking before each action, what you are about to do, and how you ought to do it. Make up standards in your own mind of faults to be avoided, of good points to be attained.

You worry yourself about persevering. Pray for the grace of perseverance every day at Mass, during the Elevation of the Chalice, and every time you receive Holy Communion, and leave it to God and His Blessed Mother. Never forget you belong to the Sacred Heart, and keep the devotion to the Sacred Heart always fresh and fervently in your heart.

Encourage the spirit of compunction *in general*, and make frequent acts of contrition, and make that spirit of compunction the foundation of your gratitude and love for Jesus Christ. Go on bravely, always looking forward. *Sursum corda.*

Dec. 2, 1887.

. . . I do not remember whether the American translation of Perhmahr contains an Appendix with self-examinations, many from St. Francis of Sales. My German edition has them, and I consider them most valuable. If you cannot find them, tell me.

You say the *Banquet of the Angels* is virtually out of print. I am glad to hear it. By the way, I see you still have a few copies. Can you spare me half a dozen? My visit to Karachi exhausted my store.

Next week, I must make the visitation of Bhaunagar, a station in the Guzerat province, two days' rail from Bombay. I shall not return here before Dec. 18th, so do not be surprised if there is a certain break in my correspondence. In case I do not write again in time, I now wish you all Christmas joys and blessings. You are past the merry Christmas side of life, but I pray you may enjoy the spiritual consolations of that blessed season and receive many graces. Add a *buon capo d'anno* for January 1, 1888.

Did I ask you in my last letter if you had any detailed list of all those prize-books? If you have, I shall be glad to have them, in order to portion out the shares of the several purchasers. If you have not, do not trouble to get them. I can make division on an average without inflicting any grievous injustice on any one.

I am tempted to ask you to get from several publishers, lists of prize-books: *v.g.*, Nimmo, the S.P.C.K., and the chief school-book publishers. Books of travel, geography, history, atlas-books, drawing-books, music-books, scientific books (elementary, of course). Next year we might order a very large box, perhaps £100, instead of £10. These prize lists tempt purchasers by the promise of considerable discount.

Dec. 15, 1887.

I sent you some account of my visit to Karachi. I have since made the visitation of Bhaunagar, in Katiawar. The place is about five hundred miles from Bombay, accessible by railway. The *Examiner* will give you the particulars. Bhaunagar is a native state, the chief of the one hundred and eighty-six states into which Katiawar is divided. A model, go-ahead state, with waterworks, fine tanks, a noble hospital (in course of erection), a college, &c. I gave the Monday up to visiting and receiving visits. Unfortunately I lost a most interesting personage, the former Dewan, or Prime Minister, who made Bhaunagar what it is. Azam Gasrishankar Udyashankar retired from the world about seven years ago, and became a *souyassi*, or monk. He is eighty-two years of age, but retains all his faculties. He is a remarkably able man, a profound Sanskrit scholar. He never goes out, but he receives visits. His whole time he divides between prayer and study. Next time I go to Bhaunagar, I hope to talk with him. On my way home I stayed a few days in Ahmadabad, to pay my respects to the Governor, Lord Reay, who was then on tour, and to see the place. I came in for some gorgeous pageants, a procession, and a durbar, both most picturesque and interesting. The place itself would occupy a week; it was a Hindoo capital and a Mahommedan capital. The remains of temples, tanks, and wells are of surpassing interest and beauty and magnificence, *e.g.*, a lake, of regular polygon form, of thirty-four sides, each side one hundred and ninety feet long, with steps down to the water, and a beautiful causeway running up to what may be called an island. Most of all I was interested in a monastery of Swami-Naryan Hindoos and their temple. I went through the monastery, visited the temple, and had a conference with the chief man. Perhaps I may one day write again about this visit.

Ahmadabad, Dec. 15, 1887.

. . . May the New Year bring you blessings of every kind, both spiritual and temporal. May it bring you many graces, and above all an increase of patience, the virtue we all need most in this life of trials. I will copy for you a sentence which occurs in the chapter of à Kempis which I read last: "All our peace in this wretched life consists rather in humbly bearing our trials than in not meeting with unpleasant things." You have had many trials during the last year, and you have been much upset sometimes. Believe à Kempis. If you can be patient, no trials will rob you of your peace of mind, and you will be happy whatever comes.

And to be patient under trials one must pray much for the gift of patience, and you must approach the sacraments regularly; never allow the enemy of your soul to keep you away from the sacraments.

Fort Chapel, Bombay, Dec. 22, 1887.

My dear ——

I must not allow the New Year to come in without sending you my wishes for a happy New Year; may it bring you many graces and consolations. I hope that time lays his hand gently on you, and that you have been well through the severe summer and now in the winter.

My health is excellent, thank God, and I can work as well as ever I did in my life. I have not much news to send you about my mission; but I may tell you of a little episode which has some interest. During a recent visit to Ahmadabad, I went to see a monastery and temple of the "Swami-Naryan" sect. My guide was an intelligent Parsee, who knew English and Gujerati perfectly. This sect dates from about a century only. The founder wishes to set up a higher standard of morals. It numbers not less than a quarter of a million of adherents. Of the laity I will only say, they pay to the treasury of their sect a quarter of their income, and twice a year visit Ahmadabad and Wadthal, their chief centres, and inscribe their names. The monastery is a large building. Some three hundred monks live there, of all ages, including mere boys, dedicated by their parents and accepted by the monks. In the part which I saw, the lower storey was a vast open verandah, in which the monks were occupied in manual works. Above this was a huge, barn-like room where the clothing was kept (very light, a huge sheet of yellow cotton, which is adapted to the fancy of the wearer) and where the monks slept. The bed consists of a strip of matting laid on the floor, and a pillow equally primitive. The monks retire about 8 p.m., and rise at 4 a.m. They eat only once in the day, at noon. They pray together five times each day. Twice or thrice in the month they pass the whole day without touching food of any kind, even water. They have no private property. They don't marry. They obey the head of the sect. A monk may leave the monastery, but I understood that he would be cut off from the sect. My Parsee interpreter told me that the superior could marry, that he occupied a splendid suite of apartments; but I have my doubts on this head. I had an interview with the head, an intelligent looking man. We talked about their practices of prayer and asceticism. They are idolaters. I went into the temple. The shrine was of gold, and silver, and stones; most costly. The idols were hideous, and I do not remember their names. Besides the idols, the shrine of the founder, Swami-Naryan, occupies a high place both in the temple and in the dormitory. The shrine consists of two compartments, one was filled by a curious, impossible portrait of the man, the other with prints of his footsteps in red, taken at four or five different periods of his life. These people go about preaching, two and two, never singly. They won't eat unless five persons sit down to the meal.

Probably I shall return to Ahmadabad before long, and then I hope to pay a second visit to this monastery, and learn more exactly their religious and philosophical ideas.

Outwardly, at least, their life is simple and somewhat ascetic. They affect no austerities beyond the fasting I have described. What a pity that so much should be done for the old gentleman! These people would make grand Christians; religious life would flourish among them, for they are animated by a deep sense of religion, and their habits are exceedingly simple. I hope you will not find my episode too long. Good-bye. God bless you.

Dec. 28, 1887.

A year to-day, I found on my table the terrible letter which destined me for Bombay. The year has brought its share of new experiences, and some worries. But I have to thank God for many graces and blessings received. Among others, the blessing of good health in an untried climate. *Deo gratias* for all.

The Archbishop of Goa's Pastoral has reached you before this, I hope. My native manager was not quite ready for the mail with his copies of the supplement, so the following mail, not to save himself any trouble (?) he decided that people in Europe would not care to see the Pastoral. More than one remonstrance came to me, so I gave orders that copies should go with the next *Examiner*.

The boxes of books for prizes turned out an immense success in this way. Furtado and Brothers had ordered out a huge chest of gaily bound books, but the ship which carried it took fire, the box was found out by the flames, and the contents were too much injured to be sold as prizes. Hence your books were easily seized, and found to be very good value. If you like, you may begin at once to make out a list of prizes for next November. The S.P.C.K. sells some very nice ones, travels, science, biography, &c., with very little anti-Popery in them. Then you might put down, Fander's *Catechism*, Schouppe's *Catechism* (Mrs. Crosier's translation), Newman's *Turks*. I was reproached for not ordering out copies of the *Banquet of the Angels*. I had never thought of it. Any way, all the books are sold.

As to Ricci, I believe you are right in supposing that Burns and Oates look upon it as a book of meditation. Works on how to meditate are not numerous, and Ricci would supply a want.

Fort Chapel, Bombay, Dec. 29, 1887.

My dear Child,

Your letters of Nov. 21st and Oct. 24th weigh on my conscience. I thank you for all your kind Christmas and New Year wishes, and in return send you my compliments of the season. May 1888 bring you many graces and blessings, and much strength of soul and body.

Christmas out here reflects Christmas at home in a small way, as far as the thermometer at 80° and 85° will allow the copy. Spiritually, our Christmas services go rather ahead of you. On Christmas Eve they repeat Matins at 11 p.m., then solemn Midnight Mass, with a sermon added in, and a good long one. They delight in long sermons, long services, and even in the late morning when the sun burns fiercely. In cribs Bombay comes behind England generally.

My health is excellent. Beyond the trifling upset in August, I have had nothing to complain of, indeed, I may say I have enjoyed very good health since I received my nomination to this place, a year ago yesterday. The heat I do not find very trying. Father Harford may have bought a long overcoat in Bombay, and he may have wanted it on the sea, and he would have wanted it up country, but scarcely in Bombay. Our climate is more even than that of the mainland. We are in winter now, and the thermometer stands generally above 80° during the day. 60° is very low for Bombay, and that point is never reached except at night or in the early morning. I was at Ahmadabad a fortnight ago. There I found I required two heavy blankets. Here I find a light blanket more than I can manage. The variations of climate in India are most wonderful. The other day I heard a doctor say he had marked his thermometer 43° in the morning and 98° in the early afternoon: rather a change.

I read with interest the grand doings in honour of Blessed Campion and companions. I expect that many conversions will follow his beatification.

All that you tell me about your general progress is very consoling to me. Have patience, pray much for grace, and persevere as you are doing, and I promise you that you will become a changed person. Not only will you be able to overcome temptations with comparative ease, but the temptations will cease and won't return unless you encourage them. I am particularly pleased that you are in Dr. ——'s hands, he understands your case perfectly. I have often told you the temptations are physical, and you require physical and kitchen remedies.

Thank God for the progress made, and pray you may continue to progress till you have obtained a complete victory. I hope the time is not far distant when you can say your *Te Deum*.

Bombay, Dec. 30, 1887.

I must wish you a happy New Year, plenty of graces and consolations and plenty of patience. I can give you a good account of myself, at least of my health. I am very well. With the exception of a trifling ailment of a few days, I have enjoyed excellent health since I came out. On Dec. 28th, I received the letter of my appointment to this place. I often wonder why I was sent here. I don't seem to be able to do anything, but I believe God has His designs; perhaps the gain is to be for my own soul.

I have two communities of nuns: (1) The Daughters of the Cross. They have charge of a large school and orphanage, just outside Bombay, at Bandora, of a foundling hospital here in Bombay, and of a fine school at Kàrachi. These nuns do very well. They are strong in numbers, they contrive to keep their health, and they get through an immense amount of work. (2) The Nuns of Jesus and Mary, a French convent from Lyons (No. 1 nuns are from Liège). They have two schools here in Bombay, but they are too few for their work. They seem nearly all quite washed out, colourless, frail: still they get through their teaching fairly well. The spirit is not wanting, but the bodily strength scarcely comes up to the work. Perhaps before long I may have another community out from Belgium. Their first work would be the teaching of deaf-mutes; but they are prepared to take up other charitable works, and they will have a fine field before them.

No movement among our heathens as yet—not a sign of it. The native Christians are what they have been for generations, a very queer set of people, most difficult to manage, ignorant and proportionately full of conceit and downright pride. In many respects their character resembles that of the negroes.

You may infer that my work does not afford me much consolation here. I hope some good is done; the sacraments and honest work must do some good, even when we do not see it.

Elsewhere in India conversions on a great scale are being made. Yesterday I heard of a Belgian Father in the diocese of Calcutta who received 10,000 within the space of a single year, the same Father has since received 5,000 more in less than a year. In Madura, too, steady progress is being made, whole villages have accepted the faith, and after a long and careful preparation the converts have been baptized. When will the day of grace dawn for Bombay? Pray that it may be accelerated.

I lately paid a visit to a Hindoo monastery. Three hundred monks live there in community, rather an ascetical life: food once a day, sleep on matting, not a very great hardship; have something like a vow of poverty, don't marry, go about preaching, pray a good deal. But nothing much seems to come out of it all, except a new sect which has a rich common treasury, out of which they build grand temples. If only they were Catholics! Good-bye. God bless you. *Sursum corda.*

Fort Chapel, Bombay, December, 1887.

Many thanks for your letter of December 2nd, and your account of all the doings and preachings at Farm Street on the occasion of Blessed Campion's feast. I am glad you can say you are better: you have still to learn that the state of weakness, as well as suffering, must be accepted with resignation and that you may derive spiritual profit from it. I conjecture that you will live it down and regain your old power of application and work. Why not substitute vocal prayer on the second or third method for meditation, till you regain your strength?

Darwin's history of his mind and his religious ideas interested me. I take his word for it, that his power of consecutive reasoning was not great. He writes readily enough that he saw the Bible was no more worthy of credit than other of the Eastern sacred books. I wonder whether he ever looked into an Eastern sacred book: he could not have written that sentence if he had, the Bible differs so completely from any of the Eastern books.

The journey to Goa never came off. I was to have made it in the company of the Bishop of Meliapur, but he fell ill and could not attempt the journey. The paper reports to-day that he is much worse again and has had a relapse. I fear for him: he has enteric fever and he does not look a strong man.

I made another journey, which I had postponed for the sake of Goa, to Bhaunagar, in Gujerat. There is a small congregation there. That visit satisfied me in many ways. On my return I stayed three days at Ahmadabad to pay my respects to Lord Reay, who was there. I saw many interesting things: a grand durbar, a native procession, &c., some wonderful temples and mosques and tanks and wells, and visited a temple and monastery of live Hindoo monks. I went with a Parsee friend and interpreter. The monks are of the Swami-Naryan sect, only one hundred years old. The founder began a reformation, in protest against the gross sensuality of most of the Hindoos. He teaches a pure and simple life. The laity of his sect pay one quarter of their income to the treasury of the head man, and every year go in pilgrimage to Ahmadabad and Wadthal, the two centres of the sect, and inscribe their names on the books of the sect. The monks profess poverty, they own nothing of their own, all goes to the common treasury, they don't marry, they go about two and two preaching their doctrines and practices. I saw their dormitory and store-room, a barn-looking place, with an open roof, the clothes (a simple yellow sheet) resting on the beams. They sleep on a strip of matting, with the simplest of pillows which looked like matting for the head to rest upon. I was taken to the reception-hall and had an interview with the head of the monastery, some thirty or forty monks crowding round to hear the talk. The monks rise at 4 a.m., but they retire early. They eat once a day at noon. They pray five times a day, all together. On three or four days each month they observe a complete fast all day, even from water. They don't practise other austerities. My time was limited, and I did not get beyond their mode of living. At the end sweets and fruits were brought in. These people are idolaters. I suspect they worship their founder. In the temple and in the dormitory I saw a shrine, evidently the object of much care; it consisted of two parts, one containing the picture of the founder, a quaint impossible portrait, the other four or five impressions of his footsteps, in red paint, taken at different times of his life. The temple was rich, the chief shrine of the idol very much so, all gold and silver and stones. The architecture interested me much. Three hundred monks live in this monastery, many of them mere boys, dedicated by their parents. Some day I shall return to Ahmadabad and repeat my visit to the Swami-Naryan, then I will go deeper into their religion and their philosophy. For the present I must conclude, wishing you good-bye and God bless you.

Fort Chapel, Bombay, Jan. 6, 1888.

I begin by wishing you a happy *festa*. The Epiphany, the revelation to the Gentiles, is the great feast in Rome, as you know, greater in a way than Christmas. Would that my poor Gentiles could see the star and find their way to Bethlehem! I said one of my Christmas Day Masses for you. I did not say Mass at midnight, because the third Mass was a Pontifical High Mass. Christmas in Bombay does not come up to the European standard. Very little is made of the crib. We hear the *Adeste Fideles* occasionally, and that is pretty much all. The *Examiner* will tell you what we did for the Pope's Jubilee. Our celebration was a modest one, but it was not possible to attempt much.

Your infirm state of health, keeping you from the services of the Church and depriving you of Holy Communion, must be a grievous trial. You will make a merit of all this and derive even some consolation from it, if you can accept it thankfully and thank God for trying you in this particular way. Perhaps the good God intends you to get out of your loss of health and out of the change from L——, and the privation of so many helps to piety you enjoyed there is that you should be taught to lean less on external props and to go more directly for strength and consolation to Himself. The feeling of one's weakness and one's helplessness, the conviction of entire dependence on God, and the full trust that He can and will be all and everything to us, if we go to Him, make up a solid spiritual life. I am glad you are feeling better. The change from tonics to no-tonics may do no harm; certainly quiet and country air and not overdoing your strength ought to carry you into a period of vigorous energy.

While you have been reading of York Convent, I have been reading the Life of the Foundress of the Filles de la Croix, who have charge of the Girl's Orphanage at Bandora. The communities are admirable for their devotedness to their work and for their religious spirit, and they seem to have inherited the virtues of their foundress and almost the type of her face. The mother-house is in Belgium. The Congregation is scarcely fifty years old. I have another community, which have the name of the Nuns of Jesus and Mary, another modern foundation. The Sisters seem good, but washed out and worn out with fatigue and overwork, and they get no help from Europe. The Provincial was old and quite blind; no wonder matters did not advance. But God has called her to her reward, and her successor is said to be young and also energetic and clever. Energy is the quality most wanted out here, where so many influences combine to bring on lassitude and weariness. . . .

. . . You remind me my fatal appointment reached me on December 28, 1886. More than a year has slipped away. It has been in more ways than one a year of trials, but, on the other hand, I have much to be thankful for. God has not left me without many graces and many blessings. I can say *Deo gratias* at the end of all. I look forward with trust to the year we have begun. God won't be wanting to us, if we do what we can. I think you can subscribe to my account of 1887. *Sursum corda.*

Fort Chapel, Bombay, January, 1888.

You appreciate French thought. Here is a French account of the death of a young foundling soon after its baptism: "La chère petite colombe se hâta d'ouvrir ses blanches ailes, encore humides des eaux du saint baptême et prit son essor vers le beau Paradis." This I take from *Histoire de la Mère Marie-Terèse, fondatrice de la Congregation des Filles de la Croix de Liège.* These nuns have a convent in Karachi, an orphanage and school in Bandora, and a foundling hospital in the city of Bombay, all three institutions, models, and the religious animated with a noble religious spirit. The *Histoire* is rather an account of the growth of the Congregation, than a life of its foundress, which I regret, as she must have been a holy and a great woman, to judge from the stamp she has left on her children.

I am glad you are feeling better. You must not attempt too much *piano*, as the Italians say. The recovery of your full strength and vigour will require time, and do not be surprised or disheartened if the feeling of lassitude comes back to you sometimes. . . .

I will tell you now an interesting miracle, related to me by an eye-witness, Father Baur (Alsatian), a member of the Congregation of the Holy Ghost and the Heart of Mary, founded by a converted Jew, Abbé Lièbermann, whose beatification is expected before long. Father Baur has been more than than twenty-five years on the Zanzibar Mission, which he began with a debt of 130,000 frs. and an empty purse. The debt has been paid and the mission now supports itself and its large colony of converts. But I am leaving the miracle. Twelve years ago Sister Mary Joseph was at death's door, a bilious fever had laid her low, she was in her agony and the *râle* was already heard. Father Baur put into her mouth a tiny particle of the coffin of their founder (after saying three Hail Marys) in a tea-spoonful of water. The dying Sister was cured instantaneously, rose, dressed herself, did not break her fast that she might communicate the following morning, communicated, and resumed work. She has never had another attack of fever, and is now working hard on the mission.

Father Baur has been sent to Bombay by his Superiors for a month's rest. The company of these holy veteran missioners is most edifying and consoling; most of them have gone through incredible privations and hardships, and naturally their experiences are full of interest. When I see these men I gain a further insight into the Kingdom of Christ upon earth and how it is carried on and extended. Father Baur promises me the Life of Abbé Liebermann; I will tell you what it is like when I have read it. . . .

The *Examiner* will tell you what we have done for the Jubilee. One of the daily papers, the *Bombay Gazette*, reported my sermon in full, so I gained many readers in addition to a very large audience. Many thanks for your prayers and good wishes. Good-bye. God bless you.

Bombay, Jan. 11, 1888.

You know that I have a Lepers' Home and an Institution for Deaf-Mutes. Can you find out for me the habitat of any central institutions of the same kind in Great Britain, and possibly induce them to send me their publications regularly? Yesterday's mail brought your letter of December 22nd, and also *Whitaker* and St. Bernard's *Homilies on our Lady*. Thanks for all. I have read one Homily; the translation is well done. I have no fear in recommending the book after seeing that specimen. St. Bernard surpasses himself on our Lady. . .

. . . Would you believe it? The old statue of Our Lady of Lourdes is to come from Farm Street to me. Father Hayes has promised it to me; it was in its case, as it returned from Leghorn untouched, and if —— comes out again, and does his duty, it ought to be on the sea for Bombay. I wonder at my good fortune; I hardly expected so much from your prayers. But I shall not feel quite safe till our Lady is lodged under this roof.

. . . I am always writing about commissions. Now, by way of change, I will tell you how I have spent this day. I left Bombay at 5.30 a.m. in a carriage and pair with my Vicar-General. After a pleasant, I might say a cool drive, we arrived at the borders of a plain about a mile across, which is covered by the sea when the tides are high. At present the tides are not high, so the plain is of mud, with occasional pools of water. Here we exchanged the carriage for bullock-carts, which carried us slowly but surely to the other side. Another short mile on *terra* in the same carts, and we found ourselves at the Church of St. Joseph, in the small island of Juvem. At 8 a.m. I said Mass before a crowded congregation of native Christians, very few of whom speak a word of English. After Mass, I confirmed, I should think, upwards of sixty persons. This was followed by the kissing of the ring, for which the natives cherish a special devotion. Every one, young and old, even babies in arms, put in an appearance. About 10 a.m. the religious ceremony was over. A cup of coffee followed. And after the coffee, the inevitable address, accompanied, as usual, by some petitions. The address and the palaver carried us to eleven o'clock. Between the address and dinner, I made the visitation of the church, the parochial books, the vestments, &c. About one o'clock we dined, the company consisting of three native priests not knowing English. However, we got through the dinner pleasantly enough. At 3 p.m. we got into the bullock-cart again; a band was hired—two tomtoms and one Indian clarionet, supposed to imitate the human voice (a very nasal, harsh model must have been copied) and the band headed a procession in easy order of all the available men and boys at Juvem, and so we journeyed, being excellently well shaken, through palm-groves on the sea-shore to Tara, where there is a small chapel, served from Juvem. Here we were met by the Christian population, men and women, old and young; again kissing of the ring, &c. From Tara back in bullock-cart to the spot where we left our carriage in the morning, and a continuation of the shaking. A very pleasant drive in the cool of the evening brought us to Fort Chapel soon after 6 p.m The country about Juvem is very pretty; the sea and the palm-groves, with ranges of small hills in the distance, make up a series of really beautiful views. These short excursions make a little change, not unwelcome in my daily desk-life here.

The *Examiner* will tell you how we kept the Jubilee. Our manifestation was a modest one, but the number of Communions was extraordinary, and many outsiders who had not been seen for many years at the altar, made their appearance that day.

Jan. 27, 1888.

What a glorious celebration the Jubilee has been throughout the world. Europeans and natives throughout India have been considerably impressed by our humble festivities. The day in St. Peter's must have been a surprise to your Western world.

We are in mid-winter. Thermometer, 75° to 80° during the day; during the night about 70°. Nothing can be imagined more delightful, except perhaps a trifle more heat during the day. I keep very well.

We must have some cross. The mosquitoes are doing duty at present; the days are short, eleven hours, and during the long night the mosquitoes enter on the scene, and hold me in a state of abject terror. If they would sting and have done with it, and be off, I imagine I could read and write; but while they are hovering about on all sides, sounding their war-trumpet, calm application becomes a difficulty. But what are the mosquitoes to some African scourges? A missioner from Zanzibar tells me of a church in his part of the world in which a grand procession of the Blessed Sacrament was organized. A strong band entered into the programme. At the appointed time the procession left the church, and band and drums struck up. But they had reckoned without a monster bee's nest, which hung up in the belfry. The bees came down in myriads, and attacked the band and the clergy so vigorously, that the line was completely broken up, and the Bishop, carrying the Blessed Sacrament, was driven to take shelter with those around him in some wretched hovel. No devotions were gone through. He told me of a nun who died within three days from the bite of a venomous insect, in great sufferings. He himself was bitten by one of the same insects, and only saved his life by cauterizing the wound; even so his body was swollen to an extraordinary size.

Bombay, Feb. 1, 1888.

My dear Child,

Your account of the state of your health is not very cheering. For the present your duty is to regain as much strength as you can. Above all, avoid extra exertion. More easily said than done. I have observed in those who suffer from weakness of the heart a certain recklessness in attempting too much. . . . Another precaution which will help you is to lie down a great deal; when the body is in a recumbent position, the heart has much less work to do. Lastly, never scruple to take food, or even a little stimulant, when you feel run down. In fine, take care of yourself, and husband your strength; with care, you may still do much good before you are called to your reward. Make up for anything that sounds like self-indulgence in this by special care and quietness and regularity in your spiritual exercises, and by moderating your natural desire to be doing something.

If you find you can say your prayers with attention

lying down, then say them lying down; some persons can pray very well lying down.

You ask me whether I have sent you all the Pastorals and sermons which I have printed? Yes; in one shape or another I have sent you all. I have only issued one Pastoral, and printed one sermon; I do not include what the *Examiner* publishes. The chances of a good congregation are few in Bombay; most of the churches are small, and a considerable portion of the congregations of the smaller churches are perfectly innocent of English. Perhaps by degrees I may be able to create more opportunities of preaching; I very much desire to have them. The sermon is the best weapon in my armoury for Bombay. The sermon on the Papacy was printed almost verbatim in the *Bombay Gazette*, one of our daily papers which has a very wide circulation. The *Examiner* reproduced it with some corrections which I supplied.

On Sunday, I addressed an immense congregation at St. Anne's, Byculla, a new Gothic church, the best in Bombay city, the most convenient to get at, the most frequented by Europeans, where the services are carried out with much decorum, and where a very fine organ and good singing complete the recommendations. The subject was the Real Presence. If the *Examiner* runs short of matter, it will be printed, not otherwise; no one thinks of buying a sermon here. My Lenten Pastoral will soon appear; that you will get.

We have had nothing new lately, either in Church or State. The Protestant Bishop of Bombay has been to Calcutta to confer with his Indian Protestant brothers about the Pan-Anglican Synod, but the consultations have not oozed out as yet; an unusual reticence has been observed. . . .

Our winter is coming to an end, and the days are already warmer, but on the whole our climate through

December and January might be called perfect. There are parts of India where the snow lies on the ground for some months; the cold is very trying, I am told, in those places. They are in the north, near the great ranges of mountains.

Good-bye. God bless you.

Bombay, Jan. 19, 1888.

... In your spiritual affairs you have ups and downs; you have suffered much, and yet on the whole I consider you have made more progress than you believe. You are more spiritual, and you are nearer to God than you were this time last year. Your chief enemy is discouragement; when the devil sees he can discourage you, he whispers, "It is useless trying to be good; give up Holy Communion, and don't waste your time in prayer." You ought to do just the contrary; when you feel discouraged, at those times be most faithful in approaching the sacraments, and take most pains in preparing yourself. When you feel low-spirited, then turn to God and pray with all your heart. Continue in this way for a month, and you will forget what it is to be sad. You will always be in peace and resolved, if you are not even joyful. *Sursum corda.* Raise your heart to God and try to be brave; you are doing very well, and you will do still better. During this year make it a point to increase your devotion to our Lady.

Bombay, Feb. 2, 1888.

In your letter of the 12th you write of a thick fog in the country. Bombay, too, is in winter; but such a winter, thermometer 70° at night, 80° during the day; the air all light and genial warmth. My memory goes back to the spring and early summer of Rome in 1857.

To some extent I realize "the intoxication of life" which Keats reserved for the Roman spring.

The article by F. Myers in the *Fortnightly* on Darwin I have not read as yet. My periodicals come to me a month behind time. I shall have some curiosity to see what he says, for he was a disciple of James Martineau. Both are or were Unitarians, and more or less rationalists. The accounts of Darwin put me out of conceit with him. The man who changes from loving Shakespeare to finding him dull, who loses as he grows old the sense of the beautiful and the grand in nature, who gives no serious thought to the problems of our moral life, does not interest me much. A world of such men would be most dull. Did you remark a story of the Duke of Argyll? He pointed out to Darwin a striking instance of design. "Yes," said Darwin, "it sometimes comes upon me with overwhelming force that there must be a cause, but after a time the impression fades away." I only give the sense of his words. They show that Darwin only cared for facts of the outer world. . . . In my last letter I think I told you of a missionary from Zanzibar, who is staying here. He has lent me the *Vie du Ven. Père Liebermann*, the founder of his Congregation, no name of author, printed Paris, Rue de Tournon 19, 1878, with silly illustrations, for which, however, the text compensates. Ven. Liebermann passed through a strange series of trials and crosses. He tells much of his history in his letters, which are largely quoted. His patience and *abandon* are admirable. God leads His servants by strange ways. . . .

You expose me to temptation by your kind offer to send me any book I may want. Generally I resist the temptation, but to-day I will yield. The *Spectator* has excited my curiosity to read *Lectures on the Book of Job*, by Dr. Bradley, Dean of Westminster (Clarendon Press).

I shall be very grateful, if you send it to me. Job is the grand master on patience, and consoles me, by showing how God allows sufferers to grumble within certain limits. Read it yourself before you send it, if it attracts you. I can wait any length of time.

Since Jan. 1st I have been rather quiet. Last Sunday I preached on the Real Presence; perhaps the sermon may appear in the *Examiner*. I have the idea of printing several dogmatic sermons. The difficulty lies in this—they must be printed in the papers, no one buys sermons here. Thousands see them and read them in the papers. The *Bombay Gazette* printed the sermon on the Papacy. I would preach one a week, if the *Bombay Gazette* would take it. . . .

Bombay, Feb. 3, 1888.

Dear Rev. Mother,

The authors of the round-robin which came to me for the New Year, will be pleased, I am sure, if I answer them all in a letter to you. . . . How far it seems away from Bombay, more than six thousand miles, which geographies and guides give as the distance. Still your letters tell me we are not so far apart; we pray for each other and for a blessing on our work, and we work for the same Master, in the same cause. We meet at the altar.

Accept my thanks and kindly convey them to my correspondents for their New Year greetings.

I condole with you much on losing your good Bishop. He will be a great loss, for he has been a true constant father to your community, and indeed to all the communities of his diocese. His place will not be easily filled.

God enables you to get through all your work, but He puts your trust in Him to the trial, not sending you more vocations. Pray, pray, they must come one day if you pray well.

I was delighted to hear that the schools had acquitted themselves so well, especially the boys' school. *Deo gratias* for that success.

And I must congratulate you on having obtained Father —— for your retreat, that will carry you through a good part of the year, if not the whole of it.

I should like to give you some account of myself, my work, and my diocese. Of myself I can say in one word that I have enjoyed excellent health, that I keep excellent spirits, and that I want to do some good for souls. The climate seems to suit me. In winter the thermometer stands about 70° at night (then we feel a trifle chilly), and 80° during the day, which is delightful. Before many days we shall be in summer heat 80°—85° during the night, 90°—95° during the day, rather warm but quite bearable. As to work, I have no confessions, no retreats, a little preaching. My days are mostly spent at my desk. The churches are small, except the Cathedral and the modern Gothic Church of St. Anne; the decorations are tawdry, the music not ecclesiastical. The services are very long, *e.g.*, three hours for Christmas Eve. European Catholics are not numerous, and we have not a dozen of the better class. The native Christians speak about half a dozen different languages, none of which I understand. The native clergy are about twenty in number, good men, hardworking. Some of the German Fathers help, and they take the chaplaincies. I have two communities of nuns. The Filles de la Croix from Liège, who take care of an Orphanage and Foundling Hospital, and do their work very well. Besides I have the Nuns of Jesus and Mary from Lyons; the teaching of the city of Bombay is in their hands. They have a difficult task to compete with the highly educated

Protestant Sisters and ladies who come out from England. The two Colleges conducted by our Fathers are splendid institutions; in St. Xavier, 1,400 boys (of whom 400 are non-Christians) frequent the schools. We have fine instruments, but to my sorrow the heathens won't listen, won't discuss, won't inquire. If they would only listen, what a field would open to us! 800,000 pagans to convert. Pray for the dawning of that day.

I must conclude now. I send you and each a very special blessing.

I remain, yours very truly in Christ,

✠ GEORGE, Archbishop of Bombay.

Feb. 10, 1888.

You ought to receive a bundle of my Pastorals for Lent, will you kindly send them to the persons whose names you have. This week I will not say anything about the list of prizes. I have been too busy to think of it. The *Serapis*, with Father Pacificus and much treasure on board, had a break-down on the voyage out from England, and had to put into Suez for repairs. The steamer is not expected here before the 14th.

As to Newman's works, I think it better to wait for a complete set. Westell or Edwards won't be long without one. I can wait. Alas! time is not much of an object in the sleepy East.

Whatever you undertake next, try to protect yourself against worry. You may still do a great deal of steady even work. I fear you are not good for much more worry or over-hurry. *Va piano* should be the motto.

Perhaps you remarked an article on the Foundling Home in the *Examiner*, taken from the *Times* of India. That article has brought me many valuable donations in money and kind.

I am going to lose a great prop of the archdiocese, the Superioress of the Daughters of the Cross. She has worked wonders here during her twelve years of government, and has won the affection and esteem of all Bombay: crown of all, she is a saintly person.

Fort Chapel, Bombay, Feb. 10, 1888.

The last mail brought me the *Notes on Mahommedanism*, for which accept my best thanks. I will try to find out whether these Mahommedans have any catechism. I have many friends among the Hindoos and Parsees, but scarcely one among the Mahommedans. They keep more aloof and have no love for the Cross or for Christians. A few, very few, send their boys to our College, and this year one of the Mahommedan boys of St. Xavier's College carried off the first prize in English.

Feb. 15.

At this point I was called away and could not continue the letter in time for the mail. The mail of Monday meanwhile brings me your letter of January 26. I will finish about the Mahommedans. They have much faith in preaching. In their mosques the pulpit or platform, raised a few steps, occupies a prominent place near the spot marked out for public prayer, and in the streets here I not unfrequently pass a Mahommedan holding forth to a crowd.

Now I come to your letter. You must not judge of 1887 so soon. When you are a little further removed from it I trust you will discover that you have made much progress and avanced in spiritual life, in greater detachment from the world, greater dependence on God and greater submission to His will, especially in trials and crosses. We cannot judge of our progress rightly at any given time. We are so prone to despond and notice only the difficulties; after an interval we are capable of a calmer and more hopeful appreciation.

Your strength is returning, I trust. The bills will be settled and put aside, and you will be free to settle down to your Lenten exercises and your literary work. Though you do not experience the same sensible pleasure in religious services which you did formerly, I hope you are conscious of a deeper peace of soul and a conviction that you are doing all you know God requires of you. If the sensible satisfaction grows weaker as we grow older, I think the consciousness of strength and steadfastness replaces it. The *élan* and vigour ought to come back with returning health. Vigour and impaired health seldom keep company. You may feel less enthusiasm than you did of old, but probably you will do more and suffer more hopefully. I do not fear for you that sort of mental and moral atrophy which overtook Darwin in his declining years. You are still quite alive to the beauties of nature and art and literature, and you run little risk of confining all your interest and effort to scientific research or any one branch of intellectual life.

Though the outgoing mail of February 10th did not carry a letter for you, it took my Lenten Pastoral. You ought to receive it before this letter reaches London.

To-day I enter on my second year of Indian life. I landed on the 14th last year; the past twelve months have given me a new experience, which I hope will do my soul much good. Our strength and comfort wherever we are must be in God; the surroundings of our life are, after all, of secondary importance, if we can live with God and do His holy will. I have to be thankful for many graces and blessings in the midst of many difficulties, and in a world not very congenial in many respects. . . .

... My diocese will soon lose a very valuable helper, Mère Provincial of the Filles de la Croix and head of the Orphanage at Bandora. She has been named Provincial of Calcutta. She is a very holy woman, entirely devoted to God and to souls. In some respects she is simplicity itself; at the same time she does not lack shrewdness and the prudence of the serpent. Her energy knows no rest. Her health suffers much from the great heat, but still she wears on, striving bravely and trusting God without limits. Every one respects her and loves her, Protestants and Pagans almost as much as the Catholics. I wish I could show you her orphanage. I must tell you a story of her life, which reveals the goodness of the woman and her simplicity. She had to make a journey of several days and nights through the jungle, in parts where wild beasts abound, and in parts infested by robbers. She travelled alone in a palanquin with twelve Pagan coolies. She had provided for relays, but the relays did not appear. One night the coolies refused to go further and laid her down in a wood. She could hear the hyenas and dreaded a visit from them. In the morning a crowd of natives gathered round her and one threatened to kill her. Fortunately a man speaking English came on the scene and befriended her. She wanted to thank him at the end, but he could not be found. The natives would not even procure her water to make a cup of tea, till some one asked her who she was; she said she was a Brahmin of the highest class, and from that time out, she was everywhere treated with the greatest respect. The Brahmins brought her food, water to wash her feet and her hands, in fact, showed her the honours due to the highest Brahmin. She saw perhaps a smile on my face, so she excused herself for the deceit she had practised. "You know, Monseigneur, as the spouse of Jesus Christ I might claim to be a Brahmin of the highest caste." God bless her. I am very sorry she leaves Bombay.

Now for a story of quite a different kind. A Catholic official up-country gave hospitality to an Anglican clergyman who was making his rounds. This gentleman recounted how in his travels he found his store of salt exhausted. He went to a hut and there saw a supply of salt. He drew forth a rupee and wanted to buy some; the native refused to sell him any. "I was not going to stand that sort of nonsense," he added, "so I took a match and set fire to his roof!" The light of the Gospel with a vengeance. Good-bye. God bless you.

CHAPTER XV.

THE LENTEN PASTORAL AND BEGINNING OF THE SECOND YEAR OF INDIAN LIFE.

Feb. to May, 1888.

Subject of Pastoral, and extract from it. Importance of Prayer. Special graces that cannot be obtained without Prayer. No limit to what God is ready to give to those who ask. Life without Prayer, not the life for which man was created. How Prayer gives a foretaste of Heaven. Mental Prayer. Vocal Prayer. The Psalms. What we should pray for. How to meet desolation arising from physical weakness. An old nun's story. Archbishop Regan's sermon. Hindoo catechumen. A great loss to the Mission. Faith cannot be trifled with. Lord and Lady Reay's visit to the Bandora Orphanage. Death of the Emperor of Germany. Charity of non-Catholics. Great heat. Custom at the death of a Parsee. Extract from Mère Theodorine's journal. Bradley's *Lectures on Job*. Conversions in India. A little lesson of hope. Hindoo Christians' attachment to customs. Difficulty of making changes in religious observances. The Apostleship of Prayer. Clergy retreat. Khandalla. Mary always our Model. The new Emperor of Germany. Advice to an invalid. Spiritual Extreme Unction. The Pope's Jubilee—a grand fact. Trials of a Bishop's life. Dean Bradley's mode of writing. Lesson about God that sufferers may learn from Job. An Armenian church. Pagan superstitions. Dr. Ullathorne's fatherly care for his nuns. Rosmini's Philosophy and the Condemned Propositions. The *Spectator* and Hutton. F. D. Maurice. Da Ponte.

The subject of the Lenten Pastoral, mentioned in the preceding letter, was Prayer. The Archbishop showed how our Lord inculcated by word and example the precept of prayer, and went on to say that " God requires from man the homage of prayer.

". . . Without prayer we cannot be pleasing to God. Without prayer we lose our hold of God: we are drawn to the things of earth. Without prayer we are hurried along by the concupiscence of the eyes, the concupiscence of the flesh, the pride of life. We sink into self-sufficiency, into most foolish pride; we are not far removed from the fool in the Psalms, who said in his heart, 'There is no God.'"[1]

After citing many of our Lord's exhortations to prayer, he continues: "Divine Providence has established the law that special graces are to be granted to prayer; the greater the grace demanded, the more prolonged, the more earnest must be the prayer. Violent and protracted temptations cannot be overcome without special graces; against such temptations our hope lies in prolonged prayer. The accomplishment of duties which involve special difficulties requires special graces. Patience under extraordinary trials, such as the death of dear relatives, loss of health, reverses in fortune, requires special graces. Perseverance in the service of God, through the several stages of life, in prosperity and adversity, in health and sickness, in joy and sorrow, in vigour and weariness, in peace and in temptation, requires very special graces. The needs, temporal and spiritual, of near relatives, of a father or mother or children; the needs of friends; the needs of our country; the needs of the Church,—these often require a special interposition of God. The weapon God has placed in our hands is prayer, special prayer, prolonged fervent prayer, which must not cease till God heeds our cry.

"How much God is prepared to grant to prayer, we learn from the Parable of the Wicked Servant 'who owed his master ten thousand talents. The servant falling down, besought him, saying: Have patience with me, and I will pay thee all. And the lord of that servant, being moved with compassion, let him go and forgave him the debt.'[2]

---

[1] Psalm xiii. 1.   [2] St. Matt. xviii. 26, 27.

"To the power of God there is no limit; to the merciful bounty of God there is no limit. The limits to His gifts are the limits of our trust and our fervour in asking.

"Whoever called on God in temptation and did not receive strength? Whoever turned to Him in deepest affliction and did not obtain peace and strength? Whoever confessed his weakness and implored aid from God without being supported from on high?

"Men murmur often against God, and complain that the burden of life weighs too heavily on them; they have neglected the chief means by which they could have lessened their burden. They confess their sin, and with Cain they say: 'My iniquity is greater than that I may deserve pardon.' Cain never besought God to pardon him. How many in the time of affliction fly for distraction and consolation to creatures, perhaps to sinful pleasures: they have neglected the great Consoler and the great consolation, God the consoler, prayer the consolation.

"Oh! who can adequately describe all that is reserved for us by God in prayer? the light, the love, the joy, the strength, the deep peace, the unconquerable patience and trust! The soul which neglects prayer may be compared to the pilgrim who enters upon the passage of a sandy desert and leaves his store of provisions behind him; or to a warrior who goes forth to encounter a mighty foe with his arms tied; or to a sick man, who refuses all remedies. Such a soul may be compared again to the merchant who would traffic without having money. Life without prayer is not the life for which God created man, it is not the life of a rational being; it is an earthly, an animal life, in which the supernatural is omitted, in which the supernatural end and the supernatural means are wholly lost sight of.

"Our life on earth, seasoned with prayer, becomes in a manner heavenly. We have through prayer a foretaste of Heaven. For Heaven consists in perfect union with God, in the vision of God, face to face, as He is in Himself; and prayer is only a less perfect union with God: it is the effort of the soul to rise to its Creator by its highest faculties of understanding and will. St. Paul and many servants of God have been rapt up to God in prayer and admitted to the very threshold of Heaven. The lowliest may in some proportion draw near to God by prayer.

"Private prayer may be in the mind only, without words or outward movement of the lips. Prayer in the mind only, or *mental* prayer, consists in the raising of mind and heart to God and His mysteries, either the mysteries of His Divine attributes, or the mysteries of His dealings with men. To exercise the understanding about these, to excite the affections of the soul upon them, is mental prayer. To all it has not been given to meditate on the Divine attributes; but to all it is possible to meditate on God's dealings with men, on the fall of man and the promise of a Redeemer, the mystery of human depravity, the mystery of God's mercy; on the history of our redemption; on the Annunciation; the Incarnation; the life, preaching, Death and Passion of our Blessed Lord; and on the completion of this Divine work in the mysteries of the Resurrection, the Ascension, and the Descent of the Holy Ghost. The Rosary is within the reach of all; it combines with the recital of our most familiar vocal prayers, the *Pater, Ave,* and *Gloria,* the thought of the mysteries of our redemption. The Stations of the Passion confine our thoughts to the Passion; but what a field for the devout mind! Again, the devotion to the Five Wounds narrows our prayer still more; but in it we may find an inexhaustible field for the exercise of our thoughts and affections. Lastly, the Real Presence on the altar offers a never-failing theme of prayer to all.

"Every cry to God from our hearts taking shape in words is a *vocal* prayer. The best vocal prayers for each one are those which arise out of his own heart. We may assist ourselves with the prayers contained in books. The model of vocal prayer for all time will be the Psalter. The Psalms express the needs, the prayers of every human soul. . . . The Psalms form one prolonged prayer, for all phases of life, for every need of the soul, for all seasons. For the season of Lent the Church dwells with especial affection on the so-called seven Penitential, the prayer of the sinner who turns to God and implores mercy and forgiveness. . . ."

Bombay, Feb. 17, 1888.

I recommend the Pastoral to your consideration. Betake yourself to prayer. But do not only pray for temporal blessings: pray for these objects, but pray still more for an increase of patience, for more faith, and more hope, and more submission to the will of God. It may be better for you or for somebody else that you should not obtain the temporal favours you ask; but He will assuredly grant you the prayer for spiritual blessings. And, moreover, you will experience *greater peace of mind*, and you will be conscious that you are strengthened to meet the trials of your daily life. Courage! *Sursum corda.* Hope and fight.

The "desolation" you have felt may be only a natural desolation, that is, it may not come from the enemy, or even from God, except indirectly. Sickness and infirmity, especially weakness of the heart, of their own nature impair the energy of the soul and induce sadness and depression of spirits. At such times to make any effort seems very difficult, and to pray almost impossible. The soul is weighed down, and rises to God with a dead weight dragging it down. The thoughts are forced on to one's aches and infirmities, to one's sufferings and chances of alleviation, to food and sleep and physic. At such times don't force yourself to meditate or even to say long vocal prayers. If you feel drawn to pray and you can bear the fatigue, then pray as you feel you best can. Otherwise satisfy yourself with short ejaculations, with Psalms, or verses from the Psalms, with a decade of the Rosary, or with looking at your cross or a pious picture, or merely simmer away, suffering without complaining, and resigning yourself to the will of God; or take your crucifix and kiss the five wounds. The chief point is, not to rebel; after that try to rejoice in God's will in your regard. Pictures often distract the mind from one's sufferings. I had a beautiful *Life of Christ*, with illustrations, by Brothers Wierx, an endless refuge from care and suffering.

I hope you have taken to heart the lesson that you must attend to your food. A weak heart requires nourishment, not much at a time, but rather often through the day, and a little stimulant also. Follow the prescription without difficulty or scruple. You will be the better able to do work for God....

Bombay, Feb. 22, 1888.

I fear your illness has been a very serious one, more serious than you liked to tell me. It is some consolation to know that you are getting better even slowly. In cases like yours, a good cure must be slow, and it will be necessary for you not to be rash and not to rush into much work; above all, you must keep within your strength. The work which tells most on the system and on the heart is work done when the system has fallen below par or when your strength has run down. For this reason among others, taking nourishment, not much, but frequently, is so strongly recommended. Stifle scruples. Your object is a good one. You wish to work longer for God. . . .

You did quite right to accept Father ——'s offer to communicate you in the house. When there is no danger of death, you may always receive Communion if you are able to fast. And when one is a prisoner in the house, deprived of Mass, and otherwise depressed, Holy Communion gives the greatest consolation. At such times Holy Communion made spiritually helps much to keep up courage.

Now for a story. I was talking with an old nun who has been forty years in India (she spent three months between Bombay and Agra, in bullock carts mostly, sometimes on elephants!) about the conversion of Pagans who had been in the service of the nuns. She only remembered one convert. The man was very ill. She went to see him. He asked her for her cross and said he wanted to go after his death where the nuns went. Up there, people say, pointing overhead; not down there where bad people go. She sent a priest, who prepared the poor fellow as best he could for mounting upwards. He thanked the nun very warmly. "I am very poor. I have nothing to give you, but when I die take this skin (it hung loosely about his bones), and make it into shoes for the Sisters." Dead men's shoes with a vengeance! I infer from the story that survivors in India have put the skins of departed relatives to such a use.

Fort Chapel, Bombay, Feb. 29, 1888.

Your letter of Feb. 9th lies before me. You were suffering from an attack of workmen, upholsterers, and other miseries, and your letter somewhat reflects your state of mind. These mundane matters must be attended to. They form a part of our life. They are the best school of patience, if we only make the most of our trials and put on a good face when our feelings are not altogether conciliatory.

I have just been laughing over a passage in a fine sermon by Archbishop Regan on the occasion of the laying of the foundation-stone of the new Irish church in Rome. The sermon may not come into your hands, so I quote the passage. "Not only was she faithful to the Church at home, but when her children had to leave that island of fidelity and sorrow, when her enemies trampled in the dust her national banner wet with her blood, she grasped the napkin of Veronica, waved it above the heads of her children, and bore it in triumph to America and Australia and India, and planted it wherever a church could be built in honour of Him Whose image it bore." The napkin of Veronica doing duty for the blackthorn tickles my fancy. . . .

. . . Good news. My Mother Theodorine does not go to Calcutta. She remains in this diocese. As she wrote to me very gravely, "Man proposes. God disposes." I am very thankful.

I have finished the Life of the Foundress of the Filles de la Croix. It is rather nunny, and tells more of the Congregation than of the foundress. Still in the latter chapters there are some instructive points. Father Baur has returned to Zanibar, much set up in health. Père Liebermann's Life is written in French. There is a longer Life from the pen of Cardinal Pitra. The Life

Father Baur lent to me was an abridgment of Cardinal Pitra's. Some volumes of Father Liebermann's letters have been published. Perhaps I may be able to furnish fuller details later, for the good Father promised to send me various volumes of life and letters.

Yesterday I began the instruction of my first Hindoo catechumen. He is editor of a paper in English and Gujerati, speaks English well. He looks less than thirty. He is intelligent. I hope he is in real earnest. He seems to be so. He has taken a month's leave in order to be baptized. Mère Theodorine sent him to me. He was drawn to her by discontent with Hindooism and admiration for the orphanage. He wanted Mère Theodorine to baptize him. What a work he has before him. His father is dead, but his mother and two sisters live with him and upon him. He is betrothed, a very serious obligation. He wants to break off his marriage, and trusts his mother will succeed. If only he were to become a priest later, for he is a true Brahmin! I must first secure him in the Church. His conversion must be a secret. Pray for him and for my work with him. By the way, on Friday Lord and Lady Reay are going to visit Mère Theodorine's orphanage.

Yesterday the mission sustained a great loss. Francis, he had no surname, the head-man of the Madrassees (I have one thousand of them), schoolmaster, catechist, sacristan, in fact, the one man amongst them for everything, died quite suddenly and was buried within twenty-four hours.—R.I.P. God will replace him, I hope. He was a remarkable man. Tall, fine-looking, very intelligent, knew Tamil perfectly, read and wrote French well, was educated. He seemed indispensable to the priest. . . .

Bombay, March 14, 1888.

... You remark on the lively faith which is often given to Jewish converts. Perhaps the explanation of the difference in their case and that of converts from Anglicanism is to be sought in the absence of questioning and doubting on the part of the Jews. As a rule they believe in Judaism up to a point, then are led to desire the truth which is given to them. The longer I live the better I realize the delicacy of faith. It won't bear being trifled with. Mental habits of doubt and scepticism and hesitation in trusting to reason, and reading unbelieving books and talking with unbelieving people, all hamper the exercise of faith, perhaps through a life-time. Miseries about faith are not unknown to born Catholics, and I have generally been able to connect them with a habit of questioning and doubting. The frequent use of acts of faith helps to break the tyranny of doubt. I have some trust in falling back on first principles in this way: If I deny the existence of God, I must go against my reason. If I deny the Divinity of Jesus Christ, I must deny the existence and attributes of God. If I deny the Church, I must deny the Divinity of Jesus Christ.

You will be glad to know that my Hindoo catechumen perseveres so far. Continue to pray for him, for his own sake, and because he may help others later on.

I shall never be surprised to see you out here. The other day at a meeting held in favour of our deaf, mutes, an account of which you will see in the *Bombay Catholic Examiner*, I found myself beside a dear old lady, aged seventy-six, who having lost her husband had sought distraction in her widowhood by a tour through Ceylon and India. Her sympathies and interests in life and its problems have not suffered from atrophy. She was all there, alive to all the complications of the Indian problem and forming her judgments very wisely. She reminded me something of your aunt, whom you will invite to join you in your holiday trip.

The *Bombay Catholic Examiner* will also tell you of a visit paid by Lord and Lady Reay to Mother Theodorine's orphanage at Bandora. I was obliged to leave before the visit was ended, as I was due in the Cathedral for a sermon. Lord and Lady Reay were delighted with everything and everybody, especially with Mother Theodorine. When I have less to write about, I will give you some histories from the annals of her orphanage. They are most interesting. . . .

The old Emperor of Germany has gone. His son holds his life by a slender thread. Will the conflict of the nations be long put off?

The weather seems to be very severe in your latitudes. Here we are still under 90°, with a good breeze for the middle of the day. *Per contra*, mosquitoes unusually numerous and energetic. I wish you a *Buona Pasqua* and many consolations.

March 15, 1888.

The *Bombay Catholic Examiner* will keep you posted in our religious history. The Governor and Lady Reay's visit to the Orphanage at Bandora, the meeting for the deaf-mutes, and a short mission in the Cathedral, have kept me very fully occupied. . . . As a rule I find good friends among the non-Catholic people in Bombay. Justice Scott and Mrs. Scott take a lively interest in the deaf-mutes; the Orphanage enjoys a wide popularity, so does the Foundling Hospital, so does the Leper's Home, though not to the same degree. The charity and benevolence of Bombay are conspicuous. They will turn aside the anger of God, which must be provoked by this huge mass of heathenism and wickedness, and I pray it may hasten the day of faith for many.

Fort Chapel, Bombay, March 23, 1888.

Your two letters of Jan. 7 and Feb. 8 lie before me waiting for an answer. The papers tell us you have had a second winter more severe than the first. What a contrast: you are perishing with cold, and here two days ago the thermometer stood at 96°, a point we seldom pass. This year the great heat has commenced before its time. And last night we had a violent storm with heavy rain, an event quite out of the common run. My health continues very good, all I could wish. Yes, I have passed the season of anniversaries, of leaving London, of arriving in Bombay, of being consecrated at Allahabad. And now I am advancing in my second year of Indian life. It goes very quickly.

The *Times* summary of the year never reached me. If it is only a newspaper, don't mind inquiring about it. It is not worth the trouble, unless you like to put the Post Office authorities on their good behaviour. You always tie up your papers so carefully and so securely, I wonder this particular one went astray. That reminds me I must thank you for the *Catholic Times*, which comes with unfailing regularity. What an amount of Catholic news it contrives to put together. You kindly offer me a copy of the notes on retreats which I preached at Roehampton. I am much obliged to you, but the compiler of the notes was good enough to send me a copy.

The other day came news of the death of Father Dykes. It seems to me that deaths have been very frequent of late among friends. We must hold ourselves in readiness. Good-bye. God bless you.

Fort Chapel, Bombay, March 23, 1888.

The P. and O. of last Monday brought me Rev. Bradley's *Job*, and the box of vestments. I cannot say much about Job as yet, as I have had a very busy week, getting ready the *Messenger of the Sacred Heart*, a sermon on St. Patrick, and the Latin Pastoral Gazette. Next week I promise myself a little quiet reading. . . .

One of the big Parsees of Bombay died lately. His death called attention to a nice custom they have. On the third day the near relatives meet and subscribe for various charities and beneficent institutions. In the present instance £60,000 were subscribed, or as we say, six lakhs of rupees. The dead man's share is a large one. He contributes a Parsee sanatorium and a Parsee orphanage. The rest of the money is divided among various libraries, &c. In this case the money was confined almost exclusively to Parsee objects. Two exceptions were made in favour of two of my charities—the Deaf-Mutes and the Lepers' Home. One thousand rupees were assigned to each. The dead man was present at our annual exhibition of the deaf-mutes, shortly before he was taken ill. This charity and the lepers have been before the public rather prominently of late. Our charities depend much on the liberality of the non-Christians, especially the Parsees, who are more liberal than the Hindoos or Mahommedans.

My young Hindoo catechumen perseveres so far. The troubles are yet to come. His mother won't hear of his breaking off his marriage. He has new schemes before him. He hopes to be sent to England by the Gaikwar of Baroda, in short, my fish is not landed yet. He has gone through a considerable part of a long catechism, the Creed, the Commandments, and now we are in the Sacraments at the Holy Eucharist. He certainly possesses much intelligence, and he is very keen for knowledge. Continue to pray for him. He has a hard battle to fight.

I promised you some extracts from the Journal of

Mother Theodorine. I take the first which comes. "At about 2 p.m. on February 15th, a native doctor called to ask if we could not go with him at once to have a child just born removed to the Foundling Hospital. We consented, and taking a companion, followed him to the house where the child was. On seeing it we felt sure that it would not live long. On our way to the Foundling Home the child opened for the first time its beautiful blue eyes and looked smilingly, as if to ask for something. We said, we know well what you want—Baptism: and forthwith we baptized it, giving it the name of Joseph. Instead of going on to the Foundling Hospital, we returned to Bandora, and about five o'clock in the evening, little Joseph joined the choir of angels, and was singing the praises of Almighty God."

Maundy Thursday, 1888.

... Bradley's *Job* interests me; but I think he has missed the deepest lessons of the book. I do not believe he has caught the real thoughts of Job; but I shall wait till I have read the book through, and then I will try to throw my criticism into shape. His entire renunciation of the mystical interpretation disappointed me. Cardinal Newman, in his *Essay on Development*, if I remember rightly, almost makes the acceptance of the mystical sense a test of orthodoxy. Those who part from the Church seem instinctively to drop all interpretation that is not exclusively literal. Bradley proves himself an able man and a good scholar. I hear that he is best known for his edition of Arnold's *Latin Exercises*. I am glad he has aspired higher....

... You remark that little has been said of Catholic work in the (missionary) controversy (in the newspapers). Our progress is very unequal. In the south, in Madura especially, much has been done, and solidly done. Whole villages and tracts of country have been made Catholic. I believe the converts might be counted by tens of thousands. The caste system has less hold in the south. Again, in the jungle on the Calcutta side the Belgian Fathers have obtained some consoling results. Up to the present, the non-Christians in the large towns are unapproachable. They won't listen, or read, or discuss. In our parts the tyranny of caste destroys all freedom of inquiry or conscience. I am not without hope of being able to do something later with the Press, but the time has not come yet, and I am not sufficiently known. Meanwhile, I trust much to prayer, and to the Apostleship of Prayer, to prepare the minds and hearts of people for the gift of faith. I recommend the conversion of the Indians as a special intention in your prayers.

I shall conclude with a little lesson of hope. The devout women asked, " Who shall roll away the stone?" It ought to be, who *can* roll away the stone—and they found it rolled away. Often we ask how can this be done? and often if we don't give up, if we do what we can and pray God to supply what is wanting, we find it is done, the stone is rolled away. In my next I may return to Mère Theodorine and Mr. John Morley. What a conjunction!

Bombay, April 5, 1888.

Last mail-day was Good Friday, and I am not sure whether I was able to write. If I did, I could only have sent a hurried note. Let me now wish you a *Buona Pasqua*, though Paschal-time will be somewhat advanced when this reaches you.

The vestments were used at the Pontifical High Mass on Easter Sunday, and were admired by my Christians, though they are accustomed to the ponderous Portuguese style. I was obliged to offer my Mass on Easter Sunday and the two following days for my flock. But on Wednesday I offered it for you and for your intentions, and put in a special *memento* for Sister R——.

On the same Easter Sunday, a very magnificent episcopal chair was set up in the Cathedral, made of our best woods, and really well carved.

Did I tell you Father Hayes was so good as to send me the old Notre Dame de Lourdes which called forth so much devotion in Farm Street, before the new chapel and statue came into existence? It looks so well in our little Fort Chapel, and has begun to work on the feelings of our people.

We are strangely behind here. In all matters of art and taste we are quite a century after the rest of the Catholic world. The month of May, I may say, is unknown. Still more strange, the Novena of Grace to St. Francis Xavier, which ends March 12th, is absolutely unknown in India, at least in Bombay. The Christians have much devotion to the Passion, to Our Lady of Dolours, to the dead Christ; and on certain occasions very much devotion to the Blessed Sacrament. And it is not easy to change the prevailing ideas, or to add to them. The Hindoo instinct is pre-eminently conservative. Once establish a custom and it may last till the day of doom. A curious example: In the rubrics it is prescribed that the *Jam exultet* on Holy Saturday should be sung *ex pulpito*, which means from the lectern, but some fifty years ago a priest of some authority understood it to be from "the pulpit," and from the pulpit it is duly sung, notwithstanding the palpable inconveniences of the practice. A very marked tendency in the Hindoo character is to observances, forms, and formalities. I believe the Brahmins maintain their authority over the people by rigorously insisting on endless observances. You may remember the Gaekwar of Baroda visited England. To cross the " black water," the sea, is reckoned a sin. The sinner on his return must go through various purifications, some decidedly nasty. One, in this case, was a payment of twenty thousand rupees, to be given in various charities. This I don't call a nasty ceremony, it is a costly one.

This mail ought to take for you the numbers of the Indian *Messenger*, from July 1, 1887. Previously it was printed in a very inconvenient form. As yet we are satisfied to cut a poor figure. Our subscribers are not much over five hundred. You may see from the Intentions that the people are very simple. My hope is that within a short time the Apostleship of Prayer will take a great development, and I trust more to prayer than to any other weapon in the present state of affairs. Should you ever feel disposed to send any articles, verse or prose, nice sayings or doings of the saints, original thoughts, &c., they will be gratefully received. Remark the translations from an MS. left by Father Druzbicki. He left them in an unfinished state, but they suggest methods of prayer which may be usefully employed.

Don't forget to tell me whether your health is improving.

St. Xavier's Villa, Khandalla,
April 11, 1888.

I think I wrote to you last year from this place, up among the Ghats, seventy-eight miles away from Bombay. The native priests (not all of them) from the dioceses of Bombay and Poona, seventeen in number, are going through their annual retreat under my direction. Last year I came to see them, and to give them one or two instructions. This year I give the whole retreat.

The climate differs much from that of Bombay. The air up here is very dry, in Bombay it is always moist and damp. The heat during the day is as great here, but the mornings and nights are cool and often breezy. The scenery would delight you. On every side great mountains thrown here and there, in the wildest fashion, of every form and shape. One is called the Duke of Wellington's nose, and the resemblance strikes every visitor.

Many of the mountains look barren and scorched, but there is plenty of verdure, if you walk a short distance. Just at present the soil looks more parched, and is more parched because we are nearing the rainy season.

St. Xavier's Villa is a bungalow built for the accommodation of some twenty (at a push thirty) Fathers. They come here during the holiday to escape the great summer heat of Bombay. It is complete: has a nice chapel, refectory, in fact everything. The situation is perhaps the finest in the whole neighbourhood.

Your fate as a "mover on" on the face of the earth, furnishing houses and then leaving them, furnishing now the eighth in succession, is indeed a strange one; it has not fallen to the lot of many. You point out one great gain which you may derive from it. You may live in the world and not of it, use it as though you used it not, directing your thoughts to an unchangeable home. I am not quite satisfied with your theology and your idea of how our Lady would have acted in similar circumstances. I cannot help thinking she would have attended to carpets and coal-scuttles and the rest as well as she could in each of the eight houses, while she tried to be patient under the endless round of mere trivialities. It is not easy to picture her in such a life, but we may feel certain she would have sanctified it by her diligence and patience and very faithful use of spiritual opportunities. How much of every one's life goes in what is only valuable in proportion as it is well done.

I find I still run some risk of losing my good Mother Theodorine, at least for a time. The matter rests with her Superioress in Liège, and we must wait one or two weeks before the decision comes to us. I can better spare her for a time, if I know she will return to Bombay.

My Hindoo catechumen has gone to Karachi for a fortnight. He has gone on well so far. The relatives are in arms against his proposal to break off the marriage. That step means the loss of all the jewels and dowry which have been promised to the lady.

The old Emperor and the new Emperor of Germany! What a contrast! And what a startling lesson on the uncertainties of life! A general idea prevails in Germany that the new Emperor, if spared, would rule wisely and justly. Innumerable prayers have been offered for his recovery. The Catholics fancy he is well disposed to them, and always disliked Bismarck's persecution.

TO AN INVALID.

April, 1888.

What you tell me of the state of your heart does not quite take me by surprise; only I had hoped you had not as yet reached the stage of the permanent invalid; perhaps even yet you may disappoint the doctor. I hope you will take certain sensible precautions: *e.g.*, always keep yourself well warmed in winter; don't face the raw morning fasting if you can help it; *never hurry*, and lastly, carry with you a tiny bottle of brandy; one single drop on the tongue often averts a serious attack. I see I must add another lastly, attend to nourishment, never let yourself run down. These are for your bodily health. Let me prescribe for the soul. Your death may be sudden. It need not be so necessarily. Pray you may have the sacraments. Make every day what some French writers have called a spiritual Extreme Unction. Read through the prayers of Extreme Unction and the prayers for the dying. Perhaps at first this devotion may give you some alarm; I do not think it will, but if it does, I beg of you to persevere with it for a few days, and I promise you that you will find in it the greatest peace and comfort. I venture to make this promise, having seen in many cases this invariable result. The practice itself forms a very fitting preparation for death, be it distant or near. One of my penitents who had a natural fear of death began this devotion with some repugnance, but she told me afterwards it had been a great consolation. She persevered in it faithfully during two years. I saw her very unexpectedly on the Friday before Whit Sunday. She died on the Monday in Whitsun week.

However, while I give you this preparation for death, I hope God will spare you long, to sanctify yourself and to do good for others.

St. Xavier's Villa, Khandalla,
April 11, 1888.

Your letter comes just at the right moment. The heading will tell you that I am absent from Bombay. Khandalla is seventy-eight miles distant from Bombay, in the midst of the finest scenery of the Ghats. The native priests of the dioceses of Bombay and Poona, to the number of seventeen, are here assembled to make their annual retreat, under my direction. The climate is very different from that of Bombay. It is more dry. The sun burns fiercely during the day, but the mornings and evenings are cool and generally breezy.

Your letter did reach me on Low Monday, towards the middle of the day, but you and your community have a daily *memento* in my Mass.

What a grand fact the Pope's Jubilee has been. I am sure great graces will come to the world. I hear the same tale everywhere, numerous conversions of souls long estranged from God. The political horizon looks dark enough, as if the days of mighty wars could not be far distant. Where will it all end? Is the civilized world hurrying to a crash, or will God grant a further reprieve to a people which flies from Him further and further? I confess the outlook fills me with anxiety. One safe conclusion will be to do more for our own sanctification.

My health is very satisfactory, thank God. I eat, sleep, and work well. My flock, my Cathedral, my palace are all wonderfully unlike anything in Brompton. If ever I can find an idle hour, I will write you a picture. The only resemblance will lie in the worries which fall to my share. I imagine the mitre always covers a world of small worries, and occasionally some big ones. My sack of small ones is full; the big ones promise an early visit. It does not matter much. Our trials are as big as we make them. And then I can console myself with the story of the bull-pup, "Bear it, father," &c. You have not forgotten it.

Thank God for a long chain of blessings, and love and serve Him as well as you can, and wish and try to love and serve Him better.

God bless you.

Bombay, April 27, 1888.

Your letter of April 5th was still wintry and snowy. Has spring yet put in an appearance? We are in summer, and our tropical light and foliage are wonderful. At times they quite take me out of myself. I wish you could see our palm-groves at sunset, or when the moon is full. The whole vegetable world is very wonderful.

I quite agree with your estimate of our Douay version of Job. It always pleased me, and whenever, reading through Bradley, I turned to the Douay, my liking for it was increased. Bradley writes like a thorough Ritualist, taking up questions, then dropping them, trying to defend doubtful causes, detracting from God's best servants, and utterly ignoring all mystical interpretation, a sure symptom of a mind not in harmony with the Church, or with Christ and His Apostles. Cardinal Newman, in his *Development*, says some strong things on the mystical sense of Scripture. Bradley's worst sin is condemning Job of impatience. I look on Job as the Scriptural proof that sufferers may complain bitterly to God without offending Him. And in very great sorrows what a comfort it is to show God, as it were, all one's wounds and their inmost horrors. My studies of Job have been interrupted. I finished Bradley. Now I want to arrange my ideas on the whole book: the three friends may represent heresy, and no doubt they do; but what is the literal drift of their persecution of Job? I like your idea that their persistent self-satisfied charging him with sin added a separate suffering to all which had gone before.

Fort Chapel, Bombay, May 4, 1888.

. . Did I tell you that my next-door neighbour is an Armenian (schismatic) church? Yesterday, they forced me to think of them by interminable devotions and the frequent ringing of a very harsh bell. The praying began about 6 a.m., then developed into singing, rather monotonous, and this lasted well on till mid-day. I did not remark when the services were resumed in the afternoon; but at 9 p.m. the singing was in full swing, and it must have continued till midnight. I was told they were keeping their Maundy Thursday. So far (9 a.m.) Good Friday has been kept in silence. The Armenian congregation was numerous and wealthy, but the chief families fell into the hands of the money-lenders, and now barely a dozen persons can be got together. The priest sends two students who live with him to the Protestant school, and some time ago an Armenian Bishop took part in Evensong, and said a prayer in Armenian over the Ritualistic congregation.

By the way, Mr. Luke Rivington's conversion has caused a commotion in the Ritualistic camp. I have hopes that one or two good men may follow his example. You may be interested in the following. The Tansa Waterworks is a colossal undertaking now in progress. The chief manager of the iron work is a Catholic. You will estimate the scale of the works when I tell you he advertised for twenty thousand hands. As a fact, he has never quite reached half that figure. One day a rumour flew through the crowd that all the male children were to be sacrificed in order to conciliate the favour of the gods on the new waterworks. Within a few minutes a regular stampede took place, and the labourers left in hundreds. Scarcely were the effects of this panic got over, when a man who had been sent up a long pipe (they are 4 feet in diameter) came out saying he had seen "Shaitan," *i.e.*, the devil. The natives live in constant fear of the devil, and this word caused another stampede, and the men would not return until a goat was sacrificed and the pipes smeared with the blood. A feast on the sacrificed goat and libations of toddy followed, and the work goes on again. These labourers were all Pagans, but two days ago a priest brought me some idols he had found in a Christian house: three silver plates set in a copper casing, not bad workmanship. The priest had gone to the house to bless it. He observed on the floor some red powder, red lead, which is much used by the worshippers of the monkey-god. He forced his way into a room which was closed, and there he found a Pagan oratory. He carried off the idols, promising to restore the broken silver. What sounds strange after this history, the priest fined the man, a fisherman, forty rupees for the church, and the man paid the fine. The next point will be to get him to the sacraments with his family. Many of the Christians are poorly instructed, and they cling to their Pagan superstitions. It is not easy to instruct them, they don't want to be instructed. Pray for them.

The great heat has not set in yet. The thermometer has never passed 90°. I find the mornings and evenings most pleasant. I keep my health, thank God. To-morrow the Archbishop of Goa comes to Bombay. He sails for Europe on the 10th, and will be absent six months, or perhaps a year. I am longing to have some news of your health and your spiritual affairs.

Fort Chapel, Bombay, May 8, 1888.

Dear Mother ——

Many thanks for your letter and for the mortuary card. They were the first intimation of your dear brother's death.—R.I.P. He was a holy man, and dear to God, and I believe he will have a high place in Heaven. He certainly received the grace of prolonged and intense suffering, and he was always most patient, and more than patient. His words on the card tell the tale of many years' familiarity with the Cross. You have much to thank God for in his illness and death, and you have a good friend in Heaven.

You have lost a very dear old Father in Bishop Ullathorne. I always said he gave a perfect example of fatherly care for his nuns. How deeply interested he was in each community and in each Sister. He has never written the great work on Humility. We are all losers by its being kept back, though I dare say much that would have appeared in it has a place in his last three great works.

Kindly thank Rev. Mother for her note. I am very glad Bishop Ilsley encourages the Apostleship of Prayer. I am confident you will find in him a kind Father, who will take much to heart the spiritual and temporal welfare of your community.

I am glad to hear that you have some hope of receiving new subjects. May they persevere and prove useful members to your community.

Remember me very kindly to Sister ——, Mother, ought I not to say? I am sorry to hear that the gout has gone upwards. Tell her that I will pray for her, that she may be very patient and merit a glorious crown by her sufferings. Please tell her I send her a special blessing.

Yes, the ties to earth are snapping one by one. Before long we may hope ourselves to be called out of this vale of tears to our rest.

Remember me very kindly to Rev. Mother and to all my old friends at ——. I pray for you all every day at Mass.

Bombay, May 8, 1888.

The last mail brought me on Sunday afternoon your welcome letter of April 19. I will begin with Rosmini. The condemned Propositions 38, 39, 40 form one end of his system. The other end, the beginning, goes with those Propositions. Rosmini held that we see God in Himself, here in this world, in some sort of a way, and only by seeing God do we see creatures. To put his idea in a rough way, we cannot say finite, without saying implicitly infinite, *i.e.*, God. This is a form of ontologism. The Church has condemned it. If ontologism assigns to the creature an undue cognition of God in the natural order, Propositions 38, 39, 40 take away from the knowledge of God which the blessed enjoy. In the Beatific Vision the blessed see God face to face, as He is in Himself. Rosmini only allows them to see Him in His works as Creator. In the *Tablet* of March 24th you have the Latin text of the condemned Propositions. It might throw light on the French translation. Rosmini's condemnation, though long delayed, was seen to be inevitable. You have Cornoldi's *Filosofia*, or Lezioni on Filosofia. If I remember rightly, he has a chapter on Rosmini. Rosmini held some dangerous opinions on Church government, and the Italian Liberals have on many occasions appealed to him as their authority. The delay of the condemnation was partly delayed by the great exertions of the Italian politicians. I have No. 1 of the *Études*, but have not had time to read it as yet. It promises well.

The rapid sale of *Spiritual Retreats* is very encouraging. I did not anticipate that the edition would go so quickly.

The *Spectator* comes to me regularly. I find it very pleasant and suggestive reading. Hutton interests me. He has been so long at the door of the Church. He understands many things, but he has not as yet reached the idea of the Church as God's witness to man on earth, as the Divine messenger. He has many Catholic friends. Of Arnold's writings I know nothing. They never came in my way. F. D. Maurice I dislike. I copied out the following from a letter of his on his second marriage: "I thank you especially for remembering my marriage, because I take it as a proof that you do not set me up as a teacher, but own me as a friend. One who marries voluntarily comes down from any oracular tripod, and declares that he has nothing to distinguish him from his fellows," &c. Not bad for a guide of English thought in matters of faith!

... Don't forget to use Da Ponte's meditations on the Divine Perfections. He was a sound theologian as well as a great saint. I am reading for my spiritual book, *Behold your Mother*—the Virgin Mother of God—by St. Bernard, his homilies in English (Richardson and Son, 1886), a really good translation, though St. Bernard must always lose something when taken apart from his Latin. The weather at present is delightful. Thermometer above 90°, and a breeze for the most part of the day and night cools the air. The deep blue sky and the balminess of the air recall the glories of a Roman spring. At times I almost feel young again. Next Sunday I go to Mahabuleshwar for the inside of a week. Lord Reay has invited me to stay with him. I hope to secure some quiet reading. I promise myself further study of holy Job, and one of Martineau's works.. Martineau was, perhaps still is, a Unitarian. He has reasoned himself out of a foolish philosophy into one which seems generally true. He writes well, sometimes eloquently. Good-bye. God bless you. I wish you a happy Pentecost. *Pasqua delle Rose*, I think the Romans call it.

CHAPTER XVI.

THE ARCHBISHOP'S ILLNESS. MAHABULESHWAR. GANESH
KHIND. KIRKEE.

May to Sept. 1888.

Confidence in God. Journey to Poona and Mahabuleshwar. Visit to Lord and Lady Reay. Interest manifested in Mr. Luke Rivington's conversion. The worries of wealth. Reviews of *Robert Elesmere*. Consideration shown to unbelievers. Malarial fever, and removal to Kirkee. Kindness of Lord and Lady Reay. Hope. God nearest to us in dark hours. Papal Decree on Boycotting and the Plan of Campaign. What to do when everything is a trouble. Portrait of St. Ignatius. On sanctifying sickness and helplessness. Ganesh Khind. Death of the Emperor Frederick of Germany. James Martineau's writings. Hettinger on the Apostolic See. More helps for strengthening hope. The Pan-Anglican Synod. Sir Henry Maine's *Ancient Law* and *Village Communities*. Bright's *Progress to Democracy*. Visit to the Cowley Fathers at Poona. *Life of Lady Georgiana Fullerton*. Kirkee. Feast of St. Ignatius. The Prerogatives of St. Peter. "Without St. Peter there can be no Church." The Lambeth Conference. Mr. Rivington's *Plain Reason*. Return to Bombay. Difficulty of taking exercise.

May 17, 1888.

My dear Child,

I must thank you for your letter of April 1st, and all your good wishes and prayers on St. George's day.

You do not give a very bright account of your health up to the present. You have passed a penitential Lent, I fear, confined all the time to your bed. Patience! this life is not our resting-place. One can never be long without trouble or suffering, of one kind or another.

Sursum corda. Keep up your courage, and try to resist all despondency; do what you can on your part, and trust to God for the rest with the fullest confidence. He won't abandon you. I am glad the spiritual account is more consoling. I am writing from Mahabuleshwar; it is a station on the hills, with a very nice climate. Bombay has become very hot and sultry. When I left on Sunday, the thermometer was at 92° on my verandah, and the air was clear and still, no breeze at all. The journey up to this place occupied nearly a day, forty miles posting, all up-hill. I think we were seven and a half hours on the road. The country is all wooded, and intersected by the most magnificent roads, the drive here quite equal to the best parts around London.

Unfortunately I must return to Bombay for next Sunday. A month here would be a delightful holiday before the rainy season sets in. I hope your next letter will give better accounts of your health, and of continued improvement in other ways. Good-bye. God bless you.

I remain, yours very truly in Christ,

✠ GEORGE, Archbishop of Bombay.

Fort Chapel, Bombay, May 21, 1888.

Your letter of May 4th was delivered this morning before six o'clock. I answer at once, for to-morrow the first monsoon mail (Tuesday instead of Friday) starts.

I have just returned from Mahabuleshwar, the first refuge of our Governors from the heats of Bombay. They linger there till the monsoon breaks. The rainfall at Mahabuleshwar is over three hundred inches during that terrible season. From Mahabuleshwar they go to Poona, where the monsoon is a mild affair. Lord Reay wrote me a very kind note, asking me to be his guest at Mahabuleshwar—so kind a note, I could not do otherwise than accept his invitation. He and Lady Reay both treat me with the most marked attention; they insist on introducing me to all the notabilities, of whatever creed or nationality. I will tell you of my visit; it will give you some idea of Indian life. The first stage to Poona was simple enough, a good railway, good carriages, good speed; about five hours. I reached Poona at 7 p.m., and had intended to post all night (seventy-five miles) to Mahabuleshwar; but at some distance from Poona we encountered a terrific storm of rain and thunder and lightning, rather out of season. No chance of getting beyond Poona, so I claimed hospitality from the Bishop, slept at his house, said Mass next morning, and by his advice changed my plan, and took the train to Watha: five hours in a narrow gauge, very slow pace, most irregular delays. I arrived about 2 p.m., dined, then posted in a phaeton forty-five miles to Mahabuleshwar—a primitive concern, no comfort or rest in it—a rather dreary drive. We only passed one village, Wai, a considerable one, however, and most picturesque, with its line of temples on the sacred Krishna. I am wrong, there was another, Pauchgunni, perhaps ten miles from Mahabuleshwar, a small hill-station, where people live all the year round without discomfort. There were huts where we changed horses. We met and overtook bullock-carts; for the rest we went on, on through a wild desert country, always mounting and mounting. The scenery rather awed me: deep gorges, large plateaux, sometimes a mountain-top, sharp and clear against the sky, not much vegetation. The landscape seemed a scorched desert. I reached Mahabuleshwar long after dark, dressed, took some refreshment, and then joined the company. What a shaking I had in those forty miles!

I said Mass every morning at the little chapel of Mahabuleshwar, two miles away; had a cup of coffee in my room on my return; then enjoyed two hours' reading, writing, praying, as the case might be; 9.30, breakfast, which did not take long; room again till 2.30 lunch; after lunch, driving, seeing what was to be seen, &c.; 8, dinner. I have not told you what sort of a place Mahabuleshwar is. You must know the soil is composed of very red earth. For miles around Mahabuleshwar you have unbroken jungle, wood, not very fine trees, but real trees, not mere brushwood, all even now of bright green; beyond the jungle, the same sort of scenery, through which I drove from Watha, piles upon piles of mountains (about 4,500 feet high), then the valley of the Konkan, and beyond the sea, which you distinguish plainly on a clear day. The jungle is intersected by a very elaborate system of roads, kept in perfect condition. I don't think you have on any side of London such glorious drives and walks. The bungalows are all scattered up and down. Each has its garden, or rather, luxuriant growth which takes the place of garden. Some very pretty, well laid-out gardens there were. An enterprizing Chinaman grows strawberries, but they are not as good as English strawberries—they are watery, and rather acid.

Mahabuleshwar quite took me by surprise. I had been too busy to take informations about the place. Hence, whence I woke up to see the jungle, and the roads, and the rest, I was, as it were, in a new and a better world. The climate was perfection, about 80° in the shade, rather less. The whole of official Bombay was there, so I never wanted for pleasant company and sensible conversation. Several of the best heads among the Hindoos were there. One, a member of the Governor's Council, sought me out to learn all he could about Mr. Luke Rivington's conversion. " I cannot understand it," he said. " Why did he leave the Church of England?" They had been near neighbours for some time in Poona, and had become intimate. Naturally I pointed out to him that Mr. Rivington had only followed his conscience. He had found the truth, and had accepted it; had discovered his duty, and performed it at every sacrifice. "But don't you think, if we keep the Ten Commandments, that will satisfy God?" That seems the highest standard a Hindoo can arrive at. When I asked him whether man had duties to his God, whether he was bound to receive a Divine message and obey it, whether God could be passed over by His creature, he had not much to say. This man likes to talk about religion, perhaps some day the light may reach him.

I left on Friday about 4 p.m., posted seventy-five miles to Poona, arrived just after 5 a.m., rested till noon, and returned to Bombay, reaching it at 7 p.m. Altogether I had a pleasant holiday, with the penalties of the two long journeys by road. On these occasions many persons talk to me about religion, and I trust some good is done; otherwise, the mere world is a dreary piece of acting.

I pity you with your life-long temptation to despondency; console yourself, though it is so trying, it is most rich in opportunities of merit. Perseverance under this ever-present cloud is a true life of faith. Mass, Holy Communion, and prayer, *Deus in adjutorium meum intende*, frequent cries for grace and help, these must be your refuge and constant occupation, when you are equal to it.

You find yourself in the midst of luxuries, of unnecessary waste or expenditure. You are not answerable for that, you come in for the cross of riches, the accounts, the worries, the unrest; you may arrive at a great detachment from the world and riches whilst in the midst of them. You are like a clerk keeping the accounts of a millionaire, with some extra worries as your salary.

Your account of Mr. Gladstone's review of *Robert*

Ellesmere interested me not a little. I did not know who Mrs. Ward was, but the *Spectator* had reviewed the book a little too gently, as I thought. I get vexed at the sort of consideration which is shown to agnostics and unbelievers generally. The world needs an angel's voice to ask, Does Truth exist? Is there such a thing? Is it a matter of indifference whether we accept it, or amuse ourselves with it, or reject it? So many writers speak of life and its problems, and the next world, much as they do of fashions which change.

You speak of St. Anselm's Society; where do they publish their lists of books? I should like to see some of them. Good reading is at a low ebb in Bombay, and good books are not easily found. You certainly owe much to your mother for giving you a taste for solid reading. Good-bye. God bless you.

Kirkee, June 25, 1888.

At least two letters of yours are waiting for an answer, one of May 18, the other of June 8 received here this morning. There may be more, for my correspondence has been interrupted. I have made my first experience of Indian malarial fever. I caught it in Bombay, towards the end of May, but how, when, or where, I cannot say. I had been getting rather low for some time; the heart gave signs of feebleness. I never had fever before, so could not understand what was the matter. I found myself unfit for head-work; mails left without letters from me. I was thankful to be able to get through Office. Then I was not able to say Mass, and the doctor was called. He took my temperature, and at once declared I had malarial fever. For a week he attacked it with his medicines, but could not reduce it one point. Then I proposed going to Kirkee; he approved. I was scarcely equal to the journey, and on my arrival became much worse, in fact, for three days I was in some danger, and received the last sacraments. Thank God, the danger is past, and the doctor tells me I am convalescent, but I must not return to Bombay for some time. Lord and Lady Reay have been kindness itself. They are now at Ganesh Khind, Poona, very near Kirkee. He came over to see me, and placed his kitchen and cellar at my disposal, and sends a carriage for me to take a drive in the evening. They want me to stay with them, and I intend to accept their invitation in two or three days. This is a great deal about myself: it will help you to understand the *Bombay Catholic Examiner*. I do not know whence the rumours of my going to Europe come from: at present I see no cause to take me there. . . .

What is the best bellows to fan your sparks of hope into a good flame? Make many acts of hope now, in anticipation of future dark hours, especially from the Psalms. The Compline Psalms will serve, and the exercise of hope, and any verses for which you have a preference. I find Job's own words a great help, even when he grumbles a bit. Then fix in your mind the truth—in dark hours God is unchanged, your soul is changed, and looks at life through different glasses; and He allows these dark hours principally to draw us nearer to Him by prayer and supplication. I often think God is often nearer to us in the dark hours than in times of consolation; but we must suffer and feel the want of Him, the need of flying to Him by prayer. I will add, in dark hours and in brighter hours the perusal of the Rules for the Discernment of Spirits, for the First Week, always gives light and hope. Good-bye.

P.S.—I said Mass on Sunday and to-day, after seventeen days of privation. *Deo gratias.*

Kirkee, June 25, 1888.

My dear ——,

    Your letter of May 23 reached me in the midst of my first experience of an Indian malarial fever. I must have caught it in Bombay itself, but how, or where, or when, I have no idea. I had it for many days without knowing that it was fever. I lost all power of work; with difficulty got through my Office. Next I found myself unable to say Mass, and finally was obliged to call in the doctor, who took my temperature, and discovered I had fever. I had been running rather low for some time, so the fever took a stronger hold. For a week the doctor tried his medicines, but all in vain: the weather in Bombay was very unfavourable. So he sent me to Kirkee, where I am staying with Father Bridges, S.J., in a very quiet bungalow. The journey was rather much for me, and for three days I was in real danger, and received the last sacraments. Thank God, the danger is past, and the doctor tells me I am convalescent, but it will be some time before I can go back to Bombay. In a day or two I am going to be the guest of Lord R——. I cannot tell you the kindness and attention they show me. I was their guest at M—— for several days, and I may say they both treated me as one of the family. They do not shun religious questions; on the contrary, they rather like them. I told them the story of the conversion of General S——, and they were very much interested by it. Who knows but that the grace of God may visit them? They have much to fill mind and heart, and both like their Indian life. I have been long in telling you of my sickness, and you must excuse me: I am too stupid to contract it and tell my tale in fewer words. I have not yet paid a second visit to the monks at Ahmadabad. The devil has long reigned supreme in this country. How his tyranny is to be broken I do not see. The missioners, in parts, do make many good converts among the poor, *v.g.*, in the south, on the Calcutta side. In the great cities very little progress is made, but the Pagan ideas and habits and usages are very much shaken: those who are educated for the most part despise their gods and priests, and if they keep up outward forms it is only to satisfy their mothers and wives and sisters, who will have the old thing.

The Papal Decree on Boycotting and the Plan of Campaign, was admirably drawn up, and appeared at a timely moment. My opinion is that it will have a great effect; first on the clergy, later on among the better part of the laity. The Decree is unanswerable, so plain, and so simple. Yes, the Jubilee of the Holy Father was a great event for the Church and the whole world. It was the hymn of the three youths in the fiery furnace from the whole Church.

You ask me to tell you honestly the sins and faults you ought to fight against most earnestly. You say everything is a *trouble* to you. Well, accept everything as a cross, by which your soul is to be purified and you are to be drawn nearer to God. Say, "Everything is a trouble; I accept it. I only pray that I may have the grace to be patient, and even thank God." And then for an ejaculation say often the *De profundis*, or some verses of it: "If Thou shalt observe iniquities," &c. And besides make frequent acts of the love of Jesus Christ. The gout furnishes great opportunities of merit. All the same I pray that you may be freed from it. Good-bye. God bless you.

Yours very truly in Christ,

✠ GEORGE, Archbishop of Bombay.

Kirkee, July 2, 1888.

By last mail I sent you a card that I had been seriously ill, that danger was past, and that I was convalescent. I am happy to say the improvement continues, but I am not allowed to return to Bombay for some time. I was rather low, when a malarial fever took hold of me, and the doctor let me go to Kirkee. The journey was rather much, and for three days I was in real danger.

In your letter of May 7th you ask for the name of a book containing a portrait of St. Ignatius said to be authentic. As well as I can remember, the book was either the new Spanish edition of the letters of St. Ignatius, or a work by Ribadeneira, containing the same portrait of St. Ignatius. If the portrait referred to by X—— as in the refectory, Mount Street, was a large photo, that is the most authentic portrait extant. Short oval face, pointed chin, very ample forehead, prominent cheek-bones, a thorough Biscayan type: it corresponds exactly with the cast I had at Manresa, taken from St. Ignatius after his death. . . .

My retreat to the native clergy was given in English: two or three who cannot follow English made private retreats at one of the Colleges. The heat was very great for our part: one day 99° in the shade. Going from my room to the open air was like facing the breath of a furnace.

July 5, 1888.

I have not written to you for several weeks for two reasons. First, not hearing from ——, I concluded you were regaining your strength. Secondly, I have been on the sick list myself, and have not escaped from the doctors yet. Your faithful secretary tells me you are not yet recovered, and she adds you have had several relapses. I am glad you have moved to ——. I have more faith in the air and the quiet of that place, though I fear you purchase these advantages by the loss of some spiritual comforts. . . . Living this invalid life so long, I hope you have learnt the lesson to sanctify it, and draw nearer and nearer to God. How this life of quiet and suffering and helplessness contrasts with your (perhaps too) active life of old. You will discover truths you did not think so much about then. The old fear of death has gone, I feel confident, and you almost wish to be released from this weary world. Still I will pray that you may be spared to work a little longer, and to be better prepared when the end comes. I will pray, too, for Z——. I fear from what I am told that she is in a critical condition. Life is full of miseries and troubles, and the longer we live, the more the miseries seem to thicken. We must pray for perseverance to the end.

Now I will tell you how I was brought to death's door. For some time I had felt myself running down; then a fever took hold of me, how or when I cannot say. This was my first fever, and naturally I did not know what was the matter. I felt myself less capable of doing anything every day, till at last I could do nothing, and then the doctor came, and at once told me I had fever. He tried for a week to master it, but in vain, so I asked him to let me go to Kirkee, five hours by rail. The journey was too much for me, and for three days I was in real danger, and received the last sacraments, but rest and a good doctor pulled me through; my fever has gone, and I am regaining my strength. But I am not allowed to return to Bombay for some time. Another warning! I have had so many since my first illness in Liverpool. I hope each one makes me more anxious to make good use of the time left to me.

Ganesh Khind, July 6, 1888.

My letters of last mail only arrived here (Ganesh Khind) after the English mail had left. The mail left 5 a.m. on Tuesday, 3rd. My letters were given to me 8 a.m. Lord and Lady Reay kindly asked me to stay with them a few days to recruit after my fever. I have spent a very restful week, with a library of modern books. My health is now fairly restored, but I must not return to Bombay for some time. I shall go back to Kirkee from Ganesh Khind; the distance is only two miles, and most probably I shall make my retreat in July, as I did last year. I give you a special *memento* for yours which is now going on.

Don't be afraid of wearying me with your letters, only be indulgent, if I sometimes allow a mail to leave without an answer.

The Emperor of Germany has gone; humanly speaking, his death seems a calamity to his country and to Europe. He gave great promise. God knows what is best, but the future looks very dark. . . .

. . . Before my fever, I began to read Martineau's *Sources of Religion*, or some such title. He is profound and reliable on the great questions of liberty, &c., rather copious, if not diffuse.

During my stay at Ganesh Khind, in addition to light reading, I have gone through a short but learned and deep book by Hettinger, author of the book on Dante, and a defence of Religion (Christianity) entitled the *Plenitude of the Ecclesiastical Power of the Apostolic See*. The German, word for word, is "The Ecclesiastical Plenitude of Power (*Vollgewahlt*) of the Apostolic See." It is a small 8vo, 220 pp. It contains two chapters. (1) The Episcopate and the Primacy. (2) The Infallible Teaching Primacy of the Holy See.

The place of the Pope as teacher of all, and the bond of union because teacher of all, is wonderfully well established. I wish I had time to put it into English.

I hope you have had no return of your neuralgia. Don't forget it often proceeds from weakness, want of food.

In a recent letter I suggested some helps towards strengthening hope. I omitted one: the Office of Martyr or Martyrs in the Breviary, and best of all, the Office of Martyrs for Paschal-time. There you will find so many thoughts full of consolation and hope and preparation for trials. . . .

Kirkee, July 23, 1888.

You will have been able to make your retreat, I trust, and I hope it has been satisfactory. The few days of a retreat must be a godsend to those who live in the world. . . .

I look forward with some curiosity to the Pan-Anglican Synod, in which they promise to issue no canons, no definitions of faith, no anything Councils ought to do.

E—— is not quite right as to Sir H. Maine's *Ancient Law*. That book and his other book on *Village Communities* have helped very powerfully to prepare the minds of statesmen for the terrible agrarian questions which now agitate the world. I think the question of private property in land, the socialist demands, are more thoroughly understood through Sir H. Maine's works than they could have been otherwise. If E—— thinks of public life, he should read some of the more modern books, beginning with (that odious) Miss Martineau's *History of the Thirty Years' Peace*. The opinions of men in politics have undergone such a revolution during this century, especially during the last thirty years, that they cannot be understood without a special preparation. I see a short English History by Dr. Bright announced in some series (the name I forget). He has just published part iv. or v., *Progress to Democracy*, 1837—1887. I have sent for this part. Dr. Bright is a very competent person to write on history, with a leaning to High Church.

I can send a good report of my health. I am nearly as well as ever I was. After spending ten days at Ganesh Khind I came back to Kirkee; here I continue to improve, but the doctors forbid my return to Bombay for some time. I have much time on my hands. As I have no library to draw upon, I have begun the translation of Hettinger's *Die Kirchliche Vollgewahlt des Apostolischen Stuhles*, an 8vo of 220 pages. The title won't run well in English. I think of putting it in this way: "The Apostolic See—the Plenitude of its Authority in the Church." I should like to go even farther: "The Supreme Authority of the Apostolic See in the Church." The idea is—Jesus Christ valued unity above all things in His Church. St. Peter is the source and bond of unity. The German book pleases me. I think it would do good in English-speaking countries. I have translated about sixty pages.

I have become rather intimate with a Hindoo Rao Bahadur (two titles), Mahader Waswdeo Barve: (1) formed by the astrologer from the horoscope of his nativity, (2) his father's name, (3) his distinguishing name from caste, &c. Mr. Barve is an old man, has held high office in native states, is C.T.E., is also Councillor of the Presidency of Bombay. He is very intelligent, speaks English fluently, likes to talk about religion, is very interested in the conversion of his friend, Mr. Rivington. . . .

July 22, 1888.

Last week I went into Poona, and paid two visits; one to a Hindoo friend, in a Hindoo house, and saw and heard much about their daily life. The other visit was to the Cowley Fathers. They have a beautiful church near my Hindoo friend. One of the Fathers showed me over it. They have just received a very fine marble altar from Devonshire, designed by Gribble (architect of the Oratory), and carried out in Devon marble, with a tabernacle, &c. Poor fellows, many of the pieces reached Bombay broken, but the frontal and the tabernacle are unhurt. In the church I observed the Stations of the Cross. The pulpit was provided with a chair, as in the Oratory. The church is really very pretty, designed by Father Black, though carried out by an architect. All the services except one, 6 or 6.30 a.m. on Sunday, are in Marathi. All the Fathers speak it and preach in it, which means they have all gone through a very heavy drudgery. The Father next showed us the workshops, carpentering, which bid fair to be a success; they keep their young boys. From the shops we went to the native schools, under Cowley Nuns. All the nuns in the school are supposed to speak Marathi. They have a high school. The one I saw was for poor children. The nuns treat them very sensibly, leave them to themselves, and some older native girls for their cooking, sleeping, recreation, and only profess to see to them in school hours. Between them, the nuns and Fathers own an immense property, and they are preparing an immense work; they are liberally supplied with money from England. The Superior is a Father Rivington, brother or cousin of the late convert. I forgot to say these Cowley Fathers form a community. They wear white flannel habits with black sash or girdle. Certainly they are very devoted, and do not spare themselves. I wish they were working with me. I think they run the risk of attempting too much. . . .

If you are prudent, that is, if you will avoid any violent exertion, and *always* keep within your strength, and never work to the end of your tether, you may still be able to go through a lot of work of a quiet kind. . . .

Yes, utter lonesomeness is not healthy for mind or body. At —— I suppose you do not suffer from that cross. Should you ever take up your quarters in ——, get a poor child or some poor person to instruct in the evening. And do it quietly, without raising your voice too much. You will find the occupation a very interesting one; you will do some good, and the duty will bring light to your life.

Does writing fatigue you much? if not, some literary work, original (the best of all) or translation, done without any hurry, for so long and no longer, makes a pleasant interruption.

In your next letter, tell me a little in detail how your retreat passed off, and what resolutions you came to. The stage of your infirmity which you have reached necessitates quite a change in your life, spiritually, intellectually, and in every way. Try to see how you can make the most of it. . . .

A copy of Lady Georgiana Fullerton's Life was sent to me. I have nearly finished it. I had the English edition. It is pleasant and edifying reading, and it is especially interesting from one's knowing so many of her friends. Did you see the *Spectator* (about July 27th) on the book. The reviewer does not like Father Coleridge's edition, and much prefers the original French. He pays a very high tribute to the character and virtues of Lady Georgiana, but not more than she was entitled to.

July 29, 1888.

My dear Child,

I am happy to be able to tell you that I am perfectly recovered from my fever and the serious illness which accompanied it. As a precaution, the doctors forbid my return to Bombay for some time; so I am staying at Kirkee, probably till the end of August: they fear a relapse. Kirkee at this season has a climate more like that of England, and the fields now are as green as those of old Lancashire, if not greener.

In your next, Father Thomas will be the occasion of much information. I hear he had fever in Rome. Tell me all about him. His visit will remind you of old days.

Matters will be easier for you now that Father —— has come over to my way of thinking, and I shall have more confidence in advising you. Of course, keep up the sacraments. At the same time, I sincerely hope and trust you will outlive most of your difficulties, only you must fight for it; fight is the word, and pray besides. God bless you.

Kirkee, July 30, 1888.

I did not write by the last mail, so I send you a letter by this, lest you might think I had had a relapse. Thank God, I feel so much better that I no longer look for improvement. I take walks every day, towards evening, 5 or 6 p.m., and spend the day in quiet work which does not overtax my head: letters, translations, reading.

Father Bridges and I had promised ourselves a most interesting visit to a large Hindoo temple, under the guidance of my friend Rao Barve. I wrote arranging an evening, but received no answer to my letter, so the visit never came off, and I must wait till I can see

Mr. Barve, who lives five miles away. I hope this visit will come off later.

To-morrow you will be in Farm Street. I shall be there in spirit. Here I shall say Mass 5.30 a.m. I hope to hear another in thanksgiving; beyond, there will be nothing to mark our holy Founder's day. He knows that we would honour him better if it were in our power, but in these distant countries we are forced to forego many of the luxuries of religion. . . .

My translation of Hettinger goes on pretty rapidly. I have finished nearly half of the text; for the notes I mean to go to recognized translations, as the notes in the main consist of extracts from the Fathers, the Council of Trent, and the Council of the Vatican. Do you remember an English translation of the Council of the Vatican? I fancy the *Tablet* published one, and I have written for a copy if such still exist. If none exists, I shall have to make one of the whole, as it is nearly all embodied in Hettinger's book. I like the book better and better. It explains very fully the prerogatives of St. Peter, always leading up to the "bond of union;" then the position and privileges of the Apostles; lastly, the Divine institution of the Episcopate, and the duties of the Episcopate *vis-a-vis* of the Primacy; all matter of the highest importance in our day. Sometimes it comes home to me that where non-Catholics are weakest is in their conception of the Church and of St. Peter's place. They quite leave out St. Peter, and without St. Peter there can be no Church. The Pan-Anglican Synod is a living illustration of my proposition. The Anglican Church is anything but a Church. Perhaps you noticed an Œcumenical Council of the Presbyterians, lately held somewhere in Scotland; they congratulate themselves on many subjects, but their own Church questions are avoided. The *Church Times* surpasses itself on the Lambeth Conference (the writer does not like the Pan-Anglican *Synod*). He quotes some Synod, perhaps in South Africa, calling upon the Pan-Anglican to salute the Archbishop of Canterbury, Bishop of Bishops, Metropolitans, &c. God may blind the Synod, and allow it to fall into this abyss of foolishness; otherwise Benson has lost his cunning, if he attempts such a high flight.

Kirkee, August 13, 1888.

The doctors wish me to prolong my stay in Kirkee till the worst of the monsoon is over in Bombay. I propose to go back at the end of this month. My health is really quite restored, and I feel as strong as ever I did. Every morning and evening I take a constitutional; I should think I walk from four to six miles every day. During the middle of the day, *i.e.*, from 8 a.m. till 5.30 p.m. (allowing for dinner and siesta), I read or write letters, or go on with my translation. I have made good resolutions not to do anything rash, and to be prudent. There will not be any question of my leaving India on account of my illness.

Have you seen Mr. Rivington's *Plain Reason*? The book is well written, and goes to the root of the important question of authority. Read it with L——, and get her to take in the idea of what a Church is; that it must be *one*, and that it cannot be one without one Head. Mr. Rivington brings out his point very forcibly. Curiously enough, the book by Hettinger, which I am translating, goes over much of the same ground as Mr. Rivington, but at greater length, and with more erudition and learning. Mr. Rivington's book will decide not a few High Church people, at least I hope it will. He is rather too learned for Bombay, and a very few even of the

Europeans could follow his argument and the historical proof.

My Hindoo catechumen wants to come to Bombay in order to be baptized by me. I have still my anxiety about his future, to see that settled before I allow him to become a member of the Church. The persecution before him is terrible to think of, and I am bound as far as I can prudently and reasonably to provide against it. Continue to pray for him.

Your news about the religious vocation of D—— and A—— was most consoling. Their father's prayers have obtained that grace for them. Their happiness and goodness will make him happier in Heaven, for he loved those children dearly.

I shall still hope for Mrs. A——. What makes me fear a little is that she has been so long looking at the Church, staying always outside. God is very patient.

The telegrams say you now have splendid weather. I pray you may have a good spell of it, and recover more vigorous health. At last I hope you will be able to work out in the open air. That is one of the delights of India. I live in the verandah except at night, the birds singing (not always sweetly), and squirrels climbing the lattice-work. Good-bye. God bless you.

August 27, 1888.

One remedy against the spiritual malady of self-worry is to live in the present, to attend to the duties of the day, of the hour, or to put off the future and the possible till they have become present realities.

As to thoughts, the important point is to control them when you advert to them, and gradually to acquire the habit of fixing your attention *quietly* on what you are saying or doing.

You say you are trying not to judge others even in

little things. Very good, try a step further sometimes, and try to discover their good qualities, good ways, edifying demeanour, &c. As St. Thomas says, "Keep your eyes open on the good in others and the evil in yourself."

Sursum corda. Keep up your courage. Thank God for one year spent in religion, and pray you may close your eyes in that blessed state.

Fort Chapel, Bombay, Sept. 4, 1888.

I returned from Kirkee on Saturday. The difference of the climate is very great, more than 10° Fahrenheit, and the Bombay air is full of steam; life in Bombay just now is life in a perpetual bath. However, I am glad to be back. I am *obliged* to be here now in order to draw up some papers for Rome which I can only prepare in my own room with all my books about me.

You ask me how I caught the fever. I cannot say. It was on me for at least a fortnight before I discovered it. The only symptom was a growing incapacity for any exertion of body or mind. At last I could not say Mass, and then I sent for the doctor. The gout, an old acquaintance, took advantage of the confusion, and probably I was somewhat below par when the fever laid hold of me. I feel *quite well* and *quite strong* now. One resolution I have come to, and that is, I must take more walking exercise. Before my illness I took none, I might say absolutely none; it is not easy or convenient to walk about in Bombay, partly on account of the sun, partly on account of the crowd, and partly on account of the lie of the ground. Bombay is a small, flat, rocky island. However, what must be done must be done. I say my Little Hours walking in the morning, and I mean to find out a way of taking a walk in the cool of the evening.

Some one has sent me the Anglican Encyclical, so I am fairly *au courant* of the proceedings. Bishop Ryle's letter is delicious; he is logical at least, if not devout, and he is a thorn to his brethren.

Up to the present, our Protestants of Bombay have not noticed Luke Rivington's book. They find it a tough morsel.

CHAPTER XVII.

END OF SECOND YEAR AS ARCHBISHOP.

Sept. to Dec. 1888.

German as a language for theology. The Pan-Anglican Synod and Bishop Ryle. The Land Question. A tiger-killing Colonel. Ghastly story of Indian life. Encouragement and advice. Counsels to an invalid. Fear of death. Extreme Unction not to be delayed. The Parsees—customs at their New Year. The Chinese and their payment of debts. Death of the Very Reverend Thomas Porter, S.J. *Robert Ellesmere*. *Moral Philosophy*, by Father Rickaby. Father Clarke's Manuals of Catholic Philosophy. Famine. Reception of the Pope's Letter in Ireland. Mr. Luke Rivington's *Plain Reason*. The English Edition of Lady G. Fullerton's Life. Scrapes. Pages of Indian life. The Divine Presence. Suggestions as to conversation. Omnipotence of prayer. Retreat at Bandora. The thought of death, pleasant. Visiting the poor in England. Value of literary occupation. St. Peter Claver. *The Holy See and the Wanderings of the Nations*. A marriage arranged by nuns. Pastoral visitation. Culvem. Dissatisfaction with self, good, if not morbid. Motives for thanksgiving. A second account of the visit to Culvem. Contempt for the body practised by St. Peter Claver. The loss of faith. Comforts and self-indulgence. Duty must come before mortification. Discouraging thoughts. *Il Diritto Naturale* of Taparelli. Druzbicki's *Devotions to the Sacred Heart*. Distribution of prizes at Bandora. Benediction and Mass. Second anniversary of the nomination to Bombay.

Bombay, Sept. 9, 1888.

I returned to Bombay on the 1st, quite restored in health and strength, thank God. Now my only care will be to avoid a return of the fever. Many thanks for your letter of August 16th, and for the Pan-Anglican Encyclical, as also for Blessed Fisher and Fonsegrieve which you tell me are on the way. My translation of Hettinger was not *quite* finished before I left Kirkee: the text was finished, but the notes of a few pages are still to be done. Hettinger enjoys a great reputation; his *Apologetik* (of which I fear my translation formed a part) many consider the very best that exists. German lends itself easily to express theological distinctions and shades of meaning. With some writers this very facility encourages obscurity, but Hettinger is clear enough. . . .

To go back to the Pan-Anglican Synod. Bishop Ryle of Liverpool is a very Low Churchman. I am told he is now living with his third wife (what would St. Paul say?), but he knows what he does and does not believe, and he logically holds to his position. He must have been a thorn in the sides of many of the 145 prelates whose names are given. I mean to give two or three articles in the *Bombay Catholic Examiner* on the Pan-Anglican Synod and the Encyclical Letter.

You do well in going through Sir H. Maine's *Ancient Law*. When you have finished that, you might read easily and quickly and pleasantly Maguire's *Irish in America*, and a book on Australia by Sir Charles Duffy. These works show how our colonists have dealt with the land question, and how it can be dealt with in other ways than our somewhat hard lines in English law. The land question must always be among the most important to a politician. And it is a wide question.

Mr. —— sees me from time to time. He is not near the Church yet, but grace can do great things, and prayer can obtain grace. The visit to the Hindoo temple did not come off: the multitude of pilgrims brought the cholera into the place, and it still rages there.

Now I will tell you a tale I heard the other day, which will show a ghastly side of Indian life. I was invited to dine with the mess of a native regiment. My place was next the Colonel, a quiet-looking man, short but very strong. I saw he could not use his left arm, he told me it had been crunched by a tiger. Later on it came out that he had been carried in a tiger's mouth for fifty or sixty yards into the jungle. Notwithstanding his crunched arm, he has killed seventy-six tigers and hopes to make up his hundred; he had killed more than a hundred before he lost the use of his left arm. Before going into the army, he had served in the Bombay police. He was driving down to Colaba Protestant church one Sunday evening, when he observed two bundles by the roadside, out of one of which he saw two human hands projecting. He got down, found in one bundle two arms and two legs; in the other the trunk, but no sign of the head. He left his assistant who was with him to sew up the body and make out what he could. The Colonel himself went on to church. After the service the assistant told him the murdered man was a fakir; this was revealed by the fact that the hair on his body was not shaved (the natives connect the idea of sin with the hair, and only saints and fakirs keep it); the great toe on one foot was wrapped up in a rag. That was all the information which could be relied upon. A reward was announced, and within twenty-four hours the sheet from which the rag had been torn was brought to the police. The clue was followed up, and resulted in the discovery of a gang of murderers and the arrest of the chief and all the associates. The chief was very chatty and told everything: within a year the gang had committed upwards of two hundred murders, the place and date of each being given. The chief gave himself out as an alchemist who could change silver into gold. When a victim brought his rupees, he was told to place them in a crucible: a blow-pipe was given him, and he was told, "Blow, brother, blow." As he stooped down to blow, he received a mortal wound from an axe on the back of his head. The chief said no one ever moved a limb after he was struck. Many were killed for trifling sums, one or two rupees: some out of sheer wanton cruelty, when no plunder was to be had. He was asked why he had killed the wretched fakir. He said he did it to keep his hand in. "Why did you leave the bundles by the roadside?" "Just to see what the police will do." "Well! you see what we have done." The chief was condemned to be hanged. He asked the Colonel when the sentence was to be carried out. "On Monday, 6 a.m." "Sahib, I shan't be hanged." And he persisted he would not be.

Two warders were placed in his cell, two outside the grilled door, and a superior officer was instructed to look in every hour and prevent any attempt at suicide. The Colonel went to the gaol at 5 a.m. to see his prisoner was safe. The officer reported his man was dead. What had happened? The condemned man slept till 4 a.m.: then rose, took his bath, said his prayers, and then sat on the ground native fashion with his arms clasped round his knees. He was found in this position with his teeth firmly clenched, so firmly they could only be opened by force. He seemed quite dead. The body lay as it was moved right or left, without any sign of life. No pulse could be distinguished, and the body was stiff and cold. The body was hanged all the same, and then the legs shot out quite straight. The Colonel supposes the man had induced some sort of a trance and was not really dead. But what a chapter of Indian life and wickedness! I finish with this ghastly story.

Fort Chapel, Bombay, Sept. 9, 1888.

My dear Child,

You do not write very often; but when you do write you send a good budget of news. Accept my best thanks for your letter of August 12th. In answer

I will tell you first of myself. My health is now quite restored. I returned to Bombay on September 1st after an absence of two and a half months. During the last six weeks I was as strong as ever and did a lot of writing every day. The doctors kept me out of Bombay, fearing a return of the fever. I will take reasonable care of myself and leave all in God's hands. I am obliged to you for your good prayers, and for the big candle at Notre Dame des Victoires. I shall not go to Europe: there is no necessity. Kindly present my congratulations to the Count and Countess on their silver wedding: I pray they may be spared to see their golden one, happy together and doing good all the time. What a beautiful mortuary card you sent me of dear old Count S—— and his lady. My acquaintance with them which I owe to you will always remain a pleasant and valued memory. May they rest in peace!

You hope to go to Rome: I trust that grace and pleasure are in store for you. When your journey is settled definitively, let me know, and I will send you a letter to a Jesuit Father, who will probably be able to obtain for you the privilege of communicating at the Pope's Mass.

As to your future, the proposed plan of your going to Count X—— pleases me: it would just suit you, and would keep you more or less in the circle of old friends, where you can never be a stranger.

The advice given you by Abbé H—— and the Curé was very sound and sensible. Your past life has not been useless: you have been where God placed you, and you have done a good work in the families of X—— and Z——. You have had crosses: who is without them? Offer them now to God, and try to forget them and remember the pleasant things of your life; the good side of those you have lived with, the facilities you have enjoyed of living a good Christian, and the opportunities of doing some good to others. God will take care of you in the future, as He has done in the past: only trust Him entirely; and wherever you are never cease to help souls when you can. God has been very good to you. Thank Him every day, and try to give Him all that remains of your life; love Him, and He will love you and watch over you. Poor Mrs. M—— carries a heavy cross: thank God she takes it in a right spirit. Tom and the flower console her; and she is happy in a good Catholic husband. I have no news of Father Tom; only he is not well.

Good-bye. I send my blessing to you and to each member of the family, and remain,

Yours very truly in Christ,

✠ GEORGE, Archbishop of Bombay.

Your own spiritual affairs I sum up in one word. Don't give up any of your Communions, and do all the good you can to your neighbour. In your next letter, tell me your order of the day: what prayers you say, how often you go to Holy Communion, what books you read on holy things. God bless you again.

Fort Chapel, Sept. 10, 1888.

Your letter of August 23 reached me yesterday. The mail arrived sooner than usual, before noon. I thank you for the two vols. of Leo XIII. I will keep them as a remembrance. I am very sorry to hear that your health does not improve, but rather grows weaker. Your preference of —— for your winter abode has my cordial approval. The advantages you enjoy there more than counterbalance the disadvantage of the climate. By all means stay, and thank God for having given you such a home. Keep faithfully to the rule of not leaving the house fasting. Indeed, keep to the house as much as you possibly can. I suppose you know that if you can hear the Mass bell (Elevation, &c.) from your room, and if you follow the Mass even from your bed, you do hear Mass and even satisfy the obligation of hearing it. Naturally you will prefer the church, but days may come when you will be glad to avail yourself of the privilege of hearing Mass without leaving your room or the house. Your state of health and the severity of the climate justify you in the use of such an indulgence, if only you hear the bell. And don't have any scruple in using the kind offer of —— to carry Holy Communion to you. I am very thankful to know you are where you are. . . . As you say, your present surroundings of priests, friends, &c., take an immense load off your mind. You may spend your days in peace, waiting God's good-will. Don't attempt too much in any way.

Now I will tell you my bulletin. I returned to Bombay on Sept. 1, quite restored in health and strength, able for a full day's work. Indeed, at Kirkee for the last month, I used to work six or seven hours a day without fatigue. The doctors would have kept me out of Bombay till November, but I was obliged to return here by pressing business, which no one else could manage. So far I keep well, and I hope the fever will not come back. If it does, I shall be obliged to fly from Bombay. The rainy season began later than usual and it ended sooner than usual, unless it resumes work again. The rain has been enough for our crops, but for a healthy season we want more.

At Kirkee I translated a work on the Holy See from the German. A few notes still remain to be done. All the text is finished. I hope to begin printing in October. The book will run to about 300 pp. 8vo. I hope an

English translation will do some good in England and America, as well as in India. My idea at present includes a Preface of some length.

Bombay, Sept. 20, 1888.

Your letter of August 27 was a surprise and a great pleasure. It tells me you are really much better again. *Deo Gratias.* You are not to be a confirmed invalid, but it will be necessary to work more moderately, to keep within your strength, and to allow yourself more rest through the day. This time of rest will not be time lost. You will find more leisure for prayer and pious reading.

You know now from experience that God gives strength and consolation when we really stand in need of it. Did I not tell you you would not be frightened when death was near? I have so often observed that those who are tried by fears and anxieties in health generally enjoy peace in sickness and death. These serious illnesses are a warning to get ready for the final one, which may come any time.

You were not able to say many prayers when you were at the worst. The prayer for such moments is patience and resignation to the will of God.

Learn a lesson about Extreme Unction. Never refuse it when your confessor advises it. It is not necessary to feel very ill in order to receive Extreme Unction. Not long ago a man came here to the church to receive all the last sacraments. The same day he went on board the steamer and died before he reached Aden.

Remember me most kindly to ——. I am glad he gives up preaching out. One can only do a certain amount of work well. Tell him to work moderately, as I always did and do.

Bombay, Sept. 28, 1888.

A press of writing has compelled me to put Hettinger on one side for the present. I hope to take it up and finish it next week. I have had to preach a panegyric on St. Alphonsus Rodriguez, our lately canonized lay-brother, and I have before me the task of preparing one on St. Peter Claver. Some one sent me from Italy three vols., Lives of these two Saints, and of St. John Berchmans. The one of St. Alphonsus by Padre Bonavenia (living), pleased me much. The other I have yet to read. . . .

. . . Some of my friends think the Parsees have reached a point when they are willing or will be willing to study the claims of Christianity. I am not so sanguine, but Freppel's *Conferences,* if they see the light in a Gujerati dress, will test them. I have made the acquaintance of Mr. M——, a fearless reformer of Hindoo grievances, infant marriages, infant widows, &c. He is a Parsee, and seems a thoroughly earnest man. We have had some talks already on Christianity.

A short while ago, great festivals of the Hindoos, Parsees, and Mahommedans all fell together. Last Monday week was the New Year's day of the Parsees— the first day of their year 1258 from the date of their being turned out of Persia by the Mahommedans. The five last days of the old year are devoted by earnest Zoroastrians to fasting, meditation, making up their accounts, paying debts, and generally putting their houses in order. On New Year's day they visit each other. After New Year's day, they give five days to "communing with the spirits of dead relatives and friends." These days are not observed with the same rigour as the last five days of the year, but business is more or less suspended and more time is given to prayer. Mr. M——

told me they take about eighteen days' rest about their New Year's day, an excellent institution. Four bank holidays in the year sound a mockery in comparison.

The great idea of the Chinese is to pay their debts at the end of the year. This they recognize as the highest duty of life. So they realize all they can, sell property if necessary, sell wife and children if driven to it, and then if they cannot meet their creditors they hang themselves, and not unfrequently invite their friends to come and witness their happy despatch. Hence there is always a large number of suicides about New Year's day. How the devil tyrannizes over his worshippers, and how he tramples on God's image in man!

Bombay, October 5, 1888.

The *Tablet* has announced the death of my brother, Very Rev. Thomas Porter, Vicar Apostolic of Jamaica, at St. Beuno's in North Wales. A telegram was sent to me. I was not quite unprepared for the intelligence. A previous mail had informed me that he was not making a good rally. In fact, he died of mere exhaustion. Kindly give him a *memento* in your prayers. Life glides past so quickly and so silently. My turn cannot be very distant. Death has its terrors, and the Judgment has greater ones; but life has not many attractions to keep one's heart attached to it. We must make the most of the time which is left.

I have been reading *Robert Ellesmere*. I find much talent in the good sketches of character, in the descriptions of scenery, and in some of the narrative. The core of the book, the contribution to the solution of the religious question, strikes me as sadly weak. Mrs. Ward's lame apology for not joining the Catholic Church some years ago when she had almost reached the gate, and her humanitarian Ellesmere, with all his go and energy, is a poor contrast to a simple humdrum priest hearing confessions or administering the sacraments or catechizing children.

Have you seen Father Joseph Rickaby's *Moral Philosophy*? It is a book quite within your grasp, beautifully written, clear, solid, compressed as a manual should be. It is a long time since I have met with a book which so completely gained my approbation. If the other volumes of the series are of equal merit, Father Clarke will have rendered good service to the English world by editing these manuals. They will be most useful out here. Herbert Spencer, Fowler, Bain, and Sedgwick, are in the hands of many non-Christians. These writers do not satisfy them (how could they?), but they make many agnostics. *Blessed John Fisher* and *Libre Arbitre* are still waiting an interval of greater leisure before I begin them.

At present we are much interested in the rain. The monsoon season has not given the usual quantity of rain, and six days more without rain means famine in many districts. Famine literally stalks the land. Within two or three weeks prices rise day by day till famine-point is reached, and then untold suffering follows. Sale of ornaments, jewels, clothes, and lastly, of the children, if any one is willing to buy. During the last famine, the hungry crowds flocked down to Bombay and a "famine camp" was formed. I understand the anxiety of the native about the rainfall. How much depends on it!

Fort Chapel, Bombay, Oct. 5, 1888.

My dear ——,

You were very good to write me that long newsy letter from Eastbourne on the Assumption. First, let me assure you that I am really quite restored and quite strong. I am not sure that I am not stronger than I was before the fever. I came back to Bombay and to work on Sept. 1, and I have been at it ever since, without any symptom of fever returning.

Yes, I was very much grieved to see how the Pope's letter was received in Ireland, especially by the clergy. All the same, I believe it has done some good and broken the back of the lawlessness. I never liked this movement in Ireland: *au fond*, it is revolutionary and hostile to the Church. There is not much hope of converting Mr. or Mrs. R——. They are both most kind, but they are both so completely taken up with the duties of their position, that they have little time for the one great question, "What is the truth?" One never knows what the future may bring. Sickness, advancing years, comparative inactivity, often lead to serious thought. The Protestants here keep "mum" about Luke Rivington. They don't write about him, neither do they talk about him. They seem to wish the ugly fact of his conversion to be buried in silence, as if it had never been. Meanwhile, I suppose more than a hundred copies of his *Plain Reason* have been sold by one man, and he tells me he hopes to sell another hundred. I like his book, but wish it had been more adapted to the general public. Mr. R—— addresses himself to the learned and reading class. I know that several of the "Cowley Fathers" and Sisters are not at rest in their minds. I read Lady G. Fullerton's Life, and I agree with your criticism. The space given to the child-life was out of proportion, and not very interesting; and the conversion and spiritual life were put out of sight in a most provoking manner. I have not seen the French edition, which is more generally liked, I find, than the English one.

In all probability I shall meet Lord and Lady M——.

If I can interest them with any of our charities, I will not fail to do so. We have some well-managed institutions here, *e.g.*, the Deaf-Mutes, the Lepers, the Foundling Home, and an excellent Girls' Orphanage.

Your anticipations of the future of S—— and its mission are not hopeful. Make them the subject of a special intention, and we may hope that God will send them a friend to continue what you have begun so well.

I hope the gout will not prove too heavy a cross to you in the coming winter. The laziness, I fear, you must accept as an infirmity. Like a headache, it is a humiliating one. You want to fight against it, and you are always beaten. Spiritually it cannot hurt you as long as you continue the unequal fight, and do not surrender entirely to your enemy. *Sursum corda! Gratias agamus Domino.* Do as well as you can, and wish always to do better.

The two conversions were a solid consolation. I hope you will have many more, and get into further scrapes on that account. Out of such scrapes good comes in the end.

Good-bye. God bless you.

Oct. 10, 1888.

... I shall tell you a little page of Indian life I had yesterday from a Portuguese gentleman, living at Kalyan. The cholera was raging there. In a single chawl (row of huts) there lived fifty-two Hindoos. Thirty-six were attacked, twenty-six died. The survivors were terrified. They held council. They said our *pujas* (sacrifices and prayers) don't save us, let us ask the sahib leave to pray in his temple. The sahib had built a chapel to Our Lady of Lourdes. To the sahib about twenty went. Three held back. Two refused to go. The sahib, my Portuguese friend, said he would open his chapel, but on condition they prayed as he taught them. He took them to the chapel, explained the Crucifixion, and bade them all say, "We have sinned, we ask pardon, save us from the cholera." Not one of the twenty was attacked, but the three who held back were struck down while the others were in the chapel. The sahib went from the chapel and gave them medicines, and did what he could, but the three died. The Pagans are greatly impressed.

Here is another page, very unpleasant. My Portuguese heard that a Mussulman had bought a Christian girl, aged twelve, for ten rupees. He sent for the Mussulman, who had been a labourer on his estate. He came, and brought the girl's mother with him. The story was quite true. The woman, who had left her husband, owed the Mussulman ten rupees. She offered the girl as payment, and the man accepted the bargain. My friend told him he made himself liable to the law, to three years' prison, &c., and insisted that he should marry the girl or provide for her maintenance. Then my friend questioned the Mussulman about himself. His parents were Catholic, but he had always lived as a Mussulman. He had no objection to being a Catholic, and the end is that he is now under instruction. My friend has four non-Christians under instruction. So far it is well, but what a state of things! The Kingdom of God on earth is a mystery.

Oct. 16, 1888.

The Presence of God.—When the clock strikes make an ejaculation. If your eyes rest on a crucifix or a holy picture, and you feel inclined to make an ejaculation, don't resist the inspiration. Or, sometimes pause in your occupation and raise mind and heart to God, as you feel inclined. Sometimes acts of praise, sometimes of thanksgiving, sometimes petitions, sometimes merely thinking on God or holy things. You will find profit in turning towards the Blessed Sacrament and addressing your ejaculation to our Lord on the altar. As a change, fix your thoughts on the Passion and its scenes, with verses from the *Stabat Mater*. But all very quietly, not in a wooden way, so many inches to the foot.

Another form of Divine Presence.—When you begin an action, pause, ask yourself, What am I going to do? How would Jesus Christ have me to perform this action?

When you feel stronger, don't attempt more, but try to do what you do with greater attention and greater love of God. When you feel you can scarcely do anything, wish you could do more, and leave yourself in God's hands.

The social difficulty.—This I understand only very imperfectly, and my remarks will be quite general. Talk rather about things than about persons. Get up an interest in Home Rule, in foreign politics, in anything, and take your side resolutely. The gossip of the parish, the new arrivals, the departures, the events. Here is a field for ingenious charity which suggests matter for talk that does not lead to sin or unfit the soul for union with God in prayer. When characters are pulled up, whenever it is possible, defend the absent, and insist on their good qualities.

Oct. 26, 1888.

I pray that this coming year may prove a brighter one for you in every way: in your spiritual life, in your health. You must make more use of prayer. We are weak; but God has given us prayer, by which we can make up for our weakness, and by which we can obtain the help of His almighty power. Hence the saying, Prayer is omnipotent, or as St. Paul represents it: "I can do all things in Him Who strengthens me."

Bombay, Oct. 26, 1888.

I went into retreat after posting my letter. It was not very satisfactory in some respects. I went to Bandora, half an hour's rail from Bombay. The thermometer was all day at 90°, and there was no convenient walking-ground. I hope I brought away with me at least a strong desire for the spirit of compunction. We have so much to be sorry for, and I see Thomas à Kempis comes back again and again, especially in bk. i., on its necessity and the advantages it brings.

Naturally the death of my brother gave me much matter for meditation. We were both ill at the same time. Why was he taken? Had I been taken, was I ready for the summons? Death has not many terrors for me, I confess; or I may say, the thought in a way fascinates me, for this world is a poor place after all, most worthy of consideration in proportion as it is the preparation for the better life.

My brother's death was a very happy one, and I thank God for granting him such an end.

You say you could resign yourself to being at Y——, if you did not feel a weight of responsibility about the poor. You cannot do much for them. Should opportunity offer, teach them short simple acts of faith, hope, and charity, and contrition. If you visit the sick poor you can say for them short acts, especially of contrition; or read them a Psalm, say Psalm 102 (Douay). It seems hopeless to get any further with the poor, who are so ignorant. As to your responsibility, if you refuse no good work which comes in your way, you may rest satisfied. You may pray God to put in your way some work that you can do. You are quite right; the thought that God is displeased with you, that you are not doing what you ought, is sheer temptation, to be disregarded and dismissed. Do what you can, what comes before you; be ready and anxious to do more, and beyond that resolutely put down trouble and anxiety. To live very much in the present, and to make the most of it, should be your aim.

Begin the translation you mention, not to worry about the work, but to have a definite occupation to fall back upon, when you find yourself with a quarter of an hour on your hands. Some definite literary task, undertaken reasonably, not pushed eagerly, I consider a real help to the whole round of duties for the day. A certain vigour communicates itself to every other duty or occupation, and even conversation.

I am rather overwhelmed with business letters just at present. My reading leisure has been very short. I have been giving what time I could to a panegyric on St. Peter Claver, the heroic slave of the slaves. I am to preach it next Sunday. Some one sent me from Rome a new Italian edition of Oddi's Life, which I think was translated for the Oratorian Series. What a life of devotedness to a very uninteresting set of big children.

October has been a most trying month, but, thank God, my health is and has been very good. I take some exercise every morning and every evening, and I fancy I am much the better for it. God bless you.

Bombay, Nov. 7, 1888.

We have had heavy showers the three last nights, and now the thermometer is only 81°, a delightful change on sultry 96° or 97°.

The *Examiner* will give you my panegyric on St. Peter Claver; the one I preached at Poona on St. John Berchmans was not printed. On St. Peter Claver I could not speak without alluding to Cardinal Lavigerie. When the anti-slavery crusade is taken up, the Parsees will come forward. One, a poor man rather than otherwise, told me he would give three hundred rupees.

Mr. Allies has sent me the *Holy See and the Wanderings of the Nations*. I promise myself a great treat; he writes with such full knowledge of his subject, such a comprehension of St. Peter's place in the Church, and with a certain stateliness of style which seems to me always to befit grand historical books. I do not remember for many years to have read a work with greater pleasure than his *Throne of the Fisherman*.

I am rather suffering from *l'embarras des richesses* at present. Your book on *Libre Arbitre* has been waiting its turn for some time. There is Father Rickaby's Manual of *Moral Philosophy*; another ponderous French book, *Les lois intimes de la Societé*. Bradley's *Job* I want to go over once more. You can imagine official engagements which are to be met, and the working-day, six or seven hours at the most. Life is short, and there remains much to be done.

Good-bye. I hope you are better and brighter than you were on October 18th, the date of your last. What weak creatures we are!

Nov. 13, 1888.

We had a curious case in our Girls' Orphanage last Sunday. I think I told you one of the good works of those who conduct it is to find husbands for the girls when they reach marriageable age. Young men write that they want to be married. When the nuns have satisfied themselves as to a young man's character, position, &c., he is invited to the Orphanage and there introduced to three or four likely girls, and makes his choice. With rare exceptions the marriages turn out well, indeed very well. In the present instance a young girl of fifteen was the favoured individual. Great rejoicing among relatives. On Sunday the girl was visited by her mother, her grandmother, her great-grandmother, and her great-great-grandmother, five generations. *The* old lady is as black as coal. Then each generation grows less dark. The girl herself is very fair.

Bombay, Nov. 30, 1888.

... Last Saturday I left Bombay on a short pastoral visitation. The first stage was an hour in a comfortable railway carriage. Then an hour in a bullock-cart, rather slow, yet not unbearable. On Sunday morning I made half an hour in bullock-cart to Candolim: crackers and fireworks on my arrival; procession for a considerable distance. Then Mass and Confirmation, breakfast, address, abuse of the parish priest before his face, and then back to my quarters in bullock-cart. At 3 p.m. I started in palanquin for Culvem: a primitive conveyance, a very short bedstead slung from a strong bamboo-cane, carried by four men, two in front and two behind, along the road, through rice-fields. An hour of this travelling brought me to a creek; there we were taken, palanquin and all, on board a stout boat and had a pleasant short passage to the other side. A Christian village stands near the landing-place. There I had a most hearty reception from the parish priest, eighty-two years old; crackers, &c., visit to his church, wine and cake, and then one hour and a half in palanquin. I must tell you the palanquin was not so very bad. I was obliged to double myself up, but the sides were open and an awning protected me from the sun. I reached Culvem, and there was a regular reception—crackers, procession, address, visit to the church. The kissing of the ring next morning after the Confirmation lasted quite an hour. I returned to Bombay by palanquin, boat, and rail on Tuesday. Culvem pleased me very much, it is a very happy parish, in the hands of an excellent native priest.

Next week we are to receive the new Viceroy, which means no end of ceremonial, dinners, &c.; very wearying, but inevitable. You won't wonder I send you no commissions by this mail or for two or three more.

Fort Chapel, Bombay, Nov. 30, 1888.

My dear ——

I thank you for your letter of October 11th, and your kind condolence on the death of my brother. He died on a very privileged day, and his end was surrounded by all that could comfort a priest and a religious. I hope I shall receive as great a grace when my time comes.

Lord M—— did call upon me, unfortunately I was not at home; he left word that he would call again in two or three days. Unfortunately the weather was very hot, and he fled to the hills. Perhaps he may return for the arrival of the new Viceroy, the Marquis of Lansdowne; in any case I hope to meet him before he leaves India.

We are living in a state of agitation here. The native priests who come from Goa are not satisfied with the decrees from Rome: they and some newspaper writers are trying to stir up the ignorant Goanese to make a schism. This most wicked movement is doing great harm among the simple people and prevents us from working all together. United, we might do much; divided, our efforts are paralyzed.

You must not mind if you feel dissatisfied, after all your efforts to please God. As you say, "When can we think ourselves other than unprofitable servants?" to feel satisfied would not be a desirable condition. God is not displeased that we feel dissatisfied, if we do not go further and yield to disappointment. Feel dissatisfied, and still strive after better and higher things in the love of Jesus Christ and in the service of God.

Above all, never cease to thank Him for calling you to the true faith, and for the privilege of your chapel, and the Blessed Sacrament, and your brother's Mass.

Remember me very kindly to him and to his good prayers and Sacrifices.

I am very well. The fever has not given any sign of returning.

God bless you, and make you a saint.

I remain, yours very truly in Christ,

✠ GEORGE, Archbishop of Bombay.

Nov. 30, 1888.

Last Saturday I made the visitation of two outlying churches in Salsette. My first stage was one hour in a comfortable railway carriage, the second another hour in a bullock-cart, but the road was a fairly good one and the journey was not too inconvenient. Crackers and fireworks greeted me on my arrival; then a visit to the chapel, supper, prayers, and rest.

The next morning half an hour in bullock-cart took me to Candolin, the church I was to visit. Crackers, fireworks, and a long procession, and finally the church, where I said Mass and confirmed some twelve persons. After breakfast I had to listen to an address, and then to a series of complaints against the parish priest, who was present and defended himself vigorously. A curious case of conscience came before me. The Pagans had consecrated a cock to one of their gods. The bird is taken to the shrine, offered to the god, and then set free. Can a

Christian kill the cock and eat what has been offered to idols? The common Christians dare not touch such a bird for the world. I fear the priest shot it and made one or two good meals of it.

Monday, 3 p.m., I set out for Culvem, in a primitive palanquin: a low, very short bedstead slung from a strong bamboo cane, two men in front and two behind trot along pretty briskly. I was obliged to double myself up on cushions for my head and feet, the sides were quite open and a good awning protected me from the sun. We took straight lines along the roads, through the rice fields, over dried-up creeks. I have made more uncomfortable journeys. The weather was very delightful, the country fertile, and the trees tropical and wonderful. We crossed a creek, palanquin and all, in a strong boat of the country. I passed several Christian villages; there I had to get out, visit the church, and let the villagers kiss my ring. A long torchlight procession led to the church entrance, where an address was read in English and Marathi. My answer was translated into Marathi. These you will see in the *Examiner*. Next day after Mass I confirmed nearly one hundred persons. The kissing of the ring occupied quite an hour. There are several Christian villages not far from Culvem, and all who could get away came to take part in the *festa*. Culvem is a very happy parish, and the native priest, who does not know English, is an excellent man, respected and beloved by all his people.

I returned to Bombay on Tuesday evening by palanquin, boat, and rail. On this journey I had a long row over an arm of the sea: the scenery was very beautiful. I ought to say we were rowed in a boat called *The Three Kings*, with flags and banners, &c., flying. The visit to Culvem was a consolation to me, and I am sure a very happy day for hundreds of the Christians.

December will be a month of distribution of prizes, breaking up of schools, reception of the new Viceroy, and many uninteresting festivities.

Bombay, Dec. 14, 1888.

I am too late to wish you a *Buona Pasqua di Natale*, but I am still in time to wish you a *Buon capo d'anno*, which I do with all my heart. May 1889 bring you many graces and blessings. I will offer one of my Christmas Masses for you and for all your intentions.

By the last mail I sent you St. Peter Claver's Life. One thing in his more personal virtues may shock some persons, that is, the sort of contempt with which he treated his body, reducing it to the most complete subjection and slavery, I might almost say degradation. At the same time, the apostolic side of his life seems to me to fall little short of that of St. Francis Xavier. I hope you will like it.

The history of —— is a very sad one: howl ye fir-trees, the cedar is fallen. Every such wreck ought to drive us nearer to the Sacred Heart. The gift of faith is very mysterious, and the loss of faith has its mysteries which are very terrible.

In your letter of November 14th, you say something about comforts and self-indulgence which makes me think you are under the idea there is merit in making the body miserable with cold, &c. A distinction must be made between pampering the body, getting all the comfort possible, and avoiding discomfort. Discomfort, cold, &c., which interferes with the entire application of the mind to prayer, or to work, or to duty of any kind may properly be avoided, and ought to be avoided if possible. To bear such discomfort patiently when it cannot be avoided is meritorious, and it is meritorious to deny the body at times. But as duty should go before pleasure, so duty should go before misery and mortification.

In the same letter you speak of the discouraging effect of the thought that God is not pleased with you. This reminds me to ask you whether you *often* read the Rules for the Discernment of Spirits for the First Week? These rules furnish the surest test of the good or evil origin of thoughts, and will put you on the safe way to obtain peace of soul, and a peace not easily disturbed; but you must make yourself very familiar with them. They seem simple and obvious, so they are, yet they have wide applications and profound ones.

Bombay, Dec. 19, 1888.

Do not fear about my health. I have been very well ever since I came back to Bombay on September 1st, and I have been, and am, very busy. My translation from Hettinger is in the press; about thirty pages have been struck off. In my German Hettinger, the book I have translated corresponds to the 18th Conference—The Episcopate and the Primacy—and the 19th, the Infallibility of the Teaching Office in the Church.

I am glad you like Father Rickaby (*Moral Philosophy*). I recommend you to go over part i. again; it is dry and somewhat difficult, but the fundamental principles are there, and you will find yourself often driven back upon them, and they help above all to clear ideas. Did I not procure for you years ago Taparelli's *Il Diritto Naturale*? There is a larger and a shorter edition; I have an idea I gave you the latter. Having read Father Rickaby, you will be better able to follow Taparelli, and you will like it and learn much on political matters.

Dec. 27, 1888.

Many thanks for Christmas and New Year good wishes, which arrived on Christmas Eve. I hope mine were in your hands somewhere near the great festival.

Have you a copy of the Marquess of Bute's *Breviary*? or will your Latin carry you through the original? If so, you would find help and devotion in reading the antiphons and prayers and hymns for this Christmas season, a few at a time. At all the chief feasts of the year there is a resource in the Breviary not to be met with elsewhere, and they serve for reading, or meditation, or vocal prayer, as you may feel disposed.

The sort of work that will suit you best would be something which might be taken up or laid down as you like, never writing under the feeling that so much must be done within a certain time. I am strongly of opinion that a little pen work, when you can feel equal to it, will be useful to body and soul.

I must thank you for your proposed Christmas card. I meant to have asked you to procure *Whitaker* and the *Catholic Directory* for me in this letter: you have anticipated my wants. My Christmas card will be my translation from Hettinger. I fear it will hardly reach you before the latter half of February; our press is rather full of work, and I have not much free time to correct proofs.

I will try to get you a copy of the *Messenger* for Dec. 1887; if I succeed it will go to you with the one for Jan. 1889. As a rule, few extra copies are printed. My own solitary copy is bound up, and I constantly require the little volume for reference, otherwise you should have my number. Druzbicki has almost come to the end; there still remain certain contemplations on the Sacred Heart. His practices teach people how to vary their prayers and how to meditate a subject in a variety of ways. He seems to me a very devout writer.

My health is excellent, save a very bad cold; few are without one at present here. The weather is very delightful, a trifle warmer than it usually is at Christmas. The thermometer is usually just above 80° in the day-time; the nights are cool, with a touch of north in the breeze: hence the colds which are so prevalent.

Bombay, Dec. 28, 1888.

Mother —— has really left us; she has been appointed Provincial of the Calcutta houses, and I fear she is lost to Bombay. We all regret her; she has done much for this place. Going to Calcutta looks like going to certain death—she suffers so much from the heat. She had been ailing for months from fever when she began her journey. She writes to me that the fever has left her, and she is well now; but the winter of Calcutta, where fire-places are actually needed, will not try her; the summer will show whether she has received a special grace with her new appointment.

She has been succeeded at Bandora by a brave Irish Sister. I wish you could have been present at the distribution of prizes; it was a pleasure to see the little black eyes so bright and so happy. The music, the recitations, and the singing, were admirably done. I have heard nothing better in Europe from children of the same age. In India many prizes are awarded. One tiny little mite was under training as to the manner she should come up to me and receive her prize and say, "Thank your Grace." When the nun thought the lesson was well learnt she asked the child, "What are you to say to his Grace?" The child said quite simply,

"Good morning, little Jesus." She had the crib in her mind.

Your account of Father H——'s stern teaching amused me. He is rather uncompromizing in his Roman allegiance. I own I go a little way with him on the point of Benediction. I like Benediction and value it highly, but I feel some grudge against it for the great popularity it enjoys; it does seems to me to dispute the supremacy of the Mass in some minds, and I am vexed when I hear how some Protestants are affected by it. I decidedly prefer a plain altar; the very plainness of the altar seems to draw the mind and imagination to the awful Sacrifice.

I believe this is the very anniversary of that black day two years ago when I received the fatal letter. Pray for me that I may do all that God intended me to do out here.

CHAPTER XVIII.

COMMENTS ON BOOKS, WITH A PREFACE TO THE TRANSLATION OF HETTINGER.

Jan. to April, 1889.

Growth and fluctuations of devotions. Devotion to St. Joseph; graces that have come from it. Constant expansion of the faith. The way to get rid of disquieting thoughts. What an invalid may do. A line of ncouragement. Blessings of sickness. Temptations and difficulties. The prayer of physical helplessness. Trial of Bishop King. Translation of Hettinger completed and forwarded to England. The native Press; its disregard to truth. The Malabar Syrian Christians. Life of Gaorishankar. Manuals of Catholic Philosophy; their sale in Bombay. How to behave in serious illness. Graces given through Extreme Unction. *The New Antigone.* A conversion. Father Clarke's *Logic.* Father Dalgairns' Preface to the *Lives of the Fathers of the Desert.* Life of Mère Marie de Sales Chappuis. Archbishop Ullathorne, his death, his interest in nuns and knowledge of religious life. An Easter meditation. The Mandatum. Maundy Thursday in Bombay. Ritualists and their impatience of authority. Archdeacon Farrar. The Constitutions of the Vatican Council. Preface to Hettinger.

Bombay, Jan. 24, 1889.

I have not read the *Life of St. Joseph*, by Healy Thompson, which you mention. The growth, the fluctuations of devotions form a subject of curious reflections. St. John Baptist has fallen quite into the background. St. Anne was formerly more frequently invoked; she is very popular out here. Something may be put down to pious fashion, something to the influence of a great preacher—*e.g.,* St. Bernardine of Siena created the devotion to the Holy Name—something to particular religious orders. Then every deep devotion naturally lends itself to development, *e.g.,* devotion to the Sacred

Humanity, to the Blessed Eucharist, to the Sacred Heart. Then devotion to our Lady has expanded and extended marvellously. In the Commentaries of the New Testament the Fathers speak worthily of St. Joseph, still he was not much invoked (invocation itself, by the way, has grown immensely in the Church). It may be, as you say, that he was considered as being one with our Lady. More probably Providence kept him back that simple people might thoroughly take in the Incarnation, and not pay undue worship to St. Joseph. Gerson first roused the attention of the Church, and since his time God has in a way made it up to the holy Patriarch by the extraordinary devotion which has entered into the daily life of the whole Church, with so many blessings in the temporal and spiritual order. The devotion to St. Joseph stands out as a legitimate development of the faith in the Incarnation. Certainly in these days of waning charity and faith it has contributed to foster and extend the love of Jesus Christ and of His Church. To me it often occurs as one of the problems of our religion, how men have advanced so slowly in the comprehension of the Incarnation and its consequences. The faith of the Church has been constantly expanding, and there is every reason to believe that it will continue to expand to the end of time. The group of the Holy Family we see in a way completed in the minds of the faithful by the devotion to St. Joseph. I sometimes fancy the next most prominent development will be in the conception of the Church, the mystical Body of Christ, and in increased love for her.

You find that sometimes there is no getting rid of teasing suggestions except by mentioning them, and you add truly the opportunity is not always there. Try this other plan: place yourself in prayer; say to God, "I have a worry. How am I to meet it? Give me grace to accept the cross, to bear the humiliation, to submit to the disappointment," &c., as the case may be. Think how our Lord would take it, what He would think and say and do, and pray earnestly to do what you believe He would have done. Half an hour's, a quarter of an hour's prayer in this spirit will bring peace. Read *Imitation*, bk. iii. c. xxx.

TO AN INVALID.

Jan. 31, 1889.

I am glad to hear that you have gained the degree of "confirmed invalid;" it is a distinct rise on your former state. A confirmed invalid may get through a great deal of work, if you never work too long, never work when you are tired; if you change your work, and above all, if you never work in a hurry. You will find moderate writing a great help; it stimulates the brain, it fixes the attention at the moment, and it awakens interest and cheerfulness. . . . Make up your mind to go your way, and let people say what they will; don't defend yourself from their attacks. . . .

You must not be discouraged by the absence of fervour, which seems to come over you when kept for some time away from church. You can't have fervour when you have a difficulty in breathing. The most you can do is to be patient, to avoid swearing and grumbling, to say some prayers mechanically, or to look at your crucifix, or to make short Stations at any pious pictures you may happen to have in your books or on your walls. At such times it is certainly better to say the Rosary very quietly than to try to meditate. St. Ignatius' third method of prayer applied to short favourite prayers you will find a great resource at such periods of the wooden and stony ages.

BB

Fort Chapel, Jan. 31, 1889.

My dear Child,

Just a line to cheer you in the midst of your pains of body and soul. Be assured I don't forget you; every morning I make a *memento* for St.—— and all its inmates.

Don't be unhappy about M——. She wrote to me some time ago from Sweden. She was going to Rome with ——. Her travelling so much explains her silence. How happy she will be to see the grand Leo XIII., and to visit the holy places of Rome!

Through much suffering we must fight our way to Heaven. *Sursum corda.*

God bless you and strengthen you.

I remain, yours very truly in Christ,

✠ GEORGE, Archbishop of Bombay.

Bombay, Jan. 31, 1889.

I thank you for your sympathetic letter of Dec. 17th, 1888. How much consolation I found in all the history of the illness and death of good Father Thomas. He is truly to be envied. I knew the prayers of all your Sisters in the diocese of Birmingham were to be counted on. We both had the privilege of helping your convents at one time or another.

Your health, I fear, does not improve much. You are in the case of verifying the word of St. Ignatius: "A sickness which is not less a gift of God than good health." You must sanctify yourself, by bearing your infirmities patiently and humbly, and by uniting your sufferings to those of our Lord. The time of sickness affords a precious opportunity of atoning for the past and accumulating a great store of merits. Make the most of the time left. *Sursum corda.* You and Sister —— must encourage each other to patience and heroism. Father —— helped you all, I hope, by his retreat. You delighted me by your few words on your good Bishop's visitation. May the healthy spirit long survive and improve.

Do the *Messengers* reach you safely? The Intentions are very Indian. We give much space to them because we find our doing so helps much to the spread of the devotion. I wish I could insert more Indian stories.

Bombay, Jan. 31, 1889.

From your silence I supposed you were stronger and very busy, and trying to do too much. I am sorry to hear that you did not write, being prevented by several relapses from attempting any letters. Thank God, you have taken a good turn; don't fall back again. I won't tell you not to attempt too much, you have friends and comforters enough to inculcate that lesson. I fear more your worrying. Try to take everything from the hands of God, and often think all in this world passes very quickly.

Have you discovered that sickness is a blessing? How many truths grow distinct when one is a prisoner and unable to move. In sickness, too, I believe the soul may make great progress in prayer, not perhaps in formal meditation, but in keeping the mind near to God, in making short ejaculations, and in having good thoughts more easily. I have found the remembrance of death comes more easily and less terribly since my big illness in Liverpool. Probably different persons are affected in different ways. You remark an increase of faith and hope and contrition. Try to keep up the fruits of your long sickness.

A—— seems to be passing to a better world. It is a comfort that she faces death so cheerfully and hopefully. Death is a great release if we are not too much attached to the things of this world; and they are not much after all. I will pray she may persevere in her present dispositions to the end..

Your judgment on the new altars interested me. If ever I go to England, I must see them and form my own opinion.

Feb. 8, 1889.

Your letter, though you say you have taken a turn for the better, does not give a very cheering account of your state of health. I do not know bronchitis from personal experience, but I have seen it in many. It makes the patient very tender, above all, if a succession of attacks has been endured. The one indispensable precaution is to avoid the early and late open air from the end of October to March or April. The restraint naturally grows irksome, and in your case will imply sacrifices of spiritual consolations which you prize highly. I knew a case of an old man past eighty who shut himself up resolutely from October to April, and so for several years entirely escaped. I used to take Holy Communion to him every fortnight. His immunity for several years made him over-confident; he renounced his rule, soon caught bronchitis, and did not recover. I hope the attack in your case has not been very severe, and that you will not find such strong measures necessary. You will do well, however, always to be careful of the open air, early and late, during the winter season.

When you are very ill, and cannot pray, don't try to pray. Don't be impatient; suffer with resignation everything, even restlessness, which is one phase of illness: that is the prayer of great sickness. If you can, look at your crucifix, or at some good picture. I remember an old priest who recommended for such states a devotion of simply kissing the crucifix five times, or seven times, or ten times in honour of one or another mystery. Even lying quiet, or tossing about, may be made a prayer without any words. When you regain strength, you will find the time has not been without its profit to you. As for the possibilities of suffering, God seems always to give the grace necessary to bear the burden of the hour, unless the sufferer rebels against God.

The *First Principles of Knowledge* has not yet reached me. Clear ideas about knowledge, opinion, doubt, certainty, and faith (human and Divine) are very precious to those who care to find and to hold the truth.

The Hettinger is almost ready. My part is completed except a portion of the Index and the correction of some of the proofs and the notes which are lengthy. I hope the book will be read. It seems to me an opportune treatise.

Fort Chapel, Bombay, Feb. 27, 1889.

My dear Child,

I have to thank you for your letter full of news, grave and gay, and of my old friends; you tell me many changes and events I should not otherwise hear of.

About your own spiritual concerns. You are suffering the consequences of the wilfulness as regards health in years long past; these consequences cannot be prevented now. The most you can do, the most you can hope for, is to lessen them as much as possible. The greater part of your temptations and trials come from the state of your health. So, in short, you must take great care of your health, and help yourself by the frequent use of the sacraments. The care of your health will diminish the temptations, the depression, &c.; the frequent use of the sacraments will obtain for you more abundant graces. Force yourself to talk to Father ——. Your temptations and difficulties only increase if you keep them to yourself.

You must not be discouraged. You have made some improvement, but if you want to make more, you will have to follow the advice I now give you.

You must fight hard. The worst is, that the malady disinclines you from fighting; still, strive all you can and pray you may have grace to strive more vigorously. With these helps and Father —— you will surely obtain a complete victory. *Sursum corda.* Keep up your courage. Fight and pray and go to the sacraments. Remember me kindly to all. God bless you each and all.

I remain, yours very truly in Christ,

✠ GEORGE, Archbishop of Bombay.

Feb. 28, 1889.

I am sorry to find that other ailments have followed the bronchitis. The doctor, I dare say, is right when he says you have tried your head by attempting to do too much, and perhaps by worrying and anticipating troubles. Whatever the cause may have been, you must now idle completely. Give up all your prayers, even the vocal ones, except some few short ejaculations, submitting patiently to the helplessness of your state, trying not to dwell on possibilities and futurities, vegetating in the hands of God—that is your prayer. If you can bear short conversations, or looking for a time at nice pictures, or listening to some one reading, you will feel enlivened even if you are a little tired. Oftentimes the presence of a silent friend soothes the wearied head. Chase away those who talk too loud or too long. At such times you can bear very little; try to have little to bear. Your religion is all right, deep down in your heart, a long way out of the reach of mere physical weariness. Do the little you can and do not care to do any more.

Bombay, March 7, 1889.

By your letter of February 14th I see that your recovery goes on slowly. Don't be impatient and wish it to be more rapid. When you are quite recovered, you will see that this time of fallowness has not been without its uses. Don't mind the inability to meditate or say vocal prayers. Your prayer consists in being submissive and satisfied and even thankful that you are good for nothing, and willing to remain good for nothing as long as it pleases Almighty God.

Easy conversation, looking at pictures, watching the outside world, even the snow, whiling away the hours and not fatiguing yourself—there is your day's task. Add a good deal of resting, lying down, if that posture does not distress you. I hope you will find your sort of illness may become very sanctifying, even though it is tedious.

The trial of Bishop King interests me immensely also. Whatever happens, a great convulsion is in store for the Established Church: the chains of State bondage will be rivetted more closely about her. I do not think all the unction and craft of Edward of Canterbury can save them from the trap which has been prepared. Very probably the protest of Bishop King, and his request to have a still more purely Ecclesiastical Court than the one now sitting, will bring down in the end a more crushing blow. If his prayer is granted, and if the Metropolitan with his comprovincial Bishops sanctions the practices of Bishop King, the Low Church prosecutors will go to the Judicial Committee of the Privy Council, and this body will not encourage the aspirations of the Ritualists to spiritual independence.

March 15, 1889.

My book does really go by this mail. If you are equal to reading it, you must tell me where it strikes you as weak and where as capable of improvement. I think myself the book is a very good one, but any book dealing with a question of so much actuality may easily omit an important point and not allow sufficiently for it: at any rate it will be capable of improvement. If it goes well, I think I may venture on an English edition.

You will be glad to hear the Rev. Mother —— has returned to Bombay. She could not stand Calcutta; the climate is much more trying than ours of Bombay. I am not sure she will be left here. I dare say she may be recalled to Europe.

The article in last week's *Examiner*, which you recognize as mine, has roused the Anglo-Lusitans to extraordinary fury. Our native Press is served by a great set of rogues and liars. I used to laugh at the Irishman who boasted he had receive the grace, no one could pick the truth out of him drunk or sober. But the natives leave Paddy far behind: how many have I heard say (Parsees, Christians), "Never believe a native, and if he offers to take an oath suspect him all the more." They say the thing which is not, which they know is not, and which they know you know is not, with an incredible audacity, and they are not in the least ashamed if they are found out, and they expect you to have as much confidence in them as before. An old Parsee told me he challenged a countryman of his to translate into their language (Gujerati), "My feeling of honour was wounded." He could not: the language has neither the words nor the ideas.

March 21, 1889.

Your letter of February 28th tells me that you are going through a new experience in your illness, though you are gaining ground slowly. The one point is not to worry about the future, about to-morrow. Live in to-day, suffer your helplessness, and as nearly as you can obey the doctors. One of the miseries of sickness is that every one will prescribe, every one takes command of the invalid; don't mind them, mind only the doctor. I am very glad the doctor does not think you are likely to have a return of bronchitis, that would be a heavy cross and entail many privations. The power of volition and the sense of responsibility will come back soon, I trust.

You must not imagine you are not capable of good works: accepting your present helplessness with patience and resignation is one of the best works you have ever had it in your power to do.

The Delegate has been making a tour on the Malabar Coast, among the Malabar Syrian Christians, some of whom are Catholic. They are in a more curious state, if possible, than the Goanese, semi-savages, with a thin coating of Christianity over them. One of the plagues of India is the speech and the inevitable address (such wonderful addresses), which always takes the form of a petition. On the Malabar Coast the petitions are written on palm-leaves, in beautiful square characters. Every Bishop has heaps of them. One Syriac Bishop was taking his bath; the petitioners actually forced their way into the bath-room and insisted on reading their petition there and then.

Bombay, March 29, 1889.

I cannot help feeling anxious about the progress you are making in your recovery. The distance of six thousand miles puts a long interval between letter and letter. I pray and hope you continue to gain strength. I am a believer in climacterics. I wonder whether you are passing through one; they recur at intervals of seven years, the old doctors used to believe.

A Hindoo friend, Taverilal Umiashankar Yajnik, now Sheriff of Bombay, presented me with a book of his, which I will send you later. It is the Life of Gaorishankar Udayashankar (not yet dead), a notable character. He ranks among the very first of native statesmen, and the Bhaunagar State owes a great debt to his wisdom and energy. The political side of his life is not without its interest. But the religious side is perhaps even more interesting. When the old gentleman had reached the age of eighty-one he retired from the world and became a Sanyasi, or ascetic of the highest order. The account is one which you will read with some curiosity. You won't fail to remark that the Sanyasi ends his sleep at 4.30 a.m., but in the order of the day, 4.30—5.30 is given up to religious thoughts *in bed;* a sensible arrangement enough for a very old man.

I take him to be a very favourable specimen of a religious Hindoo. Much reading of the *Vedas* and religious thoughts, which will be the Hindoo for meditation, and many observances in washing, bathing, &c., fill up his life.

March has been colder than usual; my thermometer has seldom reached 90°. On the whole the weather has been very pleasant.

The *Logic* manual has reached me, but I have still to prepare a review for the paper on Father John Rickaby's *Principles of Thought.* This last volume pleased me much; it is worthy to have a place [beside his brother's *Moral Philosophy.* I think it will find even a larger circle of readers. About fifty copies have been sold in Bombay, an extraordinary sale for a book on philosophy. The German Fathers here are greatly taken with these manuals; they prefer the second to the first.

Do you get your Indian *Messenger* regularly? It is an unambitious affair, but it only counts five hundred subscribers. The English *Messenger* had fifteen thousand when I left England. India is split up into Presidencies and provinces and divisions quite as distinct from each other as England and Ireland, perhaps more so. Then it is the land of petty jealousies. Then we Catholics are under different nationalities: English, German, Belgian, French, Italian, &c. If the whole Catholic clergy of India were English we might accomplish a grand work. This dream would be too much happiness for this world, so we must struggle and do, not what we wish, but what we can.

Good-bye. *Pazienza.* All will come right in its own good time.

April 4, 1889.

I hear you have had a serious attack, but are much better again. *Deo gratias.* I was glad to read that Father N—— gave you the last sacraments in good time: it does seem so unmeaning to put them off till the last.

I suppose you found in your late attack that passivity and patience were the best dispositions you could aim at: in states of continued invalidedness and in more serious crises the highest perfection is to leave oneself in God's hands, to be content to attempt little or nothing, to take each hour with its crosses and helplessness.

Make up your conscience clearly and firmly to take care of yourself, and not to try more than you have strength for. And rest quite assured God will be pleased if you follow this rule.

Bombay, April 17, 1889.

I am thankful to hear of your rapid recovery and of your feeling of comparative health having returned; may this last. Father N—— has my hearty concurrence about the last sacraments. Always ask for them soon, and don't wait till you are at the last gasp. Extreme Unction brings with it so many graces useful to a sick person, it cannot be called for too soon. How often it brings back health, to say nothing of spiritual helps, patience, resignation to God's will, &c. . . .

The summer has fairly begun. The thermometer stands in the nineties during the day, and the nights are close. So far my health is excellent; if I feel out of sorts I will run to the hills and rest there for a time. We are not the worst off; at Surat they have 108° in the shade—a temperature not favourable to study or work of any kind.

I forgot to thank you for writing me your opinion of *The New Antigone;* I have read the book myself since I first wrote about it. What rather excited my curiosity was a rumour that it was written by a Catholic priest, an eminent divine. The book is unquestionably from a superior hand, but I should not hear with unmixed satisfaction that he was a priest. Curiously enough it was eagerly sought for by our most educated natives, non-Christian; I have not had the opportunity of finding out their verdict on it.

April, 1889.

Instead of a sermon this time, I will give you a meditation, when you feel equal to "religious thoughts in bed." Point I. *Pazienza.* Point II. *Pazienza.* Point III. *Pazienza.* Colloquy. *Da Domine quod jubes et jube quod vis. Sursum corda.*

I believe I told you in my last letter of the conversion of the Chief Justice of Calcutta. We have heard no further particulars, except that he was received by our Father Lafont. We hear nothing more about his dangerous illness; very probably he owes restoration of bodily health to the sacraments. I have much confidence in the healing power of the sacraments, of God's creatures reclaimed from the service of sin to the service of holiness.

I have read the three Manuals of Philosophy which have appeared, *Logic* being the last; they are all three admirable. *Logic* ought to be very popular, the style is particularly clear, and the explanations are numerous, well-chosen, and much to the point. These books have made their mark even in Bombay; our few reading men, judges, &c., express themselves as delighted with them.

Did you ever fall in with *The Fathers of the Desert*, by Countess Hahn-Hahn, with Preface on the Spiritual Life of the first Six Centuries by Father Dalgairns (Baker, Soho Square). The Introduction is very learned and pious and interesting. I have not read many pages beyond it.

I am reading a Life of Mère Marie de Sales Chappuis, a Visitandine, who died so recently as 1875. She was a great saint of the school of St. Francis de Sales and St. Chantal. Steps have been taken for her canonization, and I am more or less obliged to read the Life; it is lengthy—722 pp., somewhat Frenchy, but contains many instructive and edifying facts. When you are stronger I will tell you more about it.

My good advice harps on the old string, *pazienza*. As much passivity and resignedness as possible. You are in God's hands; don't care to do more than He allows you to do. Be content to be helpless.

Bombay, April 19, 1889.

My dear Child,

I send you a very cordial blessing for next Sunday, and the same to your community. May you all enjoy a *Buona Pasqua*, with abundant graces and joys. . . .

You have had a great loss in the death of Dr. Ullathorne. How nicely he said, "If God shows me mercy for anything, it will be for the care I have taken of my nuns." Indeed, he was the truest father to his nuns amongst all the Bishops I have ever known. He understood religious life, and he took the deepest interest in the spiritual advancement of his nuns. He leaves behind him some very noble communities. His wide experience proved of immense use to him in directing his nuns. Then, he really knew the law of the Church, and enforced it as well as he could. He was a grand old Bishop—*Sacerdos magnus.*—R.I.P.

As we advance in life, the uncertainty of all human affairs forces itself more and more upon us. We take more notice of deaths, we see how many die, how many die young, and it is brought home that the knock at our own door may come at any hour, when we least expect it. We may make the thought of death very familiar to us, and prepare for it by many acts of contrition. It will be a relief when all is over, and we hear, "Well done, thou good and faithful servant."

Continue to thank God for all His past mercies, and try to fill your days with good works.

My health keeps up, so far. I am ready to run to the hills, if the heat proves too much for me.

Say everything most kind to Rev. Mother, and to all my old friends.

I remain, yours very truly in Christ,

✠ GEORGE, Archbishop of Bombay.

I am somewhat sleepy. Our neighbour, an Armenian schismatic, sang through the night till 2 a.m. with a healthy vigorous voice.

April 19, 1889.

. . . My last meditation was *Pazienza;* why should not the next one be *Alleluia, Alleluia, Alleluia*? The short history of those forty days is so peaceful, so alive with hope, so triumphant, you will be the better for the change from the Lenten considerations. I wonder whether you have contrived to get into London. Even to be there, though unable to assist at the long services, would be some gain. It is something to know they are going on, and that one is near them, especially if the imagination can fill up the scene, the prayers, &c.

Yesterday I went through the Mandatum in my Cathedral, and afterwards preached on the Blessed Eucharist. The Mandatum is carried out in a peculiar way. Thirteen boys, about ten to twelve years old, are dressed in surplices; they wear a broad red sash. They are seated on each side of the passage down the middle of the church. Each receives a pious book and a picture after his washing is ended.

The Cathedral was well filled. Bombay reminds me somewhat of Rome on Maundy Thursday. In the afternoon every Christian appears in his or her best, and they wander from sepulchre to sepulchre, and spend some time in prayer at each one they visit. The sepulchres are but poor affairs. Bad Portuguese taste still survives amongst us; everything is small, tawdry, and in a certain sense mean. Some excellent German statues have been imported, but our natives prefer their hideous figures, of form and colour most dreadful.

The old Fathers S.J. introduced among the natives representations of the Passion on a very large scale.

They are rather roughly done, but I think they are suited to the people. These representations are called Passos. Crowds gather to see them.

I read the letter of the Dean of Windsor, and those of Carnarvon and the Rev. Carter. They form a strange confession of the state of a Church which claims any particle of divinity. Mr. Carter's personal confession, and his assurance that he has never looked for settled authority beyond the Church of England, sound strangely from a man on the brink of the grave. How much he is to be pitied!

April 30, 1889.

While the Archbishop is preparing his judgment, the Dean of Windsor has set a nice little ball rolling. As the *Spectator* says, he drives them into a corner, *i.e.*, the Ritualists, the most lawless and the most self-willed of all the "sects of perdition." The last thing they want in this world or the next is a living authority, civil or ecclesiastical. I see Archdeacon Farrar tries to attract attention by much unseemly blasphemy. He can sink to any depth; the author of *Eternal Hope* and the *Life of Christ* belongs to a very low order of minds, and is perfectly eaten up by vanity. How wretchedly small and wicked all this must appear to the angels!

My edition of Hettinger was printed between 1885 and 1887; it is called the sixth, and is said to be thoroughly revised, much increased. The work consists of two vols. in five parts. I think it is very probable that the two lectures I have translated were new and incorporated afterwards into the book. As you say, he uses the Vatican Council largely. Have you ever read through the Constitutions of the Vatican? They are marvels of accuracy and compression, quite worthy to stand beside the noblest chapters of the Council of

Trent. Such a contrast to the solemn trifling of the Lambeth gathering!

The splitting up into short chapters was an idea of my own. That form tempts many impatient readers; they are caught by the headings. In making this change, I followed the contents printed at the beginning of each conference by Hettinger. Common readers do not care to go through the summary of a long conference, they lose themselves before they get to the end.

Your illness has not allowed you to follow E—— in his University studies. I fancy that was not the smallest of the concomitant crosses of your illness. Pray and have patience. Perfect patience and joy in your helplessness! It looks easy enough, but it tests all one's principles. I have not left Bombay as yet; the heat is nearly at its worst.

Much has been said in the preceding letters about the treatise on the Apostolic See from Hettinger's large work on Christianity which Archbishop Porter translated during his convalescence this summer, and which was printed at the *Examiner* Press, Bombay. Some copies were sent to England, and possibly, had the Archbishop lived, an English edition would have been published ere now. Archbishop Porter wrote a Preface to the translation, in which he places before his readers proofs of the Primacy of St. Peter, drawn from Scripture and from the condition of the Church at the present day as compared with that of the sects outside her pale. From this Preface we reprint what follows.

Professor Hettinger insists much on three fundamental ideas of Christ's Kingdom, viz., the idea of a Church, the idea of the unity of the Church, and the idea of Church government.

Holy Scripture describes the Church in magnificent language. She is "the city of our God," "the city of the great King," "the city of the Lord of hosts," "God

cc

hath founded it for ever" (Psalm xlvii.). She is the mountain of God, "a mountain in which God is pleased to dwell; for there the Lord shall dwell unto the end" (Psalm lxvii), "the mountain of the house of the Lord, prepared on the top of the mountains, exalted above the hills, and all nations shall flow into it" (Isaias ii. 2). She is the city of truth: "Jerusalem shall be called the city of truth and the mountain of the Lord of hosts, the sanctified mountain" (Zach. viii. 3). With Jeremias she is "the chosen vineyard" (ii. 21), "the throne of God" (iii. 17). In the Canticle of Canticles "she is all fair and there is not a spot in her" (iv. 7). The earth and its inhabitants still belong to her: "Ask of Me and I will give thee the Gentiles for thy inheritance and the utmost parts of the earth for thy possession" (Psalm ii. 8), and she "shall rule from sea to sea, and from the river unto the ends of the earth" (Psalm lxxi. 8). "Terrible as an army set in array" (Cant. vi. 3). She is invincible: "Often have they fought against me from my youth; but they could not prevail over me" (Psalm cxxviii. 2). For God set her up "a kingdom that shall never be destroyed, that shall stand for ever" (Daniel ii. 44).

In the New Testament, Christ founds His Church: "Thou art Peter, and on this rock I will build My Church" (St. Matt. xvi. 18). He Himself is the foundation on which the Church is built: "For other foundation no man can lay but that which is laid, which is Christ Jesus" (1 Cor. iii. 11). She preserves the truth, being the house of God, which is the Church of the living God, "the pillar and the ground of the truth" (1 Tim. iii. 15). She is the fold in which the lambs and sheep will feed: "There shall be one fold and one shepherd" (St. John x. 16). Christ is the door: "By Me if any man shall enter in he shall be saved; and he shall go in and go out and shall find pastures" (St. John x. 9). St. Paul again calls the Church the Body of Christ: "Now you are the Body of Christ and members of member" (1 Cor. xii. 27). In the same context he calls the Church simply "Christ" (v. 12), and to the Ephesians: "He gave some apostles, and some prophets, and other some evangelists, and other some pastors and doctors . . . for the edifying of the Body of Christ" (Ephes. iv. 11, 12). The holiness of the Church he describes in the following chapter: "As Christ also loved the Church and delivered Himself up for it, that He might sanctify it, cleansing it by the laver of water in the word of life. That He might present it to Himself a glorious Church, not having spot or wrinkle or any such thing, but that it should be holy and without blemish" (Ephes. v. 26, 27).

Christ promised to abide in His Church: "And behold I am with you all days, even to the consummation of the world" (St. Matt. xxviii. 20). For "He will reign in the house of Jacob for ever, and of His Kingdom there shall be no end" (St. Luke i. 32, 33). J. M. Capes counted in the New Testament about seventy passages in which mention is made of "the Church" by Christ.

The texts taken from the Old Testament may be found in the Christian tradition of all ages as referring to the Church.

The teaching of both Testaments may be fairly summed up in the statement that Christ founded His Church, that in it and through it men might receive the graces and blessings of the Redemption; the Church has been well called the continuation of the Incarnation to the end of time.

The second idea is that of the unity of the Church. This blessing of unity, the High Priest prayed for on the eve of His Passion. "And not for them only do I pray, but for those also who through their word shall believe in Me; that they all may be one, as Thou, Father, in

Me, and I in Thee, that they also may be one in Us; that the world may believe Thou hast sent Me" (St. John xvii. 20, 21).

The Church must be one, numerically; she must be one, there may not be many churches. She must be one within herself; she must be one in faith, one in worship, and one in corporate life. St. Paul describes the unity of the Church: "Careful to keep the *unity* of the Spirit in the bond of peace: one *Body* and one *Spirit*, as you are called in *one* hope of your vocation. One Lord, *one faith*, one baptism, ... unto the edification of the body of Christ. Till we all meet in the *unity of faith*. ... That we may not now be children tossed to and fro, and carried about with every wind of doctrine. ... But we may in all things grow up in Him Who is the Head, Christ" (Ephes. iv. 3—16). All, whatever differences in nationality, language, circumstance may separate them, must be one in faith, must reject doctrines opposed to the faith, and must grow up in Him Who is the Head.

The unity in worship follows from the unity of faith: no act of worship may contradict the faith or fail to express it.

The corporate unity, the unity of government, was established by Jesus Christ in order to preserve the unity of faith. Without corporate organic unity the unity of faith would soon perish, and the unity of worship would soon be lost. The figures under which the Church is represented in the New Testament all imply this corporate unity. She is the Kingdom of Heaven, a flock under one Shepherd, the vine from which every branch grows, a temple, a house; above all, she is the mystical Body of Christ.

The unity of government exists sometimes in sects, a mere outward material unity, as in the Church of England by law established, and in the Russian Church, where the members form one body under the headship of the reigning Sovereign. Such outward accidental unity differs widely from the essential visible unity which come from within, from the formal principle of faith, from the Holy Ghost ever abiding in the Church and uniting its members in one faith. External unity alone is a mere fact which may disappear. External unity proceeding from the internal principle forms a positive mark of the Church of Christ: "That the world may *believe* Thou has sent Me" (St. John xvii. 21). The evidence for this mark should convince the world of the Divinity of the Mission of Jesus Christ. In the Church of Christ external unity rests on the internal unity which must be referred to the indwelling of the Holy Ghost and the abiding presence of Jesus Christ. The promises of Christ assure the continuance of His presence to the end of time, and the endurance of the fact of external unity.

The third idea is that of the government of the Church.

The providence of God established the Supremacy of St. Peter and his successors in the Church as the means for the maintenance of the internal unity of faith and the external unity of creed, of worship, of communion, and of corporate cohesion.

The place of St. Peter in the Gospels cannot escape the observation of a careful reader. "In the whole New Testament, John, who is yet mentioned oftener than the rest, occurs only thirty-eight times; but in the Gospels alone Peter is mentioned twenty-three times by Matthew, eighteen by Mark, twenty by Luke, and thirty by John" (Allies' *St. Peter, his Name and Office*, p. 93).

In each of the four catalogues of the Apostles Peter is placed first (St. Matt. x. 2—5; St. Mark iii. 6—19; St. Luke vi. 14—17; Acts i. 13). St. Matthew calls him simply the first, "the first Simon, who is called Peter;" and first is not used as a mere numeral, for if it were so used, second, third, &c., would have followed.

When the Evangelists mention some of the Apostles, Peter being one, he is always placed first. Thus at the raising of Jairus' daughter to life: "And He admitted not any man to follow Him, but Peter and James and John the brother of James" (St. Mark v. 37). Again, at the Transfiguration: "Jesus taketh unto Him Peter and James and John his brother" (St. Matt. xvii. 1). Again, at the Agony in the Garden: "And He taketh Peter and James and John with Him, and He began to fear and to be heavy" (St. Mark xiv. 33).

St. Peter often appears as the chief or head: "And Simon and they who were with him followed after Him" (St. Mark i. 36). "Peter and they that were with him said" (St. Luke viii. 45). At the Transfiguration: "But Peter and they that were with him were heavy with sleep" (St. Luke ix. 32). So after the Resurrection: "Peter standing up with the Eleven". (Acts ii. 14). "They said to Peter and the rest of the Apostles" (v. 37). "Peter and the Apostles answering said" (v. 29). "Go tell His disciples and Peter" (St. Mark xvi. 7). The form, *those with him*, is never used of any other of the Apostles; it is used of David and his followers, and still more frequently of our Lord and His disciples.

The questions of St. Peter to our Lord preserved in the Gospels are numerous and of deep meaning: "Lord, how oft shall my brother sin against me, and I forgive him? Until seven times?" (St. Matt. xviii. 21). "Lord, dost Thou wash my feet? Thou shalt never wash my feet. . . . Lord, not my feet only, but also my hands and my head" (St. John xiii. 6—8). "Behold we have left all things, what therefore shall we have?" (St. Matt. xix. 27). Lord, to whom shall we go? Thou hast the words of eternal life" (St. John vi. 67). "Lord dost thou speak this parable to us or to all?" (St. Luke xii. 41). "And Peter, taking Him, began to rebuke Him, saying: Lord, be it far from Thee; this shall not be unto Thee. But He turning, said to Peter: Go after Me, Satan, thou art a scandal to Me, because thou dost not relish the things that are of God, but the things that are of men. Then Jesus said to His disciples: If any man will come after Me let him deny himself" (St. Matt. xvi. 22—24).

In how many mysterious incidents is Peter prominent?

"And when they were come to Capharnaum, they that received the didrachmas came to Peter and said to him: Doth not your Master pay the didrachma. He said, Yes.... And when thou hast opened its mouth thou shalt find a stater; take that and give it to them *for Me and thee*" (St. Matt. xvii. 23—26). Peter is the only Apostle into whose house our Lord is recorded to have entered. "And when Jesus was come into Peter's house, He saw his mother-in-law lying and sick of a fever. And He touched her hand and the fever left her; and she arose and ministered to them" (St. Matt. viii. 13—15). "And going up into one of the ships that was Simon's He desired him to thrust out a little from the land. And sitting down He taught the multitudes out of the ship. Now, when He had ceased to speak, He said to Simon, Launch out into the deep and let down your nets for a draught. And Simon answering, said to Him: Master, we have laboured all night, and have taken nothing; but at Thy word I will let down the net. And when they had done this they enclosed a very great multitude of fishes and their net was breaking, and they beckoned to their partners that were in the other ship that they should come and help them, and they came and filled both the ships, so that they were almost sinking, which when Simon Peter saw he fell down at Jesus' knees, saying, Depart from me, for I am a sinful man, O Lord. . . . And Jesus saith to Simon, Fear not; from henceforth thou shalt be taking men" (St. Luke v. 3—10).

During the Passion, Peter distinguishes himself by his too rash and too self-reliant zeal. His fall is specially foretold, though the others were equally brave and all fled in the hour of danger. For him Jesus Christ prayed by name. "But I have prayed for thee that thy faith fail not, and thou being once converted, confirm thy brethren" (St. Luke xxii. 32). To Peter he addresses a personal reproof: "What, could you not watch one hour with Me?" (St. Matt. xxvi. 40). "And the Lord, turning, looked on Peter, and Peter remembered the word of the Lord. . . . And Peter went out and wept bitterly" (St. Luke xxii. 61, 62).

During the forty days which followed the Resurrection the Angel directed the holy women: "Go tell His disciples and Peter that He goeth before you into Galilee." And St. Paul records that Christ risen "was seen by Cephas and after that by the Eleven" (1 Cor. xv. 5). Peter leads the mysterious fishing in the Lake of Tiberias, and on the beach afterwards receives the commission to feed the lambs and the sheep of Christ's flock, and hears the manner of his death on the cross foretold" (St. John xxi.).

To sum up. Peter alone received a new name from his Divine Master, and this at the first moment when Andrew led his brother to Jesus (St. John i. 42), as Abraham received a new name when God called him to be the father of many nations (Gen. xvii. 5), and as Jacob received the name of Israel: "For if thou hast been strong against God, how much more shalt thou prevail against men" (Gen. xxxii. 28). Peter alone is the Rock on which Christ builds His Church. To Peter alone was given the power of the keys. In the first instance, to Peter alone is promised the power of loosing and binding which was afterwards conferred on him and on all the other Apostles (St. John xx. 23). To Peter alone was committed the charge of strengthening or confirming his brethren (St. Luke xxii. 32). To Peter alone was entrusted the care of the whole flock, sheep and lambs (St. John xxi. 15—17). To Peter alone was addressed the mysterious command, "Follow thou Me" (St. John xxi. 22).

Such is the place held by Peter while our Lord remained on earth. Let us turn to the history of the infant Church contained in the first twelve chapters of the Acts of the Apostles.

Peter ordains the election of an Apostle in the place of Judas (Acts i. 15). He first preaches the Gospel to the Jews. But Peter, *standing up with the Eleven*, lifted up his voice (Acts ii. 14). He founds the Church of Samaria (Acts xviii. 14). He admits the Gentiles into the Church (Acts x.). He passed through visiting all (Acts ix. 32). He cuts off from the Church the first heresiarch, Simon Magus (Acts viii. 20, 21). He decides the dissension about circumcision (Acts xv. 10). Publicly and with authority Peter reproves Ananias and Sapphira, who had lied to him and to the Holy Ghost (Acts v. 3—10). Peter announced Christ before the Sanhedrin: "For there is no other Name under Heaven given to men whereby we must be saved" (Acts iv. 12). And after the miraculous deliverance of the Apostles from the common prison, *Peter then answering, and the Apostles*, said, "We ought to obey God rather than men" (Acts v. 29). When Peter was kept in prison, prayer was made without ceasing by the Church to God for him (Acts xii. 5), which was not done when St. Paul was cast into prison in the same city, because the Church without Peter was without her head. He performs the first miracle, bidding the lame man at the Beautiful Gate, "In the name of Jesus Christ of Nazareth rise up and walk" (Acts iii. 6). He raised Eneas, lying on his bed for eight years, ill of the palsy: "Eneas, the Lord Jesus Christ healeth thee, arise and make thy bed. And immediately he arose" (Acts ix. 34). He called back to life Tabitha, who was dead: "Tabitha arise. And she opened her eyes and having seen Peter, sat up" (Acts ix. 40). And such confidence did the believers feel in the power of St. Peter, people "brought out the sick into the streets and laid them on beds and couches, that when Peter came his shadow at the least might overshadow any of them and they might be delivered from their infirmities" (Acts v. 15). Lastly, St. Paul testifies, "Then, three years after, I came to Jerusalem to see Peter and stayed with him fifteen days. But other of the Apostles I saw none, except James the brother of the Lord" (Galat. i. 18, 19).

This prominence of St. Peter in the Gospels and in the Acts is not drawn out here with a view of establishing his Primacy and Supremacy or that of his successors: that Professor Hettinger will do in his two books. A more general consideration presents itself.

The position given to St. Peter during the lifetime of his Divine Master, is, to say the least, a singular one; he towers above the other Apostles, and he stands on a relation of intimacy and unity with our Lord to which no one else is admitted. He receives a new name; he is proclaimed as the foundation of the future Church; he may be described as acting with his Master and for Him, almost as one with Him. In the Acts he steps into the place of the leader of the Apostolic band and of the Church. During the subsequent history of the Church,

Peter survives; he and his successors to his See exercise a decisive influence in the Church. On the one hand, they have been looked up to and obeyed as the Vicars of Christ by the overwhelming majority of those who believe in Jesus Christ. On the other hand, those who have torn themselves away from the communion of Peter's See have forgotten him; his name is a mere memory to them, no living reality; he is almost disliked, and the annals of his successors form a tale of unceasing persecution.

To the Catholic Church to this day St. Peter holds a place not unworthy of the distinction assigned to him in the Gospels and the Acts. Our adversaries reproach us even for giving to his successors more than Holy Scripture warrants. The reproach we reject; we contend that the Catholic tradition keeps closely within Scriptural limits. What is a clear fact, called into question by no one, the sects who have separated from the Catholic Church not only do not pay an exaggerated honour to St. Peter, they almost ignore him; the least bitter denounce his successors as usurpers. We look in vain among them for a Peter who even faintly corresponds to the Peter of the Gospels and the Acts. "Save me, O Lord, for there is now no Saint; truths are decayed from among the children of men" (Psalm xi. 2). The truth about Peter has decayed among the children of men outside the Catholic Church.

The Catholic Church glories in her unity. She does not fear to take to herself the description given by St. Paul in his Epistle to the Ephesians. Nay, her enemies taunt her because her unity becomes more perfect every day. The union between the Bishops of the Catholic world and the successor of St. Peter becomes more intimate; the press, the post, the telegraph, the railway, the ocean steamers, render communication between the Head and the members more easy, and it has become more frequent. The desire for closer union grows stronger, as the war against Christ and His Church becomes more bitter.

Outside the Church what a spectacle of disunion and discord! Sects multiplied without number: the more important sects with difficulty preserved in some semblance of unity by the bonds of State authority, State funds, and State penalties; the others a very Babel of profanity and blasphemy. A few years ago an Anglican Dean maintained in a sermon that when Christ prayed that those who believed in Him might be one, He meant that they might be many. More recently an Anglican writer defended a unity, not of *subordination* but of *co-ordination*, which really means the same thing, not unity, but multiplicity. The latest theory proposes a *primary* unity of charity or faith, but the author nowhere explains his *secondary* unity, and if it means anything he champions only an invisible unity of an invisible Church. A visible mark of unity which can lead men to believe in Jesus Christ is still wanting outside the Catholic Church. It is sadly wanting in the Church by law established in England.

Truths are decayed from among the children of men, and the truth about Church unity has decayed from among the children of men outside the Catholic Church.

Nay, the very idea of a Church seems to survive only in the Catholic Church. To her children the prophecies, the descriptions, the attributes, the sufferings, the triumphs and the glories of the Church of Holy Scripture, are very real and actual. Catholics eagerly and fearlessly claim for her and for her alone all that Scripture and Tradition say of the Bride of Christ.

What sectarians do as much? Where do we find amongst them a definition of a visible Church? any claim to a supernatural origin? to any assistance of the Holy Ghost? to any promise of indefectibility? to a final triumph over Hell? Are not all feverishly hastening on the decay which began from the moment they separated from the Rock of Peter?

Earnest and sincere inquirers who do not belong to the Catholic Church may put this plain question to themselves: The Gospels and the Acts are filled with three ideas or facts; the fact of a Church, the fact of a Church one in body, one in spirit, and the fact of Peter as the leader of the Apostles. These three ideas and facts are prominent in the Catholic Church; as prominent as they are in the Gospels and the Acts. These three ideas or facts are absent in all the religious bodies which are separated from the communion of the Catholic Church. These truths have decayed from the minds of their adherents.

Which religious body would Christ claim as His Church? Which would St. Peter recognize as the Church founded on him? Which would the Evangelists confess to be the realization of their pages?

In which can I best secure the eternal salvation of my soul? Shall I follow Peter? Or remain with those who have revolted against him? To whom shall we go? Shall we not hear the words of eternal life from the successors of Peter, who gathered them from the lips of his Divine Master, and received the commission to confirm the Church in her faith?

CHAPTER XIX.

LAST LETTERS.

May to Sept. 1889.

Indisposition. Move to Khandalla. Trials of convalescence. How sickness sanctifies. Catholicism, the only remedy for India. Liturgy for Pentecost. The jungle and its aborigines. Storm at Khandalla. Sanyasis, their penances. How much can be effected by moderate work. Change to Poona. Suppressed gout and its effects. Rev. A. Richardson's *Catholic Claims*. Contemplated work on the Papacy. Power of music. Despondency. Pleasantness of Poona. Short visit to Bombay. Puzzle solved about "An Impossible Precept." A Hindoo's idea about the two chief sacraments. Conversions at Chota-Nagpore. Rules of Election. *Life of Ozanam*. Attack of fever. Enjoyment of the beauties of nature. Ritualists and the Royal Supremacy. Dr. Pusey's Life. Return to Bombay. W. G. Ward. Bryce's *American Commonwealth*. The Sacred Heart Convents in Australia. Mrs. Montgomery's theological books. *The Nun of Kenmare*. Wilfrid Ward's Life of his father. Moisture of the weather. To a Nun on her Profession. To visit Rome a great grace. Devotion of the early Christians to our Lord's Glorified Life. *The Grammar of Assent*. The ways of Providence. Sunday and the European mail. The Religious life and life in the world. Unhealthiness of Poona. Plans for the future which were cut short by death.

Khandalla, May 19, 1889.

Last Thursday I began to feel the heat was telling on me, and on Friday I came up to Khandalla. The result was, I sent no letter by the last mail. Friday was the last Friday mail for this season. We now enter on the monsoon arrangements, and the mails will start on Tuesday, beginning with the 21st of May. The change has already done me good; the fever had not fairly taken hold of me, so I hope to be quite myself again soon. The days here are very hot, always in the neighbourhood of 95°, but the mornings and nights are delightful. We are a community at present of nearly twenty Fathers: each has a room to himself. It is far away the grandest bungalow in Khandalla, and occupies the very choicest position; we have twelve acres which we are gradually planting. The change from Bombay is invaluable to the Fathers. So much for Khandalla.

Your letter of April 24th was very welcome. You do seem to be making real progress, thank God. Still, *pazienza!* Sometimes patience is more difficult in the first days of returning vigour, than in the worst period of the sickness; with vigour come back will, fancies, temper, &c., the old man. I do not quite agree with you that it is so difficult to sanctify sickness. It is very difficult to feel that sort of sanctity which we have pictured to ourselves in health; but if we don't rebel and murmur, if we submit to God's will and try to take what comes as coming from His hand, then sickness sanctifies, and it will sanctify still more if we unite our sufferings to those of our Lord. Father —— was right: when you become stronger, you will be able to see your gain and progress, more entire dependence on God, more inclination for prayer and the sacraments. The detachment from life which often comes in sickness may easily be converted into a supernatural detachment. A Kempis (bk. i. c. 12), among the uses of adversity, says what applies to sickness also: "Then he wearies to live longer and wishes death to come, *that he may be dissolved* and *be with Christ;*" then detachment from life becomes altogether supernatural. Take it for granted all has been for the best.

Your young Mahommedan friend from Hyderabad is too sanguine about reforms in India. The evils of Indian life are too deeply rooted to be changed in one or many generations. I doubt whether the Mahommedans with their swords could effect the change. 'In India the very Mahommedans catch the contagion of Hindooism: its influence is always debasing. The one remedy is the Catholic Church, and when will the day dawn for this devil-beridden land and people? Oh! it is so sad to see so many millions seemingly hopelessly lost for this life and for the next. The talk about reform sounds so empty in the presence of such wide-spread and deeply-rooted mischief through the whole family life. Perhaps later I may send you a copy of a work lately published, *The Status of Women in India*. Meanwhile, pray for us. God bless you.

Khandalla, May 27, 1889.

The stay up here has done me much good, though the days have been very hot. The mornings and evenings are deliciously cool, and the greatest heat has not the oppressive character of the Bombay heat; there you live in a perpetual bath.

You will receive this early in Pentecost week. I hope you will be sufficiently recovered to spend that week following the wonderful series of Masses and prayers throughout the octave. Pentecost-tide always seems to me one of the most perfect pieces of the Liturgy; it is certainly one of the most consoling. The presence of the Holy Ghost in the Church and in the soul must be an extraordinary gift, since it was to console the Apostles for the visible presence of Christ amongst them, and abundantly compensate for its loss. May you receive a large share of the gifts of the Holy Spirit and His consolations!

Khandalla, May 27, 1889.

The weather in Bombay has been unusually oppressive this May, and I was beginning to feel rather out of sorts, so I fled up to this place last Thursday week. The days have been very hot, the thermometer keeping 90° and above, but the mornings and evenings are very cool, sometimes chilly. The two Colleges of Bombay have each a magnificent villa up here (two thousand feet above the sea). I am in that of St. Xavier's. The country is very wild; tigers and panthers and hyenas are frequently killed about here. The Fathers have had five or six dogs carried off by panthers; now they lock their dogs up at night. There is little cultivation, except what we have introduced. The jungle is not far off, with its aborigines, far older than the Hindoos, and even than the Dravidians, who were invaded by the Hindoos; great thieves, but they tell the truth and seem good-natured people. In the jungle, besides tigers, panthers, and hyenas, there are snakes of many kinds, scorpions without number, monkeys, lizards, &c. I do not attempt long walks, but the younger Fathers make great expeditions. . . .

You must tell me whether you ventured on the trip to London, and if you did, how you fared. The quiet life of S—— would make you wish for a breath of London air and the hum of London life and the luxury of London devotions and a word with old friends. The excitement gives a momentary increase of energy, and invalid people are so tempted to go beyond their strength. I hope you were proof against the temptation. . . .

Take everything quietly and leisurely; there is plenty of time to do all you have to do. You would find the practice of always asking yourself, "What am I going to do? How ought I to do it?" a very salutary one and favourable to habits of self-control.

Khandalla, June 3, 1889.

When the illness has passed and you are quite well, then you will forget all the unpleasant memories of your illness, and you will only think of the great lessons and graces received. Human nature is very forgiving; we remember the sunny days, we forget the cold, damp, foggy December. So you will find by your experience.

Do not worry about your habits of piety. Those were for times of health and vigour; when the vigour comes back, you will resume the old habits without the least difficulty.

However exhausted and wretched you feel in the morning, receive Holy Communion whenever you have the opportunity, if only you can bear the fast, even if you are not equal to read prayers of thanksgiving.

The summer has been very trying this year. I came up to Kandalla not one day too soon. We are dying for the monsoon, and hope it may be a strong one.

Last evening, I sat more than two hours in the verandah, watching a thunderstorm raging all around us. Most vivid lightning; the clouds swept up to our feet and were carried past in a few minutes. How small man seems in the presence of a grand storm! When the monsoon breaks here, as it will do in a week or ten days, I shall go to Poona. There the rainy season is a very mild affair, in Bombay it is serious.

TO A NOVICE.

June 3, 1889.

Moments of weariness and disgust, temptations to ask for your bonnet and umbrella, wild imaginations, don't come from yourself; they are from outside, and may be forgotten as soon as you can drive them from an excited fancy. When you wonder at the goodness of God in calling you and bearing with you so long, those thoughts are your own true thoughts, prompted by grace, but really your own. I suppose you are not so simple as to believe that you are going to do it all, reform all faults, acquire all virtues, during the two years of your novitiate. How much will remain to be done after you have made your vows, and when you come to the end of your life perhaps all will not have been done.

7, Sholapur Road, Poona, June 17, 1889.

I am writing from the house of the Bishop of Poona. I came here without any accident this day week. The thermometer stands about 77°, an improvement on 96°, but we want rain sadly. We thought the monsoon had commenced, but the weather prophets are not so strong in maintaining the monsoon as they were, and the crops are crying for rain.

I read the long judgment of Edward Cantuar. It was an able paper, and his conclusion was the only one I suppose which he could arrive at. The Ritualists don't like it. The *Spectator* had a very amusing and also a very clever article on the judgment: he would have liked the Archbishop to have decided in favour of a synodical trial on grounds of broad general policy.

You ask me if I ever visited a real Sanyasi. I have not. I only learnt the fact of Gaorishankar's existence at Bhaunagar when I was on the point of leaving the place. Common Sanyasis are to be met every day in Bombay. They are a very dirty set of fellows, and I should not care to talk with them. They trade on the superstition and credulity of the people, and make a good business of it. Some go through fearful penances. In the Esplanade, one of our principal thoroughfares, one was to be seen day after day turning round over a fire.

Another sat gazing at the fierce sun for eight or ten hours. The passers-by throw money into their boxes, and so they live.

Your account of S—— is not a cheering one. I fear his office, its responsibilities, and its worries, sits heavily upon him; his is an anxious mind. It seems, in the providence of God, that we only learn how limited our strength is and how much the soul depends on the body, when we come to a breakdown. It is something to learn the lesson even then, and to accustom oneself to keep within one's strength and never go to the end of our tether. Moderate work persevered in can accomplish much; but then our old friend *pazienza* must never leave us.

I have had a visit from an old friend, "suppressed gout." The victim feels good for nothing, very much inclined to be depressed, often he cannot say what precisely ails him. The change to Poona has done me good, and the gout has gone down to my knees and feet, giving me some pain, but not enough to prevent me from going through my ordinary duties.

Poona, June 24, 1889.

I am glad to read of your splendid May weather. The fresh air and the glories of the spring will do you all the good in the world. Don't have any scruple about self-indulgence where there is question of avoiding work. Your first duty is to get well, and avoiding work and anxiety is the best remedy you have. Wait till you feel strong before you attempt any real work. Rest, rest and learn to find God in the beauties of nature.

You see I have been on the hills for more than a month. The fever does not return, but I have been for some time under an attack of suppressed gout. Poona has done me some good, but the enemy I cannot quite shake off; that must be a work of time. One curious effect is a strong inclination to despondency, which I must always fight against, a sort of general depression, not despondency about anything in particular.

We have had a week of wonderfully cool and pleasant weather, the rain threatening every day, but never coming down. The country needs it much. Our monsoon is late again this year.

Thank God, I am able to write and read a few hours every day. I have just finished a most perfect little controversial book by the Rev. Austin Richardson, *What are the Catholic Claims?* I am sure you will read it with pleasure when you are able to resume your reading.

My reading has been connected with the book I am contemplating on the Government of the Church. I am at a loss for a title. "Development of the Papacy" won't do, for the power was always there in its plenitude. The history of the Papacy I do not want to write. My idea is to trace the events and the causes which have led to the greater centralization of the government of the Church in the Pope. The subject is full of interest. I hope I may be able to do it fairly justice.

You are fortunate in having such a sympathetic, intelligent companion in M——. She must have a good head to enjoy the Manuals of Philosophy, for they are close reading. The musical taste and talent will be a real comfort to you when you can do little more than listen. What a mysterious power music has to lead the soul! It seems to me like the language of spirits. Your account of the organ makes me wish to hear it. Will that ever be? At present I see no prospect of a journey to Europe, but any day business may require my presence.

Poona, June 24, 1889.

My dear Child,

You see from the heading "Poona" that I have left Bombay. The weather in May became most trying. I thought prudence the better part of valour, and fled to a cooler atmosphere. Poona is at this time of the season from 10° to 15° cooler than Bombay. The fever did not return, but I had some symptoms of suppressed gout which require looking to. I can go about and attend to all my duties, which is a comfort.

You must not lose courage about your spiritual affairs. Now that you go to Confession and Communion pretty regularly every fortnight, I hope for better things. Regularity in approaching the sacraments must in the long run produce its result, even though many falls may occur. You have the will to serve God well and to save your soul. You will surely do so if you persevere in your fortnightly reception of Confession and Communion. Your health improves, I hope. I hear you have had a cold spring but a delightful May. Our May has been unusually hot. In one city within three days twenty-six persons died of heat apoplexy.

Good-bye. God bless you. Give my kindest remembrances to all the members of your family.

I remain, yours very truly in Christ,

✠ GEORGE, Archbishop of Bombay.

Fort Chapel, July 2, 1889.

The fever has spared me so far. Its place has been taken by gout, suppressed gout, which is tiresome even though it is not dangerous. I find it very depressing, and I am obliged to fight vigorously against gloomy thoughts and imaginations. Happily I have succeeded so far and kept up my spirits under difficult circumstances, as Mark Tapley would say.

You see I write from Bombay. A sermon and some business brought me down on Thursday last. I return to Poona by the mid-day mail train to-day. Poona I find most pleasant. Ten to fifteen degrees cooler than Bombay, very quiet, tempting one with many pleasant walks, along the finest roads in India. I stay with the Bishop, in a long straggling bungalow, only one storey high. . . .

We have had another conversion in Calcutta. The Rev. Mr. Townsend, the head of the Oxford Mission, has submitted to the Church. *Deo Gratias.*

I see that Mr. Rivington wages a very serious war with his former brethren. I like all I have seen by him. And he has found a valuable ally in Rev. Austin Richardson. In his *What are the Catholic Claims?* he demolishes the Rev. Gore, Master of Keble House, Oxford. Rivington's books are somewhat stiff reading, but Richardson's would not fatigue you. I think it would amuse you.

Some of the consecrations of families have been very splendid. The Jaffna ceremony surpassed all the others. I hope to give an account of it in the *Messenger.* The Indians love a big ceremony, and with a little training they produce very fine combinations of persons and things.

Bombay, July 1, 1889.

Your scepticism about the sanctifying effect of sickness convinces me your recovery is not complete. When you are quite well, you will then know that you are the better for it spiritually. You allude to the loss of your power of attention. How could there be much devotion or fervour without attention? You have not strength enough for holy things. Do the little you can, and wish you could do more. Don't doubt the mist will clear away. The sea-shore and the ever-moving sea will brighten you up.

Father Morris' article on "Archiepiscopal Jurisdiction" I have not read, nor yet the one you mention on an "Impossible Precept."[1] I can solve your puzzle about this last. The Council of Trent defines for one living amidst the dangers of daily life, with the ordinary allowance of human inconstancy and carelessness. Such a one requires a *special* grace, not to avoid this or that sin, but to avoid all sin. Persons, however, who really wish to avoid venial sin, who fly occasions, who make use of means of sanctification, prayer and sacraments, &c., may and do avoid venial sin for months and years together. I have seen in some of the greatest theologians that they are persuaded many persons, especially in religion, pass years without offending God by a deliberate venial sin.

I am writing from Bombay. I came down from Poona for a few days, to expedite some business. I mean to return to-morrow. Bombay is very hot and stifling.

The fever has not shown itself, but that I may not be without an occasion of merit, I have suppressed gout. In its present form with me it is not dangerous, but it is very tiresome, and I find myself obliged to wage a constant war against depression and laziness.

I have some hopes that I may make a beginning with my book on the defence of the Papacy against the charge of usurpation. The matter grows under my hands. I hope I shall be able to put it in an interesting form.

May I beg for three copies of Freppel's Conferences on the Divinity of Christ? My interesting Hindoo

[1] *The Month*, June, 1889.

catechumen has turned up again. His ideas are still much "mixed." He informs me that I taught him the two chief sacraments were Baptism and Matrimony. A possible combination in the Hindoo mind, but not one that I can accept. God is very patient. Perhaps, after all, this wandering, changeable man may settle down to be a thorough Catholic.

Did you see in the *Tablet* an account of the conversions at Chota Nagpore? The Fathers were on the point of giving up the mission, when the turn of the tide came.

Poona, July 21, 1889.

What a talent you have for going forward to meet miseries and woes! Don't think of the autumn or of the bad symptoms coming back. Try to make the most of the present, and thank God for prolonged life and opportunity of serving Him. Pray for the courage to say you can't, when you feel too weak to do what is expected. You can make use of that rule of election, "What should I advise another person to do in my place? What would be reasonable?" I am no great believer in the merit of worry and perplexity. There is greater merit in making a quiet little election and standing by it. Don't delay your refusal to work till you feel you can't. Say you can't when you know the task will be rather difficult or will fatigue you greatly. I shall be surprised if you do not feel yourself a real Christian sooner than you expected. Early Mass you won't be able to manage for some time, but vocal prayers will become easy and pleasant to you long before then, and so will good reading for a short space.

I know the translations on the Love of God from St. Bernard by Mrs. Coventry Patmore and her husband. The book is a treasure, and the translations are perfect.

DD*

I have lately read Kathleen O'Meara's *Life of Ozanam*. It is a deeply interesting book, and lets its reader into the inner history of the French Catholic movement in which so many noble and able minds devoted themselves. Cardinal Manning put a Preface to the edition I read, I think the second.

The rainy season has not proved a favourable one to me. Since I left Bombay I have been under a prolonged attack of suppressed gout, and last week Brother Fever came on the scene. The doctor attacked him, however, so vigorously with quinine and other remedies that he was soon banished. I promised myself some time for writing a book I have on the stocks. The first line has yet to be written. It must wait for brighter days. I am now recruiting. I say Mass every day and take a drive when it is fine. So far I have not done much walking. That will soon come. I am reading the *Grammar of Assent*, which speaks for my health.

Poona, July 29, 1889.

Your letter of July 10th has just come in, and I shall have time to answer by the mail which leaves Poona this afternoon. In the first place I may say I am quite well. Both fever and gout have left me, and I am now picking up strength and drinking port wine despite the gout. I hope to be in Bombay before the end of this week. I have begun to do a little head-work and read some stiff books and write some reviews for the *Examiner*, but I find it does not answer to work too long hours in India. The mind ceases to bite.

I congratulate you on having returned to C——. Enjoy the flowers and the trees and the shadows on the grass; only put in an occasional *Benedicite omnia opera Domini Domino*, and think how beautiful Heaven must be, if the earth looks so fair. Have no scruples about the idling either. Give up reading or listening when you feel you have had enough. When you are really strong enough you will use your head again as naturally as you use your hands or feet.

Short easy prayers ought now to become more possible and more devotional. Say them out in the open air, if you find that helps your devotion, or seated in your chapel.

If you did not see the *Spectator* on the judgment given in the St. Paul's reredos, especially by Lord Coleridge, it will repay you to look it up. I shall be surprised if that judgment is not reversed. The *Spectator* turns Lord Coleridge's argument against his own judgment very ably.

The Bishop of Lincoln's case tries the Ritualists more severely. They want to get rid of the Royal Supremacy entirely, but they dare not say so, and they have not the faintest hope of succeeding. If the Archbishop of Canterbury can contrive a sentence which will not be appealed against to the Privy Council, the Ritualists will be happy for a time, but only for a time.

You are not equal to following the Rivington controversy. It has been very instructive and not a little amusing. The Rev. A. Richardson, who has joined Mr. Rivington, is a new-comer of considerable ability. His book, *What are the Catholic Claims?* is admirably written. I hope we shall have much more from this pen.

Is it true that Canon Liddon's health has broken down? For many reasons I should regret it, but especially for the unfinished Life of Dr. Pusey. We want to know more of the interior life of this man, if he had one.

Fort Chapel, August 6, 1889.

I returned to Bombay last Saturday. A tiny trace of fever clung to me at Poona, and the doctor agreed that a move to Bombay for a short time would probably free me from it. Those who suffer from Poona fever often run down to Bombay to shake it off. In these local fevers a change of air seems the best remedy. I already experience the benefit of the change. If the fever returns later, I shall fly back to Poona.

When you saw Y——, did he not tell you that you had been attempting too much? It is so difficult not to go beyond the limits, notwithstanding good resolutions. Even driving out may be continued too long. You may find it a demand on your credulity, but when I am on the invalid list and my own master (the kindness of friends is sometimes a trouble), I try to cut short any exertion before I come to feel tired.

I am afraid you have not as yet discovered the spiritual advantages of your long illness. Have patience. The day will come and you will resume what you can of your spiritual life, with a deeper feeling of the overwhelming importance of the world to come and a stronger desire to come nearer to God.

Fort Chapel, Bombay, August, 1889.

I must thank you for the Life of Ward which you have sent, and which will probably be delivered to-morrow. Ward's own writings did not attract me much. He was a great logician, but he was not much besides, and logic alone is a poor guide out of the world of theory and speculation. Ward was driven to exaggerations in many practical questions by his hard and fast logic. But he was a fine character, and a very able man. I look forward to his Life with eagerness.

A friend has lent me the three volumes of Bryce, *The American Commonwealth*, a most instructive and interesting book. L—— should read it and study it. To make it doubly profitable, he should afterwards read De Tocqueville's *Democratie en Amerique*, a book now thirty years old; in itself under some respects superior to Bryce, but corrected, verified, and supplemented largely by the latter. If L—— dislikes French, there is a good translation of De Tocqueville by Reeve. Bryce and De Tocqueville form an excellent introduction to the knowledge of contemporary politics.

A gentleman just returned from a holiday in Australia gives a most glowing account of the two or three convents of the Sacred Heart. They are well placed; the buildings are sensible, and splendid (he called them), and the schools will certainly fill as time goes on. He is a good Irishman, and rejoices in the progress of religion in those young colonies.

I have little Bombay news. I am very well, and quite equal to all my ordinary duties; well tired at the end of the day, and glad to rest; sleep does not fail me.

Poona, July 29, 1889.

. . . Did you ever read Mrs. Montgomery's *The Divine Sequence*, the *Eternal Years*, and the *Divine Ideal*? They have come out in a new coat, and I have had to write a review of them. This led me to run through them again. If you can put up with preaching from one of your own sex, and are satisfied to read a little at a time, you will be much pleased. Mrs. Montgomery has attempted some of the deepest problems in theology, and she has rendered them into beautiful English.

You have a new writer amongst you, who wields a masterly pen, the Rev. A. Richardson, who seems to be an importation from Belgium. He has taken part in the

Rivington controversy. His *What are the Claims of Rome?* is one of the most complete little books I ever read. I see he writes for Catholic Truth Society too.

One of my latest readings was *The Nun of Kenmare*, by herself, of course. Report says she has become an Anglican, and now rules a Ritualist Sisterhood. She has certainly resigned the generalship of the Sisters of Peace. The book is a painful book to read; full of disappointed ambition and spiteful venom. May she see her error, and receive the grace of repentance.

Sept. 20.

I have been reading Wilfrid Ward's book on his father, W. G. Ward. Indeed, I have finished it, from cover to cover. It is an infinitely clever book. The cleverness is what strikes one most. At the same time, I found it deeply interesting, and it added not a little to my knowledge of the Tractarian movement. No wonder the author has received such big compliments on the way he has carried out his idea.

Fort Chapel, August 19, 1889.

My dear Child,

First, I must thank you for your good wishes on the return of my birthday, and for the Communion you promise to offer for me. You ask me how much our time is in advance of yours. We are not much less than five hours before you, nearly the double of what you thought. I am glad to hear of your fine weather and prospect of good crops. Here our cry is for rain: we want so much. A heavy rainy season means escape from famine, and more or less abundance of food for two hundred and fifty millions. This season the fall of rain has been all we could wish. The rainy season has some inconveniences. Everything is saturated with moisture.

A small instance: you must be very careful of your matches, or they won't light, in some places they are kept under the pillow. Envelopes have to be ungummed, a tedious performance.

Many thanks for sending the paper regularly. *Sursum corda.* God will carry you through if you don't give up. Trust in Him, and continue to strive and pray. Kindest remembrances to all. God bless you. Pray for,
    Yours very truly in Christ,
        ✠ GEORGE, Archbishop of Bombay.

Bombay, Sept. 2, 1889.

My dear Child,

    I congratulate you on having completed your novitiate and taken your holy vows. May God grant you the grace to live up to the high sanctity of your vocation!

Think each day that all is before you, that all depends on making the most of the day you are in. You must not allow your fervour to cool down with time, rather try to increase it constantly. If you do this, your happiness will always become greater, and you will be more and more grateful for the call God gave you.

I pray every day for each and every member of the English Province of the Sacred Heart, and I hope you will live many years, to come in for your share in my Masses and prayers here or in the next world.

God bless you.
    I remain, yours very truly in Christ,
        ✠ GEORGE, Archbishop of Bombay.

Bombay, Sept. 3, 1889.

Why did you not write to me from Rome, a fortnight from Bombay? However, you got on very well, and you seem to have seen all that was most worth seeing, and assisted at all the grand *festas*. What a place Rome is! and what a grace to be able to visit it. You were fortunate in having such a good and such an enthusiastic *cicerone*. I would not give much for man or woman who is not stirred up to some enthusiasm in Rome. Thank you for the message from the dear German Fathers. Well it would have been for me, if it had pleased God to leave me with them. I am so thankful you have been able to make your pilgrimage to Rome and see the Holy City under such good guides.

How your account of the X—— family consoles me! God is wonderful in all His works, but most of all in His works of grace. . . .

. . . I began this letter hoping to send it by the mail of last Tuesday, but I could not finish it in time.

Fort Chapel, Sept. 3, 1889.

Your letter of August 14th reached Bombay on the night of September 1st, and was delivered at 6 a.m. on Monday, little more than a fortnight from London.

I am quite restored now, and I may say I am not at all pulled down. The doctor has recommended me to take more nourishment. I think I am better for following his advice.

You seem to be improving in the fine weather, which has been most opportune for you. I understand that you feel much better when you rise at 7.30 and hear Mass. Add a little precaution: when you rise somewhat earlier, give yourself a little rest after breakfast; it will freshen your mind. I take it for granted that it is easier to pray and meditate in the afternoon; the brain is stronger then. But people whose rule of life provides for prayer, like to secure their devotions early, lest they may be interrupted later, and they dread the distractions of the day. The brain requires some time after the night's rest, and some food, to regain its normal power. Until you are much stronger, do not attempt long devotions in the early morning. Sickness is a time when little "dodges"—spiritual writers call them *industriæ*—are most useful.

Father Dalgairns' observation that the early Christians dwelt more on our Lord's Glorified Life is so true that they never represented the Crucifixion in its true form till the fifth or sixth century. I remember a sarcophagus of the fourth century in the museum of St. John Lateran, in which the Crucifixion appears as a simple cross with a wreath of glory above, and in the Scourging the executioners show the greatest reverence to our Lord. No crucifix or picture of the Crucifixion (except the caricature of the second century found in the Palatine) is known to exist earlier than the sixth century.

You ask me for my latest view of the *Grammar of Assent*. I had never read the book before this year. The great conclusion of Newman seems to me, that we can only have an accumulation of *probabilities* in favour of Christianity; but, he adds, such an accumulation as justifies certitude. He does not like the word *moral certitude*, which Catholic philosophers commonly admit. I have not quite satisfied my mind. Cardinal Newman would seem to admit that there might exist a sound argument against Christianity. I have always held there does not exist, there cannot exist, a single sound argument against Christianity. Difficulties there are, numerous and serious; arguments not. I don't think Father Harper's articles in *The Month* would help you. Cardinal Newman said Father Harper had not understood him. I must go over the *Grammar* once more, and I will try to see my way to a clear judgment. The book contains several beautiful and valuable passages. Cardinal Newman has studied "faith," theoretically and practically, as few others have done.

TO A YOUNG MAN IN THE WORLD.

Fort Chapel, Sept. 8, 1889.

My dear ——

I am glad to write to you on this great feast, the anniversary of my taking my vows, and no doubt a great day to you and all good Sodalists.

Your letter of last July was very welcome.

I am glad to hear all the good news you give of yourself, spiritual and temporal.

Keep on as you have begun.

I often wonder at the ways of Providence. Your father seemed to have passed beyond the ordinary trials of life; and yet see how much he has to suffer, probably more in a year now than in ten years of his early life.

Happily he is a good Christian, and he knows how to carry his cross.

You say nothing about your health. I take it for granted you are quite well. Some months ago I was not over-well, but I am all right again. My old enemy the gout got hold of me, and the fever of last year returned; but the illness was not serious. Catching fever out here is a very simple thing. Taken in time, it may easily be got under.

I read with special pleasure what you write about the Sodality and the interest you take in it.

I hope you will always continue to promote the Sodality; it is a great means of doing good.

Kindest remembrances to papa. God bless you.

Yours very truly in Christ,

✠ GEORGE, Archbishop of Bombay.

Fort Chapel, Sept. 19, 1889.

The home authorities threaten to make Sunday the European mail-day from Bombay all the year round. This would make Sunday the busiest day of the seven, would do away with the Saturday half-holiday, and leave the Sunday rest a matter of history. All Bombay, Hindoo, Mahommedan, and Parsee, joined with the Christians in a vigorous protest. Ask M—— to fight for Bombay. The smallest Australian colony refuses to run one Sunday mail-train, and so brings this trouble. I am satisfied the scandal in the estimation of the natives will be grievous. The desecration of the one religious day of the week seems to them so wanton.

I pass to a page of native Christian life. One of my priests has charge of two villages, Juvem and Tara. He has a church in both places. The cholera broke out in Tara. The whole population fled from the infected place, and moved *en masse* to the sea-side. The priest sought out, and with some difficulty found, the sick persons in Tara. Out of eight, three died. Meanwhile, his flock of Juvem met and passed a law that no one from Tara should come within a mile of Juvem: beating, perhaps worse, to be the punishment. Then they passed a second law, forbidding their priest to attend the sick at Tara. The priest paid no attention to their law. They are strange people.

I have finished Wilfrid Ward's book. It is a most able and a deeply interesting book. My estimate of W. G. Ward has been raised on several points, still I cannot say I like him unreservedly.

No doubt Sister C—— enjoys an advantage in religion, having everything marked out by obedience. You can come near it in the world. Only decide *beforehand* your order of duties, your course of action under such and such circumstances, &c., and then you may take your decision as the will of God in your case. Where perplexity comes in is where nothing has been decided on. Time presses, something must be done, the doubt continues, and in the end you do what was never laid down by a rule or reason; it is not satisfactory. The Rules of Election should be very familiar, and often put in practice.

I did not go back to Poona. I have remained all the time in Bombay. The heat was great on some few days; generally, however, the weather has been pleasant. The gout has not finally left me, but at present it does not hinder me from getting about, and leaves my brain free. Next month I shall leave Bombay and visit some of the stations. Poona has been very unhealthy this year. The Bishop of Poona has been unwell almost the whole time since I left. I had better not go there.

I remain, yours very truly in Christ,

✠ George, Archbishop of Bombay.

Thus abruptly ends the series of Archbishop Porter's letters that have been sent for publication. The plans he had formed, of which he writes in this last letter, were never carried out. He did not live to the end of the month. His letters during the summer gave indications of failing strength, but his friends in England were unaware how very precarious was his state. His last public appearance was at a meeting held to protest against Sunday being fixed as the European mail-day. A chill caught at the meeting rapidly developed into fever, which after a few days proved fatal.

Archbishop Porter died on the afternoon of Saturday, September 28, 1889.

R. J. P.